Buy and Bust

Buy and Bust

The Effective Regulation of
an Illicit Market in Heroin

Mark Harrison Moore
Harvard University

Lexington Books
D.C. Heath and Company
Lexington, Massachusetts
Toronto

Library of Congress Cataloging in Publication Data

Moore, Mark Harrison
  Buy and bust.

  1. Heroin. 2. Narcotics, Control of—New York (City). 3. Heroin-Prices—
New York (City). I. Title.
HV5822.H4M56   364.1'57'097471   73-11665
ISBN 0-669-88179-1

Published simultaneously in Canada.

Printed in the United States of America.

International Standard Book Number: 0-669-88179-1

Library of Congress Catalog Card Number: 73-11665

To My Parents

Contents

List of Figures   ix

List of Tables   xiii

Preface   xvii

Introduction: Prohibition Policy and
     Regulatory Effect   xix

Part I   *The Structure of Illicit Heroin-Distribution
     Systems*

Chapter 1   **Avoiding Arrests and Rip-offs; The General
Structure of an Illicit Market in Heroin**   5

    1.0 Dealers' Responses to the Threat of Arrest
     and Imprisonment   5
    2.0 Threats from Other Criminals   41
    3.0 Problems of Illegality: Consumers   47
    4.0 A General Model of Illegal, Domestic
     Heroin-Distribution System   51

Chapter 2   **Quantitative Estimates of the New York City
Distribution System**   67

    1.0 The Aggregate Consumption of Heroin   69
    2.0 The Number, Activity, and Profits of
     Heroin Dealers in New York City   92
    3.0 Summary   108

Part II   *The Structure of Narcotics-Enforcement
     Efforts*

Chapter 3   **Making Cases; The Structure of Enforcement
Efforts against Heroin Dealers**   121

    1.0 Legal Constraints   121
    2.0 Procedures for Making Cases   128
    3.0 Resources and Constraints   149
    4.0 Summary: The General Shape of the
     Production Function for Narcotics Enforcement   178

Chapter 4   Narcotics Enforcement in New York City   187

                 1.0 The New York City Police Department   188
                 2.0 Federal-Enforcement Agencies   201
                 3.0 Coordinating Mechanisms among Enforcement
                     Agencies   210
                 4.0 The Prosecutors and Courts   212

Part III   Policy Recommendations

Chapter 5   The Role of Narcotics-Enforcement Strategies
                 in an Overall Policy   237

                 1.0 Narcotics Enforcement as a Prevention
                     Program   238
                 2.0 Impact of Narcotics Enforcement on
                     Current Users   258
                 3.0 Summary: What We Want Narcotics
                     Enforcement to Do and What We Must Do
                     in Addition   261

Chapter 6   A Specific Enforcement Strategy for New
                 York City   263

                 1.0 Specific Objectives of an Enforcement
                     Strategy   263
                 2.0 Optimal Strategies and Tactics for Achieving
                     Operational Objectives   264
                 3.0 Obstacles to Effective Implementation in
                     New York City   268

                 Bibliography   275

                 Index   283

                 About the Author   293

List of Figures

1A-1	Model I Distribution Unit	63
1A-2	Model II Distribution Unit	64
1A-3	Model III Distribution Unit	64
1A-4	Model IV Distribution Unit	65
2-1	One Possible Model of the New York City Distribution System	100
2-2	Distribution of Prices Paid by Federal Undercover Agents Purchasing Heroin in New York City	102
2-3	Distribution of Quantities Purchased by Federal-Undercover Agents in New York City	103
2-4	Distribution of Purities Received in Federal-Undercover Purchases in New York City	104
2-5	Predicted Compared with Observed Quantity-Purity Combinations in Narcotics Transactions	107
4-1	Trends in Total Narcotics Arrests in NYCPD: 1967-74	190
4-2	Trends in the Proportion of the Total NYCPD Felony and Misdemeanor Arrests that Are Narcotics Arrests: 1967-74	191
4-3	Trends in the Distribution of Narcotics Arrests among Charges: 1968-72	192
4-4	Trends in the Share of Heroin Arrests within Narcotics Arrests: 1967-74	193
4-5	Trends in the Levels and Distribution of Arrests by the Narcotics Division: 1971-74	196
4-6	The Size Distribution of Heroin Buys Made by the Narcotics Division: 1971-74	198

4-7   Levels of Narcotics Arrests Produced by DEA's
            New York Regional Office: 1972-74   203

4-8   Distribution of DEA Narcotics Arrests among
            Classes of Violators: 1972-74   204

4-9   Heroin-Cocaine Arrests Made by DEA's
            New York Regional Office: 1972-74   206

4-10   Disposition of *Felony* Arrests for Narcotics
            Offenses in New York City Courts:
            August 1969-August 1970   214

4-11   Disposition of *Misdemeanor* Arrests for
            Narcotics Offenses in New York City
            Courts: August 1969-August 1970   215

4-12   The Growth in Court Resources: 1971-75   222

4-13   The Distribution of Adult Felony Arrests
            before and after Reclassification of
            Offenses   224

4-14   Percentage of Felony-Drug Dispositions
            Disposed by Trial   225

4-15   Comparison of Sentences for Class A Offenses
            under New Laws with Sentences for
            Similar Offenses under Old Laws   227

4-16   Comparison of Sentences for Less than Class A
            Felonies under New Laws with Sentences
            for Similar Offenses under Old Laws   228

5-1   Alternative Hypotheses about the Relation-
            ship of the Effective Price of Heroin to
            the Probability of Experimental Use   240

5-2   Retail Heroin Availability: April 1972-
            September 1974   242

5-3   Annual Trends in Hepatitis Reporting in
            the Middle Atlantic Census Division   243

5-4   The Spread of Heroin Abuse in Crawley, New
                Town, England   251

5-5   The Spread of Heroin Use in a Neighborhood
                in Chicago, Illinois   252

5-6   Possible Results of the Analytic Model   255

List of Tables

1-1   Predicted Impact of Increased Threat of Arrest
       on Gross Revenues and Attractiveness of
       Heroin Business for Alternative Assumptions
       about Industry and "Tax" Structure   14

1-2   Types of Dealers Defined in Terms of Different
       Positions and Attitudes towards Profits,
       Risk, and Violence   39

1-3   Portfolios of Defensive Strategies for Different
       Types of Dealers   40

2-1   Estimates of the Number of Users in New
       York City: 1966-72   72

2-2   Evaluations of Estimating Techniques in
       Terms of Their Ability to Control Sources
       of Error   74

2-3   Prevalence Rates of Heroin Use among Selected
       Populations Implied by Different Estimates
       of the Number of Current Users   76

2-4   The Observed Prevalence of Heroin Use among
       Various Population Groups   78

2-5   Estimated Distribution of Habit Sizes among
       Heroin-Using Population   81

2-6   A Typology of Users   83

2-7   Estimated Distribution of Types of Users
       among Different Habit Sizes   84

2-8   Existing Data Sources on Demographic
       Characteristics of Users in New York City   86

2-9   Observed Sources of Users' Incomes   88

2-10   Adjusted Estimate of Sources of Users'
       Incomes   89

2-11   Estimated Annual Aggregate Consumption
            of Heroin (100,000 Users)   90

2-12   Estimated Total Amounts of Money from
            Different Sources (100,000 Users)   92

2-13   Estimated Annual Amounts from Different
            Sources per User (100,000 Users)   96

2-14   The Size of the Heroin Industry Compared
            with Other Industries in New York City   98

2-15   Number of Levels in Distribution System
            Implied by Different Estimates of the
            Numbers of Users; the Number of Dealers
            at Top, and the Average Number of
            Customers per Dealer   99

2-16   A Simple Dilution and Packaging Process
            Consistent with Distribution of Purities
            and Quantities Observed in Federal
            Undercover Purchases   106

2-17   Calculation of the Value Added by Each Level   108

2-18   Estimated Value Added per Dealer   110

2-19   Characteristics of Distribution Levels Affecting
            Levels of Profit   111

2-20   Estimated Average Net Profits per Dealer   111

2-21   Estimated Average Lot Sizes for Purchases
            and Sales at Each Distribution Level   112

2-22   Estimated Levels of Activity for Dealers at
            Different Levels of the Distribution
            System   113

2-23   Summary of Quantitative Estimates of the
            New York City Heroin Market: 1970-74   114

3-1   Different Degrees of Generality in "Leads"   137

3-2	Summary of Outputs and Resource Requirements for Enforcement Strategies and Tactics	180
4-1	The Estimated Expected Number of Arrests per Dealer from NYCPD: 1968-73	194
4-2	The Estimated Expected Number of Arrests per Dealer at Each Level from Narcotics Division: 1971-74	199
4-3	Distribution of Types of Arrests on Lennox Avenue Near 116th Street: 1972	200
4-4	Criteria for Assigning Arrested Traffickers to Different G-DEP Classes	205
4-5	The Estimated Expected Number of Arrests per Dealer from DEA-Enforcement Efforts in New York City	207
4-6	Duplication among Cases Known to Unified Intelligence Division: September 1972-January 1973	212
4-7	Causes of Dismissals: Bronx Criminal Court November-December 1970	216
4-8	Dispositions of Undercover Cases Made by the Narcotics Division: 1970	218
4-9	Major Changes in Classification of Heroin Offenses under Rockefeller Drug Laws	220
4-10	Major Changes in Restriction on Sentencing and Processing under Rockefeller Drug Laws	221
4-11	Share of Old-Law and New-Law Cases in Court Pipeline: 1972-75	223
4-12	Proportion of Convicted Felons Receiving Prison Sentences under Old and New Laws: 1972-74	226

4-13   Fraction of Convicted A Felons Receiving
        Jail Sentences Compared with Other
        Felons: 1974   226

5-1   Dangerous Drugs Used In and Since Vietnam   244

5-2   Significant Factors in Abandoning Heroin
        Use for Neophyte Users   245

5-3   Outcomes of Policies to Restrict Access
        under Alternative Assumptions about
        Role of Access in Affecting Probability
        of Use   248

5-4   Conditions of Initiation to Heroin Use   250

5-5   Outputs of the Analytic Model of the Spread
        of Heroin Use   256

6-1   Bureaucratic Obstacles to Proposed Law-
        Enforcement Program   271

Preface

This book began in January 1970. The Hudson Institute invited me and two fellow students from the Public Policy Program in the Kennedy School of Government, Harvard University, to assist them in an analysis of the heroin problem in New York State. Our specific assignment was to gauge the importance of the heroin-distribution system in the ghetto economy. Although we never learned enough about the ghetto economy to give considered advice on this issue, we did begin a detailed description of the structure of heroin-distribution systems. The result of those efforts was published as Mark Moore, *Policy Towards Drug Abuse in New York State: Vol. 3. The Economics of Heroin Distribution*, Hudson Institute, 1970. In writing that report, I was greatly indebted to Max Singer and Ralph Salerno of the Hudson Institute staff; to Edward Preble for advice and criticism as well as for his excellent article (Edward Preble and John C. Case, "Taking Care of Business—The Heroin User's Life on the Street," *International Journal of the Addictions* 4:1 [March 1969]); and to my fellow student and friend, Mark Rosenberg.

My interest in the heroin problem continued for the next six years and broadened in scope. I worked for the Addiction Services Agency, a treatment organization in New York City, and as a consultant to the National Advisory Council on Drug Abuse Prevention, an oversight council for the Special Action Office on Drug Abuse Prevention. These experiences provided a unique opportunity to learn about the operations of many instruments of drug-abuse policy in addition to enforcement, and to develop a broad, strategic view of the problem. This work culminated in my doctoral dissertation, "Policy Towards Heroin Use in New York City" (Harvard University, 1973), which set up a conceptual framework for analyzing the problem, and recommended an overall strategy. In producing that document, I became deeply indebted to James Q. Wilson who provided the critical but responsive audience that is every writer's greatest hope. In addition, I became indebted to Richard E. Neustadt, Graham T. Allison, John D. Steinbruner, Henry Jacoby, and my other colleagues in the Faculty Seminar on Bureaucracy, Politics, and Policy of the Institute of Politics, John Fitzgerald Kennedy School of Government, Harvard University. This seminar, supported by a grant from the Ford Foundation, was devoted to developing styles of policy analysis that incorporated calculations of political and bureaucratic feasibility. In both the analysis and recommendations, this book bears unmistakable traces of their concerns and skillful advice.

My knowledge of enforcement activities and the structure of heroin-distribution systems was enormously enriched by two rather unique opportunities. In April 1972 I was invited to observe the activities and inspect the files of the Narcotics Division of the New York City Police Department by Deputy

Commissioner William P. McCarthy, head of the Organized Crime Control Bureau. I benefitted greatly from conversations with him and with William T. Bonacum. In addition, an extraordinarily generous undercover policeman named Robert Hayes invited me to stay at his house, took responsibility for explaining things to me, and opened his personal files.

In January 1974 I was invited to participate in a survey of federal-enforcement efforts by John Bartels, the administrator of the Drug Enforcement Administration (DEA). Several remarkable federal agents—Ben Thiesen, Bruce Jensen, Dave Costa, and Don Smith—joined me in interviews with a large number of federal agents, and helped interpret the responses to my questions. Following the survey, Mr. Bartels invited me to be his special assistant and chief planning officer. I am very grateful for that opportunity. Although this book is *not* about DEA or federal enforcement strategies, I learned a great deal about narcotics enforcement by being at DEA. Many people, too numerous to mention here, instructed me. However, I think particularly of my staff, Tom Hurney and Jerry Strickler, and also of Dan Casey, George Belk, William Durkin, Ed Kass, Ted Vernier, Fred Rody, and Howard Safer, as being particularly instructive.

At Harvard, I was greatly assisted by my colleagues in the Public Policy Program. The document is inspired by, and shamelessly relies on, the work of Thomas C. Shelling. Professor Philip B. Heymann of the Harvard Law School provided specialized advice on what I, to his horror, continued to call "legal constraints." Mark Kleiman and Lawrence Bacow, performing in the time-honored role of eager, skeptical, and creative students, offered insights and assistance.

All this intellectual investment would have produced nothing were it not for the able assistance of my secretary, Elizabeth A. Charney. Throughout the last year on work on the book, her diligence rebuked me for my laziness, and her enthusiasm made me think I was producing something exciting.

Finally, I would like to thank my wife, Martha, who endured my absences, tantrums, and bad moods while researching and writing the document. The enjoyment of her company and the company of my children provided the most important incentive to finish the book.

To all these people, I owe a debt. Since I would be mortified if I did them any harm by association with this analysis, I of course, assume full responsibility for the statements in the book.

Introduction: Prohibition Policy and Regulatory Effect

The design of an overall strategy towards drug abuse is a complicated enterprise. One must consider what is bad about drug abuse and compare the magnitude of the drug-abuse problem with other social problems. One must analyze what drugs and what patterns of consumption account for the largest fraction of the drug-abuse problem. One must assess the potential impact of an array of policy instruments affecting both the supply and demand for illicit drugs. Finally, one must consider how to mobilize and coordinate efforts by governmental units at different levels.

This book is *not* intended as the design of a general policy toward drug abuse, nor as an overall policy toward *heroin* use. It is not even intended as the design of a comprehensive strategy to reduce the *supply* of heroin. The book is limited to an analysis of a single piece of the strategy to reduce the supply of heroin—the piece that focuses on domestic-distribution systems and relies heavily on state and local-enforcement agencies.

There are clear risks to producing an analysis with such a limited scope—particularly if the analysis proposes to have policy implications. A major substantive risk is that the analysis and recommendations will simply be wrong. Without a sufficiently broad perspective, major effects of the proposed policy might go unnoticed, and important interdependencies between this policy instrument and others might be missed. A major commercial risk is that readers who have a high regard for their time will spend it on more ambitious efforts. In my defense, I offer the following points.

First, this analysis is in fact embedded in a systematic approach to analysis of the heroin problem. The framework is partially exposed and defended in Part III of this book. It is presented in greater detail and more convincingly defended elsewhere.[a] I would have combined the two analyses, but it became awkward to combine the overall policy analysis with this detailed analysis of a single instrument. To maintain an even balance in the design of the overall strategy, I would have been forced to write a very long book, and to include details about other policy instruments that others know much better than I. It seemed less likely to distort my position if I separated this partial analysis from the general analysis and clearly signalled that the analysis was partial. Although I cannot expect a reader to accept the legitimacy of the policy proposals simply on the basis of these bland assurances, I can direct the reader to a more comprehensive

---

[a]For a complete exposition of the analytic framework, see Mark H. Moore, *Policy Towards Heroin Use In New York City* (Ph.D. diss., Harvard University, 1973). For a shorter version of the framework, see Mark H. Moore, "Anatomy of the Heroin Problem: An Exercise in Problem Definition," *Policy Analysis* 2:1 (1976).

approach to the heroin problem and assure him that I have at least considered the relationship of the policies proposed here and other components of heroin policy.

Second, the particular instruments and effects analyzed in this book are important, controversial, and poorly understood components of heroin policy. Enforcement efforts by state and local police consume substantially more resources than federal efforts. Moreover, the police efforts raise issues of corruption, illegal police practices, and stigmatization of users. Indeed, many people believe that aggressive, domestic-enforcement efforts exacerbate rather than improve the heroin problem.[b] Although these views are passionately held and propounded, neither advocates nor opponents of strong enforcement efforts have solid analyses to buttress their positions. The analysis presented here can reasonably claim to be more deliberate than any that has previously been presented.

Third, this analysis has some significance apart from its contribution to heroin policy. It applies basic economic concepts to produce insights about the behavior of heroin dealers and the planning of enforcement operations. As such, it may prove useful in the analysis of other black markets, organized crime, and police strategies for controlling them. Moreover, it lays bare, once again, the orderliness and rationality that underlies deviant behavior. These things are intellectually satisfying in and of themselves.

Perhaps the greatest contribution of the analysis is that it transforms the perspective from which enforcement efforts against distribution systems are evaluated. This point is sufficiently important that it is worth elaborating.

A broad consensus exists that the distribution and use of heroin ought to be restricted. Heroin is sufficiently attractive and destructive that even those who minimize its harmful effects recommend that heroin be kept beyond the easy reach of at least some segments of the population.

No such consensus exists on the form that such restriction should take. The battle is usually joined on the issue of whether heroin should be prohibited or merely regulated. Advocates of regulation identify appropriate medical uses of heroin, note the disastrous effects of prohibition on the lives of addicts, and observe that enforcement has no effects other than the corruption of police and the enrichment of organized crime. Advocates of prohibition deny that heroin has legitimate medical purposes, judge that heroin would have disastrous effects on the lives of users even if legally prescribed, and argue that slight changes in strategy and administrative practice would result in law enforcement that was sufficiently effective to deter much heroin use.

This debate between prohibition and regulation creates a false dichotomy. Obviously, there is a difference between the statutory language, which prohibits

---

[b]For examples of passionate and effective critiques of narcotics enforcement, see A.R. Lindesmith, *The Addict and the Law* (New York: Vintage Books, 1965); or Abraham S. Blumberg, "Drug Control: Agenda for Repression," in Richard L. Rachin and Eugene H. Czakjoski, *Drug Abuse Control* (Lexington, Mass.: D.C. Heath and Co., 1975).

heroin use, and the language that allows particular uses of heroin. However, the restriction on the supply of heroin that *actually results* from the different statutes will not necessarily be different. Whether there will be a difference, and what it will be, depends on the tactics and scale of enforcement efforts as much as on the statutory language. A weakly enforced prohibition may result in larger aggregate supplies and easier access to heroin than a tightly enforced regulatory scheme. A well-designed law-enforcement strategy can achieve a subtle regulatory effect in spite of a crude prohibition policy.

A major purpose of this analysis is to design a piece of a strategy for *regulating* the distribution of heroin under a policy that *prohibits* all uses of heroin. This may seem a twisted purpose. It would be more straightforward to decide what restrictions ought to apply, to promulgate the restrictions in statutory language, and to design an enforcement strategy that guaranteed close compliance with the statutory provisions. Why attempt to achieve a regulatory effect with a prohibition policy?

A satisfactory response to this question rests on three observations. The first observation is that the appropriate objectives of a policy toward the supply of heroin lie closer to the notion of regulation than prohibition. Simply raising the amount of time it takes to find heroin from five minutes to two hours is an extremely valuable achievement. It discourages many new users from continuing to experiment, and it motivates experienced users to seek treatment more frequently than they otherwise would.[c] Effectively prohibiting heroin (i.e., eliminating all supplies of heroin) is impossible without unacceptable expenditures and intolerable assaults on civil liberties. Hence, regulation is a more appropriate and feasible objective than prohibition.

The second observation is that the prohibition policy is likely to remain in place for the immediate future. Although there is some erosion of support for the prohibition policy, the possibility of a significant change in this policy seems remote. Indeed, it seems unlikely that anyone will be authorized even to experiment with the legal proscription of heroin.

The third observation is that it is possible that the specific regulatory effect we want can be achieved *only* under a prohibition policy. Although statutes do not precisely determine supply conditions, they may restrict the range of possible outcomes or make some outcomes much more likely to occur. My hunch is that the prohibition policy moves us to a region of supply conditions that are preferred to the supply conditions that would result under most regulatory policies.[d]

---

[c]Of course, this assertion that inconvenience in consuming heroin will in fact discourage new users, and motivate some old users to abstain or seek treatment is controversial. For evidence and arguments supporting this position, see Chapter 5.

[d]For a brief analysis of the supply conditions likely to result from different enforcement and regulatory policies, see Mark H. Moore, "Policies to Achieve Discrimination on The Effective Price of Heroin," *American Economic Review* 63:2 (May 1973): 270-277. For an excellent description of problems in managing the regulatory system in England, see Griffith Edwards, "The British Approach to the Treatment of Heroin Addiction," *Lancet*, April 12, 1969, pp. 768-772.

Given that we want a regulatory effect, and that we can achieve this effect in spite of (or because of) the prohibition policy, it seems desirable to give detailed attention to the design of enforcement tactics under the prohibition policy. Since no one has previously investigated the potential of enforcement tactics to achieve regulatory effects, it seems likely that reflection will yield a different set of tactics than usually considered, or a different evaluation of existing strategies.

The analysis is composed of three parts. The first part describes the characteristics of an illicit-distribution system for heroin. It has two sections: one describing the general characteristics of an illicit market in heroin; the other estimating specific characteristics of the market currently operating in New York City.

The second part describes current law-enforcement efforts. It also has two sections: one presents a general view of strategies available to the police; the other is a specific description of law-enforcement efforts in New York City.

The third part designs and recommends a strategy for using domestic law-enforcement agencies to enforce the prohibition of heroin. It sets objectives of law enforcement in the context of an overall policy toward heroin use, recommends both strategies and tactics, and identifies major bureaucratic obstacles to implementation of the proposed strategies.

Part I
The Structure of Illicit Heroin-Distribution Systems

Introduction to Part I

Impressionistic evidence indicates heroin-distribution systems differ from other marketing systems. Striking anomalies include:

1. An extremely large markup between the first wholesale exchange and the final retail exchange
2. A distribution system that operates through small, highly personalized, face-to-face networks rather than through widespread advertising
3. An apparently high degree of concentration at some levels of distribution in spite of the absence of technological and capital barriers to entry

Such characteristics are inconsistent with the behavior of most profit-maximizing firms. Why, for example, isn't the industry organized into larger and more impersonal marketing systems? It is likely that such units would increase sales and decrease distribution costs. Another puzzle: how can any degree of monopolization be maintained without technological or capital barriers to entry? One would expect new firms to enter the market often.

Theoretically, there are many possible explanations of these anomalies. For example, peculiar aspects of the technology of producing heroin, or the addictive characteristics of heroin, might explain the unusual structure of the distribution system. However, it is almost certain that the single most important factor influencing the structure of heroin-distribution systems is that producing, importing, selling, and possessing heroin are all prohibited in the United States. Indeed, in New York City it is a misdemeanor even to loiter for the purpose of procuring narcotics.

Part I of this analysis systematically explores the impact of illicitness on the behavior of individual heroin dealers, consumers, and the structure of domestic-distribution systems. The first section develops a general description of the major features of illicit-distribution systems. The technique is to identify problems created by illicitness for both dealers and customers, and to identify possible solutions. Efficient solutions to these problems become hypotheses about how dealers will behave. Aggregations of the behavior of individual dealers yield hypotheses about the structure of the system. The second section uses this general model to develop quantitative estimates of the size, volume, and profitability of the illicit-distribution system currently operating in New York City. Because of the enormous uncertainty about the accuracy of the general model and the bits of evidence used in the quantitative analysis, the estimates should be considered *extremely* rough.

There are several notes to keep in mind while reading part I. First, illicitness has an effect on the structure of the heroin industry only through the concrete actions of law-enforcement agencies. Unless police arrest people who engage in

3

the sale and use of heroin, none of the tendencies described here will be visible. The corollary of this observation is that the strength of these tendencies depends on the amount of police pressure.

Second, there are serious limitations to the methodology employed in this book. The methodology is similar to that used in developing intelligence estimates. Bits of unverified, half-verified, and fully verified information are assembled into a systematic picture by combining arbitrary definitions with assumptions about how reasonable men behave. The composite picture is constantly checked for consistency. When the information seems consistent and the assumptions reasonable, an estimate or proposition is offered. The methodology offers the advantage of systematically and extensively exploiting meager information. It has the disadvantage of providing only good guesses about the nature of the phenomenon. Moreover, the guesses may be radically altered by the introduction of a single, verified piece of information.

Third, there is a small, definitional problem. The heroin industry will sometimes be treated as a single organization with peculiar problems and characteristics, at other times as a highly differentiated structure composed of many different organizations with varied problems and characteristics. When the heroin industry is described as if it were a single organization, the discussion is confined to problems experienced by all organizations within the heroin industry. When the discussion explicitly focuses on the different units of the heroin industry, the purpose is to modify the general propositions about the behavior of the industry as a whole.

Avoiding Arrests and Rip-offs; The General Structure of an Illicit Market in Heroin

The fact that the manufacture, distribution, and possession of heroin is illegal creates major problems for heroin distributors. The particular ways in which dealers respond to these problems has a decisive influence on the structure and behavior of the distribution systems. In this section, we explore problems and responses in three different areas: dealers' responses to the threat of arrest and imprisonment, dealers' efforts to protect themselves from other criminals, and consumer responses to problems created by the dealers' responses. The objective is to develop a general model of a heroin-distribution system that has been outlawed.

1.0 Dealers' Responses to the Threat of Arrest and Imprisonment

The most immediate and important consequence of legislating against the manufacture, distribution, and possession of heroin is that every heroin supplier is faced with some possibility of being arrested, convicted, and imprisoned. Lost income, restricted opportunities upon release, the loss of freedom, and isolation from normal society all represent losses associated with imprisonment. To a greater or lesser degree, depending on their activity and the activity of the police, heroin suppliers must expect to absorb these losses.

A useful technique for analyzing the effects of threatening heroin dealers with arrest and imprisonment is to assume that the expected losses represent costs to individual heroin suppliers. In this view, the threat of arrest resembles a tax imposed on dealers. The higher the probability of arrest and imprisonment, and the greater the penalties, the greater is the tax imposed on heroin dealers.

If this view is accepted, then economic theory allows two general predictions about the response of heroin suppliers to increased risks. First, they will attempt to pass the increased costs of supplying heroin onto the consumer through higher prices. Second, they will seek to reduce these risks by engaging a variety of strategies to reduce the chance that they will be arrested, convicted, and imprisoned.

1.1 Price Increases as a Response to Enforcement Pressure

The conventional analysis of the impact of enforcement efforts concentrates on the price response of heroin dealers. The reasoning is usually the following:

5

1. An expanded enforcement effort increases the risk of arrest and imprisonment to dealers.
2. To compensate themselves for the increased risk (and to cover increased operating costs) dealers raise their prices.
3. Since the demand for heroin is perfectly ineleastic, the increased price results in no reduction in the amount of heroin that is consumed.
4. Since consumption is not reduced and since the price has increased, gross revenues and profits increase.
5. The increased profits mobilize old dealers to be more aggressive and attract new dealers into the business.

The conclusion of this analysis, then, is that increased enforcement pressure results in higher prices for heroin, no less heroin consumption, and richer heroin dealers. In addition, many analysts conclude that the higher profits will motivate old dealers to seek new customers and new dealers to enter the market.[a]

This analysis is misleading. The major problems are (1) the restrictive (and probably incorrect) assumption about the elasticity of demand; and (2) logical errors in reasoning about the relationship between gross revenues, profits, and the attractiveness of the business. In addition, the conventional analysis fails to present explicit assumptions or hypotheses about the structure of the distribution system. Since industry structure will decisively influence the price response to increased threats of arrest, it is difficult to evaluate the conventional argument.

A more careful analysis of the response of the distribution system to increased enforcement pressure is presented below. However, before advancing to the more careful analysis, it is important to confront directly the misleading parts of the conventional analysis. Consequently, we explore the assumption of a perfectly inelastic demand for heroin, and the implications of relaxing this assumption. In addition, we consider the issues of whether heroin distribution is more attractive or less attractive following a general increase in the risk of arrest and imprisonment.

The conventional assumption that the demand for heroin is *perfectly* inelastic is based on beliefs about the overwhelming addictiveness of heroin. In this view, the mechanisms of tolerance and withdrawal lock heroin users onto narrow, steadily rising paths of heroin consumption. If the user falls off this path, either deliberately or by accident, he faces agonizing withdrawal symptoms. The pain of withdrawal is sufficiently agonizing (and the pleasure of relieving the pain sufficiently euphoric) to insure very strong resistance to

[a]For expositions of this conventional analysis, see Donald Phares, "The Simple Economics of Heroin and Organizing Policy," *Journal of Drug Issues*, Spring 1973, pp. 186-200; or Harold L. Votey and Llad Phillips, "Minimizing the Social Cost of Drug Abuse: An Economic Analysis of Alternatives for Policy," *Policy Sciences* 7:3 (September 1976).

reductions in heroin consumption—even if maintaining a given level of use requires extraordinary effort and imposes extraordinary risks on the user.[b]

Although this view is colorful and widely believed, there are two major problems with relying on it as a justification for the assumption of a perfectly inelastic demand for heroin. First, the aggregate demand for heroin is composed of the demand from many different kinds of users – addicts, casual users, neophyte users. The addiction model applies to only a fraction of the total users. Second, the addiction model turns out to be a poor description of the consumption of even hard-core users.

Consider, first, the demand by hard-core addicts. Within this group, one might expect the assumption of a perfectly inelastic demand to be most accurate. However, even for this group, consumption is likely to decrease at least a little and perhaps substantially as the price of heroin increases. The reasons to expect decreased consumption are the following.

First, the demand for heroin from this group will certainly be affected by the enforced periods of abstinence that result from arrests. Since the probability of arrest is likely to increase with the level of addict crime, and since the level of addict crime will increase as addicts seek to maintain their level of real income in the face of increased heroin prices, these users will take increased periods of enforced abstinence. Although we may not place any great social value on such enforced periods of abstinence, they will affect the total consumption of heroin and absolute levels of revenue to the industry.

Second, under the pressure created by high prices for heroin, and in the presence of adequate treatment capacity, many users will seek treatment rather than remain on the street hustling for heroin.[c] In New York City, users may

[b]For scientific descriptions of tolerance and withdrawal, see Hannah Steinberg, *Scientific Basis of Drug Dependence* (New York: Gruen and Stratton, 1969). For more popularized accounts of the phenomena, see Edward H. Brecher, *Licit and Illicit Drugs* (Boston: Little, Brown and Co., 1972), pp. 64-90; or James Delong, "Drugs and their Effects," in Drug Abuse Survey Project, *Dealing with Drug Abuse* (New York: Praeger Publishers, 1972). For anecdotal accounts of the subjective reactions of users to these effects, see William Burroughs, *Junkie* (New York: Ace Books, 1953); Seymour Fiddle, *Portraits from a Shooting Gallery* (New York: Harper and Row, 1967); or Jeremy Larner and Ralph Tefferteller, *The Addict in the Street* (New York: Grove Press, 1964).

[c]The extent to which high prices will motivate current users to seek treatment is controversial. However, interviews with addicts who enter treatment programs consistently show that a large fraction of these users attribute their decision to enter treatment to increased pressures of maintaining an expensive habit. In Patrick Hughes et al., "The Impact of Medical Intervention in Three Heroin Copping Areas," paper presented at the Fourth National Methadone Conference, (San Francisco: January 1972) the following results from interviews with users who were being recruited for treatment were reported: "[T]hey [the users] were not particularly interested in treatment while they had a successful hustle and access to quality heroin. Interest increased only when they came on hard times, i.e., they were arrested, lost their drug dealership role or their drug connection." (p.5) Similarly, in Gila J. Hayim, "Changes in the Criminal Behavior of Heroin Addicts: A One Year Follow-Up of Methadone Treatment" (The Center for Criminal Justice, Harvard Law

choose from methadone programs, therapeutic communities, and detoxification programs for help in reducing heroin consumption. Although it is clear that heroin consumption does not fall to zero in these institutions, it is likely that it declines significantly,[d] and these declines will affect the total consumption of heroin.

Third, even without the institutional "help" offered by jails or treatment programs, heroin users can reduce their heroin consumption. There is evidence that heroin users can consume heroin at levels far below their "habit size" without experiencing withdrawal symptoms,[e] that addicts detoxify themselves frequently,[f] that addicts voluntarily abstain from drug use for relatively long periods,[g] and that addicts substitute other drugs for heroin. Again, although we

School, 1972), p. 9, it is reported that "over 2/3 of the patients listed such factors as 'being tired of hustling,' 'the habit is getting too expensive,' or 'would like to find an honest job,' as important reasons for joining the program."

In summarizing a review of many studies of reasons for seeking treatment, McGlothlin reported that "about 25-50% of current methadone admissions appear to be largely motivated by the push of legal and other pressures. They come into treatment under legal pressure, the demands of relatives, the panic of withdrawal, the need for habit reduction, etc." (See William H. McGlothin et al., "Alternative Approaches to Opiate Addiction Control: Costs, Benefits, and Potential," Bureau of Narcotics and Dangerous Drugs, 1972, p. 20).

Finally, at an aggregate level, a strong relationship between increased prices of heroin and increased treatment enrollment is demonstrated in Robert L. DuPont and Mark H. Greene, "The Dynamics of a Heroin Addiction Epidemic," *Science* 181 (1973): 716-722.

[d]Methadone programs using urinalysis to discover heroin use routinely find "dirty urines." For example, Gearing reports: "Although many of the patients test the methadone 'blockade' of heroin one or more times in the first few months, less than 1% have returned to regular heroin usage while under methadone maintenance treatment." Similarly, Richman reports that 28 percent of a group of 587 patients treated in methadone-maintenance programs had at least one reported "dirty urine." See Frances R. Gearing, "Successes and Failures in Methadone Maintenance Treatment of Heroin Addiction in New York City," and Alex Richman, "Utilization and Review of Methadone Maintenance Patient Data," in Proceedings of the Third National Conference on Methadone Maintenance, National Institute for Mental Health (1970), pp. 8, 26.

[e]Heather Ruth, "The Street Level of Economics of Heroin Addiction in New York City: Life-styles of Active Heroin Users and Implications for Public Policy," Unpublished manuscript (New York: 1972).

In interviews with 42 street addicts, Ruth found that although the average habit size was estimated at 20.5 $2 bags of heroin per day, the estimate of the average amount of heroin necessary to avoid withdrawal was 5.4 $2 bags per day. As she states, "The most important finding is that there is room for much economic flexibility in the range between 'minimum' heroin to avoid withdrawal and 'habit.' " (p. 31).

[f]Richard Brotman and Alfred M. Freedman, *Continuities and Discontinuities in the Process of Patient Care for Narcotic Addicts* (New York: New York Medical College, 1965), p. 73. In a sample of 200 hard-core users in treatment, the median number of previous detoxication was 5. Moreover, 60 percent of those reporting detoxication reported they were undertaken voluntarily at home.

[g]Mark H. Moore, "Policy Towards Heroin Use in New York City" (Ph.D. diss., Harvard University, 1973), Appendix 1, pp. 677-701, contains descriptions and an analysis of the evidence on voluntary abstinence. The basic sources on the phenomenon are the following: John C. Ball, and Richard Snarr, "A Test of the Maturation Hypothesis," *Committee on Problems of Drug Dependence*, National Academy of Science (Washington, D.C.: National

have much different attitudes about the social value of these different responses, the fact that hard-core users have this much flexibility about their heroin consumption suggests that they can respond to price increases by reducing their consumption.

Consider, next, the demand of users of heroin who are not addicted. It used to be widely believed that nonaddicted users constituted only a small minority of all heroin users. The physiological mechanisms of tolerance and withdrawal were sufficiently powerful to insure that nearly all experimenters would become addicts. However, more recent evidence indicates that hard-core users constitute a minority of all users. There are many users who use heroin sporadically over a long period and never become deeply involved.[1] Since the physiological mechanisms that could justify the assumption of a perfectly inelastic demand have not begun to operate in this group, their demand for heroin must be considered to be relatively elastic. The inclusion of this group in the aggregate demand for heroin has the effect of making the aggregate demand much more elastic.

In sum, the aggregate demand for heroin is not likely to be perfectly inelastic. It includes the demand of consumers who are not addicted. Even those who are addicted can reduce their consumption in the face of price increases. Thus, it is not surprising that current estimates of the price elasticity of heroin resemble the price elasticities of such ordinary goods as physician services, oil and gasoline, and auto repair:[2] when prices for these goods increase, consumption declines. Specifically, in the case of heroin, it is estimated that a 10 percent increase in price results in a 2 percent decrease in consumption. Some new users are discouraged from experiments; and some chronic users seek treatment, voluntarily abstain, or wind up in jail.

Note that this estimate of elasticity indicates that the demand for heroin is "inelastic" (i.e., the percent decrease in consumption is less than the percent increase in price); but the demand is not "*perfectly inelastic*" (i.e., there is some reduction in consumption). This is an important distinction. If the elasticity lies between zero and one, we know that price increases will *reduce* heroin consumption, and *increase* gross revenues to the heroin industry. We *like* the effect of reducing consumption. We do *not* like the effect of increasing gross revenues since we are concerned that increased gross revenues may imply more

Research Council, 1969); Henrietta Duvall, Ben Locke, and Leon Brill, "Follow-up Study of Narcotic Drug Addicts Five Years After Hospitalization," *Public Health Reports* 78:3 (March 1963); John O'Donnell, "The Relapse Rate in Narcotics Addiction: A Critique of Follow-up Studies" (Albany: Narcotic Addiction Control Commission, 1968); John O'Donnell, "A Follow-up of Narcotic Addicts: Mortality Relapse and Abstinence," *American Journal Orthopsychology* 34 (1964); Lee Robins and George Murphy, "Drug Use in a Normal Population of Young Negro Men," *American Journal of Public Health* 57:9 (September 1967); George Vaillant, "A Twelve Year Follow-up of New York Narcotic Addicts: The Relation of Treatment to Outcome," *American Journal of Psychiatry* 122 (1966); "The Natural History of a Chronic Disease," *New England Journal of Medicine*, December 8, 1966; and Charles Winick, "Maturing Out of Narcotic Addiction," *United Nations Bulletin on Narcotics* 14:1 (January-March 1962).

stealing by addicts and greater profits for heroin dealers. We leave the issue of whether price increases result in increased stealing for another section. The issue of whether increased gross revenues necessarily imply greater profits and a more attractive business are discussed directly below. At this stage, the important point to understand is that the demand for heroin is *not* perfectly inelastic, consumption will *decrease* as price increases—although not by an equal amount.[h]

The fact that price increases caused by increased threats of arrest and imprisonment result in increased gross revenues leads many to assume that profits to dealers have increased and that the business has become more attractive as a result of enforcement pressure. This seems like a paradoxical result. It seems incredible that increased enforcement pressure would make the heroin business more attractive. In fact, the conclusion that the business becomes more attractive *is* incorrect. However, the problem in the reasoning that leads to the incorrect conclusion is somewhat subtle.

The basic problem comes from failing to distinguish between money profits and "utility" and failing to remember which concept is being employed at different stages of the analysis.[i] In most commercial enterprises, this distinction between money profits and utility disappears. We can assume that all the things that could potentially influence a person's view of the attractiveness of a business are small compared to the impact that money has on his total satisfaction. Consequently, in gauging the attractiveness of the business, we look only at the difference between costs and revenues defined strictly in terms of money.

In the heroin business, the assumption that money profits are all that matter is not so readily defensible. It is likely that the threat of arrest and imprisonment also looms large in a dealer's calculation of the attractiveness of the business. Indeed, it is reasonable to expect that the anxiety of living with the threat is

---

[h]There is a legitimate issue of whether a 2 percent decrease in the consumption of heroin for a 10 percent increase in price is a "significant" reduction. The answer to this question depends partly on which populations of users decrease their consumption, and partly on how hard it is to increase the price by 10 percent. If all of the decrease in consumption comes from current users marginally adjusting their consumption, then little of significance is achieved. If the decreased consumption results primarily from driving experimenting users out of the market before they advance to chronic, intensive levels of use, then a very valuable social effect is achieved. This would imply a significant decline in the growth of the heroin-using population. In addition, the fact that the price of heroin has doubled nationwide (and tripled on the East Coast) in the period from 1970 to 1974 suggests that it may not be hard to raise the price of heroin by much more than 10 percent. Thus, although the significance of this effect is uncertain, one can make an argument that says the effect is very important: one can easily increase the price of heroin by 50 percent, and thereby both prevent new use among many experimenters and drive current users into treatment.

[i]The concept of "utility" is introduced here to capture two somewhat different ideas. One idea is simply to remind us that variables other than money are included in the objective functions of heroin dealers. A second idea is to remind us that people have different attitudes toward uncertain results—some are risk favoring and some are risk avoiding. For a complete and precise description of this second idea of utility, see Howard Raiffa, *Decision Analysis* (Reading, Mass.: Addison-Wesley, 1968).

unpleasant even if the dealer is never actually arrested. Thus, in describing the calculations of heroin dealers, it is important to talk in terms of *utility* rather than simply money profits and to remember that utility will be affected not only by changes in money profits, but also by changes in levels of risk to the dealer.

The conventional analysis relies on the idea of utility in the early stages of the analysis. The threat of arrest and imprisonment enters the analysis as a cost to dealers with cost being defined in utility terms. In response to this reduced utility, dealers make two adjustments: they invest time and money in strategies to reduce the risk, and they demand more money to compensate themselves for the increased risk of staying in the business. Notice that the dealers demand more money not to *increase* their utility, but rather to *maintain* their utility at levels that existed prior to the increased threat of arrest and conviction. It is only the *reduction* in utility occasioned by the increased threat that forces the price adjustment. Presumably, if it had been possible to increase utility through price increases before the increased threat of arrest and imprisonment occurred, dealers would have done so. Whether dealers can succeed in offsetting reduced levels of utility by price increased depends on both the precise elasticity of demand and the market structure. This analysis is presented in detail below. However, it is worth noting here that there is no way that the industry as a whole can become more attractive with an increased threat of arrest and imprisonment. At best, dealers can exactly offset the reduction in utility that occurs with the increased threat. And this result occurs only with very restrictive assumptions (e.g., a competitive market operating in an inelastic portion of the demand curve). In the more likely cases, dealers' efforts to increase prices will be restrained either by consumer resistance or by competition, and the business will be *less* attractive than the situation prior to an increased threat of arrest and imprisonment.

The conventional analysis reaches a different conclusion about changes in the attractiveness of the heroin business because it suddenly changes from a calculation in terms of utility to a calculation in terms of money. In the very last step of the analysis, money suddenly becomes the terms one uses to gauge the attractiveness of the business. Gross money revenues have increased, money costs have probably not changed all that much, therefore money profits must have gone up. If money profits have increased, the business must have become more attractive. What this reasoning ignores is the fact that the analysis *began* with a significant *reduction* in utility that resulted from an increased threat of arrest and imprisonment. Thus, the conventional analysis forgets that the dealers were made worse off before prices and revenues increased, and that these increases are motivated by an effort to offset the losses.

Probably the easiest way to see the failure of the conventional analysis is to draw a strict analogy between an increase in the threat of arrest and imprisonment and a tax on the operation of the dealers. A tax is applied. Prices, amount consumed, and gross revenues change in response. But in calculating the impact of the tax on profits, the cost of paying the tax is suddenly ignored. In effect, the conventional view of high prices and high profits overstate the attractiveness of the heroin business just as looking at the pretax profits of a highly taxed industry would grossly overstate the profitability of the industry. Because there is no neat way of calculating the costs associated with the prospect of arrest and indicating this cost on a financial statement, we grossly overestimate the attractiveness of the heroin business. When we include these costs, the industry does not look so attractive in spite of the large money profits.

Thus, two major conclusions of the conventional analysis about price responses by heroin dealers are incorrect. It is likely that heroin use *decreases* rather than remains constant. It is also likely that the attractiveness of the business *decreases* rather than increases.

Given the weakness of the popular analysis of pricing responses by the heroin distribution systems, it is important to develop an alternative analysis. We are interested in predicting the impact of an increased threat of arrest and prosecution on:

1. The quantity of heroin demanded
2. The price of heroin
3. The total revenues earned by heroin distributors
4. The attractiveness of the business

Economic theory indicates that these effects will depend on:

1. The degree of competition in the distribution system
2. The price elasticity of demand in the relevant range of demand
3. Whether the threat of arrest is perceived as a lump-sum tax or as a variable-cost tax

It is not obvious what we should assume about these factors. It is not clear whether the distribution system is competitive, monopolistic, or hybrid. It is not clear whether existing supplies of heroin are in the elastic or inelastic portions of the demand curve for heroin. Finally, it is not clear whether the threat of arrest should be treated as a lump-sum tax or a variable-cost tax. Consider this last problem.

Treating the threat as a lump-sum tax implies that the heroin dealer cannot affect the magnitude of the tax by adjusting the scale of his operation. The threat of arrest could have this aspect if a dealer was known to be involved in heroin dealing and avoided arrest only by paying large bribes on a regular basis and by successfully disciplining his employees and customers. For such dealers, an increased threat of arrest adds only to fixed costs (e.g., bribes and administrative overhead to monitor and discipline employees). Moreover, such dealers must consider themselves vulnerable to informants and illegal arrests by the police in spite of their fixed cost strategies to avoid arrest. Both the heavy reliance on fixed-cost strategies and the residual risks give the threat of arrest the appearance of a lump-sum tax.

Treating the threat of arrest as a variable-cost tax implies that the dealer can adjust the magnitude of the tax he pays by adjusting the scale of his activity. The threat of arrest may have this aspect for retail dealers who are not well-known by the police. For such dealers, reducing the number of transactions or reducing the quantity they sell could significantly reduce both the probability of arrest and the magnitude of the sanctions. Thus, it is not clear what we should assume about dealers' perceptions of the threat of arrest and imprisonment.

Because of the uncertainty about these different factors, we have made predictions for each possible case. Table 1-1 defines eight different sets of assumptions about conditions prevailing in the heroin industry, and deduces the effects of increasing the threat of arrest for each set of assumptions about the industry.[j] Although Table 1-1 yields no powerful general conclusions, one can make several significant observations.

First, in every case, the supply of the product is unchanged or reduced, and the price is unaffected or increased. In *no* case does the supply increase and the price decrease. This is an important regulatory effect to achieve.

Second, a price increase is not always associated with an increase in total revenues. The only case in which a price increase occurs and yields greater total revenues is the case of competitive suppliers producing in an inelastic range of the demand curve. In all other cases, price increases yield less total revenues simply because dealers were operating in an elastic range of the demand curve prior to the increased risk. In effect, they had made everything that could be made out of the users' desires for heroin before the threat increased.

Third, even in those circumstances in which a price increase yields increased total revenues, it is not clear what happens to the utility and money profits of the industry. It is possible that the costs (i.e., the threat of arrest) have increased by a larger amount than total revenues have increased. In this case, utility will also certainly fall. It is also possible that the costs will have increased by less than the total revenues increase. In this case, money profits would obviously increase, but utility will not necessarily increase. In general, the more inelastic the demand and the smaller the costs, the more likely it is that utility will rise. This suggests that if we are working on an already restricted supply (i.e., one that is close to an *elastic* range of the demand curve), and if we impose a substantial cost, utility is unlikely to increase.

In sum, in many cases, the heroin industry does not respond at all in terms of price to an increased threat of arrest: the dealers simply have to accept the reduction in utility associated with the increased anxiety. In other cases,

---

[j] I am indebted to Francis M. Bator, professor of political economy, Kennedy School of Government, Harvard University, for assistance with this table.

Table 1-1

Predicted Impact of an Increased Threat of Arrest on Gross Revenues and the Attractiveness of the Heroin Business for Alternative Assumptions about Industry and "Tax" Structure

Assumptions about Industry Structure, Tax Characteristics, and Elasticity of Demand	Predicted Effects On:			
	Quantity Consumed	Price	Gross Revenues	Attractiveness of Business
1.0 Monopolistic structure:				
1.1 Lump-sum tax	No change	No change	No change	Decrease
1.2 Variable-cost tax[a]	Decrease	Increase	Decrease	Decrease
2.0 Competitive structure:				
2.1 Elasticity >0; and <1				
2.1.1 Lump-sum tax	No change; or decrease[b]	No change; or increase[b]	No change; or increase[b]	Decrease; or uncertain[c]
2.1.2 Variable-cost tax	Decrease	Increase	Increase	Uncertain
2.2 Elasticity >1				
2.2.1 Lump-sum tax	No change; or decrease[b]	No change; or increase[b]	No change; or decrease[b]	Decrease
2.2.2 Variable-sum tax	Decrease	Increase	Decrease	Decrease
3.0 Monopolistic competition:				
3.1 Lump-sum tax	No change; or decrease[b]	No change; or increase[b]	No change; or decrease[d]	Decrease or uncertain[c]
3.2 Variable-cost tax	Decrease	Increase	Increase	Uncertain

Note: This table is produced from simple manipulations of microeconomic theory.

[a]The reason that supply, gross revenues, and attractiveness decline is that monopolists will choose to restrict supply until they are operating in a region of the demand curve where the price elasticity is greater than 1. Consequently, when the tax hits, it forces them into an even more elastic portion of the demand curve.

[b]A decrease in supply, increase in price, and increase in gross revenues will occur if the tax is large enough to drive some marginal dealers out of business. Note that the number of marginal dealers forced out of business depends on the "opportunity costs" of dealers as well as the size of the tax.

[c]The attractiveness of the business *to dealers who remain in business* is uncertain. It depends on the size of the tax, the number of marginal dealers who leave the business, and the precise elasticity of demand. If many go out of business and the demand is very inelastic, the business may become more attractive for those dealers who stay in business. If only a few go out of business, the demand is not very inelastic, and the tax is large, then the business may become less attractive.

[d]This assumes that the dealers have already restricted supply and priced at a level that is close to the elastic portion of the demand curve.

although the dealers respond by reducing supply and increasing prices, these actions do not necessarily yield increased total revenues. In the cases where dealers can increase total revenues, their utility need not increase. Thus, dealers cannot always respond successfully to an increased threat of arrest simply by restricting supply and raising prices. Unless they are competitive dealers operating in an inelastic portion of the demand curve facing a variable-cost tax that is small relative to the gain in revenue associated with a reduction in supply, they will be worse off than they were before the threat of arrest increased.

1.2 Investment in Strategies to Reduce a
Threat of Arrest

A second response to the threat of arrest and imprisonment is for heroin dealers to spend time and money to decrease the probability of arrest and imprisonment. Since the sanctions are applied by social agencies that are susceptible to deception, corruption, and incompetence, broad opportunities exist for heroin dealers to manipulate the situation strategically to their own ends.[3] The strategies available to dealers can be grouped as different lines of defenses against the enforcement agencies; as one line of defense is penetrated, the next line may still provide sufficient protection.

The first line of defense is to conceal all connections with the heroin industry. The objective is to avoid becoming known as a dealer. The second line of defense is to avoid creating evidence that could be used to convict a dealer for criminal offenses. The third line of defense is to corrupt or manipulate the agencies that apply sanctions to heroin dealers.

1.2.1 Concealing All Connections with the Heroin Industry. To conceal one's relation with the heroin industry, one must avoid (or reduce the frequency of) activities and associations that threaten to expose one. More specifically, one must

1. Avoid activity that is visible and uniquely connected with the production, distribution, or consumption of heroin
2. Avoid associations with people known to be active in the heroin industry
3. Prevent people who know one is involved in the heroin industry from telling others that one is involved

It is not easy or inexpensive for dealers to follow these guidelines. Indeed, there are some activities and associations that must be continued in spite of the fact that they create substantial risks for those involved in the trade. Moreover, the more religiously one adheres to these guidelines, the less successful one will be in producing, selling, and using heroin.

Consider, first, the problem of avoiding activity known to be associated with the production, distribution, and consumption of heroin. If one is a producer of heroin, one must purchase anhydrous acetic acid to continue production. If one is a distributor of heroin, one must purchase adultrants (mannite, quinine) and containers (medicine capsules, glassing envelopes) to continue successful distribution. If one is a consumer, one must inject heroin into one's veins. Each of these activities leaves traces: records of transactions in the case of purchase of supplies, scars in the case of injection. These traces are both durable and visible. Moreover, to some extent, they are probative of connections with a heroin industry. Thus, the activities make association with the heroin industry quite visible. Although one can substitute other activities that produce less durable and visible signs, or are less probative of connections with the heroin industry, all substitutes are more costly to producers, dealers, and consumers. Thus, in seeking to avoid tell-tale activities, heroin dealers and consumers will find it either impossible or costly.

Consider, next, the problem of avoiding identification with people known to be involved in the heroin industry. This problem is at least as expensive to resolve as the problem of avoiding tell-tale activities. The basic problem is that suppliers and dealers must communicate among themselves to make the market work smoothly. Addicts need to talk to other addicts to find their way to heroin markets in which "good bags" are being sold. If they shun the company of known addicts to avoid identification, they cut themselves off from valuable information. Similarly, dealers need to be able to communicate with consumers. If they fail to advertise to known users to avoid identification, they cut themselves off from valuable markets in which to sell. Thus, avoiding identification with known users and dealers often results in giving up significant advantages that come from being able to communicate freely.

The third problem—keeping those who know of one's involvement in the heroin industry from telling others that one is involved—is by far the most difficult. The major problem is that the police can suddenly change the contingencies facing one's associates. Although prior to an arrest it is generally in the interests of an associate to be discreet and tight-lipped, following an arrest it may be strongly in his interests to trade information for money or reduced penalties. Unless a dealer can wield incentives contingent on an associate's silence that are at least as powerful as the incentives wielded by the police, the dealer will be betrayed.

Notice that the dealer has two strategies in guarding against betrayal. One strategy is to confront all his associates continuously with sanctions sufficient to guarantee their silence under all possible threats by the police. This strategy yields a generalized immunity from the police. A second strategy is to adjust the sanctions that confront his associates according to changes in their situations; that is, he can confront his associates with sanctions sufficient to guarantee their silence against modest pressure or inducements of police most of the time, and then change the sanctions when an associate comes under stronger police pressure or is weakened for some other reason. This strategy yields a selective immunity.

Both strategies have serious problems. The problem with the generalized immunity is that it is very expensive. It is difficult to distribute continuously a set of rewards and penalties that are sufficiently large to guard against all threats by the police. The problem with selective immunity is that it does not always work. It is difficult for a dealer to discover when an associate's incentives have changed, difficult for him to wield incentives that are as large as those wielded by the police, and difficult for him to communicate to the potential informant that the informant is now facing a different set of contingencies from the dealer as well as a new set of contingencies from the police. Thus, the dealer can neither respond selectively to a sudden need to control a potential informant, nor guarantee that there are no potential informants among his associates.

These examples indicate that there are serious problems in maintaining the first line of defense. Strategies to avoid activities and association with the industry are expensive and only partly successful. In spite of this general observation, there are several strategies that have offered some protection. Although the price of the strategies is high, many dealers have found them worth the investment.

One strategy is to limit the number of people with whom heroin is exchanged. This strategy has at least five advantages in concealing one's relation to the heroin distribution system.

First, a small number of customers and associates implies that few people have direct, first-hand knowledge of a dealer's connections with the heroin industry. This reduces the chance of a casual information leak, and reduces a dealer's vulnerability to sustained efforts from enforcement agencies to gain information.

Second, a small market allows the supplier to monitor his customers and associates closely for signs of defection. Close monitoring allows the dealer to respond more reliably and more quickly when an associate becomes likely to betray him.

Third, if customers are restricted to a single, small market, they will come to identify their interests with keeping the dealer in operation. He becomes their vital "connection." To the extent that customers do come to identify their interests with keeping the dealer in business, it will be easier for the dealer to insure against casual information leaks.

Fourth, the small market will establish face-to-face relations between customers and suppliers. Because face-to-face relations bolster norms against leaking information, these relations will facilitate the dealer's problem in disciplining his customers and associates.

Fifth, the small market allows inexpensive, simple communication between the dealer and his customers. This allows the dealer to adjust his pattern of dealing (e.g., hours of operation, place of operation, techniques for concealing the exchange of money for heroin, etc.) without having to increase significantly the time he spends with his customers. In effect, a small market is quieter and more agile in responding to new threats than a large market.

Thus, operating with 5 to 15 customers and associates has significant advantages in maintaining the first line of defense compared with operating with 30 to 50 customers and associates.

The strategy of operating in small markets is not without liabilities. One very important disadvantage is that a dealer must abandon opportunities for aggressive market expansion. Note that market expansion is dangerous for dealers at two different stages—the period in which the dealer operates and maintains a large market, and the period in which the dealer is recruiting new customers to enlarge his market. Of these stages, the second is by far the most dangerous.

The period of operating and maintaining a large market is dangerous for all the opposite reasons that operating a small market is safe. A large market implies both that there are more people who can betray the dealer, and that the dealer's ability to control and discipline his customers is less. Consequently, the dealer must consider himself more than proportionately vulnerable.

The period of recruiting new customers is dangerous simply because the dealer has the least information and control over new customers at the moment of recruitment. Moreover, the dealer must consider all potential recruits particularly suspect. Dealers must assume that other dealers avoid or exclude customers whom they judge to be risky and retain customers known to be trustworthy. Consequently, an eager, unattached customer is more than proportionately likely to be a marginal, high-risk customer. In effect, because all dealers are interested in screening out undercover agents and informants, the pool of unattached customers must be more than proportionately stocked with informants and undercover police. Thus, both because a dealer has little control over new customers, and because he must assume he is picking customers from a high-risk pool, the moment of recruiting a new customer is particularly risky.

There are several important implications of this analysis of the unusual risks associated with expanding a market. The first implication is that contrary to common beliefs, heroin dealers are not likely to be aggressive marketers of heroin. Although the industry as a whole would be better off if dealers engaged in aggressive market expansion, it is not in the interest of any individual dealer to do so. Indeed, stepping out of a protected market into an unknown market is the most dangerous move a dealer makes. Whatever incentives there are for market expansion leads dealers to try to steal their competitors' best customers rather than venture into unknown markets. Thus, the "pushing" phenomenon is probably a myth.[k]

The second implication is that dealers will rely on a variety of screening mechanisms to help them distinguish reliable customers from unreliable custom-

[k]Patrick Hughes et al., "The Social Structure of a Heroin Copping Community," *American Journal of Psychiatry* 128:5 (November 1971): p. 48. There is strong empirical evidence supporting this conclusion. In a detailed examination of activity in a heroin copping community, Hughes et al. made the following observation: "Dealers in this neighborhood were not 'pushing' heroin. The addicts, in fact, were in a seller's market—they had to seek out the dealers." Also consistent with this deduction are the findings that users only rarely report that they received their first shot of heroin from a pusher. See Table 5-4 for this evidence.

ers. They will look for track marks, insist on references or introductions from people they know, listen for false notes in the customers' use of street jargon, and look for tell-tale physical characteristics such as clean fingernails or inappropriate clothes and haircuts. These screening devices will result in discrimination against some classes of potential customers.[l]

The third implication is that dealers will choose to operate and expand in areas where there are pervasive norms against cooperating with the police. In such areas, the risks associated with recruiting additional customers and operating with a large number of customers will be less. This observation may account for the fast spread of heroin in the ghetto, and, since youth in the suburbs may now be internalizing strong norms against cooperating with the police, may not bode well for the future of drug use in suburbs.

Thus, it is difficult for dealers to expand and operate large markets without exposing themselves to significant risks. Although abandoning opportunities for expansion is a great price to pay for the protection provided by small markets, many dealers find the sacrifice worth making. Others who have become greedy have regretted the consequences.[m]

A second disadvantage of selling only in small markets is that since the supplier continues to distribute heroin, he continues to expose himself to people who cannot be completely trusted. Although the bonds between customer and supplier are greater in small markets than in large markets, they are a long way from foolproof. The fragility of these bonds implies that there is still a substantial risk in distributing heroin.

A more robust strategy is not only to restrict the size of the market, but also to invest heavily in procedures for screening and disciplining customers. This strategy differs from the first only in the relative emphasis it places on screening and discipline.

The dealer could tighten screening procedures by applying a more conservative rule in selling to new customers, or by gathering additional information about new customers. For example, the dealer could insist on three references from people known to him before deciding to sell. Or, the dealer could attempt to find out more about his customers by investigating their arrest record, asking other dealers about them, or by covertly observing their activities and encoun-

---

[l]It is argued in Part III that a fundamental objective of the enforcement strategy is to create discrimination against new users of heroin. This effect can be achieved precisely because dealers will react to the threat of arrest by setting up screening procedures. All the police must do is disguise themselves as the customers they would like to protect. In effect, the police contaminate a pool of potential customers by counterfeiting the customers.

[m]There is a general tendency for the police to arrest the least cautious heroin dealers. Many people take this as a sign of the inevitable failure of enforcement efforts. However, in many cases, it is precisely the least cautious dealers who are the most important dealers to arrest. The reason is that their aggressiveness could result in the recruitment of large numbers of new users or a dramatic increase in the aggregate supply of heroin. The caution of other dealers makes them inefficient suppliers and marketers of heroin and therefore less important targets of police action. For further discussion of this point, see page 58.

ters for a given time. The combination of more evidence and a more conservative standard could effectively reduce the risk of betrayal.[n]

The dealer could strengthen discipline by increasing the rewards and penalties he controls, and by increasing the reliability of his monitoring system. For example, the dealer can beat or kill those who betray him or share his market with those who remain silent. However, to make such rewards reliably contingent on the customer's silence, the dealer must be able to discern which of his customers is likely to have betrayed him. This requires the dealer to monitor his customers' activity and status. He can discover which have come under police pressure by monitoring arrests through newspaper accounts, court appearances, or police records.[o] He can occasionally covertly trail his customers to observe their activities and encounters. If the dealer succeeds in monitoring his customers' behavior, and can credibly threaten them with significant rewards and punishment, the dealer can, again, significantly reduce the risk of betrayal.

Note that to some extent screening and discipline are redundant. If one screens *in* customers who are naturally inclined to be discreet even when confronted with police pressure, one reduces one's need for effective discipline. Similarly, if a dealer can discipline his customers successfully, he reduces his need for effective discipline. Effective discipline implies that a customer will be strongly motivated to be discreet and silent regardless of his initial characteris-

[n]The process of screening is important throughout this analysis. Consequently, it is valuable to establish a fairly precise analytic conception of the process. Basically, dealers try to distinguish trustworthy customers from traitorous customers. They cannot directly observe the degree of trustworthiness. They can only observe characteristics they believe are correlated with this characteristic ("signals"). Because the correlation between the signals and the actual characteristics is uncertain, dealers will make errors in deciding to sell. The errors will be of two different types: they will sometimes decide to sell to traitorous customers and will sometimes refuse to sell to trustworthy clients. The frequency with which they make both types of errors will depend on the strength of the correlation between the signal and the actual characteristic: the stronger the correlation, the fewer the errors. However, dealers can adjust the proportion of errors of each type they make by adjusting their criteria for deciding to sell to a user. If they decide that a weak signal of trustworthiness is sufficient for them to sell, the dealers will reduce the frequency with which they refuse to sell to a trustworthy client, but only at the price of increasing the frequency with which they agree to sell to a traitorous customer. In effect, in setting up a screening procedure, a dealer can adjust two different components: he can change the "signals" he examines (absorbing some costs to observe signals more highly correlated with the desired characteristics than the signals that are inexpensively available); or he can alter his criterion for deciding whether to sell or not on the basis of the observed signals. Presumably increased enforcement pressure pushes dealers towards increased expenditures to observe higher quality signals and more conservative criteria in evaluating the signals. From the point of view of policy objectives, forcing dealers to invest in elaborate screening and rely on conservative standards are very valuable effects: many new users will be discouraged by the process and denied access to markets. For a brilliant analysis of the role of signals in the labor markets, see Michael Spence, *Market Signalling, Discussion Paper No. 4*, Public Policy Program, Harvard University, 1972.

[o]An analysis of a fencing operation showed that fences were heavily dependent on newspapers for information. See Carl B. Klockars, *The Professional Fence* (New York: The Free Press, 1974), pp. 74-75, footnote 1.

tics. Note, also, that effective discipline functions as a screening device. Those customers who are anxious about their ability to avoid or withstand police pressure may prefer not to participate in a market where there is effective discipline. In effect, the threat of effective discipline deters many marginal customers.

Given this redundancy, it is generally unwise for dealers to invest in both screening procedures and discipline procedures. The only case in which it would make sense to invest in both procedures is when the dealer is willing to spend large amounts of time and effort to guarantee a very high level of security. In cases where a dealer is not inclined to absorb the great expense and inconveniences of being very cautious, it is worthwhile to invest in only one procedure. Generally, it seems that effective discipline is less expensive and more valuable in providing security than effective screening. Consequently, one would expect marginal dealers to use a few rudimentary screening devices and to invest heavily in procedures to discipline their customers. As dealers become more risk averse or wealthier, they will continue to purchase improved discipline rather than improved screening. At some high level of risk averseness or wealth, dealers will begin to invest in more expensive screening devices.

The advantages of small markets combined with tight screening and effective discipline are obvious. All the natural advantages of small markets accrue. In addition, one sells only to customers who are unusually trustworthy and maintain a high degree of effective control over their behavior.

The major disadvantage of this strategy is that it is extraordinarily expensive. It is time consuming to gather evidence on the trustworthiness of customers. Monitoring the behavior of customers and rewarding or punishing them at every turn requires a great deal of time and the assumption of significant additional risks of being linked to the heroin industry.

Similarly, controlling large incentives such as a capacity to kill or injure or a willingness to share profits in the market require the assumption of additional risks or large monetary expenditures. The costs of tight screening and effective discipline make this strategy much more expensive than simply reducing the size of one's market.

This strategy also has the same disadvantages with respect to lost opportunities for market expansion as the first strategy. Indeed, problems with market expansion are exacerbated with this second strategy. Tight screening will exclude many possible customers. The effective discipline may frighten additional customers. These effects will slow, and ultimately constrain, market expansion in a way that the first strategy does not.

A third strategy is for suppliers never to engage personally in any illegal activity, and to keep their identity known only to one or two agents who do the work for them.[p] In effect, this strategy simply adds a level to the distribution

---

[p]For evidence that dealers employ this tactic see Staff and Editors of *Newsday, The Heroin Trail* (New York: Signet, 1973), p. 205. For the costs of using agents, see Richard Woodley, *Dealer* (New York: Holt, Rinehart and Winston, 1971), p. 68.

system. The advantage of adding this level is that the supplier divides by a factor of 5 to 10 the number of people with whom he must deal. All the advantages of dealing with an extremely small group follow. The supplier may more effectively screen his own activity and connections without losing control over the consumers. Indeed, he may be able to increase dramatically the number of consumers he can control.

The major disadvantage of the strategy is that a supplier often finds himself in a very precarious position vis-à-vis his agents. The agents are both an extremely valuable resource to the supplier (since they screen him from many risks) and a dangerous liability (since they are in a position to expose his apparently secure position). Because the agents have a strategic position, they may exploit their position for sizeable rewards. The supplier is faced with the difficult problem of controlling these agents without giving up all the profits that accrue to his particular heroin market.

Frequently, a critical resource that makes the supplier valuable to the agents is the supplier's relation with the supplier above him. If the agents can be made to believe that the supplier's relation to a higher level supplier is the critical factor guaranteeing the supply of heroin that keeps them all rich, then the supplier becomes the goose that lays the golden egg. Such a position allows him to maintain a hold on a share of the profits. The importance of this position to the supplier implies that the supplier will do everything in his power to keep his agents from establishing a reliable relation with the higher level supplier.

Note that the supplier's interest in limiting access to his supplier often coincides with the higher level supplier's interest. The higher level supplier prefers that he be shielded from the agents by the lower level supplier since he would like to minimize the number of people who know of his activities. It is this interest that makes the supplier's efforts to keep the agents away from his supplier likely to be successful. This probability of success, in turn, provides some stability in the strategic maneuvering between the agents and supplier.[q]

In sum, the strategies to conceal one's relation with the heroin industry are:

1.   Restricting markets to a small number of users
2.   Screening customers very carefully
3.   Monitoring and disciplining customers
4.   Using agents to shield the dealer from the customers

[q]These observations have important implications for the potential value of enforcement strategies that rely on "buying up the ladder." A common enforcement tactic is to make an escalating series of undercover buys from the same dealer. The objective is to motivate the dealer to pass the undercover agent on to the higher level dealer. In fact, both the current dealer and his supplier will resist this tendency. The current dealer will have strong incentives to retain such a good customer for himself. The higher level dealer will want to avoid being exposed to the strange customer. Thus, the incentives operating in the distribution system reduce the chance of success for this strategy. This issue is discussed more extensively below.

It is no accident that these strategies are organizational strategies. The problems to be solved in maintaining the first line of defense are to screen the inevitable transactions of the business from casual observation. The brunt of the screening efforts must lie with establishing a sharp boundary beyond which evidence of the transactions cannot be seen, and reducing the amount of activity and negotiation necessary to complete the transactions. The discipline and the number of individuals are critical variables in establishing the boundaries and determining the amount of explicit negotiation and uncoordinated activity that are necessary. Consequently, these are the variables that must be manipulated to limit the probability that a heroin supplier will be identified with the heroin industry.

1.2.2 Avoid Creating or Being Caught with Evidence. The second line of defense is to avoid creating evidence that provides probable cause for a search, justifies an arrest, or supports a conviction. In the course of their activities, dealers may create evidence that will support convictions on a variety of charges. However, the most persistent and pervasive threat is that they will be discovered while possessing or exchanging heroin. Consequently, the central problems in maintaining this line of defense are to hide or dispossess heroin while continuing to exchange and control inventories of heroin.

Maintaining this line of defense is inconvenient for dealers. Both concealing and dispossessing heroin impede the exchanges that are vital to the dealer's business. If heroin is well hidden, then it ceases to be readily accessible—either because the heroin is so well hidden that it takes a long time to disassemble and reassemble the hiding place, or because frequent access to the heroin gives away the location to any observer. As a result, to maintain the security of their heroin, dealers are restricted to a small number of transactions per day.

Dispossession of one's heroin also tends to make heroin inaccessible. In addition, dispossession carries the risk that the dealer will lose control of his inventories. Distant, unwatched caches of heroin are tempting marks for thieves. Similarly, if a dealer does not personally participate in transactions involving his heroin, he risks being defrauded. His customer can claim that the heroin he paid for was not where it was supposed to be, or can take more heroin than he paid for. Thus, in order to minimize the chance that a dealer is caught with evidence, he must sacrifice convenience and security in possessing and exchanging heroin.

Several features of the world generally facilitate the dealers' effort to avoid being caught with heroin. First, since heroin is light, small in volume, and requires no special packaging to be preserved, it can be hidden securely in many different places and dispossessed quickly if the need ever arises. It can be stored in compartments small enough to be unnoticeable, and exchanged in handshakes or kisses. It can be swallowed or flushed down toilets when the police arrive at the doorstep. If heroin was larger or heavier, it would be easier to notice and harder to dispossess.

Second, the police are restricted to looking for heroin in only a small number of places. One reason for this restriction is limited resources. There are only a small number of eyes employed to look for heroin. Equally significant are constitutional limitations on search and seizure. The police are prohibited from looking for heroin except in situations where they can establish probable cause for a search.[r] The implication of the limited capacity of the police to look for evidence of heroin is that dealers can afford to be somewhat incautious about concealing and dispossessing heroin. Even if dealers are occasionally careless, there is a good chance that the police will not notice.

Although these factors reduce the pressure on dealers to conceal and dispossess their heroin, they do not totally negate the police threat. Indeed, there are three strategies the police can use to make legitimate arrests in spite of these difficulties. First, they observe people known to be active in the heroin industry and stop them at points where they are likely to have stored or exchanged heroin. Second, they obtain information about the location of drugs from informants. Third, they penetrate the organizations that store and exchange drugs and directly observe the location of the heroin. In order to reduce their risk to very low levels, dealers must devise and employ strategies that frustrate the strategies of the police.

One effective way for dealers to frustrate police efforts to secure evidence is simply to maintain the first line of defense (i.e., avoid being identified as a dealer). If one can avoid being "known" as a dealer, one can avoid being closely observed. If one can screen out undesirable customers (e.g., informants and undercover police), one can prevent the police from learning about the location of one's heroin. Thus, the strategies that are effective in maintaining the first line of defense are also important and effective in maintaining the second line of defense. But there are additional strategies that will frustrate police efforts to secure evidence even after the first line of defense has been penetrated.

Perhaps the most important strategy is for dealers to blend their illegal activities of possessing and exchanging heroin into the normal, legitimate activities of their daily lives.[s] Heroin can be stored in the apartment of a mother or girl friend and tapped or replenished during the course of casual, routine visits. Heroin can be exchanged while shaking hands, having a beer, or buying a newspaper. Complicated arrangements to exchange heroin covertly can be negotiated during casual encounters on the street or telephone calls. In a society where citizens cannot be stopped and searched without probable cause to believe that a crime is being committed, a great deal of behavior that can be used to cover heroin transactions is constitutionally protected. As a result, heroin dealers

[r]Limitations on police activity and strategies followed by the police within these limitations are discussed extensively in Chapter 3.

[s]For the role of blending strategies in protecting heroin laboratories, see Staff and Editors of *Newsday, The Heroin Trail*, p. 76. For the importance of blending strategies in the fencing business, see Klockars, *The Professional Fence*, pp. 77-82.

can enjoy significant latitude in operating if they are careful to blend illegal activities into constitutionally protected activities.

Notice that for this blending strategy to be successful, the same activity used to cover exchanges of heroin must occur frequently and *not* involve a heroin transaction. In effect, a dealer is trying to hide a "signal" (his illegal activities) in general background "noise" (outwardly similar activities that do not involve exchanges of heroin). Consequently, for the signal to be taken merely as noise, the dealer must increase the amount of noise.

To some extent, a dealer can accomplish this himself. If a dealer wants to use his mother's apartment as a safe place to store heroin and he wants to be able to have ready access to it, he must become an extremely dutiful son. He must visit his mother on many occasions when he does not bring or take away heroin. Similarly, if a dealer wants to pass heroin on the street through casual encounters, handshakes, and embraces, he must spend a lot of time encountering, handshaking, and embracing when he is not exchanging heroin. In effect, the constant motion, interaction, and hustle that is typical of heroin dealers serves the same function as the incessant wiping, scratching, and arm crossing of major league baseball coaches: an observer attempting to figure out the sign is uncertain about which activity is the real sign. Thus, dealers can create a great deal of noise by themselves.

However, to a greater extent, dealers rely on others around them to create the background noise that conceals them. Since many others in the cultural milieu of heroin dealers behave as heroin dealers do in all respects but possessing and exchanging heroin, it is difficult to distinguish the dealers from the nondealers. Both adolescents and ghetto residents spend time "hanging out" in public areas. In addition, there is a great deal of movement and interaction. The sheer volume of activity, all of which *could* involve exchanges of heroin, makes it difficult to identify the small number of encounters that actually *do* involve exchanges of heroin. Since ordinary behavior is precisely the behavior required to continue dealing in heroin, the general background noise totally obscures the actual exchanges of heroin.[†]

One observes the same phenomenon in analyzing the behavior of heroin smugglers. Every day tons of cargo are unloaded in New York City ports and airports. Only pounds of heroin must be concealed in this huge volume to maintain the local heroin market. Sailors getting off ships, diplomats being checked through customs, bottles of wine being loaded on trucks, cars being

---

[†]Some personal experience convinced me of the difficulty of distinguishing the "signal" from the "noise." While riding in an unmarked car with New York City narcotics detectives, I asked them to point out any heroin transactions they observed. They would often point to encounters and groups of people on the street whom they believed to be involved in heroin deals. I was unable to distinguish the groups they identified from the hundreds of other encounters and groups we passed. I suspect that the differences the detective noticed were not particularly significant in identifying the transactions—particularly so because they were unable to say what distinguished the events described as heroin transactions from other events that appeared similar to me.

picked up by private purchasers may all conceal heroin. But they conceal heroin in such a small proportion of total cases, that it is not worth investigating all possible cases closely.[u] In effect, the problem that the customs official faces in attempting to single out the few bottles of wine that contain plastic bags of heroin from a large shipment of wine in a busy port is analogous to the problem that patrolmen and narcotics agents face in trying to decide which of the 40 groups standing on street corners are currently engaged in exchanging heroin.

Thus, both retail dealers and smugglers can effectively blend illegal activity into their own legal activity and the legal activity of others who look and behave much like they do. Blending protects dealers because it capitalizes on the small size of heroin and the budgetary and constitutional restrictions on the police to keep the dealers from being investigated too closely and too frequently.

A third strategy to avoid creating evidence is simply to hide the heroin well enough to frustrate a close investigation. A variety of mechanical devices are used. Heroin has been hidden in secret compartments of suitcases, cupboards, and chests; in automobile gas tanks; in specially constructed bottles that have wine only in the top third of the bottle; and in padded wire frames made to simulate a pregnant woman's stomach.[4] These devices often have the advantage of being fairly inexpensive. They have the disadvantage of being easily penetrated by a thorough police search.

Generally, this strategy of hiding heroin with mechanical devices is used merely to complement a blending strategy. The dealer relies primarily on blending to ward off a thorough search, and employs clever hiding places only to reduce the probability of a chance discovery. The devices are not designed to frustrate a very thorough search.

However, some devices are successful in frustrating very serious searches. Some hiding places can be both very carefully concealed, and very difficult to gain access to. Internal components of a car, human beings, or other large mechanisms afford both a high degree of concealment and impose a heavy burden on anyone who wants to look hard enough to find the heroin.[v] Consequently, these devices afford much greater portection to dealers.

[u]The problem Customs faces is illustrated dramatically by the following example: "An appreciation of this 'needle in a haystack' situation can be obtained from the following theoretical, but typical, example. One cargo invoice covers a shipment of 10 containers, each container holds 100 cartons, each carton contains 24 teapots in individual boxes, and one teapot contains heroin.

"Actual detection of the heroin in that teapot would be a formidable task even if it were known that the heroin was secreted somewhere within this shipment. If, however, this were not known or suspected, the task of detection becomes staggering, if not impossible, particularly when one considers the situation in its entire context—one teapot, one of 24 boxes, in one of 100 cartons, in one of 10 containers, in one of many shipments covered by one of 1.4 million invoices. This, in brief, gives an idea of the problem faced by Customs in its efforts to impede the flow of heroin into the country." See Comptroller General of the United States, "Heroin Being Smuggled Into New York City Successfully" (Washington, D.C.: General Accounting Office, 1972), p. 16.

[v]For a good example of very difficult hiding places, recall the "French Connection" case. A search of several hours failed to locate the heroin and the police were nearly discouraged

Very intricate and complicated hiding places have several disadvantages. First, they reduce the dealers access to heroin as much as they reduce the access of the police. As previously noted, this cramps the style of a dealer who needs to make transactions. Second, they tend to require the work of specialists who are knowledgeable about the mechanisms in which the heroin is concealed.[w] Unless a dealer has the necessary, specialized skills himself, he must expose his activity to an additional person. Such exposure is always a risk. Third, the hiding places tend to be expensive.

A fourth problem with intricate hiding places is of a slightly different order. Because the intricate hiding places are expensive and require the work of a specialist, a dealer may decide to use the same hiding place on several different occasions. This may lower average costs and bind the specialist closer to his organization. Moreover, because the hiding place is intricate, the dealer may feel very confident in its effectiveness. All of these factors lead the dealer to use the same device frequently. Frequent use of the same device ultimately makes the dealer vulnerable. Once discovered, the dealer's modus operandi becomes a powerful piece of evidence the police can use to discover, arrest, and convict the dealer. There is a nice paradox here: it is partly because the devices are so effective that they become the dealers' Archilles' heel. He is lulled into a false sense of confidence and comes to rely too heavily on something that becomes increasingly vulnerable as he increasingly relies on it.[x]

Thus, both simple and intricate hiding places contribute to the security of the dealers. But both have important disadvantages as well.

A fourth major strategy to prevent the police from obtaining persuasive evidence is simply to dispossess the heroin. Because the police must establish posesssion to secure a conviction, and because the police design tactics on the assumption that dealers have heroin in their immediate possession, an effective strategy for dealers is to keep heroin far away from themselves. They can do so at several different stages: while storing heroin in inventories, while exchanging heroin, or when confronted by the police.

Inventories of heroin can be dispossessed by creating caches for heroin that are remote from a dealer's daily activity.[y] The advantage of these caches is that

from continuing the search. It is also worth noting that restrictions on "strip searches" of people entering the country make internal parts of human beings effective hiding places for small, but not insignificant amounts of heroin. In reading through a sample of cases on the Southwest Border, I was surprised of how frequently heroin was concealed in body cavities.

[w]The existence of specialists in building "traps" is reported in the anecdotal literature. See Vincent Teresa with Thomas C. Renner, *Vinnie Teresa's Mafia* (Garden City: Doubleday and Co., 1975), pp. 123-128. See also, *Newsday, The Heroin Trail*, p. 71.

[x]This is an application of a general point developed in Irving Goffman, *Strategic Interaction* (Philadelphia: University of Pennsylvania, 1969). See particularly, p. 62.

[y]For the role of "caches" see Woodley, *Dealer*, pp. 31-32, *Newsday, The Heroin Trail*, p. 256. For similar operations in the fencing business, see Klockars, *The Professional Fence*, pp. 83-86.

the dealer can go about most of his daily life without fearing a police search. Then, when he needs to gain access to his heroin, he can take special measures to avoid being followed. He can lose himself in crowds or streets, outrun potential pursuers, or refuse to go when he suspects he is being successfully followed. In effect, a cache allows a dealer to economize on his efforts to avoid being followed.

A cache has several disadvantages. First, like intricate hiding places, it reduces the number of transactions a dealer may make. Second, caches are vulnerable to rip-offs. Although one can hire guards, one must worry about their trustworthiness. Third, a cache can often be linked to a particular individual. Because of the threat of rip-offs, dealers often establish their caches in property they or their friends or relatives control and own.[z] Although this device reduces the threat of a rip-off, it facilitates police efforts to prove that the dealers possessed heroin. Names on leases or titles of property where heroin is stored become powerful pieces of evidence in conspiracy or possession cases. Thus, in establishing a cache a dealer must either leave his heroin exposed hoping that it will go unremarked and confident that it will be difficult to trace the heroin to him; or he must make provisions to guard his heroin knowing that when he does so, he may not have adequately protected his heroin and has certainly made it easier for the police to connect him to the cache.

Dispossessing heroin in exchanges is slightly more complicated. But it is also very important since the police are particularly alert to and interested in any encounter of a "known dealer" with a "known junkie" that could cover a heroin transaction. The strategies that are effective in dispossessing heroin during exchanges are complicated "drop" systems. Drugs are left in locations at times when the dealer is not observed to be picked up at times when the purchaser is not observed. Such strategies have the advantage of allowing legitimate or constitutionally protected activity (e.g., meeting on the street, talking on the phone, "lending" money, etc.) to substitute partly for the illegal activity of buying and selling heroin, since the heroin part of the transaction occurs at another time in a more discreet way than would otherwise be possible. An additional advantage is that it is hard to prove that drugs in one location were in fact controlled by a man who is not there in person. Consequently, even if discovered, the behavior and purposes of the drop system are hard to prove in court.[aa]

The strategy has the disadvantage of making the dealer vulnerable to unobserved thefts (since his drugs are exposed for at least part of the time), and sometimes to absconding by the purchaser. The consumer is also vulnerable to

[z]In the distribution system described in *Newsday, The Heroin Trail*, p. 256, all the caches were controlled by relatives.

[aa]For elements of proof necessary to establish possession, see pp. 121-123 of this book; or Charles H. Whitebread and Ronald Stevens, "Constructive Possession in Narcotics Cases: To Have and Have Not," *Virginia Law Review* 58 (1972): 751.

double crosses by the dealer. The uncertainties that mark these transactions and the complex behavior that must be coordinated to make the transaction successful imply that the negotiations among consumers and suppliers consume large amounts of time. This is particularly true when communication between the supplier and the consumer is not facilitated by past experience with one another. The large amount of time required is a disadvantage of the strategy. Finally, the strategy is often vulnerable to informers since the strategies cannot change quickly without dramatically increasing the time a dealer must spend on negotiating new arrangements with his customers.

Dispossessing heroin when confronted by the police is a surprisingly effective tactic for dealers. Dealers can drop the heroin to the street, flush heroin down toilets, or swallow it when arrest and search seem imminent. This tactic is effective in subverting police efforts for three reasons.

First, because there is a demanding legal test for possession,[5] the dealer has many ways of legally disposessing the heroin. Heroin must be found in the immediate possession of a person, or in a place that is owned and used primarily by the person, for possession to be demonstrated. Since the streets are not owned by anyone, all the dealer must do is drop heroin to the street unobserved to avoid a conviction.

Second, the procedures required in conducting a legal search often provide dealers with sufficient time to dispossess their heroin. If the police must knock or otherwise announce themselves and wait a reasonable period between entering or taking custody of someone by force, the dealer may be able to throw the heroin away, swallow it, or otherwise dispossess it.

Third, since the police have often *not* followed these procedures and have given perjured testimony in narcotics cases, virtually all police testimony about the circumstances surrounding the discovery of heroin is suspect.[6] As a result, it is now possible for dealers to dispossess the heroin in a standard way, to have the police observe the dispossession and testify accurately that the dispossession occurred, and to have the court disbelieve and heavily discount the policeman's testimony. In effect, the police have given dealers additional latitude in dispossessing heroin by attempting to restrict their latitude through improper procedures and perjured testimony. Not only can dealers take advantage of the wide latitude given them if the police adhere strictly to legal procedures, but, in addition, they can often escape when their dispossession efforts have been clumsy and easily observed by the police. The courts simply do not believe the police cries of wolf, and the wolf goes undetected. Thus, dispossessing heroin when confronted by the police affords an effective strategy to avoid creating persuasive evidence of wrong doing.[bb]

[bb]Jerome M. Skolnick makes an important distinction between police "knowledge" of guilt and "evidence" necessary to show guilt, and suggests that this has a major impact on the way police use their discretion. See *Justice Without Trial* (New York: Wiley and Sons, 1966), pp. 150-151.

One thing to notice before leaving the strategy of dispossession is that using agents in transactions can serve the function of dispossessing heroin. However, it serves this function only if the agent cannot be traced to the dealer. Consequently, to dispossess heroin through the use of agents, the dealer must be able both to guarantee the silence of the agents and to instruct and direct the agent without leaving durable signs of one's communication with the agent. Using agents to dispossess heroin has the additional problem of making the dealer vulnerable to frauds and take-offs.

A fifth and final strategy to frustrate police efforts to secure evidence is to move the drugs constantly from hiding place to hiding place. This strategy has a serious liability in that the police generally watch the activity of individuals in limiting the number of places the drugs could be and this strategy dramatically increases the activity associated with storing drugs. Another disadvantage is that such a strategy often involves many people and much negotiation to keep the drugs in motion. Both requirements are liabilities. Still, the strategy has the advantage of quickly making obsolete any detailed information the police might have about the location of drugs. Consequently, it may be worth its disadvantages when there is reason to believe that the police are receiving good information about the location of heroin. This strategy works simply because there is a lag between obtaining reliable information about the location of drugs, and police action to discover the drugs in the possession of the dealer.

Thus, in addition to the strategies that maintain the first line of defense, the following strategies are effective in frustrating police efforts to secure evidence:

1. Blending illegal activities into one's own legitimate activities and the activities of others
2. Constructing simple or elaborate hiding places for heroin
3. Dispossessing heroin by:
   a. Storing it in caches
   b. Using drop systems to exchange heroin
   c. Getting rid of the heroin when confronted by police
4. Moving heroin from place to place to make any information about the location of the heroin quickly obsolete

Judicious use of these strategies allows dealers to frustrate police efforts to secure evidence even when dealers are known to the police.

1.2.3 Corruption of Enforcement Agencies. The third line of defense is to corrupt, manipulate, or demoralize enforcement agencies so they are unwilling to apply the authorized sanctions against heroin dealers. The major tactic for demoralizing enforcement agencies is bribery. The purpose of bribing law-enforcement officials is to purchase indulgence for acts that would otherwise be prosecuted. In effect, dealers purchase a "license" to continue their illicit activities.[cc] There are two interesting questions about the dealers' use of bribery. First, who will the dealers bribe? Second, what kinds of "licenses" will they be able to purchase?

The problem of whom to bribe requires a nice calculation. A bribe offered to the wrong official results in a bribery conviction. Less extreme, but still significant, is the chance that a dealer will pay an expensive bribe to one official only to be arrested shortly thereafter by another official.[dd] On the other hand, a bribe offered to the right official can prevent an imminent arrest, or relieve the dealer of having to behave cautiously. In general, dealers will decide whom to bribe by reckoning the dollar cost of the bribe (and the risk of offering it) against the protection a successful bribe can offer.[ee] A variety of factors will influence the dealers' calculations.

In gauging the *risk* of offering a bribe, the dealer will consider such factors as:

1. The number of officials involved in the bribe
2. The extent to which the actions of the officials are carefully scrutinized by others
3. The amount that an official has to lose if he is discovered taking a bribe
4. The morale and integrity of officials in specific positions

The more people who are involved, the more closely scrutinized, the more they have to lose, and the higher the morale of the organization, the more risky and expensive the bribe.

In gauging the potential *benefits* of a bribe, the dealer will consider such factors as:

1. The magnitude and immediacy of the threat posed by a specific official
2. The extent to which the official monopolizes threats against the dealer or can protect the dealer from threats posed by other officials[ff]
3. The scope of the license conferred (i.e., the variety of criminal acts that are tolerated and the period over which the license is effective)

[cc]See Simon Rottenberg, "The Clandestine Distribution of Heroin: Its Discovery and Suppression," *Journal of Political Economy* 76 (1968): 83-86. A "franchise" system for pickpockets in subways is reported in Leonard Shecter with William Phillips, *On the Pad* (New York: Berkley, 1973), p. 166.

[dd]For a description of a criminal's reaction to being arrested by different police than he was paying, see Shecter with Phillips, *On the Pad*, p. 116.

[ee]To make these calculations successfully, some kind of "brokers" would have to develop who helped criminals locate the people who were vulnerable and valuable to bribe. Such people seem to exist. William Phillips appears to have played this role. See Shecter with Phillips, *On the Pad*, p. 29.

[ff]For an explicit calculation of the adequacy of the protection provided related to the cost of the bribe, see Shecter with Phillips, *On the Pad*, p. 30.

The more substantial and immediate the threat, the more effectively an official monopolizes threats, and the broader the license conferred, the more valuable is the bribe.

Note that the potential benefits of bribing any particular official depend a great deal on the position of the dealer. Unless they happen to be neighbors, it does a street dealer operating in Bedford-Stuyvesant little good to bribe a patrolman in Richmond. Similarly, unless a large-scale importer engages in casual retail sales, it may do him little good to bribe a local narcotic detective. Because the police are geographically and functionally specialized, a dealer is threatened only by certain kinds of police. It follows, then, that only a few officials are valuable for any particular dealer to bribe. It also follows that there are few *general* propositions about the value of bribes offered to different officials. It all depends on the position of the dealer. However, to illustrate the dealer's calculations and to probe for significant weaknesses in the enforcement apparatus, it is useful to consider the problem from the point of view of an experienced street dealer. Since this group of dealers is large, any conclusions about the vulnerability of different officials are likely to identify a major portion of the existing corruption problem.

Consider, first, the choice between bribing police officials and court officials. In general, the police are the more attractive targets. Since much police work occurs without written records or close supervision, a policeman can take a bribe with little risk of exposure.[gg] Moreover, since the police initiate cases against dealers, their indulgence can totally eliminate the threat of prosecution. Court officials, on the other hand, operate with many written records and fairly close public scrutiny. Consequently, the risks of exposure are significant. Moreover, since they are restrained by written records, they can only marginally affect the outcome of a case. Thus, a heroin dealer should try to bribe police rather than court officials. The costs to them are lower, and the protection more effective.

Among kinds of police officials, the choice is less obvious. Consider three types of officials—a uniformed patrolman, a narcotic detective, and a superior officer. From the point of view of the dealer, the patrolman has the advantages of operating with significant discretion, of facing low opportunity costs if he is exposed, and often, of being judged to have relatively low morale. He has the twin disadvantage of neither posing a significant threat nor being able to protect dealers against threats posed by others. Thus, although his price is low, his protection is often not very significant.

The narcotics detective typically operates with even greater discretion than the patrolman. However, both his morale and opportunity costs if exposed may

---

[gg]For general description of the environments within which police work and the significant discretion they enjoy, see Jonathan Rubinstein, *City Police* (New York: Farrar, Straus and Giroux, 1973); Skolnick, *Justice Without Trial*; or James Q. Wilson, *Varieties of Police Behavior* (Cambridge, Mass.: Harvard University Press, 1968).

be much higher. Consequently, he may be more expensive than the patrolman. He is often worth the additional price because he poses a substantial threat to a dealer and can often offer broad, effective protection. He is certainly worth the price if his morale is judged to be low.

The superior officer is probably the least likely target. He personally rarely poses a significant threat and he cannot reliably control his subordinates without dramatically increasing his own risk of exposure. The risk of exposure is an important deterrent because he has a relatively long way to fall if discovered. Thus, a superior officer is likely to be too expensive and his protection too unreliable to be an attractive target for bribes.

Among police officers, then, a narcotics detective is the most attractive target as long as one can count on them having low morale. A uniformed patrol officer is the next most attractive target, and a superior officer the least attractive target.

Among court officials, the choice is more obvious. Consider three kinds of officials—judges, district attorneys, and court clerks. Judges and district attorneys are much alike. Since their decisions and actions are recorded and noted by others such as arresting officers, corroborating witnesses, and assorted court officials, and since there are fairly well-known standards that prescribe the appropriate conduct of a case, both D.A.'s and judges face substantial risks of exposure. Moreover, they both stand to lose significantly if they are exposed. Finally, the greatest benefit they can offer is often merely a reduction in penalties. Consequently, these officials are likely to be expensive and relatively ineffective.

Court clerks are more vulnerable and potentially more valuable because they operate without close scrutiny, and can exercise significant influence. They can lose papers, affect the pace of cases by scheduling hearings, or give cases to one judge or another. Any of these decisions could have an important effect on the outcome of a case. Because their actions are rarely noted, and because clerks face low opportunity costs if exposed, they might be easily tempted. Thus, among court officials, court clerks represent a very attractive target for bribes.

The second question about bribing officials concerns the kinds of licenses that dealers can buy. Logically, many different licenses are possible. The bribe can include only heroin dealing or can extend to a wide variety of criminal acts. It can stipulate the scale and location of the permitted activity. It can nullify a recent arrest or guarantee against a future arrest. It can require repetitive payments or include only a one-shot encounter. In spite of the variety of logically possible bribes, it seems likely that only a small number of licenses will actually be available. Moreover, the available licenses will tend to be at the extremes—broad and repetitive (the "pad"), or narrow and one-shot (the "score"). Finally, the bribes will tend to be retrospective rather than prospective.

Two arguments support the view that there will be a small number of bribes.

First, in arranging a bribe, there is not likely to be much explicit communication.[hh] To avoid creating damaging evidence, both parties will prefer to rely on tacit understandings of what is expected of each. In order for these tacit understandings to work well enough to support the market, they must be fairly simple and well-known. Complicated or detailed descriptions of mutual obligations will simply not survive. Since the contracts must be defined crudely and used tacitly, only a small number will be available.

Second, it is difficult for both parties to observe whether the other party stays within the bounds of the contract. A heroin dealer can hide a burglary ring behind his heroin dealing without being discovered by the bribed official. As a result, the official is cheated out of the larger payment he would deserve for allowing both heroin dealing and burglary to continue unmolested. A bribed policeman can "finger" the heroin dealer who is bribing him to another policeman. Consequently, the dealer is cheated out of the protection he thought he had purchased. Given that such *gross* transgressions of the terms of the contract are possible, all *detailed* stipulations about specific responsibilities are meaningless. Again, one can conclude that only crude categories of licenses will be available.

The argument supporting the view that only extreme types of licenses will be available (i.e., narrow, one-shot licenses or broad, repetitive licenses) is based on an analysis of the strategic relationship between dealers and police once the initial bribe is offered and accepted. Once the first bribe is arranged, a complicated relationship begins. Each party can continue to extort the other. The dealer can threaten to expose the official's corruption. The official can threaten a new arrest on old evidence. As in most strategic situations, the outcome of these mutual threats is uncertain. An experienced, tough, greedy cop might be able to bully an inexperienced dealer. However, in general, as the relationship continues through additional encounters, the dealer's bargaining position strengthens relative to the official.

The reason for this shift is that the dealer's threat to expose an official's corruption gradually becomes more credible than the official's threat to arrest the dealer. Immediately after the first arrest, the dealer will typically not have powerful evidence documenting the official's corruption. As a result, the official need not take the threat of exposure too seriously. As additional encounters occur, the dealer can accumulate increasingly powerful evidence of the official's corruption. The dealer can arrange to have witnesses, take photographs, or record the dealings on tape. Moreover, it becomes increasingly difficult for the official to arrange alibis or explanations for each of the dealer's specific allegations. Meanwhile, the official does not necessarily accumulate more evidence against the dealer. At best, the official will be able to charge the dealer with bribery or additional counts of narcotics offenses—charges that will be

[hh]For dialogues involved in transacting a bribe, see generally Shecter with Phillips, *On the Pad*.

relatively unimportant in court. The effect of this asymmetric accumulation of evidence is that the official's threat of a new arrest gradually becomes less credible than the dealer's counterthreat to expose the official's corruption if he is ever arrested.[ii] The official must take the dealer's threat seriously not only because he knows the dealer can make a strong case, but also because he knows it will cost the dealer very little to implicate the official if the dealer is arrested. Indeed, the dealer may have a positive incentive to "give up" the corrupt official if he thinks the betrayal will ingratiate him with the D.A. and the judge.[jj] Thus, the dealer's counterthreat often controls the strategic situation between dealers and corrupt officials.

If the official is aware of this dynamic, one of two actions is available to him in his initial encounter with the dealer. He can sell a very narrow license by agreeing to let the dealer go for that one offense and warn him that the next offense will certainly be prosecuted. Alternatively, he can sell a very broad license at a price that will compensate him for the risk he runs in granting a broad license and for the pains he must take to prevent the dealer from accumulating evidence of his corruption. If the official tries to sell a medium-broad license at a lower price, chances are that he will eventually be forced to provide the protection of a broader license without getting paid for it. Thus, due to an asymmetry in the rates at which dealers and officials accumulate threats as they continue in their relationship, a wise official will exploit the advantage he has in their initial encounter to sell either a very narrow license (minimizing the chance that he will be extorted in the future) or a very broad license (guaranteeing that he will be paid well for something he might eventually be forced to provide in any case).

The proposition that retrospective bribes (which indulge past offenses) are more common than prospective bribes (which guarantee against future arrests) is based on two different arguments. First, a prospective bribe is inherently more uncertain than a retrospective bribe. As previously noted, it is difficult to negotiate explicitly on the terms of a bribe. It is also difficult to enforce the implicit terms of the bribe. Because a prospective bribe specifies future and therefore inherently uncertain obligations, these problems of communication and enforcement will be exacerbated. On the other hand, since a retrospective bribe concerns events that have already occurred, the bargaining over the license will be facilitated. Both dealers and officials will have a relatively clear idea of what is being bought and sold. Thus, retrospective bribes will be much easier to arrange than prospective bribes.[kk]

[ii]For situations involving asymetric accumulation of evidence, see Shecter with Phillips, *On the Pad*, pp. 30, 254.

[jj]A situation in which the police are afraid of exposure by the people who bribe them appears in Shecter with Phillips, *On the Pad*, p. 202.

[kk]An important piece of indirect evidence indicating that retrospective bribes are important is the fact that dealers carry "wads" to pay off the police when they are arrested. See Shecter with Phillips, *On the Pad*, p. 111; and Woodley, *Dealer*, pp. 97-98.

Second, a prospective bribe has an additional disadvantage in that it requires a dealer to expose his position before he is certain that the police know who he is and have accumulated evidence against them. In soliciting an "insurance bribe," the dealer must abandon his first two lines of defense. For this reason, new dealers will often *not* solicit prospective bribes.

These arguments do not imply that there are *no* prospective bribes. In spite of the problems, it is not hard to see how prospective bribes could occur. As we have seen, a retrospective bribe can easily become a prospective bribe if the official's resistance crumbles before the dealer's threat of exposure and the lure of additional money.[ll] It is also possible that the police have organized their corruption by establishing "franchises" for dealers. We know that such arrangements exist.[mm] Thus, the arguments merely indicate that prospective bribes will be a little more difficult to arrange and a little less common than retrospective bribes.

This conclusion has important policy implications. If a dealer can arrange a prospective bribe, he reduces his incentives to behave cautiously to avoid arrest. He can be aggressive in seeking customers, and careless with inventories of heroin. As such, he is a particularly efficient and dangerous dealer. On the other hand, if a dealer can arrange only retrospective bribes, he continues to have strong incentives to behave cautiously. What he fears as a consequence of arrest is not jail, but extortion from the officials. As long as the officials charge a high enough price for their indulgence, the incentives for dealers to behave cautiously will remain strong, and they will continue to behave inefficiently.[nn] For this reason, we prefer that police and dealers arrange retrospective bribes rather than prospective bribes. Consequently, it is reassuring to discover that prospective bribes will be relatively easy to discourage: even if we cannot eliminate all bribery, we may be able to eliminate the most dangerous kind.

In summary, then, we can offer the following observations about bribes. First, who one should bribe depends on one's position in the distribution system. Second, for street level dealers, the police are much more attractive targets than court officials, and lower level police are more attractive targets than higher level police. Third, dealers will be restricted to a small number of kinds of licenses—very narrow, one-shot licenses, or very broad, repetitive licenses. Fourth, retrospective bribes will be more common than prospective

---

[ll]For a description of the development of prospective bribes ("pads") in narcotics, see Shecter with Phillips, *On the Pad*, p. 202.

[mm]There are several basic sources on corruption that report these arrangements. See generally, "Commission to Investigate Allegations of Police Corruption and the City's Anti-Corruption Procedures," *Commission Report* (New York: Fund for the City of New York, 1972); New York State Permanent Commission of Investigations, *Narcotics Law Enforcement in New York City* (New York: New York State Commission of Investigation, 1972) and Shecter with Phillips, *On the Pad*.

[nn]For an example of a gambler who behaves cautiously not to avoid imprisonment but rather to avoid payoffs, see Shecter with Phillips, *On the Pad* p. 238.

bribes. Thus, the most attractive bribe from the point of view of a street level dealer is a narrow, ad hoc, retrospective bribe offered to the arresting police officer.

One should keep in mind that tactics other than bribery can demoralize enforcement agencies. Narcotics dealers can become so dangerous that the police become reluctant to go after them. They can invest in so many defensive tactics that it becomes unprofitable for the police to investigate them rather than other criminals who are easier to catch. They can become so skillful and aggressive in exploiting their legal rights that enormous resources must be spent prosecuting them and few are convicted—even when there are strong cases against them. All of these tactics would have the effect of deflecting police attention from narcotic dealers to other criminals.

An apparent disadvantage of these tactics is that they depend on *collective* action by the heroin dealers. Police administrators are influenced to shift their priorities only if *many* dealers become very dangerous, very hard to catch, or very hard to convict. If only a few dealers make the investments and take the risks to become dangerous, hard to catch, and so on, the general reputation of all heroin cases will not be significantly changed. The police will continue to investigate and arrest heroin dealers.

This is only an *apparent* disadvantage because it happens that dealers face individual incentives motivating them to behave in a way that produces the collective benefit for all other dealers. The least careful dealer supplies an important externality to all other more careful dealers: he becomes the most likely target of police efforts and absorbs some portion of the police resources. As a result, the police have fewer resources to attack the next most careful dealer, and they run out of resources long before they reach the most careful dealer. Any individual dealer, then has a strong incentive to be a little more cautious than the last dealer arrested by the police. Since all dealers face these incentives, there is a general tendency to strive to be more cautious than other dealers. This leads to a high level of investment in defensive tactics for the industry as a whole and results in heroin dealers enjoying a general reputation as being very difficult to catch.

There are undoubtedly very complex dynamics in this situation. In a period when police pressure is very great, the individual incentives will cause dealers to strain to be the dealer who is slightly more careful than the last dealer caught. As a result, it will become generally more difficult for the police to make arrests in the area, and they may be dissuaded from continuing to apply the pressure. Once the police reduce the pressure, there will be some incentive for individual dealers to exploit the situation by becoming less careful. The dealers who become less cautious and do not get caught because of reduced police pressure benefit from the collective good previously provided by the strong desire of everyone not to get caught. These dynamics could easily produce the oscillation in narcotic arrests and narcotics distribution that we observe.

In summary, the main tactics for demoralizing enforcement agencies are bribery and being harder to arrest and convict than other criminals. The individual incentives of dealers cause both tactics to be employed. We observe the effect of these tactics in the low morale of agencies charged with enforcing narcotics laws, and in increasing public skepticism about the value of enforcing these laws.

1.2.4 Different Tactics for Different Types and Levels of Dealers. Virtually none of these tactics for avoiding arrest and successful prosecution are mutually exclusive. Consequently, dealers are likely to employ combinations of the tactics. In effect, dealers choose portfolios of tactics that are designed to maximize the objectives of profits and security at a low cost to themselves.

The portfolio chosen by any particular dealer depends partly on his position in the distribution system, and partly on his own individual attitudes toward risk, profit, and violence. For example, a dealer who imports heroin must be particularly concerned about the various tactics for hiding heroin since he knows there will be at least a cursory examination at the border. A dealer selling at the retail level must be interested in all the various devices for screening out informants and undercover police. A newcomer in the heroin business has the advantage of being able to rely on anonymity to protect him. But to preserve that protection, he must develop discrete procedures for advertising his product, and strong procedures for screening his customers. An old timer cannot rely on anonymity and makes larger investments in tactics to avoid producing or being caught with evidence. A dealer who is very interested in profits and less interested in security may charge high prices and aggressively market his product. A more cautious, less acquisitive dealer will charge low prices and keep his clientele small, loyal and tight-lipped. Thus, portfolios chosen by different types of dealers will vary considerably.

Table 1-2 analytically defines several different types of dealers. Table 1-3 offers hypotheses about the portfolio of tactics they will use. To some extent, these tables are drawn from specific descriptions of dealers in the literature.[oo] However, to a greater extent, the types of users are created simply by imagining the logical possibilities. The hypotheses about portfolios of tactics are based in logical inferences from assumed rational maximizing behavior. Thus, the reader should not take these tables too seriously.

What is important to understand is the general idea that types of dealers differ. The differences are important for two reasons. First, we care differently about different types of dealers—partly because some types appear more evil and

---

[oo]The major sources describing dealers are the following: Richard H. Blum et al., *The Dream Sellers: Perspectives on Drug Dealers* (San Francisco: Jossey-Bass, 1972); Burroughs, *Junkie*; Fiddle, *Portraits from a Shooting Gallery*; Evert Clark and Nicholas Horrack, *Contrabandista!* (New York: Praeger, 1973); Larner and Tefferteller, *The Addict in the Street*; Robin Moore, *The French Connection* (New York: Bantam, 1971); *Newsday, The Heroin Trail*; Preble and Casey, "Taking Care of Business"; Woodley, *Dealer.*

Table 1-2
Types of Dealers Defined in Terms of Positions and Attitudes towards Profits, Risk, and Violence

Position and Type of Dealer	Length of Time in Business	Strength and Direction of Dealer's Attitudes Towards:		
		Profits	Risk	Violence
I. Retail dealers				
A. "Accommodating dealers"				
1. Cautious	Recent	Moderate; positive	Strong; negative	Strong; negative
2. Reckless	Recent	Moderate; positive	Indifferent	Strong; negative
B. "Old Standby"				
1. Not ambitious	Old	Moderate; positive	Moderate; negative	Moderate; negative
2. Ambitious	Old	Strong; positive	Indifferent	Moderate; negative
C. Entrepreneur	Old	Strong; positive	Strong; negative	Moderate; negative
D. "Bad Actor"				
1. Not ambitious	New or old	Moderate; positive	Moderate; positive	Indifferent
2. Ambitious	New or old	Strong; positive	Indifferent	Indifferent
II. Wholesale dealers				
A. Free lance				
1. Cautious	New	Strong; positive	Moderate; negative	Moderate; negative
2. Reckless	New	Strong; positive	Indifferent	Moderate; negative
B. Independent seller	Old	Strong; positive	Strong; negative	Indifferent
C. Franchised firm	Old	Strong; positive	Strong; negative	Indifferent

Table 1-3
Portfolios of Defensive Strategies for Different Types of Dealers

| | Level of Investment in Tactics to Avoid Arrest | | | |
| | Conceal All Connections with Heroin Industry | | | |
Position and Type of Dealer	Keep Markets Small	Screen Customers	Discipline Customers	Employ Agents
I. Retail dealers				
A. "Accommodating dealers"				
1. Cautious	Heavy	Heavy	–	–
2. Reckless	Modest	Modest	–	–
B. "Old Standby"				
1. Not ambitious	Heavy	Heavy	–	–
2. Ambitious	Modest	Modest	–	Modest
C. "Entrepreneur"	Heavy	Heavy	Small	Heavy
D. "Bad Actor"				
1. Not ambitious	Modest	Modest	Heavy	–
2. Ambitious	Small	Small	Heavy	Small
II. Wholesale dealers				
A. Free lance				
1. Cautious	Heavy	Heavy	Modest	–
2. Reckless	Small	Small	Modest	–
B. Independent seller	Heavy	Heavy	Heavy	Modest
C. Franchised firm	Modest	Modest	Heavy	Heavy

criminal than the others, and partly because some types have a larger impact on the drug-abuse problem than others. Second, the different types of dealers are differentially vulnerable to different enforcement tactics. "Bad Actors" may run organizations that are difficult to penetrate by recruiting informants, but relatively easy to penetrate with "cold," undercover purchases. "Accommodating Dealers" may be extremely vulnerable to general surveillance. The implication of these observations is that we may be able to tailor the overall enforcement strategy by selectively investing in enforcement tactics that attack the types of dealers who cause the greatest problems or appear to be the most evil and criminal. We return to this possibility in part III. For now, it is sufficient merely to suggest the possibility. Thus, although one cannot be certain about the distribution of types of dealers, the potential importance of this judgment to the design of an enforcement policy encourages one to speculate and to keep the

Position and Types of Dealer	Level of Investment in Tactics to Avoid Arrest			
	Avoid Creating or Being Caught with Evidence			
	Blend Illegal Activity into Legal Activity	Conceal Heroin	Employ "Drops" and "Caches"	Move "Drops" and "Caches"
I. Retail dealers				
A. "Accommodating dealers"				
1. Cautious	Heavy	Modest	Modest	—
2. Reckless	—	—	—	—
B. "Old Standby"				
1. Not ambitious	Heavy	Heavy	Heavy	Modest
2. Ambitious	Heavy	Heavy	Heavy	Modest
C. "Entrepreneur"	Heavy	Heavy	Heavy	Heavy
D. "Bad Actor"				
1. Not ambitious	Modest	Modest	Modest	—
2. Ambitious	Modest	Modest	Modest	—
II. Wholesale dealers				
A. Free lance				
1. Cautious	Heavy	Heavy	—	Heavy
2. Reckless	Modest	Modest	—	—
B. Independent seller	Modest	Heavy	Heavy	Heavy
C. Franchised firm	Heavy	Heavy	Heavy	Heavy

issue in mind when looking at any evidence about the heroin-distribution system.[pp]

2.0 Threats from Other Criminals

The threat of arrest and imprisonment is probably the most significant problem created by illicitness. However, illicitness has an additional effect: not only are the dealers threatened by the police—they are also effectively denied police protection. No police and courts will respond to a heroin dealer's complaints that his property has been stolen, implied contracts broken, or his business

[pp]See Richard Blum et al., *The Dream Sellers*, for statistical information on types of dealers.

Table 1-3 (cont.)

Position and Type of Dealer	Level of Investment in Tactics to Avoid Arrest		
	Corrupt Enforcement Officials		
	Offer Ad Hoc; Prospective Bribes	Offer Ad Hoc; Retrospective Bribes	Purchase Licenses
I. Retail dealers			
A. "Accommodating dealers"			
1. Cautious	–	–	–
2. Reckless	–	–	–
B. "Old Standby"			
1. Not ambitious	–	Modest	–
2. Ambitious	–	Modest	Small
C. "Entrepreneur"	–	Heavy	Modest
D. "Bad Actor"			
1. Not ambitious	–	–	–
2. Ambitious	–	Modest	–
II. Wholesale dealers			
A. Free lance			
1. Cautious	Modest	Heavy	–
2. Reckless	–	Small	–
B. Independent seller	–	Heavy	Modest
C. Franchised firm	–	Heavy	Heavy

embezzled by employees.[7] No social conventions will establish strong commitments between employers and employees. The dealer can rely on nothing other than his own ability to protect, retaliate, or inspire respect among his criminal associates. In the face of enormous opportunities for gain and fragile social institutions, "honor among thieves" can disintegrate rapidly.[qq] Thus, the isolation that results from illicitness exposes heroin dealers to threats from other criminals.

These threats from other criminals create two particular problems from dealers. One problem is how to protect property and enforce contracts when the police and courts will not do so. The second is how to attract and manage reliable employees.

[qq]For evidence on the importance of threats from other criminals for heroin dealers, see Woodley, *Dealer*, pp. 5-7; Teresa with Renner, *Vinnie Teresa's Mafia*, p. 178. Klockars reports similar problems for fences. See the *Professional Fence*, pp. 113-129. For violence and rip-offs among users, see Larner and Tefferteller, *The Addict in the Street*, pp. 78-99, 206; or Fiddle, *Portraits from a Shooting Gallery*, pp. 124, 128.

2.1 The Problem of Enforcing Contracts and Protecting Property

For most businesses, the costs of enforcing contracts and protecting property are largely external. The society provides police services and courts to protect property and insure that business is carried on in an orderly fashion. Moreover, the existence of well-known laws and specialized institutions for enforcing the laws establishes norms and expectations that insure a great deal of voluntary compliance as well as enforced compliance. Although it is true that legitimate businesses pay taxes to support the legal system and must pay lawyers to take advantage of the existing legal system, it is also true that the costs of supporting the system are widely shared, and the costs of using the system are small compared to the enormous benefits.

For illegal businesses, the situation is quite different. Protection and contract enforcement are *not* provided or supported by the public at large. The full costs of the service fall directly on the illegal businesses. Moreover, these costs are likely to be very significant for two reasons.

First, the heroin business is extremely vulnerable to thefts. It is very easy to steal drugs from "drops" and strong incentives exist for addicts to do so. It is riskier, but still very profitable, for people to rob distributors for "rip-off" drugs they were supposed to sell as intermediaries or the supplier. Furthermore, because they operate in areas where there are many other criminals, distributors are often known and picked as targets by criminals. This vulnerability means that dealers must be able to provide relatively extensive protection or face significant losses.

Second, for many parts of the market there is no existing, specialized organization that performs the function cheaply and effectively. The result is that efforts at protection and contract enforcement are often undertaken by small, inefficient ad hoc organizations. The benefits that might be obtained through the economies of scale and increased efficiency of a large, specialized agency are not always available to reduce the burden of contract enforcement and protection. Thus, dealers must provide extensive services in this area. and may not be able to buy efficient forms of the service.

There are three strategies that suppliers may use in solving the problem of contract enforcement and protection. One strategy is to purchase these services from organizations that are willing and able to supply them for heroin dealers. A second is to wield rewards and penalties that make voluntary compliance with contracts desirable from the point of view of their consumers and others. A third is for the supplier to make his own activity a necessary condition for consumers or agents to enjoy any benefits from stealing or breaking contracts with him.

In the underworld, "muscle" (i.e., a capacity for violence) is a generally valuable resource. It can be used for protection, enforcing contracts, or simply for extortion.[rr] Consequently, there are many groups operating in the under-world who are in the business of "contingent violence."[ss] Included among these groups are the police, local gangs, local vigilante groups, or the "syndicate." Often the heroin dealer is a *victim* of these organizations. However, heroin dealers may also be able to use these groups to protect their property, enforce contracts, or eliminate competition. There is some evidence that heroin suppliers have used gangs they were paying off to drive competitors out of business or catch and murder consumers who absconded with goods. Other evidence indicates that police have been used selectively to arrest and jail addicts, agents, or thugs who were causing problems for the major heroin suppliers.[tt] The problem, of course, is finding muscle strong enough to stand up to other predatory muscle groups in the area, and then paying them enough to keep them loyal. To the extent that the supplier can find cheap, effective, and loyal muscle for sale, purchasing these services from others is a desirable strategy.

Note that the heroin dealer's relations with muscle groups is *very* uncertain. They can suddenly escalate their demands and seek very large shares of the dealer's profits. The dealer may have little bargaining power to fend off such moves. It is also never clear in what coin the muscle groups will demand payment. They can always ask for money, but they can also gain policy control over the dealer's organization. They can insist on more aggressive marketing or profit-maximizing strategies, and can restrict a dealer's operation to particular geographic areas. At an extreme, they can demand that a dealer occasionally "take a fall."[uu] The high cost and uncertainty of relying on outside muscle groups is a major disadvantage of this strategy.

The second alternative is for the supplier to discipline his agents and consumers with his own stock of rewards and penalties without hiring an outside enforcer and guardian. The problems in this effort are the same as those involved in trying to discipline the small market organization—a strategy considered above. The dealer must be willing to kill or give up some large share of his profits to provide sufficiently large rewards and penalties to protect himself from thefts. Note that if discipline is effective with respect to the goal of reducing the probability of arrest and conviction, it will also be effective with respect to the problem of contract enforcement. Note also that if a dealer develops his own

---

[rr]See generally, Thomas C. Schelling, "What is the Business of Organized Crime," *Journal of Public Law* 20:1 (1971), for a provocative analysis that suggests that "muscle" is the major business of organized crime.

[ss]"Contingent violence" implies that violence is threatened as a consequence of specific actions. It is designed as an incentive—not as an expressive act.

[tt]The possibility that the police might be manipulated for these purposes is a major problem in managing informants. See Malachi L. Harvey and John C. Cross, *The Informer in Law Enforcement* (Springfield, Mass.: Charles C. Thomas, 1960), pp. 33-39.

[uu]At some stage, such "muscle" groups may come to resemble what is commonly called "organized crime," but which may only be a very impressive group of extortionists. See Schelling, "What is the Business of Organized Crime."

capacity for violence, this can be used for some bargaining advantage vis-à-vis other muscle groups. It is this triple advantage of violence that justifies its enormous costs to dealers.[vv]

The third alternative is to structure the situation so that even if agents, consumers, or outsiders are successful in stealing from a supplier, they will fail to convert the fruit of their theft into a benefit without the active compliance of their victim. In most cases, this is, of course, impossible. Money stolen from a supplier is very liquid and easily convertible to benefits for the thief. Heroin stolen by an addict is also easily convertible to desired benefits. However, for one important case, there may be a serious problem.

Consider the case of a man who has just stolen a large quantity of heroin from a dealer and would like to turn it into cash. For several reasons, he has a difficult time selling the stolen heroin. Some people who might buy in quantity from him are afraid to do so since they risk their relation with the victimized supplier if they do. Since many close friends of the thief in the heroin industry may be afraid to buy from him, he may be forced to sell in strange markets. Selling in strange markets is both extremely difficult and extremely dangerous. It is difficult because he cannot "advertise" that he has some heroin to sell. It is dangerous because those consumers who do find him are likely to be people who do not have regular markets. These will be undesirable consumers and will, by definition, include an extraordinarily large percentage of informers or under-cover police. Finally, the victimized supplier can always "tip" the police about the location and activity of the thief. In such a situation, it should be clear that it is not particularly desirable to steal from a supplier even when he does not have any muscle that can be immediately applied.[ww]

In sum, contract enforcement and protection may be secured by

1. Purchasing the services from organizations that are in a position to sell muscle
2. Relying on one's own capacity for violence to discipline his own organization effectively
3. Making one's own compliance necessary for a thief or absconder to convert the stolen commodity into benefits the thief may internalize

2.2 The Problem of Reliable Employees

It is clear from previous discussions that heroin dealers are exceedingly vulnerable to activities by their employees.[8] It is also clear that strategies to

---

[vv]These observations suggest the importance of cultivating a reputation as a violent man. For the difficulty of hiring "muscle" and the importance of establishing a reputation for violence, see Woodley, *Dealer*, pp. 84-87. For the importance of a violent temperament in most underworld business, see Teresa with Renner, *Vinnie Teresa's Mafia*, pp. 118-121, 154-155.

[ww]The difficulty of people in this situation is vividly (if somewhat surrealistically) described in Robert Stone, *Dog Soldiers* (New York: Ballentine, 1974).

insure effective discipline (e.g., small numbers of employees, contingent violence, reasonable shares of large profits, etc.) are effective in controlling employees. Consequently, some of the problems of reliable employees have already been analyzed.

However, there is an additional aspect of this problem that deserves explicit attention. It is clear that there are some people who are "stand-up guys" (i.e., people who will neither expose nor steal from their associates). By definition, such people have internalized a set of norms that make them particularly valuable employees. To the extent that stand-up guys are plentiful and easy to identify, dealers will be able to reduce investments in strategies to insure effective discipline. In effect, they can substitute careful recruitment, selection, and training for later investments in control systems. Consequently, strategies to increase the supply of stand-up guys or improve dealers' ability to distinguish stand-up guys from others will be important in determining the level of security that dealers are able to achieve.

Note that the *rate* at which dealers can recruit reliable employees will have a decisive influence on the potential impact of enforcement efforts. If the police can arrest dealers and their employees faster than they can be replaced, the direct effects of enforcement action will accumulate steadily and the size of the illicit market will be steadily reduced. If employees can be replaced more quickly than they can be arrested, the direct effects of enforcement efforts will be transient. Consequently, the factors influencing the supply of reliable employees and the screening devices employed by dealers will have an important effect on the potential impact of enforcement efforts.

To a large extent, factors influencing the aggregate supply of stand-up guys are beyond the control of individual heroin dealers. Stand-up guys are the products of subcultures that distrust existing social institutions and view arrest and imprisonment as routine events. The conditions that produce such subcultures are probably deeply rooted in the structure of our society, and are not likely to be influenced by individual heroin dealers.

However, on a local and temporary basis it is entirely possible that *collectively* heroin dealers can affect the supply of stand-up guys. In areas that are badly disorganized, heroin dealers can contribute to the isolation of the community and provide examples that will influence the supply of stand-up guys. The supply of heroin will insure a high prevalence of heroin use in the community. Within the heroin using community, heroin dealers will be powerful figures. Their values and preferences are likely to be dominant. Thus, it is no accident that heroin is difficult to displace from areas where it is already endemic. Within such areas, it is likely that heroin dealers have succeeded in insuring a large supply of reliable employees.

Even if dealers are not operating in areas where there are subcultures producing stand-up guys, there are options for them to increase the supply of reliable employees. They can exploit personal relations by recruiting employees from the ranks of relatives, lovers, or friends.[xx] They can provide general services to large numbers of people to create obligations that increase the employees' reliability. Or, they can secure incriminating evidence against individuals and insure reliability through blackmail. These strategies are particularly valuable to dealers simply because they build up loyalty to a *particular* dealer. As a result, this dealer need not compete for these reliable employees with other heroin dealers. They are reliable only to the dealer who has the personal relation, owns the obligation, or controls the incriminating evidence. Thus, individual dealers can extract monopsonistic advantages from this group of employees; they will pay less for their services than for employees who are equally reliable, but whose reliability is more general across dealers.

Regardless of the actual supply of reliable employees to a given dealer, the dealer will face the problem of screening stand-up guys from others who are less reliable. There are many inexpensive screening procedures. Dealers can screen on the basis of race, addiction status, criminal record, or the testimony of others who he trusts. However, these inexpensive screens have the disadvantage of being imprecise—they screen *out* many people who would turn out to be reliable employees, and they screen *in* many unreliable types.[yy]

More expensive screening procedures are those that involve long periods of probation during which potential employees are closely observed, tested, and kept ignorant about much of the operation. Probation is expensive because one must pay for close supervision and delay the benefits of using the new employee. However, it has some enormous advantages. A common test during probation periods is the requirement that the employee commit some crime. Such tests provide an opportunity not only to gauge an employee's reliability, but also to gather incriminating evidence that can be used to blackmail the employee. In effect, these tests not only gauge reliability, but increase it. In addition, such tests will certainly screen out all police. The possibility of such elaborate tests, and the safety that comes from not exposing one's operation to untested employees are the benefits that justify the substantial costs of probationary periods.

3.0 Problems of Illegality: Consumers

The fact that heroin possession, distribution, and production is illegal has very important consequences for the *consumer's* behavior as well as the supplier's. Indeed, a consumer must make efforts to conceal his possession of heroin, protect his stock, and enforce contracts made with others just as suppliers must.

[xx]Relatives are generally among the safest people to recruit. See footnote z. It is interesting that relatives were recruited to protect the security of the "Ultra Secret" in World War II. See F.W. Winterbotham, *The Ultra Secret* (New York: Harper and Row, 1974), p. 76.

[yy]The problem is strictly analogous to the problem of screening customers. See footnote n.

Presumably, the strategies available to suppliers are available to consumers as well. However, there are some additional problems associated with being a consumer in an illegal market that have not yet been analyzed. The problems that will be considered in this section are high prices, unreliable quality, difficulty in obtaining necessary information, and difficulty in gaining access to markets.

3.1 High Prices

As we have seen, the illegality of the heroin industry increases the risks and operating costs of suppliers. The important consequences of this from the point of view of consumers is that consumers must face high prices for heroin. They often will accept these prices because they have a strong craving for the product. However, the pressure to pay the prices leads to some important effects on the way heroin consumers behave.

The most drastic and popularly known consequence of high prices for heroin is that addicts become criminals. The reason is probably that their productivity and "wages" in criminal activity are much higher than in alternative employment opportunities.

Another reason for the unusual attractiveness of criminal employment is that users are able to maintain flexible schedules—working when and as long as they like. This is important because some days the user must work long hours at irregular times to get enough money to satisfy his craving, and other days he must spend long hours locating suppliers and making exchanges.[zz] Thus, high prices encourage users to choose illegitimate employment because illegal activity often pays better and offers a more flexible schedule than legal employment.

A second consequence of high prices is that users will be motivated to find wholesale markets where they may buy drugs cheaper than on the street. Addicts will constantly be trying to be introduced to wholesale suppliers so they may buy drugs at lower cost. The wholesale opportunities also lead users to try to earn large sums of money rather than a trickle of smaller amounts because the wholesale markets require large purchases. Thus, addicts are always willing to take extra risks for a "big sting" and are always interested in establishing connections with wholesale suppliers.

A third consequence of the high prices for heroin is that heroin becomes a particularly valuable commodity to steal. Addicts shadow dealers and fellow addicts to find opportunities to steal from them.[9] Clearly such activity increases the risks of buying or selling drugs.

[zz]For an anecdote revealing the importance of irregular hours, see Larner and Tefferteller, *The Addict in the Street*, p. 216.

3.2 Unreliable Quality

A second serious problem faced by heroin consumers is that there is little guarantee that the drugs they buy will be of consistent quality.[aaa] The uncertain quality creates a dangerous situation for addicts. At times, being cheated is the problem for addicts. They purchase a white powder in a glassine envelope and find it is flour or sugar. Other times, the problem is receiving too much quality. They inject heroin that is unexpectedly pure and overdose. Death on one side and monetary loss on the other are the cutting edges of the problem of unreliably quality in the heroin purchased by users.

Sometimes, unreliability is the purpose and sometimes the undesired result of supplier policies. Because drugs are expensive, many addicts will always be looking for bargains. This situation is ripe for fraudulent suppliers who supply very low-grade heroin. Other times, dealers will penalize addicts for misbehavior by giving them a "hot shot"—a dose of heroin mixed with poison. In sum, unreliable quality may be used by dealers to make fast profits or to discipline addicts. In such cases, the unreliable quality problem may be desired and maintained by suppliers.

However, for some suppliers, who would like to control large parts of the market and turn over their inventories of drugs quickly, unreliable quality may be a serious liability.[bbb] It may be difficult for a dealer to acquire and maintain a reputation for high-quality drugs since he may not be in a position to monitor and discipline agents who sell diluted drugs. In such circumstances, unreliable quality is a marketing problem that is expensive and difficult for a distributor to solve, rather than an advantage.[ccc]

3.3 Difficulty in Obtaining Information

It is clear that the illegality of heroin distribution makes normal forms of public advertising undesirable from the point of view of the supplier. This implies that consumers will have a very difficult time obtaining information about the quality, price, and location of heroin.[ddd] This information problem is particular-

---

[aaa]A sample of "street buys" of heroin revealed concentrations of heroin varying from 3 percent to over 70 percent. In addition, a variety of adulterants with varying degrees of toxicity are added.

[bbb]Problems for dealers with low-quality heroin are described in Larner and Tefferteller, *The Addict in the Street*, p. 205.

[ccc]Problems with quality have generated efforts to establish "brand names" in the heroin business. See *Newsday, The Heroin Trail*, p. 205.

[ddd]This problem creates a specialized group of people called "touts" or "bag followers" who act as brokers for existing dealers. See Hughes et al., "The Social Structure of a Heroin Copping Community," p. 553. For a discussion of the problems involved in the use of brokers, see Section 3.4.

ly acute for heroin consumers because the price, quality, and location of drugs for sale are constantly changing.

There are two possible solutions to this problem. One solution is for consumers and suppliers to maintain routinized ways of communicating with one another. This is possible when a supplier's market is small and loyal. Another solution is for there to be places where addicts exchange information regularly about market conditions. A Hayes-Bickford cafeteria becomes the heroin industry's analogue to the stock market's tickertape and big board.[eee] It seems that both of these strategies are used to reduce the information problem.

It should be noted, though, that both strategies are expensive to consumers. In the first strategy (small, loyal markets), addicts confer monopoly advantages on the supplier, which the supplier may exploit for higher profits. In the second strategy (information centers), addicts must take the trouble to make special trips to find out how to buy drugs. The analogue might be for suburban housewives to walk to their neighborhood park to find out where to purchase meat. It should be clear that solving the information problem costs the addict time and money.

3.4 Access to Markets

Even after the addict spends time and money to obtain information about where to buy drugs, he risks not being able to buy in the markets to which he has been attracted. Most suppliers are suspicious of new customers for reasons that were previously explained.

Again, there are basically two strategies available for a user to gain access to the desired markets. One is to restrict his purchases to only his regular market. He may voluntarily give up his right to "shop around" to secure the advantageous position of being a trusted and regular customer. If he chooses this strategy, he also facilitates his information problem. The disadvantage, again, is conferring some monopoly advantages on the supplier who may or may not exploit them, plus a lack of insurance if anything happens to the supplier.

The second strategy is for a consumer to find a friend or pay another addict to introduce him into a desired market. This strategy is expensive for several reasons. First, one may have a difficult time finding someone to play this brokerage role in the desired market. Second, once the person is found, he may sell his services expensively. Third, the introducer may insist that he cannot introduce the consumer into the market, but that he will gladly make the purchase for the consumer. In this situation, the consumer immediately becomes vulnerable to a double cross by the broker.[fff] As in the case of information,

[eee]An early personal encounter with the world of heroin addicts involved "hanging out" in a Hayes-Bickford cafeteria in Brooklyn and listening to addicts talk about places to "score."

[fff]The vulnerability of users to absconding by brokers is illustrated in anecdotes described in *Newsday, The Heroin Trail*, p. 287; Fiddle, *Portraits from a Shooting Gallery*, p. 128; and Larner and Tefferteller, *The Addict in the Street*, p. 99.

solving this problem of access to markets is likely to be expensive for consumers of heroin.

In sum, the illegality of the heroin industry clearly has a substantial impact on the behavior of consumers. The high prices affect employment opportunities. Unreliable quality increases the risk of any purchase for heroin consumers. Finally, gathering information and obtaining access to markets for heroin are likely to require expensive strategies from heroin consumers.[ggg]

4.0 A General Model of Illegal, Domestic Heroin-Distribution Systems

Given the analysis of problems and possible responses of illegal dealers and users of heroin, it is possible to sketch a general model of the distribution system. The sketch is based on the assumption that dealers react to the pressures of illegality, and seek efficient solutions to the problems.[hhh]

Note that the sketch also depends on correctly aggregating the individual responses of dealers. One might think that the aggregation of individual responses would be perfectly straightforward. The process would be to calculate an efficient portfolio of strategies, assume that all dealers choose this portfolio, and solve the aggregation problem by straightforward multiplication. However,

---

[ggg]For descriptions of experienced users facing difficulties in seeking new markets, see Fiddle, *Portraits from a Shooting Gallery*, pp. 145, 309; and generally, Hughes et al., "The Social Structure of a Heroin Copping Community."

[hhh]The extent to which dealers notice and react to police pressure either by behaving cautiously or by abandoning the business is a key point. Common sense and testimony from dealers suggest that they do react to the threat of arrest. Some anecdotal pieces of evidence are the following:

Woodley in *Dealer* asked the cocaine dealer he interviewed and observed whether a "bust" would be felt on the street. The dealer responded: "Whew, is that felt on the street? You better believe that bust is felt. Everybody starts holdin' on tight to their stuff'— he clasped his arms around himself—'and they start looking around to see what's going to happen. Nobody knows how far it will go, you know, how far down the busts will go or where the supply will be cut off. Price might go up. Everybody's gonna look things over and see what's happening before they sell anything.' " (p. 42).

At another point, this dealer says the following: "It's just not out there, man. I don't know what it's because of, but man, they are bustin' people left and right. You got to be super-careful, super-cool. I'm not even carrying nothing in the street these days. I take orders, set up a meeting. But it's hot out there, man, I'm thinking about getting into another game." (p. 82).

Similarly, at the risk of oversimplifying Blum's results from interviewing a group of drug dealers, the following observation is relevant: "It is for him [the poor delinquent type dealer] that, realistically, the fear of arrest looms the greatest as a deterrent in limited dealing. One reasons that those who have quit dealing appear to do so primarily because they are arrest vulnerable and that vulnerability arises for many as soon as they begin dealing—although it is also a function of increasing exposure over time."

See Richard Blum, "Drug Pushers: A Collective Portrait," Published by permission of Transaction, Inc. from *Transaction* 8:9-10 (July-August 1971): 20. Copyright © 1971 by Transaction, Inc. For detailed pictures of drug-dealing operations in which dealers invest heavily in security measures to avoid arrest, see generally, Moore, *The French Connection;* Newsday, *The Heroin Trail* and Clark and Horrock, *Contrabandistas!*

this simple logic leaves out several complicating factors. First, since the positions, attitudes, and capabilities of dealers differ, they will not all choose the same strategies. Second, since there may be "lumpiness" in the supply of inputs necessary to employ certain strategies (e.g., the police may or may not be demoralized in an area; a dealer may or may not have a reputation for honest dealing and reliable, contingent violence), and since there may be "economies of scale" in using specific strategies (e.g., if a dealer can muster sufficient violence to protect his property, he may also be able to intimidate his competition), it is likely that some strategies will be employed only if firms achieve a certain scale. Third, the strategies chosen by one firm may produce "externalities" influencing the value of strategies chosen by other firms (e.g., if one firm develops a capacity for violence to control employees, other firms may be forced to develop similar capacities—partly to avoid becoming the easiest firm for the police to attack, and partly to avoid takeover attempts by the violent firms). In short, since the value of a given set of strategies to dealers depends partly on the position, capabilities, and preferences of individual dealers; partly on the supply of inputs and production functions associated with each strategy; and partly on the set of strategies employed by other dealers, the process of aggregation is by no means straightforward.

Given the complexity of the aggregation problem, the general model presented here should be considered a rough sketch. Still, in the light of the specific problems we have analyzed, and with attention to the aggregation problem, I argue that the major features of an illicit heroin-distribution system are the following:

1. Small, isolated distribution units and many different levels of distribution
2. A relatively centralized structure at top levels
3. Consistent upward pressure from lower levels
4. Monopolistic competition among lower level distributors
5. Occasional downward excursions by upper levels
6. Preferences for socially disorganized areas
7. Lengthy, complicated, and difficult transactions at all levels

4.1 Small Distribution Units; Many Levels; Different Requirements at Different Levels

The most distinctive and pervasive characteristic of illicit-distribution systems is that they will include only small distribution units.[iii] Most dealers will deal with only 5 to 20 customers. No one will deal with as many as 50 different individuals. Dealers choose small distribution because they have the following advantages in guarding against arrests or rip-offs:

[iii]For pictures of distribution system observed in the literature, see Appendix 1A.

1. They require only a small number of transactions.
2. Information leaks are less likely to occur.
3. Supervision and discipline of customers is facilitated.
4. Adjustments in behavior can be made quickly without elaborate planning or negotiation.

In addition, the distribution units will be isolated from one another. This will occur because each dealer will seek to limit information about his activities only to trusted customers. Moreover, although higher level dealers may have some incentives to seek to coordinate the behavior of lower level dealers, they cannot do so without making themselves and others relatively more vulnerable to arrest and rip-offs. Finally, if information is successfully restricted, dealers may exploit some monopoly advantages over consumers.

Thus, individual incentives lead to a small, relatively isolated distribution units. The basic unit is a dealer, with a small number of customers, bound to a reliable, but slightly mysterious supplier above him. These individual incentives lead to an aggregate system that has a distinctive form and a valuable characteristic.

The distinctive form is one of vertical "disintegration." Because heroin is produced in relatively large batches, and no dealer wants to handle more than a few customers, many levels are added between production and retail sales. If heroin were available in smaller quantities,[jjj] or if dealers were prepared to deal with more customers, there would be fewer levels between production and the street.

An important implication of this distinctive form is that different levels will deal in different quantities of heroin. Since penalties are linked to quantity, since theft vulnerability is linked to quantity, and since capital requirements are linked to quantity, the dealers operating at different levels will rely on different pricing and security strategies. Moreover, dealers seeking to operate at different levels will face different barriers to entry. Thus, not only will there be many different levels, but the levels will choose different pricing and security strategies.

The valuable characteristic is that the aggregate system will be very resilient to police attacks. Given some penetration (i.e., an arrest at some level of the

---

[jjj]The role of the "lumpiness" of supplies of heroin has often been overlooked. Even tiny and temporary heroin labs will turn out sufficient material to cover thousands of retail transactions. To distribute the material in a world where no one likes to make more than a few transactions requires a distribution system with many different levels. If heroin could be produced in smaller quantities, the people in the lab could sell directly to retail customers.

A comparison with the structure of distribution system for "dangerous drugs" is instructive. If much of the illicit market for amphetamines and barbiturates is supplied by diversion of legitimate products from retail levels, one will never see the elaborate structure involved in distributing heroin. The successful diverter can sell directly to retail customers because he has so few drugs that he can sell them in retail amounts without executing thousands of transactions.

system), police will find it difficult to expand the case. Horizontal development will be frustrated by dealers' efforts to restrict information about their activities. Vertical development can be resisted by effective discipline of agents and consumers. As a result, the police are limited to one small compartment of the entire distribution system.[kkk] Thus, the entire system will show great resilience even though no individual designed the system to produce that result.

4.2 Centralization at High Levels

It is often asserted that "organized crime" "monopolizes" heroin-distribution systems.[10] Unfortunately, these terms are sufficiently imprecise that the conventional wisdom fails to describe much about the behavior of upper levels of the distribution system.

The analysis here begins with necessary conditions to deal at high levels of the distribution system. We discover that satisfaction of the conditions requires capabilities that will lead to relatively high degrees of centralization. Finally, we explore the implications of a relatively centralized group at high levels for the performance of the system in general. We conclude that relatively high degrees of centralization constitute an efficient equilibrium position for the system as a whole.

To become a high-level dealer of heroin, one must develop the following resources: $50,000 to $100,000 in cash; reliable customers to whom large quantities of heroin can be sold; sufficient muscle to prevent thefts; and, most importantly, a "connection." Lacking any of these resources, an ambitious dealer will fail to score, or will become an easy mark for police or thieves.

These requirements have two important characteristics. First, the necessary resources are difficult to develop. The substantial capital requirements may be the easiest conditions to meet. It is much harder to gather arms and allies sufficient to hold off robbers attracted by $50,000 to $100,000 or several kilos of heroin; harder still to develop agents who can move heroin quickly, and who will refuse to betray their source if arrested. But probably the most demanding requirement is a connection. Even if one has put together a disciplined organization backed by significant muscle, one must find a connection. The connection is likely to be wary of powerful groups who have no track record or references. Thus, these requirements constitute strong, institutional barriers to entry by newcomers.

Second, if a dealer has these capabilities, he is in a position to control a substantial share of the market. If a dealer has sufficient muscle to prevent

---

[kkk]Many authorized intelligence systems have explicitly chosen this structure to minimize the losses from inevitable penetrations. Here, the result occurs not because of an explicit design, but because it happens to be in each individual dealer's interests to operate in a way that produces this general structure.

rip-offs with $100,000 at stake, he is likely to have sufficient muscle to intimidate small competition and to control his employees. If his distributing organization is disciplined, returns made from one deal will be sufficient to finance several more deals. Finally, a record of a few successful transactions with a given connection will facilitate future transactions. In effect, there are substantial economies of scale in moving large quantities of drugs: a generalized capacity for violence not only provides security from criminals and the police, but also allows intimidation of competition; one successful transaction facilitates the next transaction. Since the market requires only a few transactions per year at this level, a dealer who barely meets the entry requirement can control a large share of the market.

The combination of formidable barriers to entry, significant economies of scale, and a small market imply that a relatively small number of firms will be active at high levels. There is simply not very much room at the top, particularly when compared with the capabilities necessary to reach the top.

The argument for concentration at the top gains added force when it becomes apparent that a few large firms would choose to behave in ways that facilitate operations of the system as a whole. In general, heroin dealing at all levels becomes difficult if the supply of heroin is either abundant or very irregular. In a world where heroin is plentiful, prices will be low and dealers will be forced to hold inventories and seek new customers. This world implies danger and low revenues to dealers. In a world where heroin supplies fluctuate, dealers will sometimes take the losses associated with excess supplies, and other times face equally great problems with shortages. The main problems of shortages are that dealers will have to seek new connections (and be sought by others), and will lose some monopoly advantages with their customers. Since profitable and secure operations of the heroin market depend on high prices and relatively stable relationships, the market will operate most effectively if the supply of heroin is smooth and slightly restricted.

A relatively concentrated set of high-level firms will have the incentives and capabilities to produce a smooth, restricted supply of heroin. The high-level firms prefer this situation for all the same reasons as lower level firms: they can maintain high prices and avoid large inventories and disrupted relationships with customers. Indeed, because the absolute amounts handled at this level are greater, the stakes of these dealers in a smooth flow are greater: for example, a 10 percent oversupply will force them to hold inventories for long periods, tying up their capital and exposing them to arrest and thefts. Unlike lower level firms, however, these few high-level firms will have a capacity for coordination. The small number of firms will allow each firm to notice the effects of one firm's policies or the other, and will allow for either explicit or implicit negotiation among all interested parties. In addition, if the few firms achieve effective coordination, they become a monopsonist with respect to producers of heroin, and can exploit this position for better supply conditions from producers (e.g., shorter lead times, more continuous production, favorable prices, etc.). Thus, the higher level firms will have *individual* incentives and *combined* capabilities to insure a relatively smooth, slightly restricted flow of heroin.

Thus, the argument for a small number of firms at high levels rests on significant institutional barriers to entry, economies of scale in executing transactions and controlling competition, a relatively small market, and the existence of incentives and capabilities that allow centralized, high-level dealers to behave in ways that are consistent with the interests of lower level dealers.

Note that this conclusion does not imply there will be *no* "free-lance" deals for one kilo of heroin. The argument is simply that such deals will be rare and will account for only a tiny fraction of the total illicit supply. They are very difficult to set up and are extremely vulnerable to arrests and thefts. Moreover, once a deal like this is made, there is a strong incentive to make future deals. Thus, a successful, single transaction will be rare: it will either fail or expand quickly to several transactions. Since the successful, one-shot deal is an unlikely event, and since, in any case, one deal will be a small share of the market, such deals are unlikely to be a major factor in the supply of heroin.

Note, also, that the "centralization" at high levels can be achieved through several different institutional mechanisms. One can imagine the institutional forms arrayed on a continuum. At the left-hand extreme is a single, centralized organization. Less extreme is a small number of independent firms bound together through explicit negotiations and binding arbitration. Toward the right-hand extreme is a small number of firms negotiating explicitly without binding arbitration. At the right-hand extreme is a small number of firms relying on tacit negotiations. All of these structures would produce a smooth, restricted flow of heroin. However, they have different prospects for stability and different vulnerabilities to arrest. The single organization or binding arbitration structures are the most stable. However, because they depend on explicit negotiations, they are vulnerable to enforcement efforts. Tacit negotiation among a small number of firms presents few opportunities for the police to gather evidence, but can be disrupted by changes in the external environment or aggressive action by one of the firms. It is not clear which of these relatively centralized structures will be adopted. However, it seems likely that the top levels of the distribution system will have one of these relatively centralized structures rather than a very decentralized structure.

4.3 Consistent Upward Pressure from Lower Levels

Nearly everyone in the distribution system has an incentive to move to higher levels of the system. Inexpensive, reliable supplies of heroin are the incentives for the users; higher, absolute profits and greater security are the incentives for dealers. Moreover, since there are few technological or capital barriers to entry at higher levels, many low-level dealers will act aggressively to reach higher levels of the system.

This strong upward pressure is dangerous to higher level dealers. The immediate supplier risks increased competition (or even expendability) if his customers reach higher levels of the distribution system. The supplier at the next level dislikes having to deal with new people because the exposure is dangerous. Given these incentives, dealers will construct *institutional* barriers to entry to control the upward pressure: suppliers will carefully isolate their customers from their suppliers.[111]

The strength of these institutional barriers depends on the caution and discipline of the suppliers. Since caution and discipline are likely to be greater at higher levels, the consistent upward pressure is likely to be resisted more successfully at higher levels. Thus, consistent upward pressure will lead to relatively significant turnover at lower levels and very little turnover at the top.

4.4 Monopolistic Competition at Lower Levels

If small distribution units were strictly maintained at all levels, then heroin suppliers could monopolize a small piece of the market. At low levels, however, this strict discipline is impossible. Since the firms at this level cannot afford elaborate organizations to discipline their customers; and since consumers at low levels, most of whom are addicts, are highly motivated to maintain connections with several different suppliers, low-level dealers will fail to restrict consumers to a single market. In addition, since low-level dealers are arrested much more frequently than upper levels, there is a rapid turnover among low-level dealers. The rapid turnover implies that relationships between consumers and suppliers are constantly disrupted. Consequently, it is difficult for any supplier to maintain a restricted set of customers. Finally, as noted above, the upward pressure of addicts trying to get into the heroin business and the small amounts of capital necessary to get started adds to the speed at which personnel and organizations change at this level. Thus, since it is very difficult for low-level suppliers to maintain tightly knit, disciplined groups of consumers, they are unable to exploit full monopoly powers.

The system does not break down into completely free competition, however. Suppliers continue to restrict access to information and markets they control, thereby restricting the number of markets that are convenient for any particular addict. In addition, addicts often find it useful to restrict their purchases to dealers who consistently provide a high-quality product and who give them advantages as loyal and trusted clients. Thus, restricted information and product differentiation maintain shreds of monopoly advantages for the suppliers at low levels.

---

[111]Note that it is this careful guarding of sources that make good connections rare.

Thus, at low levels the inability of the organizations to resist consumer pressure or avoid large turnovers in the personnel that improve suppliers leads to a fluid, competitive system. This tendency is mitigated by imperfections in the market created by restricting information and access to markets. The equilibrium position is that of a monopolistic competition.

4.5 Occasional Downward Excursions by High-Level Dealers

Just as low-level dealers have incentives to move upward in the distribution system, higher level dealers have consistent economic incentives to cut out lower levels and deal directly with lower level customers.[11] The incentive is to capture the profits of the next level dealer, as well as those he could capture by himself.

For the most part, higher level dealers are deterred from these excursions by the risks associated with increased numbers of transactions and customers. Avoidance of these risks is the primary explanation for the existence of these levels in the first place. However, on occasion, greedy high-level dealers will cut out lower levels. When they do so, the police will have a unique opportunity to gather evidence against them. Indeed, these downward excursions will make greedy and aggressive high-level dealers particularly vulnerable to arrest.

Note that the tendency of the police to arrest the greedier and less-cautious, high-level dealers is a tendency we like. These are the kinds of dealers who threaten to expand the market significantly. Although we may be frustrated by the difficulty of catching very cautious and sophisticated dealers, and think that it is outrageous that they can earn enormous amounts of money illegally, it is important to keep in mind that these dealers avoid arrest precisely because they behave in a way that is less dangerous to the society than greedy, aggressive, careless dealers. Thus, both the direct action against the greedy dealers and the general deterrence of downward excursions are extremely important effects to achieve.

4.6 Preferences for Socially Disorganized Areas

Socially disorganized areas provide environments that are enormously attractive to heroin dealers. Among the most important advantages of these environments are the following:

1. A supply of customers and employees that have internalized norms against cooperation with the police
2. A background level of activity into which many illegal activities can be blended
3. An inability of honest citizens to demand a fair share of police services

4. The likelihood that other criminals in the area have born some of the very expensive initial costs of corrupting the local police
5. The fact that the enormous supply of criminals in the area will allow local police to reach satisfactory levels of achievement long before they arrest a large fraction of the criminals operating

Such features guarantee that dealers operating in socially disorganized areas can survive with less-cautious behavior, and less-expensive investments in strategies to reduce their risk. Although dealers operating in areas that are well-organized often have the short-run advantage of anonymity and surprise, this advantage will disappear quickly if they are not extremely careful. Thus, one would expect to find the major portions of distribution systems operating in disorganized areas. Moreover, one would expect systems operating in these areas to be particularly efficient in their operations and particularly difficult to uproot.

4.7 Complicated, Time-Consuming Transactions

In many respects, transactions are the most vulnerable aspect of the distribution system. The reasons are that several people are involved, evidence of criminal activity is immediately available, and money and drugs are on the scene to be stolen. To protect the transactions, dealers must rely on many of the strategies we identified: screening customers, drop strategies, investing in muscle, and so on. Moreover, dealers may go through several trial runs to discover what the real intentions of the participants are and to increase confidence in the procedures. The net effect of these precautions is to make transactions complicated and time consuming at all levels.[mmm] "Scoring" can be a three- to four-hour problem even for experienced users. It can be a protracted four-month negotiation among high-level dealers.

Given the time-consuming nature of the transactions, it is possible that the transactions are the major factor determining the rate at which heroin flows to retail markets. There may be sufficient demand, capital, raw materials, and ambitious entrepreneurs to triple the size of the current market. But the supply does not triple because the transactions cannot be confidently and quickly arranged. In effect, what is scarce in the system is a reliable connection.[nnn]

[mmm]For a general view of the difficulty of executing transactions, see Newsday, The Heroin Trail, pp. 226-255.

[nnn]It is very hard to demonstrate that the difficulty of executing transactions is a major constraint on the throughput capacity of the distribution system. Perhaps the strongest pieces of evidence are simply police observations of the enormous effort required to complete a deal, and the existence of the term "connection." The fact that this term exists, and is spoken of in reverant tones, suggest the importance of a relationship with someone who can execute transactions reliably.

If the time-consuming aspects of the transactions are major constraints on the rate at which heroin moves to retail markets, there are two important implications for policies to control the supply of heroin. First, the enforcement strategy should strike at the transactions rather than at other components of the system (e.g., capital, raw materials, finished inventories, etc.). This can be accomplished by undercover and surveillance operations. Second, to the extent that connections develop that succeed in reducing difficulty of the transactions simply by developing confidence in their procedures and one another, these connections should become a major target of enforcement efforts. Such connections are likely to control a substantial share of the market simply because they are more efficient than other firms.[12]

4.8 Summary: The Structure and Dynamics of the System

The overall picture of the distribution system, then, is a structure composed of small, isolated distribution units; many different levels; a small number of firms at high levels that achieve effective coordination with one another; and a relatively large number of firms at lower levels among whom competition is slightly restrained by restricted information and access to separate markets. There is movement among the levels of the distribution system: lower level dealers becoming higher level dealers, and higher level dealers occasionally cutting out lower levels to deal directly with consumers. In addition, there are new entrants. The movement and turnover is greater at lower levels than at higher levels. The major factors constraining the growth of the system are the difficulty of making transactions and the exceptional vulnerability of dealers seeking to pioneer new markets at any level. Socially disorganized areas provide a relatively favorable environment for both secure operations and safe expansion.

The response of the system to an increase in the general threat is to follow the tendencies specified in earlier sections to an even greater degree. The distribution chain will lengthen and the individual marketing operations shrink as each supplier tries to cut out his "marginal" (i.e., risky) customers and restrict his selling to only those he can trust. It will become increasingly difficult for newcomers to break into the supply network because of the pervasive suspicion. Suppliers will invest time and absorb increased organizational costs to design more elaborate drop and storage systems to conceal their activities better. Suppliers will also try to find new ways of disciplining their customers more effectively. In addition, the costs of holding inventories will increase so suppliers will be motivated to try to adjust their supply so it misses an expected demand on the low side rather than the high side. They will be constrained in all this reorganization, however, by an increase in the risk associated with negotiation and communication. People who are most likely to survive in such a situation are those who can make complicated adjustments without much negotiation. In summary, then, the markets will become more monopolized, more centralized, and more costly to run. The supply of heroin will be restricted, and customers will pay high prices.

A relaxed enforcement effort leads to the opposite adjustments. Distribution chains will shorten as bold, high-level dealers cut out levels to deal directly on the street. Individual marketing operations will seek to expand. Transactions will become easier as elaborate drop strategies and screening become less important. Newcomers will find it easy to break into the system. The market will become less monopolized and less expensive to run. The supply of heroin will increase and customers will face low prices.

Thus, enforcement pressures tend to constrain and tighten the distribution system. Aggressive marketing efforts are turned back. The flow of heroin is impeded. Given that we prefer a small, cautious distribution system to a large, aggressive system we like the effect of the enforcement pressure. However, it is important to understand that no amount of enforcement pressure will succeed in eliminating the distribution system. A very cautious dealer can avoid arrest indefinitely.[ooo] Still, the enforcement pressure can influence the equilibrium size of the residual illicit market precisely because it forces dealers to behave cautiously. As enforcement pressure increases, the illicit market shrinks. As it decreases, the market expands. This suggests that enforcement efforts should be thought of as a protracted guerrilla war to limit the incursion of heroin supplies rather than a war in which total victory is finally gained.[ppp]

Notes

1. See generally, D. Kandel, "Stages in Adolescent Involvement in Drug Use," *Science* (1975).

2. See Public Research Institute of the Center for Naval Analysis, *Heroin Supply and Urban Crime* (Washington, D.C.: Drug Abuse Council, 1976), p. 7.

3. See generally, Irving Goffman, *Strategic Interaction* (Philadelphia: University of Pennsylvania Press, 1969).

4. Comptroller General of the United States, "Heroin Being Smuggled into New York City Successfully" (Washington, D.C.: General Accounting Office, 1972), pp. 13-18.

5. Charles H. Whitebread and Ronald Stevens, "Constructive Possession in Narcotics Cases: To Have and Have Not," *Virginia Law Review* 58 (1972): 751.

[ooo]As one agent reports: "Anyone with any smarts can deal heroin for a long time and not get caught if he sticks to a couple of basic rules . . . If he doesn't sell to strangers, he isn't going to be selling to undercover agents. If he always has someone else handle the stuff and stash it for him, he's not going to get caught for possession." See *Newsday, The Heroin Trail*, p. 215.

[ppp]Strategies to control the supply of heroin are discussed in Part II.

6. See "Police Perjury in Narcotics Dropsy Cases: A New Credibility Gap," *Georgetown Law Journal* 60 (1971): 507.

7. See Thomas C. Schelling, "Economics and Criminal Enterprise," *The Public Interest* 7 (Spring 1967): 65-66.

8. Richard Woodley, *Dealer* (New York: Holt, Rinehart and Winston, 1971), p. 7.

9. Jeremy Larner and Ralph Tefferteller, *The Addict in the Street* (New York: Grove Press, 1964), pp. 98-99, 206; and Seymour Fiddle, *Portraits from a Shooting Gallery* (New York: Harper and Row, 1967), pp. 124, 128.

10. See generally, "Hearings Before the Permanent Subcommittee on Investigations of the Senate Committee on Government Operations," 88th Congress, 1st Session, Part 1 (1963).

11. See Woodley, *Dealer*, p. 68.

12. See Domestic Council Drug Abuse Task Force, *White Paper on Drug Abuse* (Washington, D.C.: U.S. Government Printing Office, 1975), pp. 35-39.

Appendix 1A
Models of Distribution Units

By sifting through anecdotal accounts of dealing activity described in the literature, one can accumulate a set of models of distribution units. The models presented below are drawn from narrative descriptions in the sources shown:

Model I

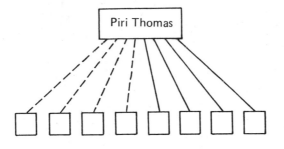

Source: Adapted from Piri Thomas, *Down These Mean Streets* (New York: Signet Books, 1967).

Figure 1A-1. Model I Distribution Unit

1. Buys "bundle" (= 25 bags) for $60 and keeps 5 for himself.
2. Sells 4-8 customers (at average of 3-5 bags) until he gets $60 to recop.
3. Sells high to people "strung out."
4. 20 percent profit finances own habit.

Model II

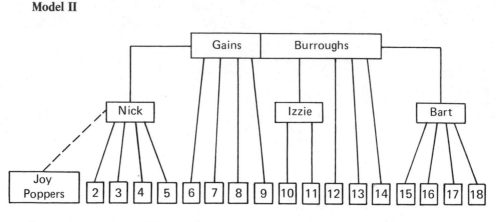

Source: Adapted from William Burroughs, *Junkie* (New York: Grove Press, 1953).

Figure 1A-2. Model II Distribution Unit

1. Buys 1/4 ounce (= 7/4 bundles) for $90 (= $52/bundle).
2. Cuts into 100 caps, @ $2/cap.
3. Sells to 7 straight customers + 3 accommodaters supplying selves and 11 others at 2-3 caps average for $90. $130 to recop.
4. Kept average of 30 caps for selves.
5. Therefore, profit of 60 percent kept two guys in own habit.

Model III

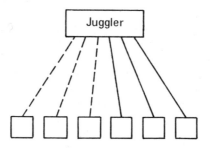

Source: Adapted from Edward Preble and John Casey, "Taking Care of Business—The Heroin User's Life on the Street," *International Journal of the Addiction* 4:1 (March 1969).

Figure 1A-3. Model III Distribution Unit

1. Buys bundle for $80.
2. Sells 5-15 bags to 2-7 customers @ about $5/bag until gets $80 to recop.
3. Keeps 10 bags for self.

4. Therefore juggler makes 40-50 percent profit, which is enough to support own habit.
5. Cycle may be repeated 2 times or more/day → juggler + clients' habits twice what appear; that is, 20 bags/juggler and 16 bags for 6 customers.

Model IV

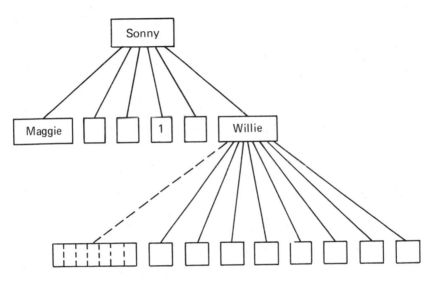

Source: Adapted from Willie Tedesco. Interview on Weight Dealers.

Figure 1A-4. Model IV Distribution Unit

1. Buys pure stuff for $750/ounce pure.
2. Cuts 2 to 1 and bags → 21 bundles at 25 bags.
3. Consigned to Willie and 5 or 6 others in lots of 1-10 bundles.
4. Willie took 6 bundles @ $75/bundle.
5. Sells 50 bags in morning to 8-10 regular customers (5-6 bags average).
6. Sells 1/2 bundle in afternoon in small lots to miscellaneous, old buyers.
7. Sells 2 bundles in evening to generally same 8-10 customers.
8. Keeps bundle → bundle and half for self.
9. Therefore, supplied 8-20 addicts/day.
10. Own habit is 3-5 times of clients.

The important thing to notice is that none of these distribution systems involves a large number of people.

Quantitative Estimates of the New York City Distribution System

Given this general model of illicit-distribution systems, what can be said quantitatively about important characteristics of a specific distribution system? How much money is spent on heroin? How much crime do heroin users commit? How big are the profits earned by dealers at different levels of the distribution system? How much money is available for corrupting the criminal-justice system?

The purpose of this chapter is to construct a rough quantitative description of the heroin-distribution system operating in New York City in the period 1970-74.[a] New York City is chosen for the analysis for three reasons. First, the distribution system operating in New York City accounts for a reasonably large fraction of the total volume of heroin distributed in the United States. Consequently, if one can successfully describe the system in New York, one will have succeeded in describing a large proportion of the domestic-heroin system.[b] Second, although scarce, data on the New York heroin market is relatively plentiful compared to other cities. Consequently, one can be slightly more confident about the conclusions of the analysis. Third, the New York City market appears to be relatively well structured and stable compared to other

---

[a] It is almost certain that the distribution system in New York City changed significantly during this period both in size and structure. Consequently, it may seem ridiculous to offer a general description of the structure for 1970-74. However, one must keep in mind that the calculations we make are extremely crude. The estimates could easily be off by a factor of 2-3. Given this imprecision, even significant changes in the character of the system could be lost in the estimating errors. Thus, the fact that we will make a single estimate for this period reveals our inability to estimate precisely rather than a belief that the system remained unaffected throughout the period.

[b] The traditional estimate is that New York accounts for 50 percent of the consumption of heroin. This estimate has no solid basis and is almost certainly wrong. For clues about the geographic distribution of heroin use that suggest New York City represents a much smaller component of national heroin consumption, see Lee Minichiello, "Indicators of Intravenous Drug Use in the United States: 1966-1973" (Washington, D.C.: Drug Enforcement Administration, 1975). Still, New York City looms large in the total consumption of heroin. Note that in addition to representing a large local market, New York City is also the location of firms involved in the transshipment of drugs to other areas. Consequently, the share of the total heroin consumed in the United States that *passes through* New York will be larger than the share of New York City consumption in the total consumption. In estimating the size of the New York City distribution system, we ignore transshipment. To the extent that transshipment occurs in New York City, this leads to an underestimate of the actual number of dealers operating there.

markets.[c] Consequently, crude estimates based on assumptions about regularity and consistency in the market will do less violence to the variety of the real market. For these reasons, New York City is a relatively attractive target for the analysis.

However, even with these advantages the analysis is *extremely* speculative. Many specific estimates must be made. Little empirical evidence is available to guide the estimate. Weak estimates made in one area are used to guide still weaker estimates in another area. Thus, the analysis resembles an elaborate confection rather than a solid piece of masonry.

Two justifications exist for making the estimate in spite of the unfavorable conditions. First, there are few competitors to this analysis.[d] Consequently, this analysis can serve as a place-holder until better analyses are done. Second, in spite of the airiness of the estimates, there are a few pieces of iron supporting them. Occasionally, empirical evidence is available for specific characteristics we wish to estimate. However, more important than empirical information on each characteristic is the requirement for consistency *among* the various estimates (e.g., the amount of heroin supplied will be equal to the amount of heroin consumed; the amount of heroin consumed cannot be more than can be purchased by users; a fixed mathematical relationship exists among the number of customers, the average number of customers supplied by a dealer, and the number of dealers; a wholesaler's selling price will be a retailer's purchasing price; etc.). These requirements for consistency allow us to anchor many weak estimates in stronger estimates, and keep the entire analysis from drifting hopelessly into the realm of disbelief.

The method is the following. First, we estimate the annual aggregate consumption of heroin in New York City. This estimate establishes a limit on the size of the local heroin-distribution system.[e] It also forces us to make some estimates of the sources of addicts' income. Second, we estimate how the distribution system is layered. When we combine estimates of the number of levels with information about prices paid and quantities exchanged at each level,

---

[c]The current conventional wisdom is that markets for drugs in California and along the Southwest border are much less structured than in New York City. There is much more entry and exit from the business, fewer levels, and less concentration at any given level. The likely reason is that the production-distribution systems operating within Mexico are penetrated by consumers at a variety of levels. Thus, the situation is more analogous to the dangerous-drug situation where there is a legitimate distribution system vulnerable to diversion. Easy entrance and exit at a variety of different levels results in much less-structured distribution units.

[d]The major exception to this general statement is Edward Preble and John C. Casey, "Taking Care of Business: The Heroin User's Life on the Street," *International Journal of the Addiction* 4:1 (March 1969). I am profoundly in their debt.

[e]Note, again, the possibility of firms engaged in transshipment—not local distribution. To the extent that such people operate in New York City, the estimates made in this chapter underestimate the number of dealers in New York City.

we can make estimates of the value added, profits, and activity of dealers at each level. Third, we summarize the observations and estimations.

The analysis we present cannot hope to describe much of the important detail and variety of the real distribution system.[f] The characterization is as rigid, stark, and lifeless as an accountant's report. But, if we are lucky and do well, the estimates of the various parameters will be within a factor of 2-3 of the real number.

1.0 The Aggregate Consumption of Heroin

Customarily, analysts make a very simple calculation of the aggregate consumption of heroin: they multiply an estimate of the number of users by an estimate of the average habit size, by 365 days per year, to yield an estimate of the annual consumption of heroin.[g] Of course, there are problems in estimating both the number of users and the average habit size of the using population. But no one feels uneasy about multiplying the habit size times 365 days per year. If there was one assumption we could be sure of, it was that heroin users consumed enough heroin to satisfy their habit—day in and day out. That was the nature of the addiction.

Recently, the chronic uncertainty about the number of users and the average habit size has been joined by increased uneasiness about the assumption that users consumed enough heroin to meet their habit 365 days a year. Analysts now note that heroin users do not spend all of their days on the street. Indeed, even in a world with limited treatment capacity for heroin users, it seemed that users spent from one-third to one-fourth of their time in jail, hospitals, or treatment programs.[1] Although there was reason to believe that heroin consumption did *not* fall to zero in such institutions, it did seem reasonable to suppose that heroin consumption was reduced to levels substantially below the user's reported daily habits.[2]

Analysts then discovered that even when users were on the street, it was not certain that they would consume heroin at the level of their daily habits. Some days, users would simply fail to earn enough money, or fail to score enough drugs to reach their habit size.[3] Moroever, it seemed that users would occasionally voluntarily abstain from heroin use or would consume other drugs instead.[4]

Thus, although the addictive quality of heroin allows one to estimate annual consumption of heroin more directly than one could estimate the consumption of other specific goods, the estimate cannot be reliably made simply by

---

[f]To imagine the variety of the real system, recall all the different types of dealers and the possible movements they can make within the distribution system.

[g]For a routine calculation of this type, see Drug Enforcement Administration, Statistical and Data Services Division, "Drug Enforcement Statistical Report," December 1974.

multiplying the number of users by the average habit size. In addition, one must take account of reduced heroin consumption associated with institutionaliza-tion, voluntary abstinence, consumption of other drugs, and failures to earn sufficient income to maintain a habit. The estimates made here are based on relatively careful estimates of the number of users, and also on estimates of the joint distribution of habit sizes with characteristics of users that make them more or less likely to maintain their consumption at specific levels for sustained periods.

1.1 The Number of Heroin Users in New York City

The actual number of heroin users in New York City is unknown. Table 2-1 presents different estimates of the number of heroin users in New York City over the period 1966-72. The table indicates a large degree of uncertainty about the number of users: for example, estimates of the number of users in 1970 vary by a factor of 10.

We can narrow this range of uncertainty in two different ways. First, we can compare the various estimating techniques and make judgments about which techniques are more likely to produce accurate estimates.[h] Second, we can compute the prevalence of heroin use that is implied by any particular estimate of the number of users and compare these implied prevalence rates with existing evidence and plausible expectations about prevalence.[i]

All the estimating techniques of Table 2-1 are structurally similar. Each is based on a count of heroin users who are identified by some government agency. In the case of the BNDD Register, it is a count of all people arrested for narcotics crimes at least once over the last five years who admit to using heroin.[j] In the case of reported deaths, it is a count of all people whose deaths were investigated by the Medical Examiner's Office and who were judged by the medical examiner to be heroin users at the time of their death.[k] Although some counts strive to be a comprehensive census of the heroin-using population, all acknowledge that they fail to identify all users. Consequently, there is a presumption that the official count of users must be inflated by some factor to correct for the bias in the counting procedure. Different combinations of counts and estimates of the bias in the counts yield the different estimates of Table 2-1.

[h]The basic underlying assumption in evaluating the different estimating techniques is that each of them exercises some claim on our credibility. However, the strength of the claim depends on the strength of the estimating procedure. The end result of evaluating the different estimates is not only to settle on a single best estimate that can be used in additional calculations, but also to develop a sense for the range of uncertainty.

[i]This is an example of relying on requirements for consistency in judging the likelihood of a given estimate.

[j]For a description of this system, write to Dr. Joseph Greenwood, Office of Science and Technology, Drug Enforcement Administration, 1405 I Street, Washington, D.C. 20005.

[k]For sources describing the system, see footnote e, Table 2-1.

Such techniques are vulnerable to three major sources of error:

1. Inaccuracy in diagnosis (i.e., an inability to reliably distinguish users from nonusers)
2. Unknown bias in surveillance (i.e., uncertainty about what portion of the heroin-using population comes to the attention of government agencies)
3. Inconsistency over time in either diagnosis or surveillance

There are several different ways of controlling these sources of error.

The accuracy of diagnosis can be controlled by investing in accurate diagnostic tests and procedures, by articulating clear operational definitions of what signs and symptoms should be taken as evidence of noteworthy heroin use, and by avoiding bureaucratic incentive structures that penalize errors of one type more than errors of another type.

One seeks to control the second source of error (unknown bias) by investing in techniques that allow accurate estimates of the bias. A useful technique is to test the counting procedure against a "tagged sample" of users. The basic procedure is to identify a random sample of the total population of users and observe the proportion of the sample identified by the counting procedure. For example, a neighborhood is surveyed to find heroin users; then the proportion of these users known to the standard counting procedure is identified. Or, one identifies all heroin users who die and observes what proportion of the dead users were known to the standard counting procedure. If the "tagged sample" accurately represents the general population of users with respect to characteristics that influence the probability of being counted (and if the tagging does not itself influence the probability of being counted), we can estimate the bias in the counting procedure simply by observing the experience of the tagged sample vis-à-vis the counting procedure.

Controlling the third source of error (inconsistency over time in diagnoses or surveillance) is the most difficult. It is hard to know whether a counting procedure remains consistent in its diagnosis and surveillance of the using population. Moreover, there is a strong tendency for the procedures to "improve." Diagnostic tests become more accurate as technology and clinical experience advance. Surveillance increases as more people become alerted to and interested in the number of users. Although improvements in diagnosis and more comprehensive reporting will, in the long run, improve our ability to estimate to number of users, in the short run, they make inter-year comparisons of the estimated number of users treacherous.[1]

Table 2-2 compares the different estimating techniques of Table 2-1 in terms of their success in controlling the different sources of error. Inspection of this table suggests that deaths among users may be the most successful

[1]For an excellent analysis of problems with changes in reporting systems and methods for handling these problems, see Lee Minichiello, "Indicators of Intravenous Drug Use in the United States."

Table 2-1
Estimates of the Number of Users in New York City: 1966-72
(In Thousands)

	1966	1967	1968	1969	1970	1971	1971
I. Direct counts							
A. BNDD register[a]	30	31	30	30	27	N.A.	49[b]
1. Expand by factor of 2.0[c]	60	62	60	60	54	N.A.	98
2. Expand by factor of 3.7[d]	111	115	111	111	100	N.A.	181
B. NYC Narcotics Register[e]	N.A.	N.A.	58	95	151	203	N.A.
1. Expand by factor of 1.28[f]	N.A.	N.A.	74	122	193	260	N.A.
2. Expand by factor of 1.67[g]	N.A.	N.A.	97	158	252	339	N.A.
II. Indirect estimates							
A. Deaths = 1.0% for using population in any given year[h]	34	65	65	101	120	126	N.A.
B. Arrested users = 0.45% of using population in any given year[i]	76	71[j]	62[j]	67[j]	102	133	76
III. Best estimate	45-50	60	65	90-100	115-125	125-140	100-150

[a]The numbers in this row represent the number of users listed by the Bureau of Narcotics and Dangerous Drugs (BNDD) as living in New York City. The information appears in Alfred Blumstein, Philip Sagi, and Marvin E. Wolfgang, "Problems of Estimating the Number of Heroin Addicts," University of Pennsylvania, 1973 (mimeographed), Table 2, p. 18.

[b]Personal communication, Bureau of Narcotics and Dangerous Drugs, Washington, D.C.

cLouria has estimated that the BNDD Register identifies only 50 percent of the active heroin users. This estimate is reported in Mary Koval, "Differential Estimates of Opiate Use in New York City," New York State Narcotic Addiction Control Commission, 1971 (mimeographed), p. 15.

dIbid. Reports DuPont's estimate that approximately 27 percent of the users that appeared for treatment in Washington, D.C. were known to the BNDD Register.

eTo discover the procedures and problems of the New York City Narcotics Register Project, see "The Development of a Case Register," by Zili Amsel et al., presented at 31st Annual Meeting of the Committee on Problems of Drug Dependence, Division of Medical Science, National Academy of Sciences, February 1969. See also, "The Narcotics Register: Problems in Data Interpretation," by J.J. Fishman and D.P. Conwell, presented at 32nd Annual Conference of Committee on Drug Dependence, National Research Council.

fKoval, "Differential Estimates of Opiate Use," reports that a small survey of the New York State Narcotics Addiction Control Commission (NACC) found that 75 percent of the users in a slum block of Manhattan were known to the Narcotics Register.

gAlan Thalinger, "A Study of Deaths of Narcotic Users in New York City—1969," Health Services Administration, New York City Department of Health, Health Research Training Program, 1970 (mimeographed). Thalinger found that 60 percent of the users who died in 1969 were known to the Narcotics Register.

hIbid. The mortality rate among users has been estimated in two different sources with remarkably consistent results. Thalinger discovered about 1,000 deaths among users in 1969. At that time, there were about 65,000 users listed in the Narcotics Register. Consequently, one could estimate a total of 108,000 users in New York City. Consequently, the mortality rate among users in the year was approximately

$$\frac{1,000 \text{ deaths}}{108,000 \text{ users}} = 1.0\% \text{ per year}$$

George Valliant, "The Natural History of a Chronic Disease," New England Journal of Medicine, December 8, 1966. Valliant observed 132 users over a 12-year period. At the end of the 12 years, 20 users had died. This implies an annual mortality rate of about 1.2 percent.

The number of deaths among users in New York City, which serves as the base for these estimates, is reported in a memorandum from the New York City Office of the chief medical examiner to the New York City Police Department, dated April 4, 1972, and from supplementary information provided to the Police Department on April 12, 1972.

iThe numbers of arrested people who admit heroin use, which serves as the bases for these estimates, were reported to me in a personal communication from the office of William P. McCarthy, deputy commissioner of the Organized Crime Control Bureau of the New York City Police Department. Mary Koval, "Drug Users among Police Department Arrestees and Arrests for Narcotic Offenses in New York City," New York State Narcotics Addiction Control Commission, 1969 (mimeograph), reports that the average user is arrested once every 2.25 years. This suggests that in any given year, roughly 45 percent of the total users are arrested.

jIn 1967 the criminal-commitment procedures began operating in New York City. Because these procedures could result in three- to five-year terms in treatment for users convicted of criminal offenses, there were strong incentives for arrested users to deny their heroin use upon arrest. Consequently, for the years 1967 to 1969, one should assume that the probability of admitting to heroin use, given that one was a user and was arrested, was lower than for the other years. From 1969 to 1972 the criminal-commitment procedures largely ceased to operate due to inadequate treatment facilities.

Table 2-2
Evaluations of Estimating Techniques in Terms of Their Ability to Control Sources of Error

	Accuracy in Diagnosis of Addiction	Ability to Estimate Bias	Consistency of Diagnosis and Bias Over Time
BNDD Register	Weak Diagnosis usually depends on either statement of arrested person, superficial examination by police or knowledge of past reputation.	Weak The register has not been tested by a tagged sample in New York City.	Weak 1. Several different police agencies with different diagnosis procedures report to the register. 2. Arrested people have different incentives to admit drug use. 3. Levels of police activity change over time.
New York City Narcotics	Variable Different agencies with widely varying loss functions for different types of errors report to the Narcotics Register.	Strong for Limited Years 1. Deaths used as effective "tagged sample" for years 1969, 1970. 2. Survey in 1968 serves as adequate "tagged sample" for 1968, 1969.	Weak The register continues to "improve" over time. More and a wider variety of of agencies report to the register each year.
Deaths among users	Strong Dead people are diagnosed as users after careful examination of the site of death and autopsy of the body by the chief medical examiner.	Reasonably Strong Several independent studies indicate mortality rate of about 1 percent per year.	Moderately Strong Procedures and personnel for investigating deaths have been fairly consistent over the last 5 to 10 years.
Arrested	Weak Same as BNDD Register.	Weak No strong evidence about the probability that a user will be arrested in any given year.	Weak 1. Arrested people have different incentives to admit heroin use. 2. Levels of police activity change over time.

estimating procedures. The adjusted counts for the Narcotics Register in the years shortly after the sample survey and prior to the inclusion of a large variety of reporting agencies may also be reasonably successful in controlling the errors. Consequently, one should not assume that all estimates of Table 2-1 are equally likely. One should assume that the estimates yielded by observed deaths among users and the adjusted counts of Narcotics Register are relatively more likely to be accurate than the other estimates. This narrows the range of uncertainty.

One can also narrow the range of uncertainty by computing an implied prevalence of heroin use in selected populations. Because we have information and expectations about the prevalence of heroin use, we can check any particular estimate of the number of users by seeing whether the estimate implies prevalence rates that are consistent with existing information and beliefs.

Table 2-3 presents estimates of the prevalence rates implied by particular estimates of the number of users for three different populations:

1. The entire population of New York City
2. The entire school-age population of New York City
3. The population of males living in low-income areas of the city (by age)

Table 2-4 presents the results of surveys that have estimated the prevalence of heroin use among several different populations.

Inspection of Tables 2-3 and 2-4 decreases one's confidence in extreme estimates of the number of users both at high or low ends of the range. It increases one's confidence in the accuracy of estimates between 70,000 and 150,000 users.

Given that both techniques for calibrating the accuracy of different estimates lead one to trust estimates in the 70,000-150,000 range and to distrust estimates either significantly below or significantly above that range, it seems reasonable to act on the basis of 70,000-150,000 users in New York City.[m] This estimate does *not* include *former* users (i.e., people who have not used heroin in the last six months), but does include casual users who have recently started using heroin.

1.2 Estimates of the Aggregate Consumption of Heroin

The amount of heroin that will be consumed by 70,000 to 150,000 users depends on many factors: the "habits" of users, the price and availability of heroin; the capacity of users to finance a given level of heroin consumption; the users' willingness to substitute other drugs for heroin; the user's motivation to

[m]For computational simplicity, we routinely rely on an estimate of 100,000 users. Consequently, to calculate the range of all additional estimates in this chapter, one should multiply the estimates by 0.7 to obtain a lower bound, and 1.5 to obtain an upper bound.

Table 2-3
Prevalence Rates of Heroin Use among Selected Populations Implied by Different Estimates of the Number of Current Users

	Estimated Number of Current Users in New York City					
	50,000	70,000	100,000	150,000	200,000	300,000
I. The total population of New York City[a]	0.6%	0.9%	1.3%	1.9%	2.5%	3.8%
II. The total secondary-school-aged population of New York City[b]						
A. Assume 10% of current users attend high school	1.1%	1.5%	2.2%	3.3%	4.4%	6.6%
B. Assume 20% of current users attend high school	2.2	3.1	4.4	6.6	8.8	13.2
III. The population of males living in low-income areas of the city (by age)[c]	3.1%	4.4%	6.3%	9.4%	12.6%	18.8%
A. Assume 45% of current users live in low-income areas						
1. Aged 16-17	4.9	7.7	9.7	14.6	19.5	29.3
2. Aged 18-27	6.4	9.0	12.8	19.2	25.6	38.4
3. Aged >27	1.2	1.7	2.4	3.6	4.8	7.3
B. Assume 55% of current users live in low-income areas	3.8%	5.4%	7.7%	11.5%	15.4%	23.0%
1. Aged 16-17	5.9	8.3	11.9	17.9	23.8	35.8
2. Aged 18-27	6.7	9.5	13.6	20.2	27.0	40.5
3. Aged >27	1.5	2.1	3.0	4.4	5.8	8.9

[a]Total population residing in central city of New York City SMSA in 1970 is estimated at 7.868 million. *Statistical Abstract of the United States–1972*, p. 859.

[b]The total number of people attending high school in New York City is estimated at 456.2 thousand. Ibid, p. 860. The estimated proportion of the heroin-using population aged less than 19 is estimated at 24 percent. Since the estimates of the age distribution are uncertain, since we are uncertain about the ages of the high school population in New York, and since many heroin users may no longer attend school, we have offered a low estimate of the proportion of heroin users who attend high school (10%) and a high estimate (20%).

cThe estimated population residing in low-income areas of city by age and sex is the following

	16-17		18-27		>27	
	Male	Female	Male	Female	Male	Female
	35,000	36,700	161,200	187,100	519,500	580,000

The source of these estimates is *Characteristics of the Persons Who Are Employed or Out of the Labor Force in Low Income Areas of New York City*. U.S. Dept. of Labor, Bureau of Employment Statistics. (Washington, D.C.: U.S. Government Printing Office, 1970). I have adjusted the data contained in this report to make the age categories consistent with the age categories of the heroin-using population, and to reflect the known tendency to under count males in low-income areas. The estimated proportions of *heroin* users in the various age and sex categories are the following:

	16-17 (9%)		18-27 (34%)		>27 (33%)	
	Male (85%)	Female (15%)	Male (85%)	Female (15%)	Male (85%)	Female (15%)
	7.65%	1.35%	45.9%	8.1%	26.05%	4.95%

The proportion of heroin users living in the particular low-income areas was estimated with the aid of New York State Narcotics Addiction Control Commission and New York City Narcotics Register, *Opiate Use in New York City* (New York City, 1969). This source presents estimates of the proportion of users who reside in each Health Center district of New York City. The BES survey areas for which the population estimates were made were *not* conterminous with the Health Center district boundaries. Consequently, the proportion of users living in Health Center districts had to be adjusted to obtain an estimate of the proportion of users living in BES survey areas. This was accomplished by a visual inspection of the two maps. I assumed that the heroin-using population was evenly spread over the various Health Center districts and estimated the proportion of the land area of each particular Health Center district that lay within each BES survey area. This yielded an estimate of 49 percent of the users currently live in BES survey areas. Because there is enormous uncertainty about this estimate, I have offered a low estimate (45%) and a high estimate (55%).

Table 2-4

The Observed Prevalence of Heroin Use among Various Population Groups

| Population Group | Observed Prevalence | | Remarks |
	Current Users	Ever Used	
I. Total population			
A. New York State[a]	0.4%	1.0%	Survey of population; interviews
B. Washington, D.C.[b]	2.4	N.A.	Estimated from deaths among users
C. Chicago, Illinois[b]	0.9	N.A.	
II. Employed males			
A. New York State[c]			
III. Unemployed males			
A. New York State[c]			
IV. Military personnel			
A. Enlisted Vietnam returnees processed at Oakland, Calif.[d]	16.2%	22.7%	Interviews
V. Ghetto populations			
A. Negro men aged 30[e] who attended elementary school and currently live in St. Louis	1.0%	14.0%	Interviews
B. Residents of Bedford-Stuyvesant in NYC[f]	2.0	N.A.	Survey of population; interviews
VI. "Hippie" populations			
A. Responding to questionnaire in *East Village Other*[g]	N.A.	18%	Self-selected; self-administered questionnaire
B. East Village hippies[g]	N.A.	13	Casual interviews of 51 "hippies"

[a]Carl Chambers, *An Assessment of Drug Use in the General Population* (Albany: New York State Narcotics Addiction Control Commission, 1971), p. 131.

[b]New York City Addiction Services Agency, "Addicts/Addicts in Treatment; Ten Largest U.S. Cities," March 1973. The estimates are based on personal communications from drug agencies in each of the various cities. I have included estimates only for those cities that I know to have effective and careful drug agencies.

[c]Numerator is taken from Chambers, *An Assessment of Drug Use*, p. 132. Denominator comes from *Statistical Abstract of the United States—1972*, pp. 222, 226.

[d]K. Eric Nelson and Jacob Panzarella, "Preliminary Findings: Prevalence of Drug Use among Enlisted Vietnam Returnees Processing from ETS Separation, Oakland Overseas Processing Center," mimeo, March 1971. *Current Use* is defined as having used at least once in the last 30 days. *Ever used* is defined as the total number who used at least once in Vietnam.

[e]Lee Robins and George Murphy, "Drug Use in a Normal Population of Young Negro Men," *American Journal of Public Health* 57:9 (September 1967): 1584-1596. Current Use is defined as having used at least once in the last year.

[f]Addiction Research and Treatment Corporation Evaluation Team, Columbia University

| | Observed Prevalence | | |
Population Group	Current Users	Ever Used	Remarks
VII. College students[h]			
A. Male undergraduates in Midwest University	N.A.	1.7%	Self-administered questionnaire
B. Random sample of 38 colleges with more than 200 students	N.A.	1.9	Self-administered questionnaire
C. University of Maine undergraduate	3.7%	6.4	Self-administered questionnaire
D. Undergraduates in 23 universities and junior colleges in Florida	N.A.	2.2	Self-administered questionnaire
E. Graduates and under-graduates at University of Michigan	N.A.	16.9	Self-administered questionnaire
F. Students in 9 colleges, universities, and business schools in Denver-Boulder metropolitan area	N.A.	2.0	Self-administered questionnaire
VIII. High school students[i]			
A. San Mateo Public High school students	N.A.	4.6%	Self-administered questionnaire
B. High school students in South Central Pennsylvania	N.A.	2.5	Self-administered questionnaire
C. High School students in Michigan		2.8	Self-administered questionnaire
D. Grades 7-12 in Dallas, Texas	1.7%	3.0	Self-administered questionnaire
E. Jr. and sr. high in Montgomery County, Maryland	0.7	1.9	Self-administered questionnaire

School of Social Work, *Progress Report* Washington, D.C.: U.S. Department of Justice, 1971), p. 41. Two percent of the population admitted using heroin themselves. Eleven percent reported heroin use by one or more of their friends.

gThese findings are reported in Dorothy F. Berg and Linell P. Broecker, "Illicit Use of Dangerous Drugs in the United States," a Compilation of Studies, Surveys, and Polls" (Washington, D.C.: BNDD, June 1972), pp. 76-77.

hIbid., pp. 48-59.

iIbid., pp. 60-72. One should be leery of these estimates. Teenagers (and probably college students as well) tend to boast about their drug use. This hypothesis is supported by a survey of students in Philadelphia in which students were asked if they used a mythical drug called JPA. Sixteen percent of the students who reported using heroin also reported using JPA. Similarly, 24 percent of the students who reported using cocaine reported they also used JPA. See "Heroin in Philadelphia: Reports of a Student Research Workshop on Heroin Abuse, Program and Policies," Fels Center of Government, University of Pennsylvania, March 1972, pp. F19-F20.

abstain from heroin use; the frequency with which they seek treatment; and the vulnerability of users to arrest and incarceration. These factors vary significantly among users. Moreover, given a certain population of users, these factors change over time—partly because of changes in government policy (e.g., expanded treatment capacity; increased prices for heroin; or more aggressive enforcement of property and violent crimes), and partly because of the internal dynamics of the heroin-using population (e.g., aging of the population). Thus, for a given population of users, it will be difficult to make a precise estimate of annual heroin consumption.

Still, if one can estimate several important characteristics of a given population of users, one can make a rough calculation of the aggregate consumption of heroin. The steps are the following. First, one estimates the distribution of "habit sizes" within the heroin-using population. However, the habit sizes are assumed to represent *intended* levels of consumption rather than *actual* levels of consumption. Second, since *actual* levels of consumption depend on many characteristics of the users beyond their habit size (e.g., their ability to finance a given level of consumption, their willingness to abstain voluntarily from heroin, their vulnerability to arrest, etc.), it is important to estimate the distribution of the characteristics within habit sizes. A simple way to accommodate these differences is to construct a typology of users defined in terms of variables affecting actual consumption, and to estimate the distribution of these types of users within habit sizes. Third, since there is great interest in the sources of users' incomes, and since knowing something about sources of income helps us to estimate users' financial capacities and vulnerabilities to arrest, it is valuable to estimate the sources of users' incomes. Fourth, the information about habit sizes, types of users, and sources of users' incomes can be combined to permit estimates of the annual consumption of heroin in New York City that reflect more on the variables affecting heroin consumption than are usually considered.

Table 2-5 presents data from several different sources on the habit sizes of users in New York City. Parallel to the data, a "best estimate" is presented. The best estimate adjusts the existing data on the basis of two different judgments. First, among these sources, the data from the Narcotics Addiction Control Commission was considered to be the strongest (row V). The data was from a relatively large sample, and there were relatively few incentives for users to distort their responses to questions about their heroin consumption. Second, it seemed likely that *all* of these data (with the exception of the general survey data) would be biased towards larger habits. The reason is that all of the data was collected in either jail or in treatment programs, and users with small habits are relatively less likely to appear in these institutions.[n] Thus, the best estimate

[n]For a description and analysis of the lag in seeking treatment, see Mark H. Greene, Nicholas J. Kozel, and Roy L. Appletree, "An Epidemiologic Study of Heroin Use Patterns and Trends in Four Cities on the Mexican-American Border" (Washington, D.C.: Special Action Office for Drug Abuse Prevention, 1975), p. 4.

Table 2-5
Estimated Distribution of Habit Sizes among Heroin-Using Population

Source of Sample: Reference	Distribution of Habit Sizes[a]				
	≤2 bags	>2 bags, ≤6 bags	>6 bags ≤10 bags	>10 bags	Average Habit Size
I. Universe:					
A. Chambers (1970)	50%	−	−	−	−
II. Arrested Users					
A. Koval (1969)	−	−	−	−	4.0
B. Nash and Cohen (1969)	−	−	−	−	3.8;4.3
III. Sentenced Users:					
A. Babst (1969)	23%	−	−	−	−
IV. Users in Treatment:					
A. Freedman and Brotman (1965)	7%	62%	21%	9%	5.4
V. Certified Users					
A. NACC (1968)	22%	42%	22%	14%	5.9
VI. Best Estimate	30%	42%	20%	8%	4.5

Sources: Dean V. Babst, Daniel Glaser, and James Inciardi. 1969 *Predicting Post-Release Adjustment of Institutionalized Addicts: An Analysis of New York and California Parole Experience and California Civil Commitment Experience* (Albany: New York State Narcotic Addiction Control Commission). Richard Brotman and Alfred M. Freedman. 1965. *Continuities and Discontinuities in the Process of Patient Care for Narcotics Addicts* (New York City: New York Medical College). Carl Chambers. 1970. *An Assessment of Drug Use in the General Population* (Albany: New York State Narcotic Addiction Control Commission). Mary Koval, "Drug Users Among Police Department Arrestees and Arrests for Narcotic Offenses in New York City." 1969 (Albany: New York State Narcotic Addiction Control Commission), mimeographed. New York State Narcotic Addiction Control Commission. 1968. *First Annual Statistical Report* (Albany). George Nash and Eli Cohen. 1969. "An Analysis of New York City Police Statistics for Narcotic Arrests During the Period 1957-1967" (New York City: Columbia University Bureau of Applied Social Research), mimeograph.

[a]All habit sizes are estimated in terms of the number of $5 bags of heroin consumed each day.

is based on a shift towards smaller habits while trying to stay close to the distribution of habit sizes observed in the NACC sample.

The major factors influencing a user's ability to maintain a given level of heroin consumption are fairly well-known. Habit size is itself one of the major factors. Since the mechanism of tolerance and withdrawal only become powerful at high levels of consumption, a user's desire to maintain a given level of consumption becomes stronger as his habit size increases. Thus, low-habit users will be less religious in maintaining habits than high-habit users.

Duration of use is also a major factor—partly because it is correlated with habit size.[5] However, duration of use seems to exercise influence on levels of consumption independently of habit size. As users move from experimental use to regular use, duration of use seems to increase the user's regularity in consuming heroin. The mechanism is probably acculturation to an addict subculture in which opportunities to earn and "score" heroin increase and incentives to abstain from heroin are attenuated. Then, as users get older and have longer histories of use, duration of use has a negative effect on a user's regularity in consuming heroin. Periods of abstinence come more frequently and last longer;[o] the user is more likely to seek treatment. The mechanism producing this effect is more obscure. Perhaps it is a combination of fatigue, dwindling enthusiasm for previously exciting activities, and decreasing opportunities for anonymous illegal activity.

A third major factor affecting a user's interest in maintaining a given level of heroin use is the level of multiple-drug abuse. High levels of multiple-drug abuse give strong indications that users like being "stoned" and will work hard to get "stoned." This distinguishes multiple-drug users from users who consume heroin simply to maintain a habit, or to garner whatever status accrues to heroin users in specific subcultures.[6] On the other hand, multiple-drug use also signals a willingness to substitute other drugs for heroin.

Finally, criminal activity is a major factor influencing a user's actual level of consumption. The variable is important partly because it provides clues about the size and regularity of a user's income. But it is also important because it indicates a user's vulnerability to arrest and imprisonment.

Thus, over the course of a year, habit size, duration of use, levels of multiple-drug abuse, and levels of criminal activity will influence a user's desire and ability to maintain a consistent level of heroin use. A simple way to accommodate these factors is to develop a typology of users. Table 2-6 presents a typology of users defined in terms of these characteristics. The specific characteristics *imputed* to the different types of users (beyond the characteristics *defining* the types of users) are informed by several different sources. The characteristics are consistent with anecdotal information about the behavior of users,[p] with known correlations of single variables,[7] and with the finding of other researchers who have developed typologies of users for different purposes.[8]

Table 2-7 estimates the distribution of these types of users within habit sizes (columns 1, 2, 3). These estimates were developed by the following procedure. First, a variety of secondary sources describing different characteristics of the population of users in New York City were collected and organized. Table 2-8

---

oFor basic sources on the "maturing out" phenomenon, see Chapter 1, footnote g.

PFor anecdotal accounts of users lives, see Seymour Fiddle, *Portraits from a Shooting Gallery* (New York: Harper and Row, 1967); or Jeremy Larner and Ralph Tefferteller, *The Addict in the Street* (New York: Grove Press, 1964).

Table 2-6
A Typology of Users

Types of Users	Characteristics of Users						
	Characteristics *Defining* Types of Users				Characteristics *Imputed* To Types of Users		
	Duration of Use	Habit Size	Level of Multiple-Drug Use	Level of Criminality	Health of User	Level of Legitimate Employment	Motivation to Seek Treatment
Joy poppers	Short		Low	Moderate-high	Moderate	Low	Low
Drug dabblers	Short	Small-medium	Moderate-high	Low-moderate	Moderate	Low	Low-moderate
Addicts	Moderate	Medium-high	Medium-high	Medium high	Poor	Low	Low
Hustlers	Moderate	Small-medium	Low	High	Moderate	Low	Low
Drug dependents	Moderate	Medium-high	High	Low	Poor	Low	Low
Conformists	Moderate	Small-medium	Low	Low	Moderate	Medium-high	Medium-low
Maturing-out users	Long	Varies	Low	Low	Moderate	Moderate	High
Burned-out users	Long	High	High	Low-medium	Poor	Low	Low

Table 2-7
Estimated Distribution of Types of Users among Different Habit Sizes

Types of Users	Habit Size			
	(1) Small Habits ≤2 bags per day	(2) Moderate Habits ≤6 bags per day	(3) Large Habits >6 bags per day	(4) Total
1. Joy poppers	6.5 (85%)	1.4 (15%)	– (–)	7.9
2. Drug dabblers	7.0 (90%)	0.8 (10%)		7.8
3. Addicts	1.7 (05%)	18.9 (60%)	11.6 (35%)	32.2
4. Hustlers	5.4 (35%)	7.4 (45%)	3.2 (20%)	16.0
5. Drug dependents	2.5 (10%)	10.0 (40%)	12.3 (50%)	24.8
6. Conformists	5.1 (85%)	0.6 (10%)	0.3 (05%)	6.0
7. Maturing-out users	0.9 (30%)	1.2 (40%)	1.0 (30%)	3.1
8. Burned-out users	0.3 (25%)	0.5 (40%)	0.4 (35%)	1.2
Total	29.4 (30%)	40.8 (40%)	28.8 (30%)	99.0[a]

[a]Totals to 99 percent because of rounding errors in original estimates of the distribution of types of users among the population.

lists the sources. Second, estimates of the distribution of users with respect to age, habit size, extent of multiple-drug abuse, criminal activity, age at onset of use, and duration of use were made by pooling the various sources and adjusting for known biases in the samples. In effect, one looked down the columns of Table 2-8. Third, data on the joint distributions of pairs of variables were inspected. The estimates presented in Table 2-7 were adjusted to be consistent with observed distributions of single variables in the population and with observed joint distributions.[q] Thus, one can have some confidence in the estimates of Table 2-7.

Given that we have gone this far in speculating about types of users and levels of heroin consumption, there is little harm in going one step further to estimate the sources of users income. Indeed, there is much in the characteristics of types of users that provide clues about sources of income. Unfortunately,

[q]For a complete presentation of the data and the analysis, see Mark H. Moore, "Policy Towards Heroin Use in New York City" (Ph.D. diss., Harvard University, 1973).

there is very little additional empirical information to guide our estimates. Data on the fraction of users reporting "some" income from various sources is available.[9] However, these data can be "fit" by many possible distributions of sources of income. What we need is information about the fractions of a user's income that come from various sources.

The only data available on this issue is a small study of 58 New York City users conducted by Heather Ruth.[10] Table 2-9 presents the results of her interviews concerning the relative importance of different sources of income. The sample she interviewed was constructed by referrals from one "street user" to another. No doubt, the resulting sample is biased. In particular, it is likely to be biased in favor of relatively careful street users of heroin. Highly criminal street users will be underrepresented, as will relatively straight, working-class or middle-class users. If the sample is biased in this way, it is likely that the importance of thefts from institutions and dealing in drugs will be overestimated, and the importance of legitimate sources of income and violent thefts will be underestimated.

Table 2-10 presents adjusted estimates of the sources of users' incomes. The estimates are guided partly by the typology of users, partly by Ruth's data, and partly by informal interviews with heroin users.[r] Given the weak basis for these estimates, they should not be taken too seriously.

Given that we now know something about (1) the habit sizes of users, (2) the distribution of characteristics that influence users' motivations and capabilities to maintain their habits over the course of a year, and (3) the users' sources of income, it is possible to make a relatively informed estimate of the annual consumption of heroin in New York City. Table 2-11 presents the calculations based on 100,000 users in New York City. The estimated fraction of habit size consumed (column 3) is based primarily on habit size, and secondarily on levels of multiple-drug abuse. Earning capacity also influences the estimates. The estimated fraction of days on the street (column 4) is based on the users' motivation for voluntary abstinence or treatment, and vulnerability to arrest. Columns 5, 6, and 7 report calculated total consumption in three different units: bags of heroin, amounts of pure heroin, and dollars.

Tables 2-12 and 2-13 present calculated aggregate and individual financing of heroin use from different sources. In reviewing these tables, it is important to keep in mind that heroin users spend income on many things besides heroin.[s] Consequently, to estimate annual user incomes, one must inflate these figures. In addition, one should keep in mind that most users will spend some portion of

---

[r]During a study with the Hudson Institute in 1970, I interviewed an addict named Willie Tedesco extensively as well as a few of his friends.

[s]Ruth found that users spent approximately three-fourths of their budget on heroin and one-fourth on other things. See Heather Ruth, "The Street Level Economics of Heroin Addiction in New York City: Life-Styles of Active Heroin Users and Implications for Public Policy," Unpublished manuscript (New York: 1972), Table 23, p. 50.

Table 2-8
Existing Data Sources on Demographic Characteristics of Users in New York City

Source of Sample	Demographic Characteristic					
	Age Distribution	Habit-Size Distribution	Patterns of Multiple-Drug Abuse	Criminal History	Age at Onset Distribution	Duration of Use Distribution
I. Total population (census or survey)	1. Chambers (1970) 2. Medical Examiner's Office (1971) 3. Narcotics Register (1969) 4. Thalinger (1970)	—	1. Chambers (1970)	—	—	—
II. Arrested users	1. Nash and Cohen (1969) 2. Koval (1969)	1. Koval (1969) 2. Nash & Cohen (1969)	—	1. Koval (1969)	—	1. NYCPD (1970) 2. Koval (1969) 3. Nash and Cohen (1969)
III. Sentenced users	1. McLean (1970) 2. Babst et al. (1969) 3. Stanton (1969)	1. Babst et al. (1969)	1. Stanton (1969) 2. Babst et al. (1969)	1. McLean (1970) 2. Babst et al. (1969) 3. Stanton (1969)	1. Babst et al. (1969) 2. Stanton (1969)	—
IV. Users in treatment	1. ASA Census (1971) 2. Brotman and Freedman (1965) 3. Gearing (1970) 4. ARTC (1971)	1. Brotman and Freedman (1965) 2. Langrod (1970)	1. ASA Census (1971) 2. Langrod (1969) 3. Brotman and Freedman (1965) 4. Perkins and Bloch (1970)	1. Gearing (1970;1971) 2. Perkins and Bloch (1970) 3. ARTC (1971)	1. Brotman and Freedman (1965) 2. ARTC (1971)	1. ARTC (1971)

V. Certified users	1. NACC Statistical Report (1968)	1. NACC Statistical Report (1968)	—	1. Estimated from data on age and duration of use	1. NACC Statistical Report (1968)

Sources: Addiction Research and Treatment Corporation Evaluation Team (ARTC). 1971. Columbia University School of Social Work, *Progress Report* (Washington, D.C.: U.S. Department of Justice). New York City Addiction Services Agency (ASA). 1971. *Report of City-Wide Census of Drug Treatment Programs* (New York City). Dean V. Babst, Daniel Glaser, and James Inciardi. 1969. *Predicting Post-Release Adjustment of Institutionalized Addicts: An Analysis of New York and California Parole Experience and California Civil Commitment Experience* (Albany: New York State Narcotic Addiction Control Commission). Richard Brotman and Alfred M. Freedman. 1965. *Continuities and Discontinuities in the Process of Patient Care for Narcotics Addicts* (New York City: New York Medical College). Carl D. Chambers. 1970. *An Assessment of Drug Use in the General Population* (Albany: New York State Narcotic Addiction Control Commission). Frances Gearing. 1969, 1970, 1971, 1972. "Evaluation of the Methadone Maintenance Treatment Program," Columbia University School of Public Health and Administrative Medicare (Albany: New York State Narcotic Addiction Control Commission). Mary Koval. 1969. "Drug Users Among Police Department Arrestees and Arrests for Narcotic Offenses in New York City" (Albany: New York State Narcotic Addiction Control Commission), mimeograph. John Langrod. 1970. "Secondary Drug Use Among Heroin Users," *International Journal of Addiction* 5:4 (December). Robert McLean. 1970. "Drug Use Among the Sentenced Population of the New York City Department of Correction" (New York City: RAND internal document D20131), mimeograph. Office of Chief Medical Examiner. 1971. "Drug Abuse, Homicides and Suicides, from 1960-1970 with Ethnic Groups" mimeograph memo. New York State Narcotic Addiction Control Commission. 1968. *First Annual Statistical Report* (Albany). New York City Department of Health, Narcotics Register. 1969. "Narcotics Register Statistical Report–1969" (New York City, mimeograph). George Nash and Eli Cohen. 1969. "An Analysis of New York City Police Statistics for Narcotic Arrests During the Period 1957-1967" (New York City: Columbia University Bureau of Applied Social Research), mimeograph. Marvin Perkins and Harriet Bloch. 1970. "Survey of a Methadone Maintenance Treatment Program," *American Journal of Psychiatry* 126:10 (April). John M. Stanton. 1969. *Lawbreaking and Drug Dependence* (State of New York: Bureau of Research and Statistics, Executive Department, Division of Parole). Alan Thalinger. 1970. "A Study of Deaths of Narcotic Users in New York City–1969" (New York City: Health Services Administration, Department of Health, Health Research Training Program), mimeograph.

Table 2-9
Observed Sources of Users' Incomes

	Sources of Income							
	Legitimate Sources of Income			Illegitimate Sources of Income				
Sample	Legitimate Job	Welfare	Borrowing from Family & Friends	Thefts Involving Encounters with Individuals[a]	Thefts Involving Nonviolent Encounters with Individuals[b]	Thefts from Institutions (No Encounters)[c]	Provision of Illegal Goods and Services (Except Narcotics)[d]	Narcotics-Distribution and Related Services[e]
Total "good sample"[f] (N = 42)	5.8%	0.7%	6.9%	1.1%	8.1%	28.3%	6.3%	42.8%
Men (all data)[f] (N = 42)	6.9	0.2	2.6	1.1	5.4	25.4	1.5	56.9
Women (all data)[f] (N = 16)	0.1	1.0	5.1	0.0	10.0	5.0	11.3	67.5

Source: Heather Ruth, "The Street Level of Economics of Heroin Addiction in New York City: Life-styles of Active Heroin Users and Implications for Public Policy" (New York City, 1972), Unpublished Manuscript. Reprinted by permission.

[a]This category includes robbery, mugging, and preying on dealers.

[b]This category includes jostling, boosting, and forgery.

[c]This category includes shoplifting, burglary, stealing from trucks, and stealing at work.

[d]This category includes fencing, running numbers, prostitution, and gambling.

[e]This category includes selling drugs and lending works.

[f]"Good" sample includes only those cases that gave relatively consistent estimates of expenditures and revenues. Men and Women rows give data for all people in sample. This difference explains why estimates for "good" sample are not merely the weighted average of "men" and "women" estimates.

Table 2-10
Adjusted Estimates of Sources of Users' Incomes

	Sources of Income							
	Legitimate Income			Illegitimate Income				
Types of Users	Legitimate Employment	Welfare	Borrowing from Family & Friends	Thefts Involving Violent Encounters with Others	Thefts Involving Nonviolent Encounters	Thefts from Institutions (No Encounter)	Illegal Goods and Services (Except Narcotics)	Selling Narcotics
Joy poppers	15%		10%			50%	25%	
Drug dabblers	10		50			25	5	10%
Addicts				10%	5%	25	5	55
Hustlers				25	15	50		10
Drug dependents		5%			20	20	10	45
Conformists	60	10	10			5	10	5
Maturing-out users	40	30	10				15	5
Burned-out users		20			40	10	20	10
Total	7	3	6	7	9	28	8	32

Table 2-11
Estimated Annual Aggregate Consumption of Heroin (100,000 Users)

	(1)	(2)	(3)	(4)	Levels of Heroin Consumption			
					Implied Consumption of Heroin			
					(5)	(6)	(7)	(8)
Types of Users	Estimated Number of Users[a]	Estimated Habit Size[b]	Estimated Fraction of Habit Consumed Each "Day on Street"[c]	Estimated Fraction of "Days on Street"[d]	Bags per Year (millions)	Pure Heroin per Year (kilograms)[e]	Dollars per Year (Millions)[f]	Fraction of Total Consumption (Percent)
Joy poppers (8%)	8,000	1.2	0.30	1.00	1.0	10	5.0	1.1
Drug dabblers (8%)	8,000	1.0	0.30	0.80	0.7	7	3.5	0.7
Addicts (32%)	32,000	5.6	0.95	0.75	46.6	466	233.0	49.6
Hustlers (16%)	16,000	3.8	0.70	0.70	10.9	109	54.5	11.6
Drug dependents (25%)	25,000	6.5	0.60	0.80	28.5	285	142.5	30.3
Conformists (6%)	6,000	1.5	0.95	1.00	3.1	31	15.5	3.3
Maturing-out users (3%)	3,000	4.6	0.80	0.50	2.0	20	10.0	2.1
Burned-out users (1%)	1,000	5.1	0.60	1.00	1.1	11	5.5	1.2
Total	99,000	4.6	0.70	0.78	94.0	940	470	100

[a]Assumes 100,000 users. Total of 99,000 comes from rounding errors.

[b]Assume: μ of small habits = 0.75 bag per day; μ of moderate habits = 3.5 bags per day; μ of large habits = 10.00 bags per day.

[c]Based on combination of habit size, willingness to substitute other drugs, capacity to finance.

[d]Based on combination of desire for treatment and vulnerability to arrest.

[e]Based on an estimte of 10 milligrams pure heroin per bag. This is consistent with dilution process to be described later, and with observed quantities of material and purity of drugs.

[f]Based on $5 per bag.

the year in institutions of some kind. Although the estimated annual incomes for users may seem low compared to one's expectations, I think they are reasonable. Users appear as people who struggle to make $10,000 in the periods in which they are not institutionalized. If the incomes were much higher than this, it would be hard to explain why more ghetto residents were not addicts since the users' incomes would be substantially above the mean.

Given the speculative nature of this effort, one should not take the precise estimates too seriously. However, these calculations highlight several general observations that are worth taking seriously.

First, actual heroin consumption is likely to be much smaller than average habit size times the number of users times 365 days per year. Heroin users are simply not able to consume heroin at this rate. Moreover, as treatment efforts expand, enforcement efforts against property and violent crimes expand, and enforcement efforts against narcotics offenses expand, the gap between this estimate and actual consumption will grow larger.

Second, property offenses finance a much smaller proportion of the total heroin consumption than is usually assumed. A common calculation is to estimate the total amount of property stolen by heroin users by estimating the cost of the users' annual heroin consumption, and multiplying this number by a factor of 3 to 5 to reflect a fence's discount. This procedure generates truly heroic estimates of the total amount of property stolen by heroin users. Indeed, the estimates are so large that simple comparisons of the estimates with data on the total amount of property available to be stolen indicates that the estimates are preposterous[11]—particularly if people other than heroin users also steal property. The calculation presented here makes much more modest estimates of the property crimes committed by users. Heroin users consume less heroin, finance very large proportions of their consumption from nonproperty offenses such as dealing drugs and prostitution, and occasionally manage to steal money rather than property that is not subject to "discounting" by fences.

Third, the consumption of *new* users (e.g., drug dabblers, joy poppers) accounts for a very small proportion of the total consumption of heroin. This observation has two important implications. One implication is that marginal changes in supply conditions have unusual importance. For many reasons, new users will be marginal customers. They will have a difficult time locating markets. Dealers will be particularly wary of them. However, because these users consume so little heroin, small changes in the aggregate supply can have a dramatic effect on the number of new users that can be supported. Thus, one should be wildly enthusiastic about small reductions in the aggregate supply, and extremely concerned about slight increases. The margin of this market is terribly important and sensitive.

A second implication of the small amount of heroin necessary to support a large number of new users is that it may be difficult to develop a competing legitimate system that would succeed in reducing availability to new users. It

Table 2-12
Estimated Total Amounts of Money from Different Sources
(100,000 Users)

| | Sources of Income | | |
| | Legitimate Income | | |
Types of Users	Legitimate Employment (Millions of Dollars)	Welfare (millions of Dollars)	Borrowing from Family and Friends (Millions of Dollars)
Joy poppers	0.8	–	0.5
Drug dabblers	0.3	–	1.8
Addicts	–	–	–
Hustlers	–	–	–
Drug dependents	–	7.1	–
Conformists	9.3	1.6	1.6
Maturing-out users	4.0	3.0	1.0
Burned-out users	–	1.1	–
Total	14.4	12.8	4.9

would not be enough to eliminate 90 percent of the illegal market: the legitimate would have to drive 98 percent to 99 percent of the illegal dealers out of business to reduce the market to new users below current levels. Thus, the small amount of heroin necessary to support significant levels of new use makes legalization of heroin a less attractive strategy.[t]

2.0 The Number, Activity, and Profits of Heroin Dealers in New York City

The estimate of $470 million in gross revenues is an impressive number. It sounds like a great deal of money to place in the hands of criminals. However, several observations put this number in perspective.

First, the gross revenues are distributed among many different dealers operating at many different levels. The entire sum does *not* accrue to a single, organized firm. The money cannot be shifted in one direction or another on the authoritative command of a single individual, of even a small group of individuals. It is spread among a variety of firms that differ in objectives, marketing strategies, and scale.

[t]See Mark H. Moore, "Policies to Achieve Discrimination on the Effective Price of Heroin," *American Economic Review* LXIII:2 (May 1973): 276-277, for more detail on this problem.

Types of Users	Sources of Income		
	Illegitimate Sources of Income		
	Thefts Involving Violent Encounters with Others	Thefts Involving Nonviolent Encounters	Thefts from Institutions (No encounters)[a]
Joy poppers	–	–	2.5
Drug dabblers	–	–	0.9
Addicts	23.3	11.6	58.2
Hustlers	13.6	8.2	27.2
Drug dependents	–	28.5	28.5
Conformists	–	–	0.8
Maturing-out users	–	–	–
Burned-out users	–	2.2	0.6
Total	36.9	50.5	118.7

Second, gross revenues are not the same as profits. Bills for raw materials and packaging equipment; salaries to packagers, agents, and guards; and bribes to police and court officials must be paid out of these revenues before a dealer sees his net profit. Moreover, since money profits ignore the risks of the business (from both police and other criminals), even these net profits may exaggerate the attractiveness of the business.[u]

Third, not all of this revenue will actually be realized. Many users will have incomes and connections that enable them to buy wholesale. Similarly, many consumers will also work as dealers and take their profits in the form of heroin consumption. In effect, users are buying at wholesale prices. Since these consumers will account for a substantial share of the total consumption, these wholesale purchases will significantly reduce the actual revenues from retail purchases.

Fourth, when one compares the heroin industry with other industries in New York City, the size does not seem so impressive. Table 2-14 compares annual retail sales for selected legitimate industries in New York City with the estimated retail sales of heroin.

Thus, the $470 million figure can easily be misunderstood. It does not tell us much about the attractiveness of the business or the potential power of the

---

[u]See pp. 10-12 of this book for a more detailed discussion of the difference between "profits" and the attractiveness of the business.

Table 2-12 (cont.)

| | Sources of Income | | |
| | Illegitimate Sources of Income | | |
Types of Users	Illegal Goods and Services (Except Narcotics)	Selling Narcotics	Total
Joy poppers	1.2	–	5.0
Drug dabblers	0.2	0.3	3.5
Addicts	11.6	128.2	233.0
Hustlers	–	5.5	54.5
Drug dependents	14.2	64.1	142.5
Conformists	1.6	0.8	15.5
Maturing-out users	1.5	0.5	10.0
Burned-out users	1.1	0.6	5.5
Total	31.4	200.0	470.0

firms involved. To gauge how many millionaires are created by heroin distribution, or how much money is available to corrupt the criminal justice system, one must probe more deeply into the detailed structure of the distribution system. That is the purpose of this section.

The general model of the distribution provides some guidance in probing for the detailed structure. We know that heroin users will try to buy wholesale and will often deal in heroin. Consequently, we know that the actual cash that changes hands will be less than the maximum retail value. We know that dealers will keep their markets small and use agents to screen them from their customers. Consequently, we know that the distribution system will have many different levels and many dealers at each level who will have to be compensated for their work. We know that dealers operating at different levels face different threats and incur different kinds of expenses. Consequently, we know that profits will vary by level and that different outside parties such as police and organized crime will receive different amounts of money from the different levels.

However, to go beyond these general characteristics to specific quantitative estimates, we must combine the general insights with specific quantitative information. Although data is even scarcer in this area than others, one can follow an estimating procedure that fully exploits the available information.

The first step is to estimate the number of levels in the distribution system, and the number of dealers at each level. These estimates will be based on necessary mathematical relationships among the number of levels, the average number of customers per dealer, and the number of users; anecdotal information from interviews with addicts;[1,2] and judgments about which dealers are likely to invest heavily in the strategy of small markets.

The second step is to estimate the total value added by each level of the distribution system. These estimates will be based on a model of dilution, packaging, and pricing at each level of the distribution system. The hypothesized model was selected as a simple procedure that approximates the quantity-purity combinations observed in the market.

The third step is to estimate the profits and levels of activity of the various dealers. These estimates are calculated from estimates of market conditions at each level and the average size of transactions made at each level.

2.1 Levels of the Distribution System

Dealers' preferences for small distribution units necessarily imply the existence of many levels in the distribution system. Exactly how many levels is uncertain.

Mathematically, the number of levels is determined by the number of users, the average of customers per dealer, and the number of dealers at the highest levels. Table 2-15 presents calculations of the number of levels implied by different estimates of these parameters. Since we have estimated 70,000 to 150,000 users; and since the general model of the distribution system suggests a small number of dealers at the top, and a small number of customers per dealer, it seems that a hypothesis of four to six levels is reasonable.

Other analysts, working with data from interviews with addicts, have identified six different levels in the New York City distribution system.[13] The proposed levels are: importers, kilo connections, weight dealers, street dealers, and jugglers. This data is not wildly out of line with the mathematical implications of 100,000 users, a small number of dealers at the top, and a small number of customers per dealer. However, to believe that there are six levels arrayed in a strict mathematical progression, one must believe in a very small number of high-level dealers (e.g., five high-level dealers) and a very small number of customers per dealer (e.g., five customers per dealer).

If one is willing to relax the assumption of a strict mathematical progression, it is possible to retain the hypothesis that there are six distinct levels and also be consistent with more reasonable estimates of the number of high-level dealers and the average number of customers per dealer. Specific adjustments consistent with the general model are the following.

First, we will assume that many "street dealers" deal directly with customers. This is consistent with the view that users will seek higher level connections. It also has the effect of removing a level of distribution for some portion of the market, and allowing more room for customers among lower level distribution units.

Table 2-13
Estimated Annual Amounts from Different Sources per User
(100,000 Users)

Types of Users	Sources of Income		
	Legitimate Income		
	Legitimate Employment	Welfare	Borrowing from Family and Friends
Joy poppers	$ 100		$ 63
Drug dabblers	38		225
Addicts			
Hustlers			
Drug dependents		$ 284	
Conformists	1,550	266	266
Maturing-out users	1,330	1,000	333
Burned-out users		1,100	

Second, we will assume that the average number of customers per dealer vary from level to level. Specifically, we will assume that high-level dealers have fewer customers than lower level dealers. This is consistent with the hypothesis that higher level dealers will invest heavily in security measures, and particularly heavily in the strategy of keeping markets small.

Third, we will assume that importers are primarily concerned about organizing shipments and smuggling heroin into the United States rather than domestic distribution. Consequently, we will assume that they deal directly with kilo connections on a one-to-one basis. This is consistent with the idea that high-level dealers invest heavily in small markets.

Figure 2-1 presents one model of a distribution system. The model has the virtues of being consistent with estimates of the number of users, the number of levels, reasonable guesses about the number of customers per dealer, and with the implications of the general model. This is sufficient justification for using this model to make speculative calculations. However, it should be kept in mind that there are many other specific forms that will fit within these general constraints.

2.2 "Value Added" by Each Level

The *value added*[v] by each level of the distribution system can be calculated by subtracting the cost of the heroin to each level from the revenues made in selling

[v]*Value added* is defined as the difference between the purchase price of the total materials bought at each level and the selling price of the materials sold from the same level. The

| | Sources of Income | | |
| | Illegitimate Sources of Income | | |
Types of Users	Thefts Involving Encounters with others	Thefts Involving Nonviolent Encounters	Thefts from Institutions (No Encounters)
Joy poppers			$ 320
Drug dabblers			113
Addicts	$728	$ 362	1,819
Hustlers	850	512	1,700
Drug dependents		1,140	1,140
Conformists			133
Maturing-out users			
Burned-out users		2,200	600

the heroin at each level. This requires us to estimate purchase price of each level, dilution carried out at each level, and selling prices at each level. Moreover, to make the calculations simple and general, we must assume that everyone at each level purchases at the same prices, dilutes the same amount, and sells for the same prices.

Of course, the assumption that all dealers at each level behave identically is ludicrous. Any market system will produce astonishing variety in prices, quality, and packaging. However, it is not unreasonable to suppose that there would be some standard practices with respect to pricing, dilution, and packaging. Since standard practices facilitate negotiations on transactions,[w] and since heroin markets operate in a world where transactions are very difficult (but also very expensive to prolong), one would expect standard practices to play a relatively important role in the heroin market. If we identify the standard practices, they may provide the best estimates of the value added by given distribution levels.

Empirical information about prices, quantities, and purities for the New York City distribution system is available from the records of undercover purchases by federal agents.[x] We have searched this data to identify standard

concept differs from *gross revenues*, which is simply the total sales of a given level times the price; also from *net profits*, which is gross revenues minus costs of all types rather than simply material costs; and also from the *utility* of the business, which is the dealer's subjective evaluation of his satisfaction with the business.

[w]Standard practices facilitate negotiation by allowing dealers to accumulate market experience and to establish prices. In a world of infrequent, secretive transactions, it may be difficult to establish prices without a relatively small number of standard deals.

[x]Data was culled from Mellonics Systems Development Corporation, "Project Impact," Drug Enforcement Administration, 1975.

Table 2-13 (cont.)

| Types of Users | Sources of Income | | |
| | Illegitimate Sources of Income | | |
	Illegal Goods and Services (Except Narcotics)	Selling Narcotics	Total
Joy poppers	$ 150		$ 633
Drug dabblers	25	$ 38	439
Addicts	362	4,006	7,277
Hustlers		344	3,406
Drug dependents	568	2,564	5,696
Conformists	266	133	2,614
Maturing-out users	500	166	3,332
Burned-out users	1,100	600	5,600

Table 2-14
The Size of the Heroin Industry Compared with Other Industries in New York City

Industry	Annual Retail Sales[a] (Millions of Dollars)
Grocery stores	7,634
Automotive dealers	6,920
Department stores	4,215
Eating and drinking places	3,422
Gas stations	3,038
Furniture	1,752
Apparel and accessories	1,680
Drugs and proprietary stores	1,162
Heroin retail sales	470

[a]Estimated from "Monthly Retail Trade," *Current Business Reports*, U.S. Bureau of Census. Monthly figures for Mid-Atlantic States were totaled for year. The sum was adjusted for New York City by multiplying the annual total by New York City's share of the population of the Mid-Atlantic States.

practices that can be linked to specific levels of the distribution system. Three things should be kept in mind in using these data.

First, even if there are standard practices, one should expect great variability in the observed transactions. There are two reasons to expect significant variability. The first reason is that given the unreliability and difficulty of controlling employees who cut and package heroin, and the crudeness of their

Table 2-15
Numbers of Levels in Distribution System Implied by Different Estimates of the Numbers of Users, the Numbers of Dealers at Top, and the Average Number of Customers per Dealer

Average Number of Customers per Dealers[a]	100,000 Users				150,000 Users			
	Number of High-Level Dealers							
	5 High-Level Dealers	25 High-Level Dealers	50 High-Level Dealers	100 High-Level Dealers	5 High-Level Dealers	25 High-Level Dealers	50 High-Level Dealers	100 High-Level Dealers
5 customers per dealer	6	5	5	4	6	5	5	5
10 customers per dealer	4	4	3	3	4	4	3	3
25 customers per dealer	3	3	2	2	3	3	2	2
50 customers per dealer	3	2	2	2	3	2	2	2
	4.3	3.6	3.3	3.0	4.48	3.78	3.48	3.18

Note: Computation Formula: Number of Levels = $\dfrac{\text{Log (Number of Users)} - \text{Log (Number of High Level Dealers)}}{\text{Log (Average Number of Customers/Dealer)}}$

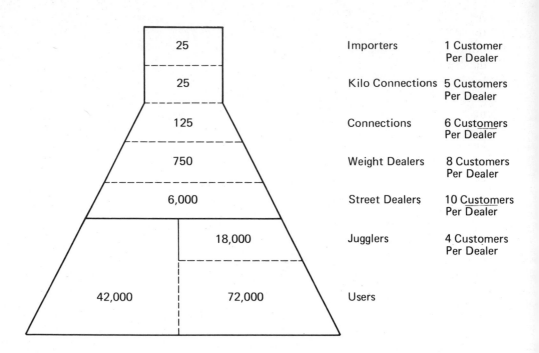

25	Importers	1 Customer Per Dealer
25	Kilo Connections	5 Customers Per Dealer
125	Connections	6 Customers Per Dealer
750	Weight Dealers	8 Customers Per Dealer
6,000	Street Dealers	10 Customers Per Dealer
18,000	Jugglers	4 Customers Per Dealer
42,000 72,000	Users	

Figure 2-1. One Possible Model of the New York City Distribution System (100,000-150,000 Users)

equipment and procedures, it would be very surprising if a standard practice religiously followed produced a consistent product.[y] Second, in heroin transactions, there are strong incentives for suppliers to cheat, and little capability for customers to protect themselves. Given the cost of maintaining a precision scale, it may be difficult to control *quantities* purchased. However, since the instruments required to calibrate *purity* are even more clumsy, it will be virtually impossible to control *purities*. Thus, some variability will be deliberately introduced.

Note that the problems of calibrating quantities and purities differ between high levels and low levels. At high levels, there may be sufficient time and security to make measurements with expensive instruments. Moreover, since there are large quantities and high purities involved, the precision necessary in the measurements may not be great. Consequently, transactions can be success-

[y]For a description of a cutting operation, see Staff and Editors of *Newsday, The Heroin Trail* (New York: Signet, 1973), pp. 181-186.

fully policed. At low levels, the opposite is true. There will be too little time and too little security for accurate measurements to be made. In addition, since small quantities and low purities are involved, the tests must be very precise to discover significant cheating. Thus, one would expect greater variability at low levels than at high levels.

Second, these data will show greater variability than is true of the regular market for heroin. Since undercover agents are likely to be marginal customers, they are likely to encounter marginal dealers.[z] Free-lance dealers with a pure kilo of heroin "copped" in Mexico may sell small quantities at very high purities simply because they have no other way to distribute the heroin. "Rip-off" dealers may try to sell quantities of low-quality heroin. Both types of dealers are relatively likely to sell to agents simply because the dealers are forced to be more aggressive. As a result, the federal-undercover transactions are likely to be more variable than those of the regular market.

Third, these data show only three levels of the distribution system. Both the highest and the lowest levels are not represented in federal-undercover purchases in New York City. Consequently, we remain uncertain about standard practices at these other levels.

Given these limitations on the data, the search for standard practices proves somewhat frustrating. The standard practices show up as small peaks in otherwise smooth distributions if at all. Moreover, when we use the estimated standard transactions to calculate value added, we know that we are describing only a portion of the real activity. Still, we may capture the central tendencies of the different levels.

Figure 2-2 presents data on the distribution of *prices* for federal-undercover buys in New York City. One can observe fairly standard prices: $5,000, $4,500, $4,000, $1,500, $1,300, $1,200, $1,000, $175, $100, $50, appear with unusual frequency. This provides some weak evidence that there may be more or less standard transactions.

Figure 2-3 presents data on the distribution of *quantities* purchased in federal-undercover buys. Again, there are peaks in the distribution at strategic locations. There is a peak around one-eighth kilo (or four ounces) of heroin; another peak at one ounce of heroin, and a peak at one gram or less. These peaks in quantities correspond to the peaks in prices: $4,000 to $5,000 for an eighth kilo, $1,000 to $1,500 for an ounce, and $75 to $150 for a gram or less. Thus, the evidence on price and quantities suggests the existence of three different standard transactions at three different levels.[aa]

Unfortunately, to compute value added at each level, this simple picture

[z]The implications of this tendency for the police to encounter marginal dealers have been discussed above, see p. 52, and will be discussed further below.

[aa]Note that it is possible that the standard transactions observed here are the result of standard *police* procedures rather than standard dealer practices. We have no way of excluding this hypothesis from the available information.

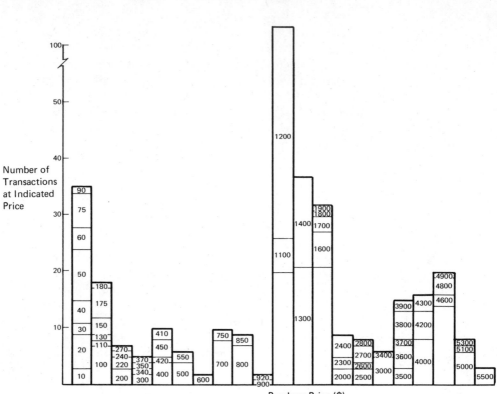

Source: Mellonic Systems Development, "Project Impact" (Washington, D.C.: Drug Enforcement Administration, 1975), Appendix E.

Figure 2-2. Distribution of Prices Paid by Federal Undercover Agents Purchasing Heroin in New York City

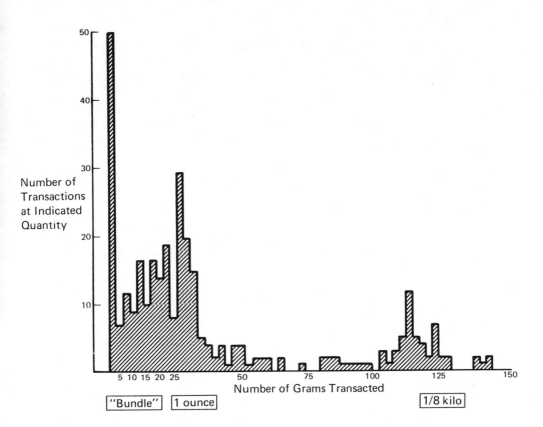

Source: Mellonics Systems Development, "Project Impact" (Washington, D.C.: Drug Enforcement Administration, 1975), Appendix E.

Figure 2-3. Distribution of Quantities Purchased by Federal-Undercover Agents in New York City

must be complicated by the dilution process. A variety of explanations for the dilution of heroin have been advanced. One explanation is that diluting heroin with such products as quinine, caffeine, or procaine enhances the quality of the product. A second explanation is that dilution solves a material-handling problem: ten milligrams of pure heroin would be difficult to handle if it were not "fluffed up" with ten times as many adulterants.[bb] However, the most likely explanation is that dilution is the expected way in which dealers increase their revenues. The importance of dilution for increasing revenues can be seen in the price-quantity data above. There are about four ounces in an eighth kilo. Consequently, if a man buys an eighth kilo for $4,000 to $5,000 and sells four ounces for $1,000 to $1,500 an ounce, his value added is negligible. On the other hand, if the four ounces he sells are diluted ounces, his value added will be significant. The problem is to guess the form of the dilution process and its relationship to the prices and quantities described above.

Figure 2-4 presents data on the distribution of *purities* in the market. As

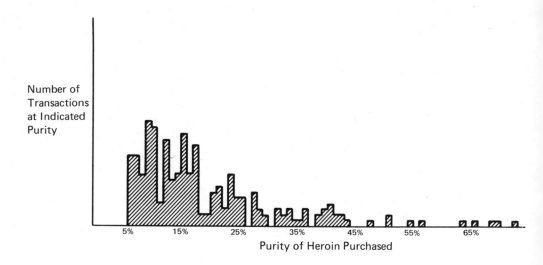

Source: Mellonics Systems Development, "Project Impact" (Washington, D.C.: Drug Enforcement Administration, 1975), Appendix E.

Figure 2-4. Distribution of Purities Received in Federal-Undercover Purchases in New York City

---

[bb]I am indebted to Professor Thomas C. Schelling, Lucius N. Littauer Professor of Political Economy, Kennedy School of Government, Harvard University, for this observation.

one would expect, there is enormous variability.[cc] If one looks hard enough at this data and insists on seeing a pattern, it is possible to see peaks at 40 percent, 23 percent, 15 percent, 10 percent, and 7 percent. These numbers have ratios that suggest very simple dilution procedures.

Table 2-16 presents a model of the dilution and packaging that produces purities and quantities similar to what we observe in the market. Figure 2-5 illustrates the results of each step in the process described in Table 2-16 (with margins of error) on a scatter plot of observed quantities and purities. If the model in Table 2-16 were accurate and general, most points would lie in the boxes that are drawn. As one can observe, many data points lie outside these boxes. It may be possible to invent a more complicated dilution process that explains these points more effectively. However, since it is likely that if there is a standard practice, it will be simple, and since the dilution process described in Table 2-16 is simple and does reasonably well in explaining the points, it is used in estimating the value added.

Table 2-17 presents calculations of the value added by each level of the distribution system. The estimates are consistent with estimates of the number of levels, and with the observed set of prices quantities and purities exchanged in the market.

2.3 Profits and Activity of Dealers at Each Level

Given estimates of the number of dealers and the value added at each level, it is possible to make some rough calculations of profits and levels of activity.

One can get a quick fix on profits simply by dividing the value added at each level by the number of dealers at that level. Table 2-18 presents the calculations. However, this calculation significantly overestimates net profits because it fails to deduct expenses of the business (e.g., payments to employees, equipment purchases, bribes to police, etc.). Although it is difficult to know how to distribute the total value added among factors of production, and between factors of production and profits, some reflection about the activities of the different levels, the strategies they employ to prevent arrest, and their market power can guide one's judgment about profits. Table 2-19 characterizes the distribution levels in terms of their operating costs, and in terms of factors that would influence the equilibrium level of profitability.[dd] Using these

[cc]This variability in purities can create a substantial problem in the market. Indeed, under some conditions, the market will simply disappear. See George Ackerloff, "The Market for Lemons: Qualitative Uncertainty and the Market Mechanism," *Quarterly Journal of Economics* 84 (August 1970).

[dd]For arguments supporting these judgments, see Mark H. Moore, "The Economics of Heroin Distribution," Teaching and Research Materials No. 4, Public Policy Program, Kennedy School of Government (Cambridge, Mass.: Harvard University, 1971), pp. 38-44.

Table 2-16
A Simple Dilution and Packaging Process Consistent with Distribution of Purities and Quantities Observed in Federal Undercover Purchases

Dilution Process	Implied Results		
	Characteristics of Heroin		
	Total Material	Percent Purity	No. of Marketing Units
Step 1:			
1 kilo of "pure" heroin	1 kilo	80%	
Packaged as: kilo ———————————————————————→			1 kilo
Step 2:			
Cut 1:1	2 kilos	40%	
Packaged as: "quarter kilos" ———————————————→			8 "quarters"
"eighth kilos" ———————————————————→			16 "eighths"
Step 3:			
Cut 1:3/4	3 1/2 kilos	23%	
Packaged as: ounces ——————————————————————→			140 "ounces"
Step 4(a):			
Cut 1:1	7 kilos	10%	
(or) Packaged as: bundles ——————————————————→			1,960 "bundles"
Step 4(b)			
Cut 1:1/2	5 1/4 kilos	16%	
Packaged as: ounces ——————————————————————→			210 "ounces"
half-ounces ———————————————————→			420 "half-ounces"
Step 5:			
Cut 1:1	10 1/2 kilos	6%	
Packaged as: bundles ——————————————————→			2,940 "bundles"
bags ———————————————————————→			73,500 bags

characteristics as a rough guide, Table 2-20 presents very rough estimates of average net annual profits at each level of the distribution system.

One can get a handle on levels of activity simply by estimating the average amount of heroin exchanged in transactions at each level. Since we know the total amount of heroin consumed, we can calculate the number of transactions by dividing the total amount of heroin by the total number of dealers, and then by the average size of the transaction. Table 2-21 presents estimates of the average "lot sizes" transacted among dealers at different levels. Table 2-22

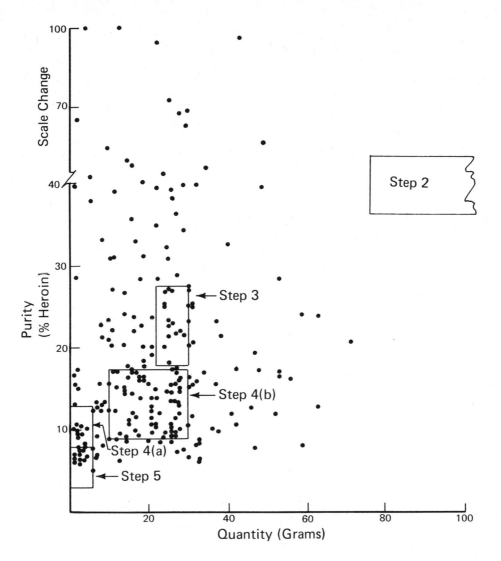

Source: Mellonics Systems Development, "Project Impact" (Washington, D.C.: Drug Enforcement Administration, 1975), Appendix E.

Figure 2-5. Predicted Compared with Observed Quantity-Purity Combinations in Narcotics Transactions (Assumes 15 Percent Error in Dilution Process)

Table 2-17
Calculation of the Value Added by Each Level

	Value Added per Kilo of Heroin		
	Calculation of Value Added		
	Purchases		
Level of Distribution Systems	(1) Amount Purchased	(2) Price	(1×2) Cost to Level
Importers	1 kilo	$5,000 per kilo	$ 5,000
Kilo connections	1 kilo	15,000 per kilo	15,000
Connections	1 kilo	38,000 per kilo	38,000
Weight dealers	16	4,500 per kilo	72,000
Street dealers (selling to jugglers) (30%)	140 ounces	1,200 per ounce	168,000
Street dealers (selling to users) (70%)			
Jugglers	120 half-ounces	450 per half-ounce	54,000

calculates the level of activity implied by these estimates of lot sizes.[ee] It is reassuring to discover that the implied levels of activity are quite plausible.

3.0 Summary

The quantitative estimates presented in this chapter should be considered the results of an elaborate "back-of-the-envelope" calculation. The exercise is valuable in providing rough estimates of the size and characteristics of the local distribution system. But the estimates should be treated as rough and ready approximations rather than "scientific" conclusions. The most important estimates are shown in Table 2-23. Although one cannot be certain about any of

[ee]I am indebted to Max Singer, president of the Hudson Institute, Croton-on-Hudson, New York, for the idea of making this calculation.

		Value Added per Kilo of Heroin		
		Calculation of Value Added		
			Sales	
Level of Distribution Systems	(4) Dilution Process	(5) Amount Sold	(6) Price	(5×6) Revenues to Level
Importers	None	1 kilo	$15,000	$ 15,000
Kilo connections	None	1 kilo	38,000	38,000
Connections	1:1	16 "eighths"	4,500 per "eighths"	72,000
Weight dealers	1:3/4	140 "ounces"	1,200 ounces	168,000
Street dealers (selling to jugglers) (30%)	1:1/2	120 half-ounces	450 per half-ounce	59,000
Street dealers (selling to users) (70%)	1:1	1,400 "bundles"	150 per bundle	210,000
Jugglers	1:1	14,000 bags	5 per bag	170,000

these estimates, their great virtues are that no single estimate seems outrageous, and that the estimates taken together are internally consistent. Readers outraged by any given estimate are invited to change the estimates and trace the effects of that change throughout the entire system.

In addition to producing these specific quantitative estimates, the process of making the estimates highlighted several general observations about the distribution system that are rarely noticed. First, it is almost certainly true that conventional estimates of crimes committed by users are exaggerated. The conventional estimates err in overestimating actual consumption of heroin, and the relative importance of theft in financing heroin consumption.

Second, one should not assume that enormous sums of money are under the control of a few criminals. There are a handful of dealers making $500,000 a year, perhaps 100 to 200 making $150,000 to $200,000, perhaps 1,000 making $75,000, and perhaps 6,000 making $15,000. Moreover, for the most part, the

Table 2-17 (cont.)

Level of Distribution Systems	Value Added per Kilo of Heroin		
	Calculation of Value Added		
	Value Added		Value Added for Annual Consumption[a] (millions)
	[7−3] Total Dollars	Percent Increase	
Importers	$10,000	200	12
Kilo connections	23,000	153	27
Connections	34,000	90	40
Weight dealers	96,000	133	113
Street dealers (selling to jugglers) (30%)	96,000	57	113
Street dealers (selling to users) (70%)			
Jugglers	16,000	30	19

[a]This number is calculated simply by multiplying the value added per kilo of heroin by the number of kilos consumed in New York City. The estimated number of *pure* kilos of heroin was 940. Since kilos are usually only 80 percent pure when they are produced, the estimated number of actual kilograms is 1,175.

Table 2-18
Estimated Value Added per Dealer

Level of the Distribution System	No. of Dealers	Value Added	Value Added per Dealer
Importers	25	$ 12 million	$ 480,000
Kilo connections	25	27 million	1,080,000
Connections	125	40 million	320,000
Weight dealers	750	113 million	150,000
Street dealers	6,000	113 million	19,000
Jugglers	18,000	19 million	1,000

dealers behave fairly independently. Although these estimates suggest a substantial amount of financial power, it is less significant than usually assumed. In terms of scale and effective coordination, the appropriate analogy is not General Motors, but rather the "legal profession" in New York City.

These general observations are probably more valuable than the specific quantitative estimates.

Table 2-19
Characteristics of Distribution Levels Affecting Levels of Profit

Distribution Level	Operational Costs				Net Profits		
	Employ-ment	Equip-ment	Finance	Bribes	Risk	Mon-opoly	Oppor-tunity Costs
1. Importer	M	H	M	M	L-M	M	L
2. Kilo connections	M	L	M	M	L	H	H
3. Connections	M	L	M	M-H	M	M	L
4. Weight dealers	M	L	L	H-M	H-M	M	L
5. Street dealers	L	L	L	L	H-M	L	L
6. Jugglers	L	L	L	L	H	L	L

Source: Mark H. Moore, "Economics of Heroin Distribution," Teaching and Research Materials No. 4 (Cambridge: Harvard University, 1971).

Table 2-20
Estimated Average Net Profits per Dealer

Level of Distribution System	Number of Dealers	Value Added per Dealer	Net Profits per Dealer
Importers	25	$ 480,000	$200,000
Kilo connections	25	1,080,000	500,000
Connections	125	320,000	160,000
Weight dealers	750	150,000	75,000
Street dealers	6,000	19,000	15,000
Jugglers	18,000	1,000	1,000

Table 2-21
Estimated Average Lot Sizes for Purchases and Sales at Each Distribution Level

	Average Size of Transactions					
	Average Purchase Lot Sizes			Average Sales Lot Sizes		
Level of Distribution System	Volume	Purity	Pure Heroin	Volume	Purity	Pure Heroin
Importers	10-50 kilos	80%	8-40 kilos	10-50 kilos	80%	8-40 kilos
Kilo connections	10-50 kilos	80	8-40 kilos	2-10 kilos	80	1.6-8.0 kilos
Connections	2-10 kilos	80	1.6-8.0 kilos	1-4 eighths	40	0.05-0.20 kilos
Weight dealers	1-4 eighths	40	0.05-0.20 kilos	1-2 ounces	23	6-12 grams
Street dealers (dealing to jugglers) (30%)	1-2 ounces	23	6-12 grams	1/4-1/2 ounces	16	1-2 grams
Street dealers (dealing to users) (70%)	1-2 ounces	23	6-12 grams	1-2 bundles	10	0.4-0.8 grams
Jugglers	1/4-1/2 ounces	10	1-2 grams	1 Bags-1/4 bags	6	8-50 milligrams

Table 2-22
Estimated Levels of Activity for Dealers at Different Levels of the Distribution System

Level of the Distribution System	Number of Dealers	Purchase Transactions per Dealer		Sales Transactions per Dealer		Total Transactions per Dealer	
		Average Lot Size of Purchase	Average Number of Purchases per Dealer per Year	Average Lot Size of Sales	Average Number of Transactions per Dealer per Year	Per Year	Per Week
Importers	25	8-40 kilos	1-5	8-40 kilos	1-5	2-10	—
Kilo connections	25	8-40 kilos	1-5	1.6-8.0 kilos	5-23	6-28	—
Connections	125	1.6-8.0 kilos	1-4	0.05-0.20 kilos	40-150	45-173	1-3
Weight dealers	750	0.05-0.20 kilos	6-20	6-12 grams	100-200	110-220	2-4
Street dealers (selling to jugglers)	6,000	6-12 grams	13-26	1-2 grams	25-50		
Street dealers (selling to users)	6,000	6-12 grams	13-26	0.4-0.8 grams	140-270	180-520	3-10
Jugglers	18,000	1-2 grams	8-16	8-15 milligrams	310-2,000	320-2,000	6-40

Table 2-23
Summary of Quantitative Estimates of the New York City Heroin Market: 1970-74

Number of heroin users in New York City:	70-000-150,000
Average habit size:	4.5 $5.00 bags per day
Fraction of users' income from legitimate sources:	16%
Fraction of users' income from thefts:	44%
Fraction of users' income from narcotics dealing:	32%
Fraction of year on street:	78%
Total amount of heroin consumed:	940 kilograms pure heroin
Maximum annual retail sales:	$470 million
Total amount of property stolen:	$540 million[a]
Average amoung spent by users:	$4,700
Number of different levels in system:	6
Number of dealers at each level:	
Importers	25
Kilo connections	25
Connections	125
Weight dealers	750
Street dealers	6,000
Jugglers	18,000

Estimated value added and net profits		
Importers (25)	$ 480,000	$200,000
Kilo connections (25)	1,080,000	500,000
Connections (125)	320,000	160,000
Weight dealers (750)	150,000	75,000
Street dealers (6,000)	19,000	15,000
Jugglers (18,000)	1,000	1,000

[a]This number is adjusted to accommodate fences' discounts for property stolen, but obviously not for money. For the purposes of this calculation, it was assumed that all thefts involving violent encounters produced money not subject to discounting. All other thefts were assumed to involve property and were subject to discounting.

Notes

1. See George E. Vaillant, "The Natural History of a Chronic Disease," *New England Journal of Medicine*, December 8, 1966.

2. See Chapter 1, footnote d.

3. See Heather Ruth, "The Street Level Economics of Heroin Addiction in New York City: Life-Styles of Active Heroin Users and Implications for Public Policy," Unpublished manuscript (New York: 1972), pp. 31-36.

4. See Richard Brotman and Alfred M. Freedman, *Continuities and Discontinuities in the Process of Patient Care for Narcotics Addicts* (New York: New York Medical College, 1965), pp. 138-140.

5. Brotman and Freedman, *Continuities and Discontinuities of Patient Care*, p. 72.

6. Brotman and Freedman, *Continuities and Discontinuities of Patient Care*, pp. 123-124.

7. See generally, Brotman and Freedman, *Continuities and Discontinuities of Patient Care*.

8. Ibid.

9. See, for example, Carl D. Chambers, "Narcotic Addiction and Crime: An Empirical Review," or Leroy C. Gould, "Crime and the Addict—Beyond Common Sense," both in James A. Inciardi and Carl D. Chambers, *Drugs and the Criminal Justice System* (Beverly Hills, Calif.: Sage, 1974).

10. See Ruth, "The Street Level Economics of Heroin Addiction in New York City," pp. 55, 57, 62.

11. See Max Singer, "Addict Crime: The Vitality of Mythical Numbers," *Public Interest*, no. 23 (Spring 1971).

12. See generally, Edward Preble and John C. Casey, "Taking Care of Business: The Heroin User's Life on the Street," *International Journal of the Addiction* 4:1 (March 1969).

13. Ibid.

**Part II
The Structure of Narcotics-
Enforcement Efforts**

Introduction to Part II

Part I indicated that the general characteristics of illicit heroin-distribution systems could be significantly influenced by police action. If the threat of arrest and imprisonment is substantial, then dealers will invest heavily in all the strategies that defend them against arrest and successful prosecution. They will operate in small markets, carefully screen customers, use elaborate drop strategies to avoid creating evidence, seek to bribe officials, and so on. As a result, the equilibrium size of the distribution system will be small, growth dynamics will be dampened, prices will be high, access to markets will be difficult, and so on. Thus, the general level of enforcement pressure has a profound impact on the general behavior of the illicit-distribution system.

Implicit in the analysis of Part I is a more subtle point. *Specific* tactics chosen by the police to make cases can have discreet effects on the behavior of heroin dealers. The reason is that some police tactics will make some defensive tactics more valuable than others. Consider the following examples.

Suppose the police relied heavily on young police to make cases through undercover purchases of heroin. If this were the major police tactic, dealers would gradually learn to be afraid of young strangers. As a result, all young strangers, including those who were not police, would experience unusual difficulty in gaining access to heroin markets. This effect enhances the preventive benefits of enforcing narcotics laws.

Now suppose the police relied primarily on experienced addict informants to obtain search warrants against suspected dealers. If this were the major police tactic, gradually dealers would learn to be wary of experienced users who have had significant contact with the police. All users who resembled well-known users would face difficulty in gaining access to heroin markets. This tactic might succeed in motivating old users to seek treatment, but would not be likely to prevent heroin use among susceptible populations.

Clearly, the outcomes of spending the same amount of resources on these two tactics would be quite different, both in terms of the behavior of the distribution system and in terms of the social consequences of heroin use. Since different enforcement tactics stimulate different defensive responses by dealers, judicious selection of enforcement tactics can exert subtle influence over the character of the illicit-distribution systems.

The purpose of Part II is to analyze the array of strategies and tactics available to enforcement officials in attacking the illicit-distribution system. The strategies are analyzed in terms of their direct and indirect effects on the character of heroin-distribution systems. *Direct effects* are the set of cases developed against traffickers. *Indirect effects* are the incentives created for dealers on the street by the threat of being arrested through the same tactics that resulted in the arrest of their peers. The strategies are also analyzed in terms of the resources they require—both the total resources and the specialized resources that are likely to be in short supply.

It is important to develop a rich array of possible strategies and tactics, to have an appreciation of the scope of their direct and indirect effects, and to know what resources are required so when we come to the problem of designing an enforcement strategy in Part III, we have a large selection of tactics from which to choose.

Throughout the analysis of Part II, I rely on a simple economic metaphor. I assume that the activities of enforcement agencies can be analyzed in much the same way as the production activities of more traditional firms. The *output* of the firm is a set of cases against individuals involved in the distribution of heroin. A set of *resources* exist, which can be used to produce this output (e.g., agent manpower; surveillance and communication equipment; money to purchase narcotics or pay for information; and information that is volunteered by citizens, grudgingly provided by defendants, stored in the files of the organization, or kept in the minds of agents). There is also a set of *technologies*, which determine the rate at which resources can be converted into outputs (e.g., undercover buys; extended surveillance; random patrol, etc.). Finally, there is an environment and a set of external constraints, which limit the available resources, the possible technologies, and influence the actual effectiveness of the technologies.

Note that the technologies for producing cases are basically the standard operating procedures of the investigative agencies. Probably in all manpower-intensive activities, the standard operating procedures can be taken as the relevant technologies. The reason is simply that these procedures determine the rate at which resources can be converted to desired outputs.

At best, these terms are only crude approximations of the activities of law-enforcement organizations. However, the general logic of outputs, resources, technologies, and environmental constraints has significant power in analyzing the options for attacking illicit-distribution systems.

Making Cases; The Structure of Enforcement Efforts against Heroin Dealers

The basic products of narcotics-enforcement agencies are cases against heroin dealers. In analytic terms, a case consists of evidence supporting hypotheses about a person's behavior and intentions that, if true, would describe a criminal offense. In general, enforcement efforts are designed to accumulate evidence against traffickers. In this chapter, we analyze the various factors that shape police efforts to make cases. Specifically, we analyze the impact of legal requirements, case-making technologies, and resources on the potential scope of enforcement efforts.

1.0 Legal Constraints

Statutes and precedents constrain police efforts to make cases by defining criminal offenses, by specifying the amount and kind of evidence that must be gathered to secure a conviction, and by limiting the procedures that police may use to gather evidence. Limited space (as well as limited expertise) prevent a full analysis of the complex legal issues that arise in making cases against narcotics traffickers. However, in investigating the possibilities available to the police, it is important to have a rough sense of how the law constrains their efforts and imposes significant resource penalties in making some kinds of cases. Consequently, this section identifies those aspects of law and practice that significantly constrain police efforts to make cases against narcotics traffickers.[a]

1.1 Narcotics Offenses: What Must Be Shown

Individuals who deal or use heroin may be arrested for several different offenses. The most important offenses are possession of narcotics; sale of narcotics; or conspiracy to import, sell, or distribute narcotics.[b]

---

[a]I am deeply indebted to Philip Heymann, professor of law, Harvard University, and Lawrence S. Bacow, law student and friend, for assistance in preparing this section on legal constraints. In addition to their excellent counsel, I have relied extensively on the following materials: Jerold H. Israel and Wayne R. LaFave, *Criminal Procedure in a Nutshell* (St. Paul, Minn.: West, 1975), and U.S. Department of Justice, "Handbook: Proving Federal Crimes" (Washington, D.C.: 1971).

[b]In both federal and state laws, narcotics dealers may be arrested on many charges other than these. However, these are by far the most common and important charges.

To convict an individual for illegal *possession* of heroin, it must be shown that the individual had "immediate" and "exclusive" access to heroin, or that the heroin was under his "dominion and control." Moreover, it must be shown that the individual knew the substance was heroin.[1]

Of course, a variety of fact situations will establish possession. Possession can be directly established if heroin is found on the person in the course of a lawful search.[c] It can also be established if the police fail to find the heroin on the person, but observe the individual dropping the heroin.[d] In addition, the courts have established a doctrine of "constructive possession," which allows the police to charge individuals who do not have immediate, physical possession of heroin, but do have either proprietary interests in the place where heroin is found, or are close to the heroin at the time of discovery.[2] This doctrine clearly broadens the definition of the offense and allows prosecution of individuals who could not otherwise be prosecuted.

Similarly, a variety of fact situations can establish knowledge that the substance was heroin. Offers to sell heroin, or observations of use of heroin would clearly establish knowledge. With somewhat less certainty, previous narcotics convictions or testimony of conversations in which knowledge was revealed would establish knowledge. Finally, observed efforts to discard or conceal the substance when police approached would establish knowledge.

Thus, a strong possession case would involve the police discovering heroin in the pocket of a previously convicted user during a lawful search. A weak possession case would involve the police charging the owner of a vehicle in which heroin was found.

Note that the possession statutes create a subtle dilemma for dealers: the more carefully dealers conceal heroin, the smaller the chance that a casual search would discover the heroin, but the stronger the possession case would be if the heroin is discovered. Similarly, the dealers may be able to defeat a possession case if they successfully discard the heroin. However, if the police observe them discarding the heroin, the police will have both probable cause for an arrest and a strong possession case. In effect, the possession law has developed so that many defensive strategies followed by dealers decrease the probability of an arrest, but strengthen the case against them if arrested.

To convict an individual for *sale* of heroin, it must be shown that the individual "sold, exchanged, gave, or disposed" of heroin to another person, or

[c]What constitutes a lawful search is, of course, a key issue dealt with briefly below. Basically, a *lawful search* includes the following situations: a search within the scope of a warrant issued by a magistrate upon a demonstration that there is probable cause to believe that a search will produce evidence of a crime, a search incident to a lawful arrest (again, both the scope of the search and the basis for a lawful arrest are limited), and a "frisk" of a person stopped on the street for questioning where the purpose of the frisk is limited to the discovery of weapons and the techniques of the frisk are limited to "patting down" the suspect's clothes.

[d]This situation gives rise to notorious "drop-see testimony" by the police.

"offered or agreed" to do any of these things.[e] Given the broad definition of "sale," many different fact situations will establish that a "sale" occurred. All that the police must do is observe, participate in, or secure testimony that some kind of transaction involving heroin occurred.

Basically, three defenses are available to dealers accused of sale. First, they can seek to create doubt about whether the alleged transaction occurred. The usual mechanism is to impeach police or informant testimony about the transaction. This defense is often successful when the case is based solely on police surveillance of the self-interested testimony of an addicted informant. It usually fails when the police have participated in the transaction or "wired" an informant with a listening device. Note that compared with the weaker case, the stronger case requires additional specialized resources from the police—a recording device, an undercover policeman, or both.

Second, the dealers can claim to be acting on a one-time basis to "accommodate" an insistent buyer.[3] This defense is rarely used and rarely successful—probably because the police can easily overcome the defense by showing a continuous pattern of transactions on the part of the defendant, and a limited relationship between the buyer and the defendant. Still, the threat of this defense is sufficient to cause the police to make several buys from the same dealer as a matter of procedure, in spite of the fact that this procedure is extremely expensive. Note that the obligation to complete several purchases imposes a significant resource requirement on the police.

Third, the defendant can claim to have been "entrapped" by the police; that is, the defendant can seek to show that without active police encouragement, the defendant would not have committed the offense. The success of this defense usually turns on the issue of the defendant's predisposition to commit the crime. It is not enough to show that the police arranged an opportunity for the crime to be committed.[4] The defense must show that in the normal course of events, the defendant would not be involved in transactions of this type. In rebuttal, the prosecution may present evidence bearing on the intentions of the dealer. Testimony about the details of the transaction, evidence about other transactions, and even the defendant's prior record may be presented to rebut the defense assertion of entrapment. Indeed, the latitude given the prosecutors in presenting evidence about a defendant's character in rebuttal to an entrapment defense is often sufficient to discourage defense lawyers from asserting it.

Thus, a *strong sale case* would be a case in which several undercover purchases were made from the same dealer, the meetings with the undercover agent were observed by other police, and the conversations between the dealer and the agent were monitored by a recording device. A *weak sale case* would be one in which the police observed a meeting between two individuals on the street, saw money change hands, and found heroin on both individuals. In effect,

---

[e]The specific language is from the New York State Statute. See *McKinney's Consolidated Laws of New York: Annotated* (Brooklyn: Edward Thompson, 1975), Art. 220.00.

if the police have extensive documentation of a single transaction, and some evidence of a continuing series of transactions, most common defenses to the charge of sale can be overcome.

To convict an individual of conspiracy to violate narcotic laws, all that must be shown is that two or more people agreed to violate the laws, and made at least one overt act to further their conspiracy.[f] It is not necessary for the objective of the conspiracy actually to be accomplished.[5] Nor is it necessary to show that the accused individuals actually handled or possessed narcotics.[6] Moreover, the offense may be proved by circumstantial evidence.[7] In effect, all that must be shown to establish the agreement that serves as the basis for a conspiracy prosecution is that several individuals had a serious conversation about importing or distributing narcotics and took some step to further their plans.

In practice, the crucial components of a conspiracy case consist of detailed testimony by one conspirator implicating others that is corroborated by independent sources of information such as telephone records or the statements of uninvolved witnesses. In addition, it is extremely valuable if clear evidence of a substantive offense (e.g., possession or sale of heroin) can be presented for at least one of the conspirators. Without these elements, juries seem bewildered by the case and are reluctant to convict.[g]

In addition, the prosecution must overcome several demanding legal technicalities. Demonstration of a conspiracy usually depends on testimony about conversations among the conspirators. Ordinarily, under the hearsay rule, any defendant who was not a party to a conversation described in a witness's testimony may successfully object to such testimony as hearsay. In conspiracy cases, a special exception to the hearsay rule applies which allows testimony about conversations to be admitted even when not all conspirators were involved in the conversation.[h] The exception is necessary to prevent a situation where all testimony about conversations could be prevented by having one or more conspirators not involved in the conversation present an objection. However, in order for this special exception to come into effect, the court must have a reasonable basis for believing that a conspiracy existed. If the testimony in question is necessary to create a reasonable basis to assume the existence of a conspiracy, but cannot be admitted until after such a basis is established, the prosecution may face serious problems with the order of proof. A similar

---

[f]The issue of what constitutes an overt act in furtherance of the conspiracy is very uncertain. See, U.S. Department of Justice, "Handbook: Proving Federal Crimes," Chapter 13, p. 132.

[g]This judgment is supported by personal conversations with many federal narcotics agents and several experienced federal prosecutors.

[h]I am indebted to Philip B. Heymann, professor of law, Harvard University, for his detailed explanation of the conspiracy exception to the hearsay rule. If I have stated it incorrectly, in spite of his tutelage, it is my error.

problem is that since the testimony of one conspirator often involves some degree of self-incrimination, this testimony can only be compelled if the prosecutor grants immunity to the witness. Since granting immunity means losing that defendant, the price of compelling some kinds of testimony may be very high.[i] The ideal situation is one where one low-level defendant is arrested carrying large amounts of heroin, but is able to testify about conversations with many higher level traffickers. This was the situation for several major cases in the recent history of narcotics enforcement.[j]

Thus, although the conspiracy offense seems very broad in principle, in practice, proving the offense turns out to be exceedingly difficult. It is hard to develop a witness, hard to establish his credibility, hard to document all his allegations, hard to insure that his testimony on the stand will be consistent with previous statements; yet, all too easy to make technical errors in the handling of the case, or to fail to convince jurors who become bewildered by the definition of the offense, the complicated maze of evidence that must be presented, and the constant fights over legal technicalities. The enormous costs of developing these cases combine with substantial risks of losing them to cause most prosecutors to shift their attention to other more profitable prosecutions. As a result, the statutes are not widely used. Given the potential for abuse in these offenses, limited prosecutions may not be bad. However, given also that conspiracy is one of the only ways to prosecute high-level dealers who invest heavily in defensive strategies, there is some reason to be concerned that we use the statute too infrequently.

1.2 The Standard and Burden of Proof

In prosecuting narcotics offenses (as in prosecuting all criminal offenses), the state must prove beyond a reasonable doubt every element necessary to constitute the crime charged.[8] Although the burden of meeting this high standard of proof never shifts, several presumptions in key areas have the effect of reducing the amount of evidence the police must present to secure convictions of narcotics offenders.

First, the doctrine of constructive possession allows judge or jury to infer possession from very general circumstantial evidence. A proprietary interest in a location where drugs are found or mere proximity to drugs have been sufficient to support convictions for possession—even when no direct evidence is presented to show either immediate and exclusive access or direct control of the drugs. Second, in moving for dismissal of a sale charge on grounds of entrapment, the defense must show an innocent intent on the part of the defendant against the

---

[i]I am indebted to Lawrence S. Bacow, esq. for emphasizing this point.

[j]See, for example, how the case against Auguste Ricord was made in Evert Clark and Nicholas Horrock, *Contrabandista!* (New York: Praeger Publishers, 1973).

fact that the sale occurred and any evidence introduced by the prosecution that casts doubt on the defendant's innocent intent. In effect, the defense must maintain a high standard of proof of innocence against broad, substantial assaults from the prosecution. Third, there is presumption that a conspiracy continues once it is established and includes everyone originally involved unless a defendant explicitly removes himself from the conspiracy.[9] In effect, the prosecution need not show continuing, active participation by a conspirator—it is sufficient merely to show that the defendant made no strenuous effort to remove himself from the conspiracy. Thus, in each kind of case, the prosecution need not exclude every plausible hypothesis advanced by the defense: some hypotheses can be excluded as a matter of doctrine; others can be excluded at low cost to the prosecution simply by relaxing standards for the admission of evidence.

1.3 Restrictions on Gathering Evidence

In seeking to gather evidence sufficient to prove elements of these offenses beyond a reasonable doubt, the police face significant constitutional restrictions.[k] The most important restriction is the fourth amendment, which protects citizens against unreasonable searches and seizures. The fourth amendment constrains police searches and their use of electronic surveillance. In addition, other legal principles constrain the use of informants and undercover police.

The police are prohibited from searches of individuals, vehicles, or property except in specific, well-defined circumstances. First, they can search property if they obtain a search warrant. To obtain a search warrant, the police must establish probable cause that specific items sought are connected with criminal activity, and that a search of a specified premise will yield the desired items. Ideally, evidence establishing probable cause should include elements other than the testimony of informants. However, if an informant's statements are important in establishing probable cause, the warrant application must establish the reliability of the informant, and the basis for the specific conclusions of the informant. Once a warrant is obtained, the police can only search a limited location in a limited time, and seize only the items indicated in the warrant. However, the police are also entitled to seize evidence that is "in plain view" while executing a reasonable search for the particular items identified in the warrant.

Second, the police may search individuals, vehicles, or premises incident to a lawful arrest without a warrant. The general principle authorizing the search is that the police may search to remove weapons or to prevent the concealment of destruction of evidence. This means that an extensive search of the person of

kThis section relies heavily on Israel and LaFave, *Criminal Procedure in a Nutshell.*

arrested individuals is allowed even if the arrest is for a minor offense.[1] In addition, any part of a vehicle or premise within reach of the defendant can be searched. Finally, the police can seize evidence that is in plain view, in executing the arrest. Note what will in fact be in plain view depends on the way that the police execute the arrest. If police come through several doors rather than just one, more of the premises may be vulnerable to a "plain-view" search.

Third, under "stop and frisk" rules, the police are entitled to make an extremely limited search when they stop an individual who may be dangerous for questioning.[m] They are authorized to pat down the outside clothing of an individual in a search for weapons. They may not intrude into a person's clothing unless there is a reasonable basis to assume there is a concealed weapon.

The constitutional principles that restrain physical searches by the police also restrain electronic surveillance. The police may listen to conversations with the consent of one of the parties of the conversation. However, to overhear conversations without the consent of participants, the police must seek a warrant. In either case, police must specify the identity of the individuals involved, the particular communication facility to be monitored, a particular description of the types of communication to be overheard, the relationship of the conversations to a particular offense, and the period over which the surveillance will be maintained.[10] The basic principle seems to be that electronic surveillance will be permitted if it is limited in scope and probable cause is established that the surveillance will yield evidence of significant offenses.

The police use of secret agents and informants to gather evidence is also restrained by legal principles—although not by constitutional principles. The most important restraints on the use of informants are created indirectly by legal principles that require the prosecution to identify informants to the defense. This obligation can arise in several ways. The defense can file a motion to discover the name of an informant, or require the government to produce an informant. These motions must be supported by a demonstration that the testimony of the informant could have a substantive impact on the question of the defendant's guilt or innocence. Alternately, the defense may file a motion to obtain records of investigations and conversations that could include exculpatory evidence held by the prosecution. Included in these materials might be records that happened to identify the informant. Although the police can reduce the vulnerability of their informants by adjusting their evidence gathering and

---

[l]The extent of the right to search arrested persons remains somewhat uncertain. A recent Supreme Court decision appeared to permit full searches of individuals arrested for traffic offenses, but it seems likely that future court decisions will narrow this interpretation. Again, I am indebted to Philip Heymann for this observation, and absolve him of any part if I have erred in stating his observation.

[m]Who, *precisely*, may be "stopped and frisked" remains uncertain. It seems likely that some grounds to suspect both criminal activity and danger must be shown to permit the search, but the court has not yet been clear on the limits of the stop and frisk power.

record-keeping procedures, these defense efforts can often succeed in exposing informants. Since the police are generally unwilling to expose informants to retaliation by the defendant, and since the future value of the informants will, in any event, be compromised by his exposure, these legal principles restrain the police capacity to use informants.

2.0 Procedures for Making Cases

Within these legal constraints the police must allocate their resources to gather evidence documenting specific narcotics offenses by specific individuals at specific points in time. The fundamental strategic problem for the police is the vastness of the space within which offenses can theoretically occur, the ease with which offenses can be concealed, and the perishability or ambiguity of physical evidence.

Note that these problems are particularly severe for "victimless crimes."[n] In most situations, the police are extremely dependent on victims. It is their complaints that mobilize the police, their recollection and descriptions that guide investigative efforts, and their testimony that convicts offenders. If everyone involved in a crime colludes to conceal the crime from the police, and if they exercise some care to conceal the offense from casual observers, the police problems become enormous. No signs or traces of the crime will come to police attention.

These observations suggest that the vast majority of narcotics offenses will go undetected. If we could define and measure something analogous to "clearance rates" for continuous daily offenses such as narcotics possession, we would certainly find that rate at which actual narcotics offenses were solved was extremely low. The observations also suggest that the police will face a continuing struggle against probability. They will search a very large haystack to find needles that are neither bright enough nor sharp enough to call attention to themselves.

2.1 General Strategies

Three general strategies are available to the police in seeking to gather evidence that will make cases against narcotics traffickers.[o]

[n]Although many significant implications are now routinely associated with the idea of "victimless crimes," the most important implication may well be simply the difficulty of enforcing the laws. See Peter Reuter, "Gambling Prohibition: Unenforced or Unenforceable Laws," Paper prepared for the meeting of the American Society for Criminology, Washington, D.C., 1975.

[o]In analyzing the strategies and tactics available to the police, I have relied heavily on my personal experience. I interviewed a large number of narcotics detectives in New York City

One strategy is *patrol*—an effort to monitor more or less superficially and more or less indiscriminately the entire "space" of possible offenses.[P] The objective of patrol is to "happen across" offenses as they are occurring, or arrive so quickly after an offense was committed that reconstruction of the offense is trivial. To achieve these objectives, the patrol strategy typically relies on large numbers of men, rapid mobility, and rapid communication. In general, the success of patrol efforts depends on the vigilance of the patrol officers, the general pattern of deployment, the willingness of citizens to complain about offenses they observe, and the physical and social ecologies that influence the visibility of the offenses.

A second strategy is *retrospective investigation*—an effort to reconstruct offenses that have already occurred, and to corroborate each element of the reconstruction with physical evidence or the testimony of credible witnesses. Unlike the patrol strategy, retrospective investigation allows the police to focus their surveillance and investigative efforts on relatively small nooks of the space of possible offenses. The particular nook that comes to their attention is the nook surrounding an offense that has already occurred and has been reported to them. The techniques of retrospective investigation are familiar to any reader of detective novels. The police interview witnesses and participants; examine physical evidence such as fingerprints, tire tracks, bloodstains, or bullets; check accounts of each witness against physical evidence and the testimony of other witnesses; and develop a story consistent with the testimony and physical evidence that explains how the crime was committed. The success of retrospective investigative efforts depends on the durability and probative value of the physical evidence created by the offense, the willingness of witnesses to testify (and their credibility), and the skill and persistence of the police in gathering the evidence and inventing plausible accounts of the offense.

A third strategy is *prospective investigation*—an effort to solicit specific information about offenses likely to be committed in the future. Like retrospective investigation, prospective investigation seeks to focus police attention on relatively small nooks of the total space of possible offenses. However, the

in April-May 1971 on assignment from William P. McCarthy, deputy commissioner of the New York City Police Department in charge of the Organized Crime Control Bureau. In addition, from January 1974 to September 1975, I served as chief planning officer of the Drug Enforcement Administration.

In addition to this experience with narcotics-enforcement agencies, the following secondary sources were very helpful: Comptroller General of the United States, "Heroin Being Smuggled into New York City Successfully," B164031 (2) (1972), and "Difficulty in Immobilizing Major Traffickers," B-175424 (1973) (Washington, D.C.: General Accounting Office); New York State Commission of Investigation, *Narcotics Law Enforcement in New York City* (New York: 1972); and Jerome H. Skolnick, *Justice Without Trial* (New York: Wiley and Sons, 1966).

For a devastating anecdotal view of narcotics enforcement, see Joe Eszterhas, *Nark!* (San Francisco: Straight Arrow Books, 1974).

[P]Note that *space* is defined in terms of several dimensions in addition to geographic area. It includes time and descriptions of kinds of activity and people as well as geographic area.

objective is not to wait until offenses are committed and find historical traces, but to anticipate the offense so that the police can observe the offense directly. To achieve this objective, prospective investigation must rely on sources of specific information (e.g., informants, wiretaps, observations combined with intelligence from previous cases) and techniques of covert surveillance to monitor the indicated nook. In addition, on some occasions, the strategy of prospective investigation relies on creating the antecedent conditions for an offense to be committed in the full view of the police (e.g., offers to purchase narcotics).[q] The success of prospective-investigative efforts depends on the number and quality of the leads developed from sources of information, the skill of the investigations in evaluating the importance and reliability of the leads, and the skill and diligence of the police in developing the leads.

These general strategies differ in terms of their likely impact on narcotics-distribution systems. Moreover, within these general strategies, there are important variants. The impact of the strategies and their significant variants are analyzed below.

2.2 The Patrol Strategy

The patrol strategy has serious limitations as a device for making cases against narcotics offenders. The ease with which narcotics can be concealed combines with constitutional restrictions on search and seizure to make patrol efforts ineffective in producing evidence of narcotics offenses. In fact, if the police adhere to constitutional search procedures, patrol efforts will discover narcotics offenses in only three circumstances:

1. The offender exposes narcotics to the plain view of patrolling police.
2. The offender commits a more visible offense that attracts the police and justifies a search of the offender and adjacent areas.
3. The offender is searched under stop and frisk authority, and the narcotics are discovered in the course of a search for a weapon.[11]

Since anyone with small amounts of caution and experience can arrange to commit narcotics offenses without necessarily involving himself in any of these circumstances, most narcotics offenders most of the time will easily evade legitimate police patrol strategies. Since only blatant or inexperienced offenders will be vulnerable, and since blatant offenders are relatively more abundant among the ranks of inexperienced, low-level dealers than among the ranks of

[q]Although most people think of these tactics being used exclusively in narcotics-enforcement efforts, these tactics have been employed effectively in enforcing other laws as well. The most dramatic example are the operations of "Anti-Crime Squads" which disguise the police as easy robbery victims such as drunks or old women.

serious long-term dealers, the direct effects of the patrol strategy are likely to be a set of cases against inexperienced, low-level dealers.

There are two important variants to the legitimate patrol strategy. First, the restrictions on police patrol that are described above apply to domestic-police forces. They do not apply to the U.S. Customs Service. Customs has a special search authority that allows them to search everything that crosses the United States border without probable cause.[12] Of course, Customs still faces the problem of finding a small volume (although not necessarily small amount) of heroin in the enormous volume of individuals and material crossing the border.[13] Moreover, like all patrol efforts, they are much more likely to turn up blatant and inexperienced users of drugs than serious dealers. However, because Customs does not have to justify their search, the patrol efforts of customs inspectors and customs patrol officers are likely to be more effective (per unit of resources given equally well-designed deployment strategies) than the patrol efforts of urban-police forces.

Second, if the police are willing to conduct unconstitutional searches and to protect illegally gathered evidence by perjuring themselves, the limitations on the patrol strategy do not apply. Nearly any dealer becomes vulnerable to police-patrol strategies. Dealers could defend themselves against illegitimate police-patrol strategies only through two devices: staying in plain view of credible witnesses, or maintaining a sufficiently low profile that the police judge them not worth the risk of perjury. This suggests that dealers with very bad reputations operating in areas where there are few credible witnesses may be relatively vulnerable to illegal police-patrol practices.[r]

Note that although illegal-patrol strategies might broaden the reach of patrol efforts in the short run, in the long run, illegitimate-patrol strategies will weaken the overall effectiveness of patrol efforts. Prosecutors and judges will become suspicious of police testimony.[14] As a result, legitimate cases as well as illegitimate cases will be dismissed, and the potential impact of patrol strategies weakened.

All of the patrol strategies have important indirect effects on the behavior of dealers as well as the direct effects of producing defendants. Patrol efforts force dealers and users to be discreet about possessing, using, or selling drugs. They are motivated to avoid doing any of these things in plain view,[s] to seek intimate settings or blend their drug-taking activity into normal activity, and to avoid routine patterns that might help organize their market, but would also

---

[r]The existence of *flaking* (i.e., planting evidence on suspected narcotics dealers) is reported in: Commission to Investigate Allegations of Police Corruption and the City's Anti-Corruption Procedures, *Commission Report*, New York City, 1972, pp. 103-104; New York State Commission of Investigation, *Narcotics Law Enforcement in New York City*, 1972, p. 140; and Leonard Shecter with William Phillips, *On the Pad* (New York: Berkley, 1973), pp. 88-89, 202.

[s]For an anecdotal description of the impact of patrol operations on street-level narcotics dealing, see Richard Woodley, *Dealer* (New York: Holt, Rinehart and Winston, 1971), p. 3.

arouse suspicions of patrolling police and eventually serve as probable cause for a search. These incentives to be discreet and unpredictable have the effect of disrupting markets for heroin. It is hard for people who are not well-connected to information about drugs to locate opportunities to buy drugs. Even experienced users will often be inconvenienced in completing drug transactions.[15] For patrol strategies, these indirect, incentive effects are probably much more important effects than the direct effects of producing cases.[t]

It is also important to understand that the patrol strategies complement the investigative strategies. Part of the complementary relationship is based on the indirect effects described above. The modest, but extremely general incentives to be discreet in public places is a unique feature of the patrol strategy. Neither of the investigative strategies would have as general a deterrent effect on the behavior of users and dealers. However, there are two additional complementary relationships worth noting.

First, the defendants produced by patrol strategies often become valuable sources of leads for prospective investigations and valuable sources of evidence for retrospective investigations.[u] Although the vast majority of defendants created by patrol efforts are either unable or unwilling to implicate other more important narcotics offenders, a few defendants will be both willing and able to assist additional investigative efforts. Debriefings may provide indirect intelligence that is valuable in making tactical choices in an investigation or in establishing probable cause for a search. Sworn testimony may serve as viable evidence of past offenses.[v] Active cooperation may result in successful prospective investigations. In short, patrol strategies will produce some grist for the investigative mill.

Second, the patrol strategies check the comprehensiveness of the intelligence systems used by investigative agencies. Investigative strategies proceed by making connections to individuals and events that are known. The dependence on what is already known is dangerous because one can never be sure how much of the universe of narcotics' trafficking is currently known to the police. If it is a large fraction, the weakness is not crippling. If it is a small fraction, the enforcement effort may be targeted on the wrong pieces of the distribution system. The only way to find out if a large or small fraction of the universe is known to the police is to look occasionally in areas that were previously

---

[t]The importance of disrupting stable markets is discussed below. See pp. 266-267.

[u]It is useful to think of narcotics investigations as having two distinct phases. The first phase is *penetration*, which usually means developing an informant within trafficking organization. The second phase is *development*, which means relying on the informant to help gather evidence against other members of the organization. Patrol efforts assist in making "penetrations" by creating defendants.

[v]To some extent, the process of taking sworn testimony can be seen as a process of "producing" or "preserving" evidence. Unrecorded recollections of narcotics traffickers are not useful pieces of evidence. Sworn testimony about these events is. This fact tempts grand juries into "fishing expeditions."

unknown to the police. If these random probes turn up leads to significant trafficking networks that were unknown, one should assume that only a small fraction of the universe is known to the police. Patrol efforts, precisely because they are random, serve this valuable function of checking and further developing the information available to investigative organizations. Without patrol, investigative agencies could become involved in endlessly chasing their own tails.

In sum, the patrol strategy has a limited, but valuable role to play in making cases against narcotics offenders. Since patrol efforts develop evidence only against aggressive, low-level, inexperienced users, the direct effects of this strategy will not be particularly significant. However, the indirect effects of the strategy are to disrupt retail markets by forcing street-level dealers to disguise and alter their retailing activities, and these are extremely valuable. In addition, the patrol strategies complement investigative strategies by producing defendants who can provide leads or evidence valuable in other kinds of investigations and by checking on the comprehensiveness of existing intelligence systems. Thus, the patrol strategy guarantees that all offenders will be motivated to be at least somewhat discreet about narcotics offenses and that no dealer can rely completely on the lack of previous records or anonymity to protect him from police investigative efforts.

2.3 Retrospective Investigations

Most crimes leave evidence in their wake. Spent bullets, complaining victims, outraged witnesses, fingerprints, broken clocks, photographs, and marked bills may litter the scene of the crime and provide powerful proof that a crime was committed in a particular way by a specific individual. In such situations, the investigative job is to collect, preserve, and interpret this evidence.

Many have argued that narcotics offenses do not leave this kind of evidence. There is hardly ever a complaining victim. With modest security efforts, outraged witnesses can be excluded. By the time the police arrive, the evidence is consumed, dispossessed, or hidden. The crime survives only in the recollection of the participants. The implication of this argument is that retrospective investigation has no role in a narcotics enforcement strategy—if we waited for a crime to occur and tried to preserve the evidence, we would never be able to make a case against anyone.

To a great extent this argument is correct. However, there is a special case in which it is wrong. Evidence of all narcotics offenses does survive in the recollection of the participants. If they would testify to the crime, and if their testimony could be corroborated by records, observations, or other kinds of physical evidence, historical offenses could be exposed. Indeed, for narcotics *conspiracy* offenses, the only compelling evidence of the crime is the recollections and testimony of participants. Thus, if recollections can be preserved in a form suitable for evidentiary purposes, and if the recollections can be corroborated, historical offenses can be uncovered and proved.

It is clear, of course, that this kind of evidence differs significantly from marked bills, fingerprints, and so on. It even differs from testimony of witnesses in other kinds of cases: it is relatively hard to get co-conspirators to testify against one another, hard to establish the credibility of the witnesses,[w] and hard to gather and interpret the evidence corroborating the person's testimony. Since this kind of evidence is more expensive to develop and less compelling than other kinds of evidence, these cases will only occasionally be worth developing.

The one situation in which the enormous expense and uncertain results are justified is when the potential defendant is a major narcotics trafficker. The direct and indirect effects of arresting such individuals are sufficiently large to justify the expense of the case. Moreover, this kind of case is the *only* kind of case that can be made against well-defended traffickers.

The *direct* effects are large for two reasons. First, by definition, the individual is currently responsible for a large volume of narcotics reaching illicit markets. Consequently, the short-run effects of his arrest and immobilization will be large. Second, the dealer may be fairly difficult to replace. In a world that is exceedingly vulnerable to rip-offs and betrayals, a reputation for trustworthiness and a track record of successful transactions will be extremely valuable characteristics. Moreover, they are likely to be seen as characteristics of an individual rather than an organization or institutional arrangement. The immobilization of a reliable connection will leave an awkward gap. New candidates to fill the gap will have to be subjected to a long period of screening and testing. In the interim, elaborate safeguards will have to be established to provide security that is no longer cheaply provided by personal trust. It could be a year or two before the connection is replaced.[x] Thus, the direct effects on the throughput capability of the distribution system will be large and relatively durable.

The *indirect* effects are also large. If dealers who have invested heavily in a variety of security devices are arrested and successfully prosecuted, all dealers with similar or lesser investments must reevaluate their position. They must consider themselves to be more vulnerable than they thought. They can respond

---

[w]See Vincent Teresa with Thomas Renner, *Vinnie Teresa's Mafia*, (New York: Doubleday and Co., 1975), pp. 66-69, for description of a conspiracy trial of Meyer Lansky. See Clark and Horrock, *Contrabandista!* for a description of a conspiracy trial of Auguste Ricord. In both cases, the witnesses have serious credibility problems.

[x]Indirect evidence of the difficulty of establishing connections is the relatively slow penetration of the East Coast market by Mexican heroin in the period 1972-74. It is almost certain that raw and finished materials were adequate to supply the New York market. However, there were few wholesale transactions of Mexican heroin in New York City until late 1973. See Institute for Defense Analysis, "Trends in Heroin Indicators: Availability Sources, Supply, and Use" (Washington, D.C.: Drug Enforcement Administration, 1975), pp. 20-33, 54-57.

by being more anxious or by making increased investments in security. Those who can see no effective defensive strategies may suffer such large increases in anxiety that they will leave the business. Those who see possible defensive strategies will make the investments and reduce their efficiency as distributors.[y] In addition, many dealers who are known to the major traffickers must consider themselves extremely vulnerable since the major trafficker facing long prison sentences may implicate them. Since the major traffickers are likely to know of many other traffickers, many dealers will be impressed by their arrest and make adjustments. In effect, not only is a major piece of the pipeline dismantled, but all the pieces that remain intact are constricted. The total throughput capacity of the system diminishes through both effects.

These dealers are vulnerable only to this type of case because they will invest heavily in the first and second lines of defense. They will keep their markets small, invest in heavy discipline, execute only a few transactions, blend their criminal activity into constitutionally protected activities, invest in expensive hiding places, and never come into direct contact with the drugs. Thus, the only evidence of their crimes will be the observations and recollections of close associates.

Thus, there is a group of narcotics offenders who are worth the enormous difficulty of retrospective investigations and who are vulnerable only to this kind of investigation. Consequently, retrospective investigations have a critical role in narcotics enforcement strategies.

The requirements for this type of case making should be apparent from the discussion above. Basically one needs four things: an associate of a major trafficker who is willing to implicate the major trafficker, a thorough debriefing of these witnesses guided by an effective intelligence system, the development of evidence from these debriefings through the taking of sworn testimony, and the location of physical and documentary evidence that corroborates the testimony of the witnesses.

Of these requirements, the most difficult is developing an associate who is willing to testify. The police seek to develop these witnesses by offering financial incentives for information. However, a more important source of these reluctant witnesses is from the defendants developed through other investigative procedures. The police trade the imminent threat of imprisonment and protection against the trafficker for cooperation from the defendant. The traffickers try to defend themselves by threatening and assisting their arrested associates. Who wins this battle over the associate's loyalty depends on which group the associate fears more. If the police have a strong case, and the case will be tried before a severe judge, the defendant may be willing to cooperate. If the trafficker is ruthless, the police case weak or the judge lenient, the associate will remain silent.

---

[y]It is reported that wiretaps placed on heroin distribution in France revealed that these dealers became much more cautious following significant arrests in Marseilles. The caution took the form of a significantly reduced rate of transactions.

Although a witness is the most important requirement, one should not underestimate the importance of debriefing techniques; intelligence systems; access to hotel records, airplane tickets, and telephone company records; and the patience and diligence of investigators who must put all the information together. If debriefings are guided by good intelligence, the defendant may give up information even when he did not intend to. If hotels and airlines destroyed records after one year instead of after five, a valuable source of corroborating evidence would be lost. If agents do not have the patience and skill to put all the pieces together, a potentially valuable witness may go unused.

2.4 Prospective Investigations

By far the most common enforcement strategy is prospective investigation. The police seek specific information about offenses that are likely to occur, or create the antecedent conditions for the offense. They then monitor the indicated area to observe and document the offense.

It is important to understand that there is a fine line between some kinds of prospective investigations and some kinds of patrol. Strictly defined, patrol is a completely random search of the space of possible offenses. The randomness is valuable because it maximizes the deterrent value of patrol efforts, and also provides a check on the comprehensiveness of investigative-intelligence systems. However, most patrol strategies are not strictly random. Analyses are conducted to reveal areas and times in which narcotics offenses are particularly likely to occur. Patrol deployments are then designed to reflect the differences in the likelihood of offenses being committed. In addition, patrol units often respond to complaints or anonymous tips about narcotics offenses. Both characteristics alter the distribution of surveillance activities over the space of all possible offenses: areas more likely to contain criminal offenses receive somewhat more attention. Insofar as the space and events to be examined are divided up into small nooks, and those that have relatively greater chances of containing narcotics offenses receive more intensive scrutiny, a patrol strategy that is strategically deployed and equipped to respond to complaints resembles the prospective-investigation strategy.

The major difference here is one of degree. One can think of a *lead* as defining a piece of the world in which an offense is likely to occur. It is apparent that leads can be more or less general. Table 3-1 illustrates leads that vary in terms of their specificity. It is also apparent that leads can be more or less reliable. Some leads will be very certain to be true; others will most likely turn out to be false. Finally, it is apparent that leads can come from different sources. They can come by analyzing past patterns of criminal offenses, from anonymous tips or complaints, or from informants or police operating in undercover roles. In general, forces following the strategy of prospective investigation will restrict

Table 3-1
Different Degrees of Generality in "Leads"

Dimension of Information	Degree of Generality			
	Properly Affects Patrol Allocation	Grey Area		Properly Requires Investigative Response
	Very General	Less General	More Specific	Very Specific
Space	S.W. border	Near San Diego	Around 14th Street	2337 Elm Street
Time	Afternoons or evenings	In the next two weeks	June 28th	Between 2:00 -3:00 Aug. 2
Descriptions of individuals	White, males; aged 15-25	People who hang out in Joe's Bar and Grill	A guy in checked pants with a scar on his face; named Willy something	Sam Jones; aka "Thin Man"; Mug shots available
Activities	Young white females with black male companions	Young white females with black male companions meeting on U.S. side of border; coming across in 5-10 min. intervals	Trucks bearing the name Gonzalez' produce	A green Chevrolet with license #562; junk in trunk

their attention to very specific, very reliable leads. These are most likely to come from informants or undercover activities. Forces following patrol strategies will rely on more general and less reliable leads. These leads are most likely to come from analyses of aggregate patterns of offenses or from complaints and tips.

In spite of these distinctions, there is a genuine grey area between patrol and prospective investigation. In some cases, the grey area will become a battle-ground as two different organizations fight for control of a given lead.[z] In describing specific tactics within the strategy of prospective investigation, we will begin with tactics that can be employed either by patrol forces or prospective investigations and move to tactics that are reserved for investigative organizations.

[z]The chronic feuding between the U.S. Customs Service and the Drug Enforcement Administration is partly caused by this problem. See United States Congress, House of Representatives, Committee on Government Operations, "Law Enforcement on the Southwest Border: Committee Report," 93rd Congress, 2nd Session (July-August 1974).

2.4.1 Observation-Sale Cases. The simplest tactic within the strategy of prospective investigation is an "observation-sale case": the police observe a narcotics transaction and arrest the dealer for selling narcotics. These cases can be made by patrol forces during the course of routine patrol, or in the course of investigating complaints. The cases can also be made by investigators who have received information from a reliable informant or have sustained a surveillance of an individual or location sufficiently long to have identified a tell-tale pattern.

There are two major problems in developing cases of this type. The first problem is persuading judges and juries that there was probable cause for police intervention. Given blending tactics, drop systems, and other forms of concealment or dispossession, even well-known dealers can avoid creating probable cause for an arrest. New, unknown dealers may never be noticed. To establish probable cause, the police will be forced to rely on arguments that their experience and expertise allows them to detect the offenses behind the screen of diversionary, legitimate activity. Alternatively, they can rely on extended surveillance or the corroborated allegations of a reliable informant. The dilemma for the police in choosing among these methods of establishing probable cause is that arguments based on special expertise may not be persuasive, and that the use of reliable informants or lengthy surveillance involves the use of relatively rare and expensive resources. Thus, it will be difficult for the police to establish probable cause inexpensively and effectively.[16]

The second problem is presenting compelling evidence that a sale occurred. Ordinarily, this requires that the police succeed in arresting both buyer and seller, that the seller have large amounts of money and heroin in his possession, and that the buyer have small amounts of heroin at the time of arrest.[aa] Clearly, the timing of the arrest must be nicely calculated, and the arrest situation must be well under the control to allow the police to come up with all this evidence. Given the difficulty, the police will have to have good information, or commit large amounts of manpower, or both, to insure an effective case.

Note that even if the police commit expensive resources to this type of case, there are serious limits to the reach of these cases. People who never make a direct sale are invulnerable to this tactic. People who make direct sales only in private locations where escape routes and ways of dispossessing heroin have been carefully laid out can significantly reduce the chance of successful prosecution even if the police commit significant resources and have good information. The only dealers who are likely to be vulnerable are those that conduct their businesses somewhat casually in public locations. These are likely to be fairly low-level dealers.[17]

Given that the dealers who are vulnerable to this tactic are relatively low-level traffickers, the police do not commit extensive resources to this type

---

[aa]These requirements were the prevailing views among narcotics detectives I interviewed in New York City. If any of these pieces of evidence is lacking, it is difficult to demonstrate that a sale occurred.

of case. Consequently, they will tend to choose less expensive ways of establishing probable cause and executing arrests. They will rely on their expertise or will exaggerate the amount and quality of prior information they had from either informants or surveillance, or both. Over time, this testimony will be given and received with some cynicism—further diluting the effectiveness of this type of case. Moreover, because the case will often turn on small details of police testimony, it will become easy for the police to disguise deliberately weakened testimony as an innocent error.[18] Because these cases produce only small direct effects and have so much potential for corruption (both abuses and subversion of authority) they are discouraged.

Thus, the direct effects of these cases is the immobilization of a relatively small number of careless, low-level dealers. The indirect effects of these cases are to motivate dealers not to make transactions in public, well-known locations.

2.4.2 Search-Warrant Cases. Search-warrant cases differ from observation-sale cases in two respects. First, they usually involve possession of heroin rather than a heroin transaction. (However, they may involve possession of such large amounts of heroin that there is a presumption of sales.) Second, they are made with the probable cause issue already resolved by obtaining a search warrant. Thus, they require a little more groundwork than observation-sale arrests, but require less precision at the moment of arrest.

There are three major problems in making search-warrant cases. The first problem is to generate enough evidence to secure a search warrant. This evidence can be created by extended surveillance, or by information from a reliable informant. Because the standard of evidence for a search warrant is relatively high, the most likely source is information from an informant that is corroborated by a small amount of surveillance and investigation.

The second problem is timing the execution of the warrant. The police must execute the warrant at a time when the location is "dirty." Ideally, they would also like to execute the warrant when the suspected violator was present since this will minimize the problem of tying the violator to the drugs.[bb]

The third problem is finding the heroin in the specified location. Although police searches are usually thorough enough to locate heroin if it is in a particular location, there may be some intricate "traps" that will frustrate significant searches.[cc]

Given these problems, a reliable informant is an extremely valuable resource in making this type of case. Without an informant these problems are all very difficult to surmount. Large amounts of investigative time must be spent on

---

[bb]The physical proximity of dealers to seized supplies of heroin has important evidentiary value. Consequently, the police try to arrest the dealers at the scene. Television police shows suggest the elaborate deceptions and contortions necessary to bring a wary violator close to the drugs. Although these stories wildly exaggerate the subtlety of police operations, they do emphasize the problem of arresting a major figure close to the supply of drugs.
[cc]See Teresa with Renner, *Vinnie Teresa's Mafia*, pp. 123-128, for description of "traps."

surveillance to persuade a judge that there is justification for a warrant. Once secured, the warrant must be executed blindly without knowledge of the violator's inventories or hiding places. It may prove surprisingly difficult to link the violator to his own heroin. With an informant who has knowledge of the violator's activities, the investigation is significantly advantaged. The warrant can be obtained more easily and executed more reliably. Moreover, the police need not "burn" the informant in a search-warrant case. The police may succeed in developing sufficient evidence of the defendant's guilt that a judge can reasonably reject a defense motion to discover the identity of the informant on the grounds that the informant's testimony would be redundant.[19] Thus, the informant can make a significant contribution to these cases at very low cost.

In principle, these cases can reach a wide spectrum of traffickers. If the police rely on surveillance to gather evidence for a search warrant they will be restricted to dealers whose transactions are sufficiently frequent that a pattern of activity can be observed with continuous observation over a limited time. However, if informants are used to secure the search warrant, time the arrest, and guide the search, the reach of the police is as broad as the knowledge of their informants. If their informants know the operations of major traffickers, then major traffickers will be vulnerable to this kind of arrest. If they know only insignificant dealers, the police attack will be restricted to these minor dealers. The dealers who will be vulnerable to this kind of case, then, are those that make transactions frequently enough to reveal a pattern, those that cannot control their employees and agents, and those that have not invested sufficiently in strategies to hide or dispossess their heroin. Some "big fish" may be caught in this net. However, the most vulnerable dealers are those at lower levels, or those at higher levels who have not invested in developing a large organization that is effectively disciplined by threats of violence.

Thus, the direct effects of search-warrant cases will be a set of solid cases against a spectrum of traffickers. Low-level dealers will be overrepresented, but will not be the only dealers arrested. Among high-level dealers, the dealers who have not built up buffers or who fail to control their buffers reliably will be vulnerable.[dd] The indirect effects will be to motivate dealers to reduce the frequency of transactions, to invest in hiding and dispossessing strategies, and to invest in devices to control associates.

2.4.3 Buy and Bust Cases. Observation-sale and search-warrant cases can be conducted by uniformed or plainclothes policemen. Some secrecy is required to prevent dealers from guessing that they will be observed and taking strong, short-run countermeasures. But the secrecy requires only surreptitiousness or sudden action, or both. It does not require the police to imitate people in the drug culture for the purpose of penetrating trafficking organizations.

[dd]Note that many cases initiated and developed through more substantial investigative tactics will culminate with search-warrant arrests.

Undercover operations require a specialized resource: policemen who can successfully imitate the behavior of drug users and dealers. Although the need for the specialized resource increases the cost of these operations, undercover operations provide some distinct advantages over observation-sale and search-warrant cases in terms of producing strong cases with small amounts of resources. There are two major inefficiencies of observation-sale and search-warrant cases. First, the police must monitor many situations that turn out *not* to show evidence of heroin violations. Second, the evidence they manage to secure even when violations occurred and were observed is often unpersuasive. The use of undercover police reduces both problems. Since a police offer to buy heroin may *attract* violations, the police may be able to economize on expensive searches for cautious violators. Similarly, since the police will actually participate in the transaction, it will be possible to protect physical evidence and provide detailed testimony of what occurred. In addition, by keeping their eyes and ears open, undercover police may develop additional leads suitable for exploitations by other investigative tactics. These features of undercover operations provide advantages over observation-sale and search-warrant cases even when the cost of undercover police is properly reckoned.

But there are some distinct disadvantages of undercover operations as well. One problem is avoiding a successful "entrapment" defense. In an extreme case, the defendant may claim that the police supplied the motivation, money, and connections to make the deal. In a less-extreme case, the defendant may claim that the police put sufficient pressure on him to provide heroin, that he "accommodated" them to get them off his back. If the defendant can persuade the courts he was entrapped, the case will be defeated. The most effective countermeasures to the entrapment defense are to make several buys from the same dealer, and to secure testimony about the reputation of the accused defendant. The necessity for these countermeasures reduces some of the advantages of undercover arrests over observation-sale and search-warrant cases by increasing the amount of resources that must be spent on each case.

A second major problem with undercover operations is the risk of corruption—both abuses of authority and subversions of authority.[ee] Undercover operations are unusually corrupting for several different reasons. First, by necessity, undercover police will develop an intimate relationship to the world of heroin dealers and addicts. They will know more about the violation and violators they attack than police usually do, and will sometimes have personal interests at stake in the arrests. This invites them to exercise their authority in accordance with their intimate knowledge rather than what the law requires: known, "evil" drug dealers will be "flaked" when it is only rules of police

---

[ee]The distinction drawn here between *abuses* and *subversions* of authority refers to whether the police assert their authority to secure some benefit when they are not legally entitled (e.g., extortion, "flaking"), or fail to assert their authority in a situation where they were legally obligated to do so (e.g., overlooking an offense). The former is an "abuse" of authority, the latter is a "subversion" of authority.

procedure and their canniness that protects them from arrest; relatively "inno-cent" violators will be protected even when they commit crimes in a way that makes them vulnerable to arrest. The close relationship also invites the police to change their views of what the law requires. They may become more or less zealous in the enforcement of narcotics laws than the society as a whole would like.

Second, the police will have access to money to purchase narcotics or reward informants. The sums involved are fairly large relative to a policeman's salary.[20] Moreover, he may operate in intimate settings where it is difficult for many people to observe, and where the testimony of everyone is suspect. In such situations, it may become tempting to steal all or some portion of the money. If the policeman does this with the knowledge of drug violations, he becomes open to blackmail and extortion by these individuals.[ff] Thus, there are substantial risks in conducting undercover operations.

Note that these risks also exist with observation-sale and search-warrant arrests—particularly when informants are used in making the cases. Close associations with informants and payments to informants can corrupt patrolmen and plain-clothes police in the same way as frequent undercover purchases. The difference is one of degree. The relations are not likely to be as intimate, and the exchanges of money are not likely to be as large or as frequent for patrolmen and plainclothesmen as for undercover operations.

Undercover operations can be of many different types. The most important distinctions involve the duration of the operation and the elaborateness of the undercover man's "cover." The simplest undercover operation is a buy and bust operation. An undercover policeman goes to a location where open narcotics activity is suspected and tries to make a deal. As soon as a deal is made, the dealer is arrested. The immediate arrest of the dealer usually "burns" the undercover policeman.

Dealers who are vulnerable to these operations include those who make a large number of transactions and do not make much of an effort to screen customers. These are likely to be low-level dealers who are marketing their product aggressively.

Note that a group that is particularly vulnerable to arrest with these tactics is the group of dealers who cheat their customers. Dealers who aggressively market talcum powder and milk sugar as heroin, and who are shunned by knowledgeable customers, will attract undercover police like flies. This is unfortunate not only because police resources will be wasted on the investiga-tion of a nondealer, but also because it is desirable from the point of view of

---

[ff]People often forget that the police are vulnerable to "flaking" and extortion as well as narcotics dealers—particularly in a world that is deeply suspicious of the police, and where police behavior is regulated by an enormous number of rules, many of which will be broken by the police. See the discussion of "dropping a dime" in Jonathan Rubinstein, *City Police* (New York: Farrar, Straus and Giroux, 1973).

police objectives to leave these frauds in operation. The frauds waste the time and money of inexperienced bonafide customers as well as police. If many frauds are operating, and if it is hard for the customers to distinguish them from the real dealers, many customers may be discouraged from trying to buy heroin.

Buy and bust cases have serious problems. The evidence of a sale is not particularly powerful primarily because they are vulnerable to an entrapment defense. With only one casual sale as evidence, it is fairly easy for the defendant to claim the sale was simply an "accommodating sale." The violators who are vulnerable to the tactic are not likely to be major figures. Finally, extensive use of this tactic may "use up" undercover police. Although there is reason to suppose that low-level dealers do not have efficient procedures for sharing information about the identity of undercover police, it is still true that the probability that an undercover policeman will be identified increases with the number of people who know his identity. Since buy and bust operations will routinely "burn" the undercover police, and may do so in sight of large numbers of people, this type of case uses up a great deal of the undercover policeman's anonymity and future value. Since good undercover police are relatively rare, this loss is substantially more than his yearly salary.

Given the weaknesses of these cases and their high cost, the police tend to use them for only limited purposes. First, they use buy and bust tactics in situations where the dealers are not likely to be in the same place the next day. In effect, if they do not bust the dealer immediately, they will never get the chance to gather additional information or to use the evidence they have already secured. This condition implies that buy and bust tactics will be used to police rock concerts and other large gatherings that imply a large, but temporary market for heroin. Second, the police will use buy and bust tactics in response to complaints about large amounts of open dealing in specific locations. Schools, street corners, bars, and pool halls may be singled out for quick cleanup operations by police conducting buy and bust operations as a result of complaints, public pressure, or police intelligence analyses. Third, the police will use these tactics when they are under pressure to increase the volume of cases and have no more effective uses of their undercover police. If the undercover police cannot be kept occupied in longer term, higher level operations where introductions and impressive credentials are required, they will be turned loose to see what they can get for themselves on the street.

Thus, buy and bust cases will produce a reasonably large number of weak cases against low-level traffickers. The indirect effects of buy and bust operations will be to motivate even low-level dealers to invest in improved methods of screening their customers. Since buy and bust cases do not require the undercover police to operate in a prolonged, intimate association with the narcotics underworld, they represent only a modest corrupting influence on the police. Since they burn many undercover police in front of many individuals, they must be considered expensive cases.

2.4.4 Standard, Undercover-Buy Operations. A more common type of undercover operation is one that lasts longer and provides a little bit deeper cover to
undercover police. These operations usually start with an informant who
introduces an undercover policeman to a heroin dealer. The introduction implies
a recommendation, and the recommendation establishes some cover for the
undercover policeman. If the dealer trusts the informant, and if the undercover
policeman's attitudes and actions are consistent with the dealer's expectations
about how a real customer behaves, then the undercover policeman will be able
to "score."

Unlike buy and bust cases, the standard, undercover operation does not end
with the first score. Instead, the undercover man will try to make several scores,
will try to score larger and larger quantities of drugs, and will hang out in the
area of operation. The arrest may not be made until several weeks after the last
transaction was executed.

The reason for these procedures are the following. The undercover policeman makes several buys to minimize the chance of some technical error in the
arrest, and to insure that an entrapment offense will be unpersuasive. The
undercover policeman tries to make larger and larger transactions to increase the
charge that can be brought against the dealer and to lay the groundwork for
gaining an introduction to a higher level dealer. If the undercover man can
persuade the dealer he wants to buy more than the dealer can provide, or if the
undercover policeman gains a local reputation as a man who can move large
inventories of drugs, he may be introduced to or sought out by a larger dealer.
The undercover man hangs out in the area of operation to strengthen his
reputation for reliability and to pick up information that will be useful in
extensions of the current operation or in new operations. The arrest is delayed
to make it more difficult for dealers to guess which customers were informants
and undercover agents.

It is important to see that these operations have a powerful dynamic that
leads to significant economies of scale. The operations begin with the informant
"giving up" the least cautious, least dangerous, and least significant dealer he
knows. This suits the informant's interest because it minimizes his risk.[gg] He gets
away with it because the police may not have any way of knowing who is
relatively important, and who is relatively unimportant. Then, as the operation
continues, the undercover man becomes increasingly independent of the original
informant. He begins to develop an independent reputation—partly because he
hangs out, and partly because the transactions were made and no one has been
arrested yet. In addition, he begins to develop other sources of information—
people who are not his informant and do not know he is a policeman will begin
to talk to him. These events dramatically expand the undercover man's

---

[gg]The informant has obvious, strong incentives to "give up" the least *dangerous* dealer he
knows. Since the *importance* of the dealer is likely to be positively correlated with his
capacity for violence, the informant will usually give up unimportant dealers.

capability. He may score from people unknown to his informant or may direct his informant to the people he really wants. If the second stage results in several more buys and no one is arrested, the undercover man's capabilities increase still more. In effect, the longer an operation continues, the easier it is to take the next step.

There are several factors that limit the scope of these operations or slow the pace of development in spite of the favorable dynamics. First, it is not in the interests of either the informant or the first dealer to whom the undercover man is introduced to let the undercover man develop the independence described above. It is against the informant's interests because he may ultimately be judged to be responsible for the arrest of several dealers if the operation is successful, and he will be afraid of retaliation. It is against the dealer's interest because he does not want to lose this valuable new customer. In fact, he regards the desire of the new customer to buy larger and larger amounts of heroin as a great opportunity for himself. He can either reduce his risk by selling to fewer customers as this new customer demands more and more, or he can ask his supplier for more heroin. The last thing this dealer would want to do is to introduce the exceptional new customer to his supplier, since he would then be unnecessary. Only in the case that the dealer's supplier hears of this new customer, is greedy enough to risk dealing with him, and is powerful enough to control the original dealer will the original dealer be forced to introduce his new customers to his supplier. In short, both informants and initial targets will have incentives to hem the undercover man in, although their reasons will be strikingly different.

Second, screening procedures of higher levels of the distribution system may become very stringent. Although a half-hearted recommendation by an unimportant person and two weeks of heavy spending and hanging out in an area may be sufficient to get through the screens of reasonably careful, intermediate dealers, they may not be sufficient to do business with cautious, high-level dealers. One may need much more important references, and a longer period of initiation to be acceptable. These tight procedures are not necessarily impenetrable, but they do require a much longer and larger investment in the undercover agent's cover.

Third, the operation becomes increasingly vulnerable as it continues. This is true partly because the probability of an error by the undercover man increases as a function of time, partly because the undercover man comes under closer and more demanding scrutiny as the operation reaches higher levels, partly because the initial informant may become afraid of the potential success of the operation, and partly because the probability of coincidences that would pierce the undercover man's cover increases. In short, the operation becomes more fragile as more (and more determined) people are brought into the net.

Fourth, bureaucratic pressures will eventually limit the scope of the operation. As the operation continues, there will be a larger and larger investment in the success of the operation. There will be large numbers of dealers with effective cases against them. There will be lots of money in the operation. There will be a risk that all of the violators may disappear before the net is finally thrown. Thus, to a police commander who stands to lose a great deal if the case finally blows up, and stands to gain a great deal if he consolidates the gains already made, the temptation to shut off an operation can be overwhelming. Similarly, for police who are under pressure to produce frequent tangible results of their activity, it will soon seem better to round up all the current defendants rather than reach for more.

Given these constraining factors, undercover operations will only occasionally achieve their maximum level of development. This suggests that the direct effects of these operations will be to produce a large number of strong cases against low- to intermediate-level dealers, and a few against high-level dealers who fail to invest in strong screening procedures. The indirect effects of undercover operations will be to motivate dealers to invest in strong screening procedures.

Note that undercover operations have a problem that is analogous to the situation where buy and bust cases sweep up fraudulent dealers, but is more serious. On the peripheries of illegal-distribution systems are *take-off artists*, armed robbers who will rob illegal businesses as well as legitimate businesses.[21] Inexperienced people trying to purchase a large quantity of drugs are easy marks for such people. They will pose as connections, set up a deal, and then steal the money that was intended to purchase heroin. Given the eagerness of the undercover police to make a deal, and given that they are dealing with government money rather than their own funds, the undercover police are likely to be somewhat less cautious than regular dealers. Being somewhat less cautious, they are somewhat more likely to encounter take-off artists. This is unfortunate. It would be better from the point of view of controlling the flow of drugs to leave these take-off artists to prey on real drug dealers. However, the greatest problem in these encounters is that there is apt to be violence. The police will fight to regain the money, and the armed robbers are likely to return their fire. Situations like this have been a major cause of serious shooting incidents among narcotics policemen.[22]

2.4.5 Long-Term Covert Operations. On the other extreme from buy and bust cases are long-term, covert undercover operations. A false background is built up for the undercover police. He is allowed to operate for a long period without making cases and even without making contact with his straight world. Gradually, a few cases will be made when it is possible for the undercover man to insulate himself from the cases. The undercover man may eventually be surfaced when he has developed compelling evidence against major trafficking networks.

In spite of what one sees on television, these operations practically never occur. There are too many troubling legal issues (e.g., can the undercover man participate in a crime and be exonerated; can he observe crimes and fail to report them; etc.). Moreover, the resources, personnel, and technical skills necessary to conduct these operations are beyond the capability of most enforcement organizations. The remote possibility of this kind of operation implies that reasonably tight screening procedures can succeed in keeping major dealers from ever having to confront an undercover policeman directly. The only people a major trafficker who maintains a tight screen must fear are his associates and competitors. Evidence of his crimes exist only in their recollections and actions.

2.5 Interrelationship among the Strategies and Tactics

Separating the strategies and tactics for-making cases is both artificial and misleading. It is artificial because the distinctions among these tactics blur in practice, and because any given operation may involve several different tactics. It is misleading because it seems to suggest that one tactic should be chosen from the entire set and made the dominant tactic.

The real situation is quite different. In any given case, one should (and to some extent will) be able to choose from a variety of tactics. The case may begin with an observation sale, a buy and bust, or even a patrol arrest. The defendant, facing a prison sentence, may agree to introduce an undercover agent to a regular street dealer. Through skillful management of the informant and a large investment in hanging out, the undercover agent may discover the location of a dealer's "cache," obtain a search warrant, and have him arrested without exposing the original informant. As several intermediate dealers are arrested, they may be debriefed and their observations and recollections checked with other intelligence available to the police. These allegations may eventually justify testimony before a grand jury that will result in a conspiracy indictment against major traffickers. Thus, a given case or operation can require many different tactics to insure its maximum development.

Similarly, looking not at the development of a particular case but at the aggregate pattern of cases, it is clear that the different strategies complement one another. The patrol strategy turns up defendants who are potentially valuable sources of leads for prospective investigations. In addition, patrol efforts check the comprehensiveness of the intelligence available to investigative efforts and provide a small, but generalized, deterrent effect that motivates low-level dealers to be discrete in their heroin transactions. The tactics of prospective investigation produce relatively strong cases against low and intermediate traffickers, and motivate dealers to make expensive investments in screening customers, keeping markets small, and hiding and dispossessing heroin. The cases produced by prospective investigation provides the basis for the fullest possible development of these cases, and for the development of retrospective conspiracy cases. Thus, at an aggregate level these strategies and tactics are complementary in several different senses: one tactic provides inputs that are necessary for another tactic to operate successfully; each tactic directly attacks a different part of the distribution system; and each tactic motivates dealers to invest in different security measures. All together the tactics permit a broad and powerful attack on the distribution system.

The implication of this interdependence is that at both micro and macro levels, there is a great need for coordination among the various tactics. At the individual-case level, tactical decisions about the development of specific cases should be made by optimizing over the full set of investigative procedures. At the aggregate level, strategic decisions about how to minimize the throughput capability of the distribution system should be made by choosing the optimal allocation of resources among patrol, prospective investigation, and retrospective investigative strategies. Unfortunately, this coordination will be somewhat difficult to achieve.

At the individual-case level, bureaucratic factors intervene to frustrate effective coordination. For a variety of reasons, different organizational units will come to specialize in different tactics.[hh] In addition, the organizational units will jealously guard any lead available to them because they will be evaluated on the basis of their production. These two factors operating together guarantee that the choice of investigative tactics will be suboptimal: tactics to develop a lead owned by a specific organizational unit will not be adjusted to fit the lead. The tactics will always be the same. Unless it happens by coincidence that the leads distribute themselves to the organization that employs the investigative procedure which maximizes the potential of this lead, some potential development will be lost. The only way to change this situation is to develop better procedures for sharing leads among organizational units, or to enlarge the set of investigative procedures used by any given organizational unit.

At the macro level, coordination is more difficult to define. Presumably, some optimal allocation of resources among strategies and tactics exists that would minimize the throughput capability of the distribution system within a given budget constraint. Unfortunately, we do not currently know what the optimal allocation is. We do not know whether 60 percent of our resources should be spent on patrol strategies or 16 percent; we do not know whether 30 percent of our resources should be spent on retrospective investigations or 3 percent. Beyond the problem of defining optimal coordination at the macro level, there is the problem of insuring that allocation decisions are consistent with the desired allocation. No single organization controls all the resources devoted to narcotics enforcement. Many separate organizations make separate

[hh]The specialization in tactics is partly the result of personnel systems that select, train, and motivate limited sets of skills; partly the result of different levels of investment in different kinds of support systems such as intelligence and technical equipment that have the effect of limiting types of investigation; and partly from a desire to establish "product differentiation" to insure the continued vitality of an organization within the narcotics-enforcement area.

decisions. No mechanisms or incentives force the different organizations to take account of the allocation decisions of the other organizations. Thus, there is neither the analytic models to calculate nor the bureaucratic mechanisms to execute a strategy that properly allocates resources among the diverse strategies and tactics.[ii]

Although it is clearly desirable to use all of the strategies and tactics outlined above, and although our strategy necessarily does involve all of the diverse strategies and tactics, it is difficult to achieve optimal coordination. At the micro level, specialized institutions and parochial interests will keep specific cases from being fully developed. At the macro level, it is not clear how resources should be allocated among the various strategies, and there is no institutional mechanism that can reliably control the allocation.

3.0 Resources and Constraints

Section 2 looked primarily at one side of making cases—the output side. The various strategies and tactics were analyzed to determine the kinds of cases that could be made against traffickers at different levels investing in different security arrangements, and the indirect effects of these strategies and tactics on dealers who were not arrested. We saw the potential for a broad, coordinated attack on all levels of the distribution system.

The attack that is actually mounted (and maintained over a long period) depends not only on our desires to achieve specific direct and indirect effects, but also on the availability of resources. To some extent, the problem of resources may seem analytically trivial: the scale of the attack will be determined by the amount of money we are willing to spend. However, there are several subtle features of the resource problem for narcotics enforcement that have not received detailed attention. For example, the availability of many of the required resources will not be determined by market forces, but by government policies. The corollary is that more money may not increase the supply of these resources. Another example: since the various tactics make differential claims on specific types of resources, constraints on the availability of some specialized resources or very high prices for the resources may force the portfolio of tactics we employ in a direction other than the one we might desire. Finally, we will find that the various resources can substitute for one another in making cases. These observations are not so bizarre for people accustomed to analyzing complex production processes for things like automobiles or electronic components, but they are not routinely made by managers of enforcement organizations.

Thus, in this section, we look at the major kinds of resources required to make narcotics cases. For each kind of resource, we analyze the relative

---

[ii]For an example of how complicated the coordination problem can become, see Chapter 4.

availability of the resource, the extent to which the resource can substitute for or must be complemented by other resources, and the tactics and strategies that place unusually heavy or unusually light demands on the specific resources. The analysis is not entirely systematic. We focus on those resources that seem likely to constrain either the scale or the specific shape of the attack. This implies that we often look at resources that cannot be easily purchased in unlimited quantities in ordinary markets.

3.1 Investigative and Patrol Manpower

Like guerrilla warfare, elementary-school education, and many health services, narcotics enforcement is a labor-intensive operation. Since labor accounts for the largest share of total expenditures, the quality of the individual labor units has a decisive impact on the character of the output. We examine the supply of manpower to narcotics-enforcement agencies along three dimensions: professional skills, cultural identification, and stocks of specific local knowledge of heroin trafficking. Each has a significant impact on the scale and shape of the enforcement strategy.

3.1.1 Professional Skills of Enforcement Agents. The different tactics (or technologies) for making cases require different kinds of professional skills. Patrol strategies require capacities for sustained vigilance. Retrospective-investigation strategies require detailed imagination to reconstruct the events, and a capacity for dogged, thorough, meticulous corroboration of a large set of allegations. Prospective investigations require a capacity to work with informants and to conduct surreptitious surveillance. The police must be able to motivate their informants, and calibrate the information provided. Undercover tactics require police who are capable of dissembling and operating in an alien and threatening environment. Moreover, since an undercover agent's success and safety depend on the agent's ability to guess correctly about the motives and actions of their informants, the undercover agent must have superior skill in controlling and managing informants.

An important question is the relative availability of personnel with these skills to narcotics-enforcement organizations. Probably the most common skills are the vigilance skills necessary for patrol strategies. Although people undoubtedly differ in the skill with which they can pick "signals" (actual offenses) from "noise" (ordinary activity), and in the tact they show in intervening when a signal is detected, the basic vigilance capability is fairly common. Thus, one would not expect vigilance skills to be an important constraint in designing an enforcement strategy.

The rarest skill is harder to guess. A priori, one might think that the skills required for undercover operations would be the least common. It is unusual to find people in the general population who combine the necessary courage, initiative, skill, and bravado to do this job well. However, among the self-selected population that applies for jobs in narcotics enforcement organizations, these skills are, if not common, at least significantly less rare than in the general population.

The basic skill that seems to be rare in narcotics-enforcement organizations are the skills required for retrospective investigation. Narcotics detectives are rarely enthusiastic about or proficient in "gumshoeing." They prefer action over reflection, and intuitive debriefings of informants over carefully prepared, deliberate debriefings, which are constantly checked for corroborating evidence.[jj]

To a great extent, this situation exists because of a combination of government policies and psychological characteristics. It is clear that a narcotics-enforcement strategy must depend to some extent on undercover operations. These operations provide strong cases at several levels of the traffic, and produce very effective incentives affecting the behavior of dealers who remain on the street. It is also clear that these skills are somewhat rare. Consequently, organizations have been developed whose personnel systems are designed to prepare people to undertake these difficult operations. Eventually, as the organization develops a style, personnel systems begin to be complemented by self-selection. As a result, the supply of effective undercover operators to enforcement organizations is maximized.

The problem with this development is that undercover operations eventually come to dominate the style of the organizations. The psychological experience of undercover work is so compelling that many undercover agents become zealots. Moreover, since they are so essential to many enforcement actions, and since their work is dangerous, the undercover agents become high-status individuals in the organization. This eventually leads to intolerance of other less demanding skills within the organization. The problem is analogous to efforts to combine paratroopers, or troops specially trained for amphibious assaults with infantry units. Thus, the problem is to mount an enforcement attack that depends primarily, but not exclusively, on undercover operations: it is hard to design a narcotics-enforcement organization that devotes 60 percent of its resources to undercover operations.

The problem is particularly difficult because it is not enough to achieve coordination between "undercover narcs" and "gumshoes" at an aggregate level—one must achieve this coordination with specific cases. Cases begun by undercover operatives may have to be further developed by the gumshoes. Since all enforcement agents are evaluated on the basis of case production and wish to retain control over cases they initiate, this sharing of cases is unlikely to occur.

Thus, the rarest and most valuable of all professional skills is a man who combines the skills of an undercover agent with the skills of a gumshoe. Slightly

[jj]For anecdotal information on the temperaments of narcotics agents, see Eszterhas, *Nark!*.

less rare and almost as valuable is a man who has the skills to be an undercover agent, but relies on and tolerates gumshoes. Indeed, if we want a balanced enforcement attack, we may have to take steps that will reduce the supply of undercover police to narcotics enforcement organizations and attract the slightly more common group of people who can be effective gumshoes.

3.1.2 Cultural Identification of the Police. Nearly all enforcement strategies and tactics require the police to blend into the cultural milieux of the policed population and become perceptive observers of the activity they observe. Patrol strategies impose the smallest requirements for cultural identification on the police, but they are not insignificant. Undercover operations impose the largest requirements. Indeed, the success of these operations will be almost strictly determined by the ability of the police to become part of and understand the activities of their targets. Consequently, to the extent that the police are unable to blend into or interpret the activity they observe, their potential success is strikingly limited.

The simple case of demographic characteristics (e.g., age, race, language) and undercover operations provides a dramatic illustration of this principle. We know from Chapter 1 that dealers will rely on screening mechanisms to protect their market from infiltration by informants or undercover police. Among the most valuable screening mechanisms are demographic characteristics. Demographic characteristics are valuable for screening partly because it may be known that the police rarely have certain characteristics, partly because the demographic characteristics may be correlated with antipolice attitudes so the dealer can be relatively confident that the customer will not be an informant, and partly because the dealer may be able to rely on some empathy and identification with the customer to bolster his influence over the customer. As a result of these mechanisms, it is difficult for Irish undercover police to buy heroin in Harlem, and for black undercover police to exploit effectively a high-class Italian informant.

The implication of this observation is that if there is a shortage of specific cultural types among the narcotics-enforcement organizations, that cultural type may enjoy immunity in dealing heroin among his own type. Chinese on the lower east side of New York, Cubans in Florida, Mexicans in the Saginaw Valley of Michigan, and 15-year-old junior high school students on Long Island may all be able to exploit the inability of the police to infiltrate their subculture. This effect is the opposite side of the coin of dealers' preferences for socially disorganized areas.

Constraints on the variety of cultural identification are likely to be a major problem for narcotics enforcement. Many diverse, "fringe" groups are likely to be involved in heroin dealing. Because few members of fringe groups will want to become police; formal selection procedures may make the fringe groups ineligible for employment; and enforcement organizations are discriminatory;

the police will have difficulty maintaining sufficient cultural heterogeniety among their agents and informants. Ironies abound in this situation. The procedures established to insure that the police are qualified may actually reduce their effectiveness in making cases. Police prejudice against fringe groups will reduce their ability to police the people who are most likely to be offenders and victims. In short, barriers established with the objective of increasing police effectiveness may actually reduce police effectiveness.

It is important to keep in mind that limitations on police capabilities for cultural identification affect not only whom they can attack, but also whom they protect. This point can be made clear by the following example. Many observers of narcotics-enforcement efforts have suspected that police efforts would be unsuccessful because the police would be unable to imitate real junkies. Their fingernails would be too clean, their hair would be too well combed, their "street patter" would be off-key, and their arms would be smooth and unscarred. In effect, they would fail to penetrate rather modest screens set up by cautious dealers. However, police efforts always have indirect, incentive effects as well as direct effects in terms of cases. If the police look like inexperienced users, then the dealers will have an incentive to discriminate against inexperienced users. Because this is a group that we are particularly eager to protect, we may be grateful that the police are unable to look like "real junkies," and that their failure to do so gives heroin dealers strong incentives to discriminate against new users. By extension, it should be easy to see that the inability of the police to resemble or effectively employ young blacks means not only that black dealers will not be arrested, but that young black children may find it easy to find heroin.

Finally, it is important to note that to some extent, both the society and the police like the fact that it is difficult for them to maintain sufficient cultural diversity to attack and protect many different groups. The police like it for the same reasons that most people like cultural homogeneity in the organizations in which they work. They like to spend their long, demanding work days with people who agree with them, reliably fulfill their expectations, reflect well on their activity, and who otherwise bolster their current beliefs and roles. The society likes the police to be different from the narcotics traffickers because we are concerned about the potentially corrupting effect of having the police identify too closely with the policed groups. Personal stakes and idiosyncratic interpretations of events may influence the way they enforce the law.[kk] Some people will be arrested who would not be if the police "played it by the book"; others will be ignored who would otherwise be arrested. Thus, we like the police to be forced to rely on formal rules and limited, insensitive perception to enforce the law because we believe that this preserves equality before the law. In

[kk]For general analyses of the exercise of police discretion, see Skolnick, *Justice Without Trial*; James Q. Wilson, *Varieties of Police Behavior* (Cambridge: Harvard University Press, 1968); and Rubinstein, *City Police*.

effect, by allowing the police to be culturally homogenous, we trade a limitation on the scope of the narcotics enforcement strategy for a gain in terms of "equity" in enforcement efforts and increased police solidarity.

3.1.3 Local Experience and Knowledge.

Just as it is possible to analyze the professional skills and cultural identities of police officials as characteristics of individual policemen that have an important resource value in making cases, it is also possible to discuss the role of local experience and information as a resource owned by a given officer. To some extent, one can look at local experience and knowledge as a resource that can compensate for poor cultural identification. With sufficient experience, a policeman can learn to be a surreptitious and close observer of the local scene. There are clear limits to this possibility. Experience will not make a middle-aged man young, nor a black man white. It may not even smooth the inflections of a foreign language or a complicated street jargon. But a policeman can learn how people with his unalterable characteristics might be made to fit in.

However, local experiences and knowledge has a value quite apart from compensating for problems with cultural identification. It has to do with the police officer's capability to manage informants effectively.

The discussion of technologies for making cases should have made it clear that informants play a vital role in all investigative tactics. They provide the information that justifies search-warrant arrests, and the introductions that initiate or accelerate undercover operations. Their testimony taken before grand juries and corroborated with standard police investigations become the pieces of evidence that convict major traffickers on conspiracy charges. Thus, in the midst of all the most important cases, one will find an informant.

The value of a set of informants in making cases is variable. The reason is that informants differ in terms of the value of the information they can provide, and in their willingness to provide the best information they process. Consequently, police effectiveness will depend on the ability of the police to screen informants, and to motivate good informants to "give up" the best dealers they know. The complexity of this problem can be indicated by some examples.

Consider, first, the informants who volunteer information. These people have a variety of motives and the quality of their information differs markedly. A narcotics dealer may inform on his competition. A paid police informant desperate to continue earning rewards may stretch facts or frame a man he suspects of dealing. A scorned woman may inform on her heroin-dealing boyfriend. A frightened mother can file a complaint against her son's newest friend. A landlord can complain about one of his tenants to harass the tenant, and force him to leave. The police must be able to evaluate these enormously varied "leads" to see which are worth pursuing, which should be quickly forgotten, and which suggest that the informant may be a more important target than the man against whom information was provided. To make these decisions reliably and quickly is exceedingly difficult.

Relationships with informants who provide information for a reduced sentence are equally complex. The police officer must first persuade a defendant to cooperate. He does so through a combination of threats, assurances that the informant will be protected, and personal relationships. Once the defendant has agreed to cooperate, the narcotics officer must persuade him to give up the most important traffickers the informant knows. Since the most important dealers are likely also to be the most careful and dangerous dealers an informant knows (and, therefore, most likely to discover the informant's identity and retaliate if he is arrested), the informant has a large incentive to steer the narcotics agent in other directions. In fact, he would like to give up the least cautious and least dangerous dealer he knows. Like B'rer Fox, a narcotics agent is vulnerable when he allows the defendant-informant to name his own punishment: a dealer who can be made to appear formidable and terrifying can turn out to be utterly insignificant.

Given the central role of informants in making cases, and given the incentives of informants, wittingly or unwittingly, to divert and deflect the police from major targets, the entire narcotics-enforcement effort is always in some danger of being misdirected. Resources will be wasted by relying on worthless informants. Potentially good informants will manage to divert the police to unimportant targets.

The best defense against this possibility is for the police to know a great deal about local traffickers before they talk to informants. If they know a great deal, and disguise how much they know, they will have an opportunity to calibrate the credibility of informants. They can invite the informant to tell lies, reveal ignorance or knowledge, and know with some confidence when he is dissembling. Thus, since local knowledge about traffickers is a vital resource in screening and managing informants, and since informants play a key role in most enforcement tactics, the amount of local knowledge that individual police officers have will have a decisive impact on the aggregate pattern of cases made against heroin dealers.

It might seem odd to consider the stock of local knowledge as a characteristic of individual policemen. One would think that the information would be sufficiently durable and transferable to become a common resource for the entire organization. However, it turns out that there are substantial barriers to sharing this information effectively. First, there is the sheer mechanical problem of recording all the information in a form that can be circulated and understood.[11] (This is one of the most powerful arguments for providing the police with extensive secretarial help.) Second, there is the problem of filing and retrieving the information so that many different people operating in different geographic locations (and sometimes in different organizations) can have convenient access to the information. Third, there is the problem of providing

---

[11]For a rough idea of the cost of this problem, it is worth noting that DEA spent $1.5 million each year to convert a very limited amount of information to machine-readable form.

adequate security for information that circulates widely. Fourth, and probably most importantly, there is the problem of motivating individual officers to share their information. Since individual officers are rewarded for making arrests, since the man who walks through the door of the police station with the defendant is the man who receives all the credit for the arrest, and since information is vital to making arrests, there are very few incentives for individual officers to share information. These barriers have proved sufficiently formidable that for all practical and analytic purposes, it is appropriate to assume that information is locked up within individual policemen, and that the stock available to them is a direct function of their personal experience.[mm]

It is worth noting that seeking to maximize the amount of local experience being brought to bear in the process of making cases conflicts with many anticorruption procedures.[nn] In general, we get nervous about policemen who have operated in the same area for a long time for the same reasons we worry about close cultural identification. We worry that the police will see too precisely and will develop personal stakes in who is arrested. As a result, they will be tempted to assume prosecutorial and judicial roles, and use evidence that would not be admitted in courts to mete out punishment or pardon offenses. Consequently, as a matter of anticorruption policy, we routinely move policemen from narcotics-enforcement operations in given geographic areas to other geographic areas or other enforcement functions. The discussion above suggests that although we undoubtedly gain a benefit from doing this, we also pay a substantial price. We leave the police vulnerable to manipulation by large numbers of informants with widely varying motives.

3.2 Information: Sources of Leads and Evidence

Much of the process of making cases involves collecting and processing information. The technologies for making cases are designed to permit the police to gather information and to turn information into evidence. The attributes of the police work force discussed above are important primarily because they affect the police capability to gather information by themselves.

In this subsection, we analyze the sources of information to the police beyond the capabilities of individual police officers to observe and infiltrate. We are concerned about complaints from private citizens, the supply of informants, procedures for disseminating information among individual policemen, and the

[mm]Overcoming this tendency to have information locked up in the minds of individual agents is both the major objectives and the major stumbling block of intelligence programs within narcotics-enforcement organizations.

[nn]For an excellent review of anticorruption strategies in the New York City Police Department, see Alan Kornblum, *The Moral Hazards* (Lexington, Mass.: D.C. Heath and Co., 1976).

supply of documentary evidence to corroborate less well-established information. In effect, we examine the supply of information in the environment in which the police pursue their case-making procedures. Depending on whether this environment is rich or poor, a given level of police effort will be more or less successful.

3.2.1 Complaints from Private Citizens. Some heroin offenses occur in public locations. Moreover, even when transactions are conducted in relatively intimate settings, the activity may be visible to bystanders. To the extent that private citizens do observe the offenses and complain to the police, and to the extent most of the police respond sufficiently quickly to observe the offense, an arrest will result. Since the private citizens have borne the entire cost of the surveillance, these arrests will be inexpensive from the point of view of the police.

Unfortunately, complaints turn out not to be a particularly valuable source of information. This is true partly because relatively modest security efforts by dealers will successfully defeat casual surveillance by private citizens. Only a few violations will be discovered, and those that are discovered are likely to involve low-level, inexperienced dealers.

However, a more important reason why complaints turn out to be unimportant is that there are large numbers of "false alarms." Perceptive, well-intentioned citizens may report too slowly or too ambiguously to allow a successful arrest. Alarmed citizens may make honest errors. Malicious citizens may harass others by filing false complaints. Of course, there are screening procedures that filter out some false alarms. For example, the police can refuse to accept anonymous or ambiguous complaints. However, even with these procedures, there will be many false alarms.[oo]

The large number of false alarms produce a harmful effect beyond the waste of police resources.[pp] Over time, the false alarms create a casual attitude towards complaints. The police stop responding. This, in turn, leads to a cynical attitude on the part of the public. The police are assumed to be indifferent or corrupt. These cynical public attitudes cut the police off from the few accurate, timely complaints that might be filed. Moreover, because the police rely on

[oo]A preliminary research effort by Jan Chaiken of the New York City Rand Institute attempted to establish screening criteria that would distinguish narcotics complaints that were relatively likely to lead to an arrest from those that were relatively unlikely to result in an arrest. He found that all narcotics complaints were very unlikely to result in arrests, and that it was very difficult to distinguish among the relative likelihood of a complaint leading to an arrest. Personal communication with Jan Chaiken, New York City Rand Institute (1972).

[pp]While I was working with the New York City Police Department, there was an ongoing debate on whether the Narcotics Division or the Patrol Bureau was responsible for narcotics complaints. Neither wanted the responsibility because both perceived responding to the complaints as a waste of resources.

public tolerance to make arrests and conduct undercover operations, these operations may eventually be hampered by a hostile public.[qq] Thus, complaints may eventually hurt rather than help narcotics-enforcement efforts.

These observations suggest an optimal policy for exploiting complaints by private citizens. The police must respond to a sufficiently large fraction of the complaints to guard against public cynicism. In addition, they should use screening procedures to filter out the complaints most likely to be false positives. However, even when these procedures are followed, the most likely benefit of these complaints is to maintain public confidence in the police. This benefit is gained at the significant cost of diverted police efforts.

3.2.2 Informants. As a matter of definition, informants differ from complainants in several ways. First, the informant's identity is always known to the police but a complainant may be anonymous. Second, the informant usually receives some tangible, personal benefit from providing information; the complainant usually offers information for free. Third, the relationship between the informant and the police is likely to last through several transactions; a complainant's contribution will typically be a one-shot deal. In short, informants have a more intimate and durable relationship with the police than complainants.

These differences in the relationships usually imply significant differences in the value of information from the different sources. Although there is great variability in the specificity, accuracy, and importance of the information from both sources, it is generally true that informants will have information that is more specific, reliable, and significant than complainants have. That this is true is largely a matter of police policy. If an informant routinely failed to provide quality information, the police would terminate their relationship—in effect, relegating a would-be informant to the status of complainant. If a complainant routinely supplied specific, reliable, and valuable information, he would quickly be cultivated as an informant.

As noted above, informants are far from a homogeneous group. Their motivations for providing information to the police vary dramatically. Dealers may inform on their competition to enlarge their own markets. Agents of a dealer may inform on the dealer to take over his operation, to revenge themselves for some insult, or to avoid punishment for some sin. Scorned lovers and disappointed relatives may inform on dealers out of spite. Finally, some people will provide information because it increases their status and power in the world: a neglected and patronized hanger-on can surprise patrons who failed to appreciate his nerve and ambition.

Similarly, the capabilities of informants will also differ. Some will enjoy the full confidence of major dealers and know current, intimate details of the man's

---

[qq]Narcotics arrests in a crowd of hostile people can be extremely dangerous for the police. The police need at least the indulgence and probably the active support of communities to make street-level arrests of drug dealers.

operation. Still others will know only insignificant violators, and have only vague and uncertain information about even these violators.

However, a fundamental distinction among informants is between "cooperating defendants" who provide information to the police to secure reductions in the charges or sentences they face, and "nondefendant informants" who provide information for a variety of other motives. The distinction is important because the quality of information from the sources differ, because the different sources support much different shares of the overall enforcement effort, and because the factors influencing the supply of informants from the different sources differ markedly. Thus, each source of informants is analyzed separately.

3.2.2.1 Cooperating Defendants. Cooperating defendants have a central role in the overall narcotics-enforcement effort. The expected value of the information from these sources is high because narcotics defendants are likely to have specific, reliable information about valuable targets. Moreover, the government has unusual leverage in securing the full cooperation of this type of informant. Consequently, any given informant of this type will be a relatively valuable resource in making cases.

In addition, these will be a relatively large number of this type of informant. Since a large number of people are arrested on narcotics offenses, since many of these will become defendant-informants, and since each defendant-informant must produce several cases to earn consideration on his charge or sentence, there will be a large supply of defendant-informants. Compared with the idiosyncratic momentary conditions that produce other types of informants, this system will routinely create large numbers of informants. Since the average quality of these informants will be high, and since there will be a large number of them, it is clear that this type of informant will account for a very large share of the total cases made by the narcotics-enforcement effort.

Given the central importance of these informants, the factors that determine the supply deserve relatively close scrutiny. We analyze three major factors: the general level of enforcement activity, options to motivate effective cooperation from the defendant-informants, and options to protect informants from exposure and retaliation. One should keep in mind that although these factors may have a major impact on the potential contributions of defendant-informants to narcotics-enforcement efforts, their actual contribution will depend on the skill and local knowledge of the investigator as well.

Level and Type of Enforcement Efforts in Previous Periods. The supply of defendant-informants to fuel future enforcement operations depends a great deal on the success of past enforcement efforts. If patrol forces have produced a large number of incidental narcotics arrests, if retrospective investigations have secured conspiracy indictments against some portion of a trafficking network, if prospective investigations have made observation-sale arrests at street levels and executed search warrants at a variety of levels, and if undercover operations have produced large numbers of defendants, the supply of defendant-informants for the future will be large and high quality. If these efforts have flagged, future efforts will be handicapped by a relatively small, low-quality supply of defendant-informants. The effect is much like the breeder reactor: some portion of the outputs of yesterday's activity can be used as an input to tomorrow's new activity.

The recursive structure of the enforcement efforts may seem to imply that a constant level of enforcement resources applied over a given set of years would result in ever-increasing output. In effect, the police would be starting every new period with lower cost, higher quality inputs. In fact, there are several conditions that constrain this apparently unlimited expansion.

First, there is a cost associated with using a defendant as an informant. One must give up the opportunity to "immobilize" the defendant by imprisonment. Obviously, the police should abandon this immediate opportunity only if the uncertain prospect of additional higher quality arrests in the future outweighs the cost of the lost opportunity. In effect, the police must decide whether a bird-in-hand is worth more or less than two different birds in the bush. Because the police are fairly risk averse (as a result of decentralized accounting schemes and assymetric loss functions for errors), the police choose too frequently to take the bird in the hand: a possibility that is attractive from a statistical view (namely, future development) will appear unattractive at the place where the decision is made—by the individual policeman who has just completed a successful operation.

Second, because the decision to use a defendant as an informant has an uncertain result, there is some chance that even if the police made decisions on the basis of the expected value of the uncertain decision, the result would be a large number of petered out leads occurring simultaneously. If this occurred (and it would occur in a certain number of periods depending on the criteria one set for deciding to pursue uncertain future possibilities and chance), the recursive structure would work against the police. A relatively poor set of defendant-informants that occurred as a result of an unexpectedly large number of failures in the previous period would hamper enforcement efforts for several periods.

Third, it is likely that police organizations have satisficing objectives rather than maximizing objectives. They control performance by establishing quotas everyone must meet. These quotas are not adjusted for the "breeder" effect. As a result, police units that strain to make the quota in one period and achieved it will find making the quota in the next period much easier. Rather than fully exploiting their new-found capabilities to exceed the established quotas, they are likely to take some of this newly developed productivity in the form of increased leisure and reduced pressure on the job. This will soon put them back to their previous level of resources where they will have to start working hard again. In the meantime, some potential will be lost forever.

Fourth, police efforts will eventually run into harder going as they forage within the distribution systems. If the police have arrested a large number of dealers, "turned them," and given them immunity for a while, the number of people remaining to be arrested will shrink. It will be increasingly difficult to find a defendant-informant who can give up one of the few remaining dealers. Similarly, the police will gradually be going up against dealers who have tougher security measures. This will increase the difficulty of capturing them. Indeed, strong efforts by major heroin dealers to control and discipline their associates will effectively dry up the stock of defendant-informants in spite of (or perhaps because of) strong showings by the police in previous periods. Thus, limits on the size of the distribution system and reactions by dealers will slow the momentum that the police develop as a result of the recursive structure of their efforts.

The role of defendants as informants in future cases provides a new dimension to consider in evaluating the effects of specific tactics and in designing an optimal portfolio of enforcement tactics. We must look not only at the specific people who get arrested and at the incentives created for dealers who remain on the street, but also at the potential of the defendants in future cases. In effect, tactics have value as devices for *penetrating* trafficking networks as well as for arresting specific individuals and creating incentives for dealers. This observation suggests that some tactics which seemed to have little value in producing direct and indirect effects may have some significant value in producing defendants for future cases. A variety of prospective investigation tactics may be riding on the success of patrol strategies. Retrospective-conspiracy investigations may be built on foundations laid by previous prospective investigations. Consequently, these tactics should be part of the overall enforcement strategy. If they were eliminated, the other tactics would be weakened. The problem is to decide which penetration tactics are relatively more valuable.

There is a lively debate about the relative value of different penetration tactics.[23] Customs often argues that patrol at the border is by far the most effective tactic. The special search authority makes it inexpensive to search large numbers of people. Moreover, major international traffickers are alleged to take close, personal responsibility for moving drugs across the border. Critics argue that the "space" that must be patrolled is sufficiently large to nullify the advantages of search authority, and that traffickers can choose to divide their drug shipments into many small lots and insulate themselves from arrest by interposing several different levels of organization between them and the "mules" carrying the contraband. Although this tactic may result in several arrests and betrayals at the border, the trafficker will be well protected by a screen of intermediaries.[24] Similar debates can be held over the value of patrols in cities and relatively undirected undercover operations.

The best that can be offered towards the resolution of this issue is several general observations about how to make the calculation. What one is looking for is tactics that produce a large number of defendants inexpensively, where the probability of any given defendant producing a valuable contribution to a large case is small, but where the probability that the defendant will be valuable is slightly higher than for defendants developed from other tactics. The key to gauging the value of a penetration tactic is the "organizational distance" between the defendants developed by a particular tactic and the major traffickers. The issue is how many cut-out men, or how many different organizational levels, must be penetrated before major traffickers are reached. This, in turn, will depend on the structure of distribution systems. Some dealers may operate with one level of aggressive agents who are vulnerable to undercover buys. They will be relatively vulnerable to undercover penetration tactics. Other dealers may operate with several levels of agents with the lowest level being cautious about their customers, but brazen in the way they conduct their business. These dealers may be vulnerable to patrol tactics. Which penetration tactics will be relatively attractive is likely to change as the distribution of types of dealers change, and as dealers react to police successes with particular penetration devices.

Motivating Cooperation. Not all people who are arrested and have some knowledge of narcotics trafficking networks will agree to cooperate with the police. Those who are afraid of other dealers, or who are bound to them by a web of obligation, or have strong antipolice ideologies, may prefer to go to jail rather than to cooperate. In general, the police capability to motivate cooperation will depend on the magnitude and credibility of the threat of imprisonment, and the procedural opportunities to make reductions in this threat contingent on effective cooperation with the police.

Probably the single most important factor influencing the willingness of defendants to cooperate with the police is the magnitude of the threat of punishment. This in turn will depend on the charges filed against the defendant, the strength of the evidence supporting these charges, and the expected sentencing decision of the judge. If a serious charge is filed, if the evidence is compelling, and if the sentence is likely to be severe, the police will have a strong hand to play. If the opposites are true, the police will have little to use in motivating cooperation.

This simple observation suggests that the choice of penetration tactics cannot be made wholly without consideration for the strength of the cases that can be made. Since insignificant charges and weak cases will fail to motivate defendants, tactics that are justified as penetration tactics, but that fail to produce strong cases, must be rejected. Police efforts to develop defendant-informants will be tightly restrained by the legal framework establishing requirements for arrests and convictions.

The observation also suggests that the sentencing policies of judges will be extremely important to the police—not because the police are deeply concerned about vengeance and the effective immobilization of arrested dealers (although they undoubtedly are concerned about these effects), but because the sentencing decision will have a major impact on the cooperation that the police receive from defendants. Thus, other things being equal, a large proportion of "hanging judges" on the bench, or legislation establishing minimum mandatory sentences, will induce greater cooperation from narcotics defendants.[2 5]

Given a strong hand for the police, the problem becomes finding a way in the complicated process of arraignment, bail, prosecution, and sentencing to maintain control over the defendant and to make the magnitude of his punishment contingent on his cooperation with the police. Current procedures are not formally designed to create these possibilities. The usual mechanism is the informal process of bargaining. Arraignment may be deferred to make the formal charges that are filed contingent on the defendant's cooperation. Alternatively, charges may be filed, but the prosecutor may delay trial and alter his sentencing recommendations depending on the cooperation of the defendant. These procedures have grave problems. Unarraigned defendants may disappear; indicted defendants may jump bail and become fugitives; the judge may refuse to honor a deal struck between prosecutor and defendant. Because the system is an informal one, problems of accountability, control, and consistency in treatment are severe. But, it provides some opportunities to motivate defendants.

Of course, we could design a system that formally incorporated incentives for cooperation. Legislation could be written to make sentences contingent on levels of cooperation. Judges could agree to postpone sentencing decisions until the defendant has delivered on promises of cooperation, or to make cooperation an explicit condition of probation. Rules forbidding judges to change sentences could be relaxed to motivate defendants who have already served some time to cooperate. Levels of cooperation could be explicitly considered in parole decisions. There are many opportunities to provide incentives for cooperation.

For the most part, we resist developing such procedures. There are two good reasons for our reluctance. First, we hate to see the coercive power of the state brought to bear directly on an individual to motivate him to do something he does not want to do. We do not have great difficulty with the idea that the state establishes limits on behavior and impersonally administers punishment to those who go beyond those limits. But we do not like the idea that some positive acts the individual does not want to perform can be extracted from him by making the state's enormous power to punish contingent on those acts. This situation reveals far too nakedly the power of the state to intervene in personal affairs.

Second, we are concerned that decisions involving charges, prosecution, and sentencing will eventually become distorted by this desire to increase the cooperation of defendants. We like to think that we decide which acts are criminal, establish penalties, and determine guilt and innocence without reference to how these decisions will affect the costs and effectiveness of criminal-justice institutions. To have these costs enter our calculation violates Learned

Hand's injunction to avoid "rationing justice." In effect, we might end up prosecuting and sentencing more harshly than the dictates of justice and protection of civil rights require, only to make the enforcement job easier and implicitly save tax revenues. This ultimately will have a corrupting influence on our perception of justice and civil rights.

Given these major concerns about making punishment contingent on cooperation, it is likely that we will continue to reject formal procedures to accomplish this objective. Consequently, the prosecution and sentencing decisions will continue to involve complicated, ad hoc negotiations among police, prosecutors, judges, and defendants. The police will be the only ones who care very strongly about motivations for cooperation. Prosecutors will be concerned about convictions. Judges will be concerned about protecting the integrity of the criminal-justice process, and making sentencing decisions that nicely balance crime-reduction objectives (achieved through incapacitation, deterrence, and rehabilitation), and different conceptions of justice (e.g., equity in sentencing, the moral value of mercy and vengeance, and the "fit" between the punishment and the crime). Given that the police interests in motivating cooperation will usually not be decisive in this situation, the police will be forced to seize opportunities rather than rely on the routine production of incentives for cooperation.

Preserving the Stock of Informants. The informants available to be used in enforcement operations will depend not only on how many people are arrested and the fraction that are motivated to cooperate, but also on how long-existing informants are preserved. If the working life of informants can be extended, they will be able to make additional cases, or the choice about which cases should be made can be optimized over a larger set of possibilities. Consequently, the productivity of any given set of informants can be increased if they can be preserved for extended periods.

A variety of events not under the control of the police can intervene to end the working life of an informant. The dealers he knows may be arrested, go out of business, or leave the area. They may even come to suspect the informant for incorrect reasons. Anything that separates informants from positions and relationships where they used to receive reliable information will eliminate their value.

However, the most common factors influencing the working life of the informant are the efforts the police take and the skills they employ in seeking to protect the informants from exposure. If the police keep an informant's arrest and cooperation secret; if they can create uncertainty among arrested dealers by suggesting plausible, alternative explanations for the arrest of the dealer;[rr] and if

---

[rr]For the importance of providing plausible alternative explanations of how one came to know of an enemy's action to protect a valuable, continuing source of information, see F.W. Winterbotham, *The Ultra Secret* (New York: Harper and Row, 1974).

they can avoid situations where the court is forced to order that the identity of an informant be revealed, informants can be protected and their working life extended.

Note that legal rules of evidence constitute the greatest threats to expose informants. Defense attorneys in narcotics will routinely file discovery motions to learn the identity of informants and force them to testify. They do this partly to discredit the informants' testimony and partly to raise the cost to the police of prosecuting the case. Judges will order disclosure if the testimony of the informant can make a material contribution to the determination of guilt and innocence.[26] To guard against this possibility, the police will try to keep informants from being intimate participants in the circumstances surrounding the arrest, and to collect a great deal of evidence that resolves issues the informant might be called in to resolve. Such moves make it possible for judges to rule against defense discovery motions and preserve the anonymity of informants. Thus, police skill in keeping the identity of defendants secret and in arranging arrests so judges will rule against discovery motions is the key to extending the working life of informants.

There is an important effect of failing to protect informants beyond the loss of the future potential of the particular informant. Exposed informants may suffer consequences beyond being shut off from information about narcotics trafficking. They, and their relatives, may be threatened, beaten, or killed.[ss] If informants are injured as a result of exposure, the willingness of other defendants to cooperate will be diminished. In effect, the example of exposed and injured informants instructs defendants considering cooperation. To reduce this effect, the police must have to offer various forms of protection to exposed informants. They can guard the informants, place them in protective custody, move them to new areas, and/or provide new identities to the informants. Such actions are very expensive.[tt] Given the importance of protecting exposed informants and the cost of this protection, preserving the anonymity of informants takes on additional significance.

Thus, the supply of defendant-informants will be determined by previous enforcement efforts, the magnitude of the threat of imprisonment and the possibilities of making this threat contingent on cooperation, and the skill of the police in preserving the anonymity of informants and protecting exposed informants. Note that these factors rely more on government authority than expenditures of government resources. In this, the defendant-informants resemble conscript soldiers—a resource is provided to the government at a price substantially below its market value as a result of the exercise of coercive government

[ss]In spite of serious efforts, I have been unable to discover how often informants are physically harmed by narcotics dealers. Records of informants' status and activity are neither comprehensive nor readily accessible. The usual excuse is security requirements.

[tt]The U.S. Marshal's Service spends $4.0 million per year to protect federal witnesses: *The Budget of the United States Government: Fiscal Year 1977*, p. 498.

authority. Defendant-informants resemble conscript soldiers in another respect: they fight most of the battles and take a large share of the casualties. The war could not be fought without them.

3.2.2.2 Nondefendant Informants. Nondefendant informants play a much less central role in narcotics-enforcement efforts. If dealers are careful to conceal their activities and make heavy investments in efforts to maintain the loyalty of intimate friends and associates, it will be a rare event when a nondefendant has both reliable information and a motivation to supply it to the police. Still, the event does occur and on occasion has produced some very significant cases.

The supply of nondefendant information will be determined largely by factors outside the control of the police. The motives are likely to be personal, idiosyncratic, and momentary. A wife gets angry; a neglected associate becomes resentful; an aggressive competitor plays a dangerous game with the police; a "buff" happens to be in the right place to overhear some significant information. These are the situations that will turn up an erratic supply of good nondefendant informants.

The police have a limited number of devices for increasing this supply. Basically all they can do is offer money and protection. If the police are very effective, they can make these offers consistently to key people over a long period to maximize the chance of exploiting some momentary condition. However, to motivate knowledgeable nondefendants to become informants, one must offer relatively large amounts of money and very reliable protection. Since these services are expensive, and since taxpayers have never been enthusiastic about paying thousands of dollars to "shady characters" for information about narcotics trafficking, the police have not made very persuasive offers to very many people. Apparently, taxpayers prefer the police to use the cheaper and more effective authority of the state to motivate cooperation from people who know narcotics dealers.

3.2.3 Intelligence Systems. Information from complainants and informants is usually provided to individual policemen or to small groups of policemen. It is not necessarily available to other police, and the information may perish.

The obvious implication of these observations is that individual policemen will be working with only a tiny fraction of the total information available to the organization as a whole. Consequently, there is a reasonable chance that less than optimal decisions will be made about which leads to follow-up, and how to develop them. Of course, the situation is not quite as bad as I have suggested. Complaints will survive in recordings of dispatchers' calls. Cases that result in arrests will be at least partly documented by investigative reports. These reports are likely to be cross-indexed by name. However, it is safe to say that these data bases will usually contain only a fraction of the information known to investigators, and that it will be difficult for individual police to retrieve information from these sources where they need it.

The potential value of making more efficient use of the information available to enforcement organizations has attracted investment in intelligence systems. The definition of intelligence systems in enforcement organizations is slightly different than in intelligence organizations.[uu] Intelligence systems in intelligence organizations include systems for collecting, analyzing, and disseminating information. In enforcement organizations, intelligence systems usually include only increased expenditures for analyzing and disseminating information. Basic enforcement operations usually include significant collection systems (e.g., complaints and informants) and some modest analytic efforts (e.g., individual investigators putting together cases from recollection, reviews of files, and conversations with other investigators). Consequently, in an enforcement organization, it is not necessary to put the whole system together: one can rely on reasonably good collection. It is only analysis and dissemination that are likely to be weak and require additional investment.

The most rudimentary form of an intelligence system is a cross-indexed name file of completed cases.[vv] To the extent that the files are complete, to the extent that investigators can gain access to them, and to the extent that the case files can be searched quickly for information about a given individual, this system can provide increased information to investigators evaluating a lead. This is by far the most common intelligence system.

A slightly more sophisticated intelligence system includes not only names involved in past cases, but names involved in current cases as well. This requires a slightly increased investment in collection efforts. Investigators must report names involved in cases that are ongoing. If such a capability exists, the police can use it not only to increase the information available to other investigations, but also to improve coordination. They can discover when two units are working the same case. The improved coordination implies savings not only because duplicated investigations are eliminated, but also because the chance of interference and premature disclosure of the investigation is reduced. The case can be developed to the fullest possible degree. Of course, these systems can be defeated. Police can wait to disclose that they are working on a case or announce that they are working on hundreds of cases. However, with a few administrative controls, these systems can be valuable within a given enforcement organization. They are even more valuable when used among several enforcement organizations.[27]

These rudimentary intelligence systems involve no investment in analysis—merely slightly increased efforts to preserve and disseminate a limited portion of the information available to the organization. More sophisticated intelligence

[uu]For more detail on intelligence systems within DEA, see "Testimony of Mark H. Moore," in U.S. Congress, House of Representatives, Select Committee on Intelligence, "Hearings on U.S. Intelligence Agencies and Activities: Domestic Intelligence Programs," 94th Congress, 1st Session, November 1975.

[vv]Examples of such systems includes DEA's NADDIS system, and the U.S. Customs' TECS system.

systems involve increased investments in analysis. The basic idea is that raw data from investigative reports should be reviewed and related on dimensions other than simply names. Common addresses, telephone numbers, operating procedures, ethnic characteristics, prison experience, coincidences of time and space, even mannerisms, if discovered, can establish connections between previously unrelated cases and point to directions for further development. Slight elaborations of this idea would involve the analysts in expanded collection activities through debriefing of investigators or through direct contact with informants. One can even imagine a sophisticated system for calibrating and indicating the reliability of specific pieces of information. If all of these capabilities existed, the following benefits might be expected: improved coordination among individual investigating units, additional leads developed from previously unnoticed information in case files, and a fuller development of existing cases.ww

Unfortunately, these capabilities are not free. One must support specially trained people to do nothing but sift through case files. In addition, one must pay to maintain very flexible filing systems and elaborate, decentralized communication systems between investigators and the files. Because the files contain sensitive information, large amounts of security must be purchased through technical and procedural safeguards. Finally, because it takes time to reorganize the existing files of the organization, a certain period will elapse before operational benefits are secured.

Given the costs of such sophisticated systems, the magnitude of the potential benefits is very important. Unfortunately, the marginal benefits of investments in intelligence systems that expand analysis and dissemination capabilities are uncertain. Since few enforcement organizations have made large investments, one might assume that the potential benefits are small. However, one can explain the failure to invest in intelligence systems as a result of bureaucratic constraints rather than a close calculation revealing that the investment would not be cost-effective.

There is a basic hostility towards intelligence functions in enforcement organizations. Although the exact reasons for this hostility remain somewhat obscure, one can point to a few major features of the situation. The functions of an intelligence analyst are almost wholly included in the functions of an investigator. No investigator would be happy to admit that he had not mined the files of his organization for every nugget of relevant information. Consequently, investigators think they should be doing what the intelligence analysts are doing, and also believe that they can perform this function more effectively and less expensively than analysts. A corollary of this contempt is the fear that the analysts may do the job better than the agents. There is a fear that the analysts will discover things the agent did not notice, or suggest things that agent would never take seriously, or steal credit for cases that agents helped to make. The

---

wwFor problems in developing an elaborate system, see Mark H. Moore, "Testimony Before the Select Committee on Intelligence."

possibility that intelligence analysts could embarrass, propose to guide, or steal credit from agents is particularly galling to agents because the intelligence analysts face no risks. They do not know how hard it is to debrief a defendant or crash a door. They sit secure in their offices to embarrass and guide street agents who risk their neck and work long and irregular hours. These bureaucratic factors may have prevented enforcement organizations from investing in intelligence systems even though their productivity could have been increased by such investments. The problem is not resources; it is a managerial problem of changing the style of an organization.

3.2.4 Documents and Records. The sources of information analyzed above are important primarily because they provide leads for police investigators. To be valuable in prosecutions, these leads must be turned into persuasive evidence. Of course, the most important resource for turning leads into a solid case is police manpower employed in any of the investigative strategies.

However, there is an important external source of information that can be used for evidentiary purposes. This source is the enormous volume of records held by private companies and the government, which record some portion of the activity of people who own telephones, travel by commercial transportation, stay in public hotels, have bank accounts, and pay taxes. These records preserve information about private actions that may be related to criminal activity. The police can never begin with this information: the volume is simply too large. However, if they have information or testimony that describes an event which would have created such records, the existence of the records can powerfully corroborate the information or testimony.

The supply of this information to the police will depend on the record-keeping practices of the companies and agencies involved and their willingness to provide records to the police. If hotels and airlines destroy their records at the end of one year rather than five, a stock of potentially valuable evidence will be destroyed. If banks and government agencies either refuse or are prohibited from making these records available to the police, potentially valuable evidence will be lost or become much more expensive to gather. The most vivid and frustrating example of how tightly these practices and policies will constrain police efforts is the example of anonymous, numbered bank accounts in Switzerland. If these records became public, it is conceivable that cases against major traffickers could be made much more easily. In the immediate future, privacy legislation may have a major impact on the supply of this information to the police.

This source of information is important primarily for retrospective-conspiracy cases. As indicated above, a major problem in developing these cases will be corroborating the testimony of participants in heroin transactions. Since these records are often the most reliable and valuable source for documenting the case, changes in the supply of these records to the police will force them to shift to other enforcement strategies and tactics.

3.3 Capital Equipment

Although manpower and information are probably the most important resources available to narcotics-enforcement organizations, they also rely on capital equipment. Cars, guns, radios, binoculars, helicopters, tape recorders, "bugs," "wire taps," electronic beepers, and computers all play a role in narcotics enforcement. As with all capital equipment, the important question is to what extent the equipment can economize on human labor either by increasing the quality of the output or by reducing requirements for human inputs. Moreover, the existence of capital equipment raises the issue of research and development. What new pieces of equipment could be developed that would dramatically improve performance or reduce costs of enforcement efforts?

In this subsection, we briefly examine capital equipment designed to increase police capability in three basic functions: surveillance, recording events for evidentiary purposes, and protecting investigators. In each of these areas we look at available equipment, discover the ways in which the equipment can influence enforcement operations, and consider the possibility of new devices that will dramatically influence productivity. The process resembles a very crude analysis of technical requirements.[xx]

3.3.1 Surveillance Equipment. A very large fraction of police work can be described as surveillance. Patroling, setting up stake-outs, tapping telephones, following suspects, and bugging individuals and rooms are common surveillance tasks. Because these activities consume a large portion of the police efforts, and because a great deal of surveillance technology exists, there is a strong presumption that technical (capital) equipment can make a major contribution in this area. To analyze the potential contribution of current or future technology in this area, it is necessary (1) to develop a crude analytic structure for defining surveillance requirements, (2) to get a feel for how technology will help meet these requirements, and (3) to develop rough assumptions about how often different kinds of requirements will appear in operational settings.

A surveillance task can generally be described in terms of the amount of territory and time that has to be covered, the range of activity that must be observed within the spaces of time and territory, and the discrimination that must be achieved for the surveillance to be useful. In these terms, a *stake-out* could be described as a surveillance system designed to observe gross physical activity at a single location. It would not overhear conversations, could not easily move if suspects moved, and could not reliably distinguish a handshake from a heroin transaction or a meeting between a suspect and an innocent friend from a meeting between a suspect and a conspirator who resembled the innocent

---

[xx]For an excellent example of a formal requirements study for vehicle tracking technology, see Lee Afflerback et al., "Vehicle Tracking and Locating Systems," The Mitre Corporation, 1974.

friend. The usual moving surveillance would be similar to the stake-out except for the fact that it would cover more space. A wired undercover agent would allow surveillance of conversations with very good discrimination over a wide range of physical locations. In general, the broader the range of activity that can be observed, the greater the territory that can be covered, and the more precise the discrimination that can be achieved, the more effective the surveillance system.

There are three factors that keep the police from using very effective surveillance systems. An obvious factor is cost: only a limited amount of men and equipment will be available for any given surveillance task. To some extent, the cost of fielding a very comprehensive surveillance system for the critical periods will force the police to do more homework. Crude surveillance by several men can be mounted to learn the habits of a dealer. As a result, a given surveillance force can be efficiently used at the culmination of the operation: teams can be positioned more effectively; crude aspects of a dealer's behavior can be interpreted more sensitively. If this option is not available, the police may be forced to accept higher probabilities of failure in the surveillance task.

A second obvious factor is legal constraints. Many kinds of surveillance must be authorized by courts.[yy] Problems of inadequate probable cause, or timing, prevent the police from employing very sensitive surveillance systems. Moreover, the courts may place restrictions on the use of surveillance systems that raise the costs of using them to levels that can no longer be managed within the cost constraint.

A third factor, which is less obvious, is the requirement to conceal the surveillance from the suspect. A policeman following a dealer within the range of normal conversation is a very broad, comprehensive, and sensitive system. The only problem is that the dealer is likely to discover he is under surveillance and avoid producing any evidence of his illegal activity. The requirement for covertness implies that surveillance systems must be disguised and kept far away from the dealer. Maintaining covertness usually has the effect of reducing the comprehensiveness and sensitivity of the surveillance systems.

In general, then, the police must set up surveillance systems capable of achieving a required level of comprehensiveness and sensitivity within the constraints of existing resources, legal restrictions, and requirements for covertness. The most appropriate trade-offs among these different attributes will differ for different operations. Moreover, the physical setting of the operation will rule out some surveillance systems and give others a comparative advantage. Thus, surveillance systems will be designed to fit within the requirements of specific operations in specific settings.

Although the variety of requirements make generalizations treacherous, it is

---

[yy]It is well established that extremely intrusive devices such as wiretaps and bugs require court authorization. It is less clear whether less sensitive devices such as electronic sensors, radars, and tags require court authorization.

possible to see the substantial contribution of different pieces of technical equipment.

The basic surveillance unit is plainclothesmen in a single, unmarked vehicle. The surveillance capabilities of this unit are strikingly limited. Activity on the street can be observed, but not with great sensitivity. Moreover, it cannot be observed for long periods without attracting attention. Activity within buildings remains beyond reach unless the plainclothesmen are willing to get out and walk. Such action may increase the probability of being discovered. If the dealer moves in a vehicle, he can be covered, but only with great difficulty. A dealer can lose himself in traffic if the police stay far back to avoid burning the surveillance; or he can force the police to expose the surveillance by making odd maneuvers that force the police to follow suit or lose him (e.g., going down one-way streets the wrong way or making sudden U turns or speeding up). Thus, a reasonably alert and discreet dealer can easily defeat a single unit surveillance.

One can add to the capabilities of this basic surveillance unit simply by adding surveillance units. Additional units increase the probability of a successful surveillance partly through redundancy, and partly by making it easier to disguise the surveillance operation. The system is insured against random errors by the fact that several units must fail simultaneously for the entire surveillance to fail. Frequent changes in the surveillance units will make it more difficult for a trafficker to pick a continuous surveillance out of the background activity. Thus, multiunit surveillance systems have much greater capabilities for comprehensiveness, sensitivity, and discreteness than single-unit systems.

Note that the basic piece of equipment required in these simple surveillance systems are vehicles. Moreover, the vehicles are fairly vulnerable components of the system.[zz] The vehicles must be inconspicuous in a variety of settings and capable of keeping up with the vehicles of traffickers. Maintaining a sufficiently diverse set of vehicles is an expensive proposition.[aaa] Surveillance vans, undercover vehicles, even helicopters and slow airplanes may be required in different settings. Moreover, the stock must keep changing to keep the vehicles from being commonly known as police vehicles. These requirements put a strain on police budget and procurement systems, which are geared up to buy large fleets of standard, heavy sedans from United States manufacturers. (Indeed, it is likely that these plain, heavy sedans, which looked suspicious in the 1960s, will look increasingly suspicious in a world of rising gasoline prices.)

[zz]The area of vehicle procurement provides a classic example of a bureaucratic foul-up. For the purposes of covert surveillance, the police would like to have many different kinds of vehicles (to avoid becoming identified with one type of vehicle), or should own the kind of vehicles owned by many other people (to provide background noise), or both. However, procurement policies encourage large orders of a standard product. Moreover, one year, a procurement officer was offered a special price on cars that had not been sold. Consequently, the procurement officer, doing extremely well by his lights, ordered a fleet of unsold cars all of which turned out to be lime-green—a situation that uniquely identified the police with some rare vehicles.

[aaa]This problem is remarkably similar analytically to the problem of maintaining sufficient diversity among police undercover personnel.

The full exploitation of multiunit surveillance systems requires radio communication as well as several units. Although communication systems increase the degree of coordination possible among the units, communication among police vehicles is potentially vulnerable to monitoring by dealers. Technical devices to insure "voice privacy" are sometimes considered. But such devices are extremely expensive. Moreover, the use of codes in radio communications may achieve the same degree of covertness at substantially lower costs.

Finally, these vehicle-surveillance systems can be improved by the development of electronic "tags" to be attached to suspect vehicles.[28] Current tags allow the police to maintain a surveillance with fewer vehicles and greater discreetness than is possible without the tags. Future systems might allow the police to monitor the movements of suspect vehicles without any commitment of men or vehicles. Note that the most vulnerable aspect of these systems is the installation of the tag. Traffickers may discover and silence the tag. Worse yet, they can discover it and use the tagged vehicle as a decoy, which attracts the attention of the complacent police while the traffickers operate in some other area.[bbb]

Thus, capital equipment such as specialized vehicles; effective, secure communications systems; and electronic tagging devices can reduce labor requirements, or increase the effectiveness of surveillance systems that monitor gross physical activity over larger pieces of territory. Since most enforcement operations have these surveillance requirements at some stage, the amount and quality of this type of capital equipment will have an important effect on the effectiveness of enforcement operations. Note, however, the limitations on these surveillance systems. Large chunks of territory are denied to them; maintaining the systems over time is extremely expensive; and they are capable of monitoring only gross physical activity.

Other forms of technical equipment can be used to expand the police surveillance capabilities. The most important devices are electronic devices that allow the police to overhear conversations as well as observe activity. In addition, these devices can reach beyond the public streets—penetrating relatively private and intimate locations.

Among these devices, wiretaps are the most common, but also the most limited. Legal obstacles make them difficult to install and expensive to maintain.[ccc] Moreover, once in place, they cannot be moved. They simply

---

[bbb]This is another application of the principle developed in Irving Goffman, *Strategic Interaction* (Philadelphia: University of Pennsylvania Press, 1969). The more one relies on a particular piece of information, the more vulnerable he becomes to counterfeits of that information.

[ccc]Currently, wiretaps must be monitored continuously to turn off recording equipment when conversations occur that were not within the scope of the warrant. This places an enormous drain on manpower. Moreover, if the conversations are in a foreign language, the requirements may drain a particularly scarce resource. A DEA wiretap operation in Florida in 1972 absorbed so many Spanish-speaking personnel that nearly all undercover operations against Spanish-speaking traffickers came to a halt.

monitor phone conversations from one location. Consequently, wiretaps can be defeated by simple codes or by substituting other phones or other forms of communication.

Putting transmitters on individuals dramatically increases the scope of the surveillance possibilities. Nonphone conversations can be overheard; the individual can move if the violator moves. In spite of the gains in coverage, there are problems with this surveillance system. First, there are technical problems with transmitters that are hidden close to the body.[ddd] Effective concealment dramatically reduces the strength and clarity of the signals. Second, such systems obviously require the cooperation of the wearer of the transmitter. This usually means that the police have succeeded in inserting someone they trust directly into the criminal activity. If he is completely trustworthy and directly observes the offenses, the transmitter is redundant: his testimony will serve the same purpose. If he is completely unreliable and the police have no way of observing him directly, one must worry about the authenticity of the transmitted messages: one cannot guarantee that the man with the transmitter has not given signals to the offenders that changes their actions. Thus, these transmitters will be used primarily to corroborate police testimony rather than be the sole basis of evidence. As a result, they reduce the requirements for police manpower less than might ordinarily be assumed.

Electronic devices for overhearing conversations increase police capabilities for surveillance, but only with substantial additional expenditures on manpower as well. These technical devices, then, increase efficiency not so much by reducing manpower inputs as by increasing the effectiveness of a given level of expenditure for gathering evidence.

3.3.2 Recording Devices and Forensic Tests. The surveillance systems described above are designed to increase police capabilities to observe criminal events directly. Such systems have value in making cases only if police testimony is credible. If police testimony is not widely believed, increasing police capability to observe criminal offenses will have relatively little impact on their ability to make cases against traffickers.

This observation suggests another critical role for technical equipment—as recording devices that produce objective evidence to corroborate police testimony. Photographs, tape recordings, procedures for disclosing latent fingerprints, devices that register distinctive characteristics of seized drug samples and reveal common origins for the different samples—all have the important capability to corroborate police testimony with physical evidence.

Such devices are extremely valuable in narcotics-enforcement operations precisely because most narcotics cases are so often based on the uncorroborated

[ddd]Dr. Donald Sheldon, chief of the Advanced Technology Division of DEA's Office of Science and Technology, explains that from a technical-communication point of view, the "body is a huge bag of water" that creates problems for electronic transmission.

testimony of the police. Most narcotics cases contain four substantial pieces of evidence: the testimony of the police, the testimony of the defendant, the drugs that are seized or purchased, and the previous record of the defendant. Neither physical evidence (other than the drugs) nor corroborating testimony by disinterested participants is often presented. Consequently, the cases turn critically on the credibility of police testimony.

Unfortunately, because cases where corroborating evidence exists are so rare, the courts have little opportunity to gauge independently the credibility of the police testimony. Moreover, police testimony in these cases tends to become stylized and repetitive. Consequently, since the courts hear the same stories repeatedly and since they rarely have independent corroboration, they are apt to form impressions of police credibility from the general reputation of the police. If the police have a bad general reputation, the police testimony will be ineffective. The only way for the police to counteract this general deterioration of their credibility is to produce independent means of corroborating their testimony. Thus, technical recording devices and forensic procedures are absolutely vital to narcotics-enforcement procedures—particularly when they are under general attack. A few cases with corroborating physical evidence can have a dramatic effect on the credibility of police witnesses.

A major reason the police have not used these devices widely is that there are substantial dangers in using this evidence as well as opportunities. Blurred photographs; conflicting laboratory findings; and muffled, coded conversations heard on tapes may create ambiguity rather than resolve it. This means that the precision and quality of these recording systems must be very great for them to be useful in specific cases.

Two major problems emerge in trying to insure very high-quality recording systems. The first is technical limitations on the equipment. It is difficult to take clear photos at night, to get clear recordings of people who mumble, and to pick out unambiguous, distinctive characteristics of drug processing or packaging. A more important problem is human failure to exploit the full potential of the technical systems. This happens as a result of poor maintenance of equipment, poor judgment about when to use the equipment, or poor technical skills in using the equipment.[eee] If there are no high-quality technical specialists in enforcement organizations, or if they are not sufficiently available to be conveniently employed in operations that suddenly develop, these human error problems will guarantee the failure of the technical equipment.

3.3.3 Devices for Protecting Police.
The last area in which technical devices may make a substantial contribution to narcotics-enforcement efforts is in the area of

---

[eee]A consultant's analysis of DEA's inability to develop and use technical equipment effectively placed a large part of the blame on inadequate maintenance and technical advice *in the field*. Personal communication with Dr. Sidney Gottlieb, technology consultant to the Drug Enforcement Administration.

safety and protection. Bullet-proof vests and alarms are major devices in this area. In addition, effective communication systems can make a substantial contribution to the safety and protection of the police. The major benefits of these devices are improvements in the morale of the police and a broadening of the police capability to confront traffickers. Without these capabilities, the police would refuse some encounters and transactions that would produce cases.[fff] With these capabilities, the police can be more aggressive in seeking encounters and transactions with dealers.

3.4 Money to Purchase Evidence and Information

If manpower, information, and technical equipment are the cogs of the narcotics-enforcement machine, money to purchase evidence and information (PE/PI money) is the oil that keeps the machine running smoothly. One can observe the small but essential role of this money in two different areas: running undercover operations and recruiting nondefendant informants.

It will be recalled that undercover operations play a major role in narcotics enforcement. They bring a wide array of defendants into the police net. They produce very important indirect effects. The defendants that are produced may become valuable inputs to future cases. In addition, it will be recalled that the most effective kinds of undercover operations involve multiple, escalating buys from several dealers stretched over a long perod. It should be apparent that these undercover operations depend on a supply of money for the police to use in the undercover buys. Moreover, since the arrests will frequently occur long after the buy has been made, much of the money will not be recoverable.[ggg] Thus, there must be a large stock of buy money to permit the fullest possible use of undercover operations. Constraints on this kind of money will simply stop undercover operations—forcing a shift to other tactics.

It will also be recalled that occasionally nondefendant informants will have valuable information to offer. They will only do so if they are offered money and guaranteed protection. Although it is unlikely that money will ever be as important as threats of imprisonment in motivating cooperation from informants (simply because it is hard to pay enough money to be an effective equivalent to the threat of imprisonment), money will occasionally be the

[fff]Interviews with narcotics detectives in New York City indicated that most were reluctant to conduct operations in houses at night. This reluctance, although certainly understandable, conferred a virtual immunity on "house connections." If the police could have been made to feel safer, this immunity would have been stripped away.

[ggg]Typically, less than 5 percent of DEA's purchase evidence-purchase information money is recovered. U.S. Congress, House of Representatives, Committee on Appropriations, Sub-committee on Departments of State, Justice, and Commerce, The Judiciary and Related Agencies, "Hearings on Appropriations for 1976" 94th Congress, 1st Session, 1976, p. 860.

inducement that is needed for specific informants with specific pieces of information to be supplied. Thus, money plays a vital role in determining the scale of undercover operations, and a smaller, but occasionally very important, role in influencing the supply of information to the police.

In spite of the importance of this kind of money, the supply to the police has been very tightly constrained. Indeed, only the federal-enforcement agencies have had PE/PI money routinely available to them in large quantities.[hhh] The primary reason for tightly controlling the supply of PE/PI money is a profound public unease about the implications and potential problems associated with the use of the money. It simply seems wrong to use hard-earned tax revenues to pay quasi-criminals who cooperate with the police or to buy narcotics from criminals. For some reason, we prefer the idea of using tax revenues to buy additional police rather than to help the existing set of police conduct more effective operations to procure evidence against narcotics dealers. Moreover, there is a fear that these expenditures may provide incentives for illegal dealers to expand drug markets or create new capabilities.[iii] Finally, the availability of this money often seems like an open invitation to police corruption. The police can create records indicating pay-offs to nonexistent informants and keep the money for themselves. The difficulty of keeping track and gauging the credibility of informants makes verification of the transactions difficult and expensive. Faced with these attitudes and problems, legislators and police administrators have been reluctant to provide PE/PI money.

In spite of these potential problems, denying money to purchase evidence and information to the police is probably an irrational policy. The money can be made available to the police under conditions that minimize the potential problems. For example, the total amount expended by the police in local markets can be kept small relative to the size of the market to avoid becoming a major component of demand and providing stimulation to local distribution networks. Record-keeping and inspection procedures can be established and maintained to insure that the police do not steal the money. Effective intelligence and supervisory systems can insure that undercover operations and purchases of information will be targeted against violators whose importance justifies expenditures of loose money for evidence or information. If PE/PI money were provided under these conditions, the benefits of the resource could be secured in enforcement operations without paying the prices usually associated with using this resource.

Note, also, that failing to provide PE/PI money under these conditions also produces undesirable effects. Part of the cost is that police are denied some

[hhh]In 1972 the New York City Police Department increased the amount of buy money from $86,000 to $840,000. At that time, they were the only city police department spending more than $50,000 for buy money. See New York City Police Department, "Activity of the Narcotics Division for 1972," Internal Memorandum of the Deputy Commissioner for Organized Crime Control, No. 90-73.

[iii]For an example of this "stimulating" process, see *Newsday, The Heroin Trail*, p. 230.

kinds of tactics and resources that are valuable in making cases. But another part of the cost is that the police will use other methods to provide the resources they need.[jjj] They may keep part of seized narcotics to pay off informants. Or, they will use their own money to pay informants. These possibilities increase as the public puts pressure on the police for more effective cases and denies them basic resources to exploit specific tactics.

Thus, as in the case of technical equipment, it is not appropriate simply to provide PE/PI money. In addition, one must buy supporting systems to insure that the money will be effectively used. Failing to provide money implies that the police will be denied a very important tactic and a small amount of information. Failing to provide money and continued pressure on the police for effective enforcement implies that the police will develop other undesirable ways of rewarding informants. Supplying the money but failing to insure adequate controls implies a host of ineffective, shady uses of tax revenues. In this situation, the best policy is almost certainly to provide the money with adequate controls.

4.0 Summary: The General Shape of the Production Function for Narcotics Enforcement

A useful way to summarize the analysis of enforcement operations is to describe the general shape of the production function. We define the outputs, compare the technologies in terms of their outputs and resource requirements, and explore the relationships among the various technologies. The section concludes with some tentative conclusions about which constraints on current operations seem to be particularly costly.

4.1 The Outputs: Arrests, Incentives, and Informants

The government commits authority and resources to enforce narcotics laws. The direct effects of these commitments is a set of cases against alleged heroin dealers. The set of cases can differ in terms of the total number of defendants, the distribution of levels and types of dealers among the arrested defendants, and the strength of the cases against the dealers. To the extent that these cases result in arrests, successful prosecutions and convictions; and to the extent that this process effectively immobilizes the individual involved, some portion of the throughput capability of distribution systems will be eliminated.[kkk]

[jjj]For evidence that police use their own funds or divert narcotics to users to motivate cooperation, see Shecter with Phillips, *On the Pad*, p. 148.

[kkk]There is some reason to believe that arrests fail to immobilize traffickers. Indeed, a DEA study indicated that 45 percent of a group of traffickers on bail were implicated in postarrest traffickers. Office of Congressional Relations, "Report on Post Arrest Drug Trafficking," Drug Enforcement Administration (Washington, D.C.: U.S. Department of Justice, 1974).

Beyond these direct effects, narcotics-enforcement effects have two additional effects on the narcotics-enforcement system. First, enforcement efforts create incentives for dealers to invest in defensive strategies. Which dealers react, and the specific defensive strategies they adopt, will depend a great deal on the scale and shape of enforcement efforts. Second, enforcement efforts create defendant-informants who can be exploited to penetrate trafficking networks more deeply than would otherwise be possible. In effect, the results of enforcement efforts in one period alter the potential of enforcement action in the next period.

Thus, narcotics-enforcement efforts immobilize a certain population of traffickers, establish incentives for dealers left on the street to adopt defensive strategies, and influence the potential of narcotics-enforcement efforts in subsequent periods. Since each of these effects is an important component of the output of enforcement efforts, an enforcement strategy should be chosen that maximizes some combination of these effects.

4.2 Technologies and Resource Requirements

A variety of strategies and tactics are available for the police to utilize in making cases against heroin dealers. Table 3-2 summarizes the potential outputs of the various tactics and identifies unusually large or small requirements for specific resources. Thus, Table 3-2 indicates that patrol strategies produce a limited number of low-level defendants; create incentives for dealers to be discrete in public locations; usually fail to provide valuable defendant-informants; and require unusual amounts of manpower, vehicles, and communication systems. The patrol strategy economizes on informants. Retrospective-conspiracy strategies produce a small number of high-level defendants; create incentives for high-level dealers to discipline their associates; provide substantial opportunities for additional cases; and require unusual amounts of manpower, intelligence analysis, and informants. The strategy economizes on technical equipment. Buy and bust tactics produce a large number of defendants, create incentives for dealers to avoid customers whom they do not know (and have characteristics that the police can imitate), and produce defendants who are occasionally valuable in future operations. The tactic requires large amounts of PE/PI money, but economizes on manpower, informants, and intelligence.

4.3 Interdependence among the Technologies

A close review of Table 3-2 reveals the complementary relationships among the diverse tactics. The tactics strike at different levels and kinds of dealers. They create somewhat different incentives for dealers who are not arrested. In addition, since many of the tactics depend on (or are helped by) defendant-informants, and since a defendant produced by any given tactic can be used in

Table 3-2
Summary of Outputs and Resource Requirements for Enforcement Strategies and Tactics

Strategies and Tactics	"Outputs" of Strategy		
	Arrested Defendants	Incentive Effects	Value of Defendants as Informants
Patrol strategies	Large number; low level or careless dealers; weak cases.	General incentives to behave discreetly	Fraction of valuable defendants is small, but large absolute numbers
Retrospective-conspiracy investigations	Small number; intermediate-high levels; difficult cases	Motivates high-level dealers to screen and discipline	Very valuable
Prospective investigations			
Observation-sale cases	Small number; low-level, careless dealers; weak cases	Motivates low-level dealers to change routines and conceal transactions	Occasionally valuable
Search-warrant cases	Uncertain number; many low-level but some high-level; good cases	Motivates dealers to hide and dispossess heroin; discipline agents	Occasionally valuable
Buy and bust cases	Small-moderate number; low-level aggressive dealers; weak cases	Motivates retail dealers to screen customers	Occasionally valuable
Extended undercover operations	Small-moderate number; low-intermediate levels; strong cases	Motivates dealers at all levels to screen customers and invest in small markets	Valuable

several different tactics, each tactic can make a substantial contribution to the effectiveness of other tactics. Given these close, complementary relationships among tactics, the strategic problem for the police is to choose an optimal *portfolio* of expenditures on *diverse* tactics rather than choose any single tactic.

4.4 The Availability of Resources

Since the different tactics make differential claims on specific resources, the relative availability of the resources can have a profound impact on the portfolio

Strategies and Tactics	"Inputs" Required		
		Personnel	
	Skills	Cultural Identification	Local Knowledge
Patrol strategies	Vigilance	—	Valuable
Retrospective-conspiracy investigations	"Gumshoe"	—	—
Prospective investigations			
Observation-sale cases	Vigilance	—	Valuable
Search-Warrant cases	"Gumshoe"	—	Valuable
Buy and bust cases	Undercover	Very valuable	—
Extended undercover operations	Undercover	Very valuable	Very valuable

of tactics that is ultimately chosen. Constraints on money to purchase evidence combined with a plentiful amount of manpower will shift the portfolio in the direction of patrol strategies and retrospective investigation and away from undercover operations. Plentiful supplies of money to purchase evidence and constraints on men and informants will force the portfolio toward buy and bust operations. Note that some of the factors influencing the availability of the resources are beyond the effective control of the government; some can be purchased at a money price by the government; some can be influenced by changes in *government* policy, but not necessarily by changes in *police* policy; some can be influenced by changes in police policy, but not by changes in the

Table 3-2 (Cont.)

Strategies and Tactics	"Inputs" Required		
		Information	
			Informants
	Complaints	Defendant	Non-defendant
Patrol strategies	Valuable	—	—
Retrospective-conspiracy investigations	—	Very valuable	Occasionally valuable
Prospective investigations			
Observation-sale cases	Occasionally valuable	Occasionally valuable	Occasionally valuable
Search-warrant cases	—	Valuable	Occasionally valuable
Buy and bust cases	Valuable	Valuable	Valuable
Extended undercover operations	—	Very valuable	Occasionally valuable

behavior of individual policemen; and some can be changed only by changes in the behavior of individual police. Although it is not clear which of these resources are generally in short supply relative to the optimal portfolio of tactics, some crude guesses about chronic shortages among state- and local-enforcement efforts can be offered.

Probably the most binding constraint is high-quality informants. This is partly a chicken and egg problem. Because the police cannot get close to significant traffickers and cannot make strong cases against them, the police are denied effective informants. Because they have no effective informants, they fail to get close to major traffickers. However, any given level of enforcement effort could become much more effective in producing informants if the police could credibly threaten long jail terms. Lacking this leverage, the police will find it difficult to motivate cooperation from a defendant whose unarrested associate has invested heavily in strategies to discipline him.

The second most binding constraint is probably underinvestment in intelligence systems (e.g., files and intelligence analysts). The lack of intelligence systems implies that different enforcement units will make cases against the

Strategies and Tactics	"Inputs" Required			
	Information			
	Intelligence System	Documents and Records	Purchase Evidence- Purchase Information	Capital Equipment
Patrol strategies	−	−	−	Cars and communications equipment
Retrospective-conspiracy investigations	Very valuable	Very valuable	Occasionally valuable	Recording and surveillance equipment
Prospective investigations Observation-sale cases	−	−	−	Surveillance equipment
Search-warrant cases	−	−	Occasionally valuable	Surveillance equipment
Buy and bust cases	−	−	Very valuable	−
Extended undercover operations	Valuable	−	Very valuable	Surveillance and recording equipment

same traffickers, and that given informants will not be fully exploited. Indeed, if only weak intelligence systems exist, and if the police seek to control corruption by shifting investigators around frequently, the narcotics-enforcement effort may be directed almost entirely by informants. Thus, to the extent that informants are rare and valuable, it is essential to invest in intelligence systems to insure that their full value is exploited.

The third most binding constraint is money to purchase evidence. Without this money, the police are denied the use of all undercover tactics. With limited supplies, the police are restricted to buy and bust operations. Extended buy operations require large stocks of money. Since state and local police have not been supplied routinely with this money, and since extended undercover operations produce very attractive direct and indirect effects, slight changes in the availability of this money could have a significant impact on the effectiveness of state and local narcotics-enforcement efforts.

If all the constraints above were loosened (i.e., intelligence systems were suddenly available, money was available to make several high-level purchases, and the supply of defendant-informants had been increased by significant threats of imprisonment), we would likely discover that we had a shortage of manpower with the skills necessary to make retrospective-conspiracy cases. Our current operations are geared so much to prospective-investigative strategies, and the skills required for these operations are so different, that most narcotic-enforcement organizations have simply lost the capability for retrospective conspiracy cases. Thus, suddenly in a position to make these cases, we would lack the investigators to carry them off.

Current constraints on resources confine the scope of enforcement operations. The portfolio is shifted in the direction of patrol strategies, undocumented observation-sale arrests, low-level search-warrant cases, and buy and bust operations. We lack the resources necessary to maintain extended undercover operations, to manage retrospective-conspiracy investigations, and to mount extended, documented search-warrant cases against high-level traffickers. This means that our efforts are directed primarily at low-level, careless dealers, and that we rarely manage to use them as successful penetrations against larger trafficking networks. For the most part, we have a costly and limited narcotics-enforcement capability. How best to use the limited capability we have, is discussed in Part III. An example of an enforcement strategy in a specific city is presented in Chapter 4.

Notes

1. Charles B. Whitebread and Ronald Stevens, "Constructive Possession in Narcotics Cases: To Have and Have Not," *Virginia Law Review* 58 (1972): 751.

2. Whitebread and Stevens, "Constructive Possession in Narcotics Cases."

3. *McKinney's Consolidated Laws of New York: Annotated* (Brooklyn: Edward Thompson, 1975), note 5; Art. 220.31, note 2.

4. *Annotated Federal Laws*, 21 USCA 841 notes 12, 13, 14, 15, 16.

5. U.S. Department of Justice, "Handbook: Proving Federal Crimes," (Washington, D.C.: 1971), p. 127.

6. Ibid., p. 130.

7. Ibid.

8. U.S. Department of Justice, "Handbook: Proving Federal Crimes," p. 75.

9. Ibid., p. 133.

10. Jerold H. Israel and Wayne R. LaFave, *Criminal Procedure in a Nutshell* (St. Paul, Minn.: West, 1975), p. 175.

11. See pp. 121-128.

12. United States Congress, House of Representatives, Committee on Government Operations, "Law Enforcement on the Southwest Border: "Hearings Before a Subcommittee," 93rd Congress, 2nd Session, July-August 1974.

13. Comptroller General of the United States, "Heroin Being Smuggled into New York City Successfully," B164031 (2) (1972).

14. "Police Perjury in Narcotics 'Dropsy' Cases: A New Credibility Gap," *The Georgetown Law Journal* 60 (1971): 507.

15. See Chapter 1, Section 3.4.

16. Jerome H. Skolnick, *Justice Without Trial*, (New York: Wiley and Sons, 1966), pp. 144-148.

17. Jeremy Larner and Ralph Tefferteller, *The Addict in the Street* (New York: Grove Press, 1964), p. 64.

18. Leonard Shecter with William Phillips, *On the Pad*, (New York: Berkley, 1973), p. 90.

19. Office of Chief Counsel, Drug Enforcement Administration, "Disclosure of Informants," *DEA Legal Comment*, no. 5 (May 1974): 5.

20. New York State Commission of Investigation, *Narcotics Law Enforcement in New York City*, 1972, p. 138; Shecter with Phillips, *On the Pad*, pp. 292-293.

21. The Staff and Editors of *Newsday, The Heroin Trail* (New York: Signet, 1973), p. 183; Richard Woodley, *Dealer*, (New York: Holt, Rinehart and Winston, 1971), p. 5.

22. Office of Statistical and Data Services, Drug Enforcement Administration, "Causes of Shooting Incidents," Drug Enforcement Administration, 1972.

23. United States Congress, United States Senate, Committee on Government Operations, Permanent Subcommittee on Investigations, "Federal Drug Enforcement: Hearings Before the Permanent Subcommittee on Investigations," 94th Congress, First Session, 1975.

24. Ibid.

25. Domestic Council Task Force on Drug Abuse, *White Paper on Drug Abuse* (Washington, D.C.: U.S. Government Printing Office, 1975), pp. 41-43.

26. Office of the Chief Counsel, Drug Enforcement Administration, "Disclosure of Informants," DEA Legal Comment No. 5, May 1974.

27. See the discussion of The Unified Intelligence Division below, pp. 211-212.

28. Lee Afflerback et al., "Vehicle Tracking and Locating Systems," The Mitre Corporation, 1974.

Narcotics Enforcement in New York City

Chapter 3 presented a general, somewhat abstract model of narcotics enforcement. To get closer to the machinery of the system, it is useful to focus on a law-enforcement program in a specific area. New York City is the obvious candidate—partly because of the importance of New York City, partly because of the availability of information, and partly because New York City was the city whose distribution system was analyzed in Part I. The enforcement program in New York City differs to some extent from enforcement programs in other areas. It is larger and more cluttered with institutions. The problems in court processing and corruption may be more severe than other places. However, the basic institutions and their procedures are likely to be similar for almost all major metropolitan areas.

The institutions involved in narcotics enforcement in New York City are the following.[a] Within the New York City Police Department, two different units are involved: the Patrol Bureau, which manages the uniformed patrol force; and the Narcotics Division, which is the central unit responsible for narcotics investigations.[b] In addition, two different federal-enforcement agencies are directly involved: the U.S. Customs Service, which patrols the ports and borders of the United States; and the Drug Enforcement Administration, which is responsible for narcotics investigations. Both federal agencies have regional offices in New York City. To facilitate coordination among these different agencies, two different institutions have been created: the Joint Task Force, manned by both city police and federal agents; and the Unified Intelligence Division, which maintains a file of violators known to and being investigated by the different enforcement agencies. Finally, there are the prosecutors and courts.[c] Each of these institutions is described briefly below. In each case, we

[a]The description presented is current for 1975-76. In previous periods, the situation was more complex. In 1972, for example, the enforcement agencies included the New York City Police Department, the Bureau of Narcotics and Dangerous Drugs (BNDD), the U.S. Customs Service, the Office of Drug Abuse Law Enforcement, and the Joint Task Force.

[b]Obviously, other units in the NYCPD make narcotics arrests or arrest narcotics offenders on other charges. Still, the Patrol Bureau and the Narcotics Division account for nearly all narcotics arrests.

[c]Generalizations about prosecutors and courts are likely to be particularly weak for two reasons. First, we have less data on their activities than the police. Second, they are a sufficiently diverse group that there will be significant exceptions to any general statement. As James Q. Wilson once remarked, "Our idea of judicial *policy* is each judge at home in bed thinking of what he should do the next day." Personal communication with James Q. Wilson.

are interested in the tactics employed to make narcotics cases, the scale of their activity relative to the size of the problem, and the trends in both tactics and scale. The most important issue is to gauge the pressure these institutions bring to bear on heroin distribution in New York City.

1.0 The New York City Police Department

The New York City Police Department (NYPD) is a very large institution.[d] It has a force of about 30,000 men, and an annual budget of approximately $800 million.[1] As indicated above, two units routinely make narcotics arrests: the Patrol Bureau (approximately 25,000 men) and the Narcotics Division (approximately 200 men prior to June 1969 and approximately 500-600 men thereafter).[2]

1.1 The Patrol Bureau

The Patrol Bureau manages the uniformed patrol force in New York City. As one would expect, this unit relies primarily on patrol strategies. Loitering arrests stimulated by complaints, possession cases incidental to other arrests, and possession and observation-sale cases made as a result of short periods of surveillance are the Patrol Bureau's dominant tactics.

Since the Patrol Bureau is *generally* responsible for enforcement in New York City, its resources must be distributed across many different offenses. How much effort will be devoted to narcotics offenses (and within narcotics offenses, to *heroin* offenses) depends partly on the volume of complaints from the public, and partly on management decisions within the police department (e.g., to establish quotas for narcotics arrests or not, to use narcotics arrests as a signal of aptitude for investigative work among patrolmen or not, to enlarge special units devoted to narcotics enforcement or not). These factors have combined to produce dramatic variations in the level of effort against narcotics violators. Figure 4-1 illustrates the trends in narcotics arrests for the New York City Police

[d]The description of the activities of the New York City Police Department presented in this section is based partly on my personal observations and interviews while working with the Narcotics Division for one month in 1972, and partly on the following secondary sources: Commission to Investigate Allegations of Police Corruption, *Commission Report*, New York City, 1972; Deputy Commissioner of Organized Crime Control, "Activity of the Narcotics Division for 1972," Internal Memorandum No. 90-73, New York City Police Department, February 1973; New York State Commission of Investigation, *Narcotics Law Enforcement in New York City* (New York: 1972). In addition, I am deeply indebted to Joseph Bauman and Anthony Japha, director, Drug Law Evaluation Project of the Association of the Bar of New York, who provided statistical data and other information to bring my knowledge up-to-date. If I have failed to describe events accurately even with all this help, it is my error.

Department from 1967 to 1974.[e] Arrests for all charges have varied from about 28,000 in 1968 to over 70,000 in 1970. Arrests for felonies have varied from 7,000 in 1968 to 27,000 in 1970. Figure 4-2 indicates the share of narcotics arrests in the total number of arrests by the NYPD over the same period. Both absolute levels of narcotics arrests, and the share of narcotics arrests within total arrests peak in 1970. The fact that 1970 was also the year of the greatest concern about the heroin problem in New York City indicates the important role of public opinion in mobilizing and targeting the patrol force: when complaints and management policies have focused on narcotics violations, the Patrol Bureau has dramatically increased its level of arrests.

Many have expressed concern that dramatic increases in narcotics arrests stimulated by intense public concern are secured only at the price of a decline in quality and focus: more cases would be thrown out of court for illegal police practices; the proportion of insignificant charges would increase; and the proportion of *heroin* arrests within total narcotics arrests would decline. The data from New York City suggests that although reasonable, these fears are exaggerated. Although the fraction of narcotics cases dismissed by the courts was high throughout this period (as it was for all types of cases), the fraction dismissed did not increase dramatically in the years in which narcotics arrests increased dramatically. Similarly, the distribution of charges did not change dramatically with charges in levels of arrest. Figure 4-3 illustrates the distribution of narcotics arrests among charges for the period 1968-72. As one can see, felony arrests were a large fraction of arrests in the peak year (37% in 1970) and a relatively small fraction in a relatively low year (32% in 1968). Thus, high levels of arrests did not necessarily lead to lower charges. Finally, the concentration on heroin *increased* during the peak years of police narcotics arrests. Figure 4-4 illustrates the share of *heroin* arrests among narcotics felonies and the narcotics misdemeanors (possession only).[f] Of course, arrest data are always suspect: the charges may not accurately reflect the circumstances of arrest. However, to the extent one has confidence in these numbers, one can conclude that the dramatic increases in narcotics arrests in 1969-71 were secured without dramatic losses in quality or focus.

Given that large-scale police efforts always present some potential for abuse,

[e]New York City Police Department, *Annual Statistical Reports.* Note that these figures are for the department as a whole. Consequently, they include arrests by the Narcotics Division and other units as well as arrests made by the Patrol Bureau. The reason for presenting figures for the entire department is simply that the New York City Police Department does not reliably separate arrests made by the Patrol Bureau from other units. Since the Patrol Bureau accounts for the overwhelming majority of the arrests in any event, the statistics for the department as a whole reflects primarily their activity. If one wanted a more accurate estimate of Patrol Bureau arrests, one could simply subtract the arrests made by the Narcotics Division (which are reported separately below) from the totals presented here. The trends noted here would be even more obvious.

[f]The share of narcotics arrests that are *heroin* arrests is likely to be influenced by the relative availability of drugs on the street as well as by targeting.

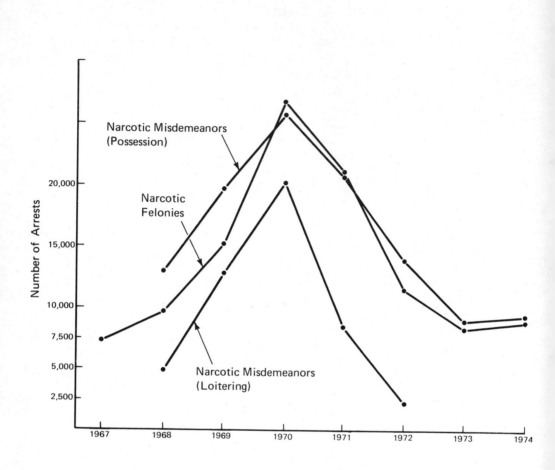

Source: *Statistical Reports*, New York City Police Department, 1967-74.

Figure 4-1. Trends in Total Narcotics Arrests NYCPD: 1967-74

and that levels of police activity have been declining in recent years, a key policy issue is to determine whether the scale of activity achieved in 1970 is necessary to put adequate pressure on the distribution system to produce indirect deterrent effects. Table 4-1 provides some rough calculations that allow one to compare the scale of the city police effort with the scale of the distribution

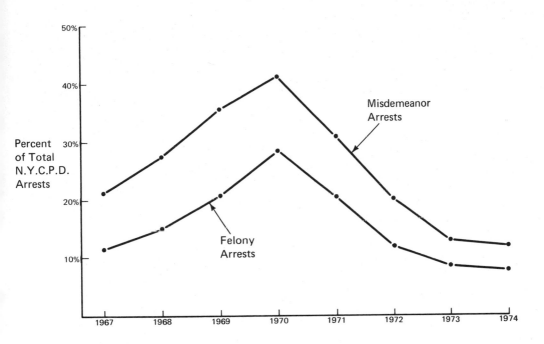

Source: *Statistical Reports*, New York City Police Department, 1967-74.

Figure 4-2. Trends in the Proportion of Total N.Y.C.P.D. Felony and Misdemeanor Arrests that Are Narcotics Arrests: 1967-74

system. One should take these calculations with a grain of salt. Not only is there uncertainty about the number of users and dealers, there is also uncertainty about how to adjust arrest information to correspond to a given number of arrests at different levels. However, the calculations may provide a rough order of magnitude estimate of the threat from the NYCPD. Simple reflection on these numbers suggest that arrests must stay in the mid-upper range of the distribution of activity to maintain a reasonable deterrent.

In sum, the New York City Police Department has made an impressive attack on the lower levels of the distribution system. However, the recent trend has been towards diminished scale and loss of focus on heroin.

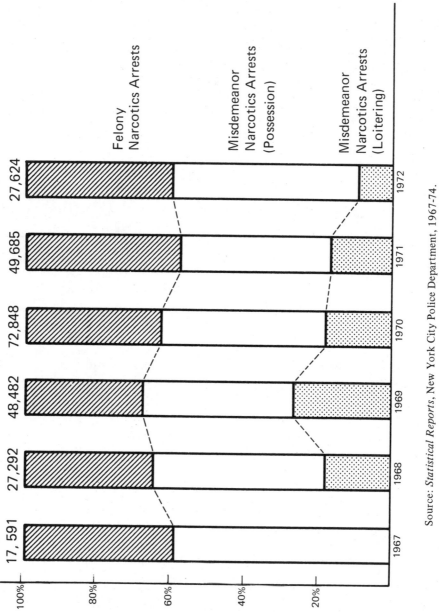

Source: *Statistical Reports*, New York City Police Department, 1967-74.

Figure 4-3. Trends in the Distribution of Narcotics Arrests among Charges: 1968-72

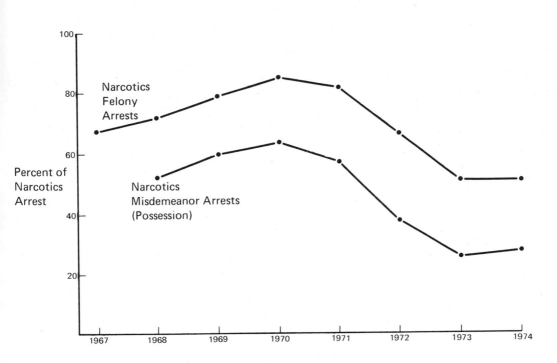

Source: *Statistical Reports*, New York City Police Department, 1967-74.

Figure 4-4. Trends in the Share of Heroin Arrests within Narcotics Arrests: 1967-74

1.2 The Narcotics Division

The Narcotics Division is the unit within the New York City Police Department that is responsible for narcotics investigations. As a result, it relies heavily on the tactics of prospective investigation (e.g., search-warrant cases, undercover purchases, extended undercover police operations tied to wiretaps, etc.). In fact, this is the only unit that makes undercover narcotics investigations in New York City.

The Narcotics Division has had a stormy history. In 1969 and 1970 the division was severely criticized by two different investigating commissions—the

Table 4-1

The Estimated Expected Number of Arrests per Dealer from NYCPD: 1968-73

Level of Distribution System	Number of People	Expected No. of Arrests[a]					
		1968	1969	1970	1971	1972	1973
		7,000 Felony 7,000 Possession 5,000 Loitering	12,000 Felony 12,000 Possession 13,000 Loitering	23,000 Felony 16,000 Possession 20,000 Loitering	17,000 Felony 12,000 Possession 8,000 Loitering	7,000 Felony 6,100 Possession 2,000 Loitering	4,000 Felony 2,000 Possession N.A.
Importers	25	0	0	0	0	0	0
Kilo connections	25	0	0	0	0	0	0
Connections	125	0	0	0	0	0	0
Weight dealers	750	0	0	0	0	0	0
Street dealers	6,000	0.35	0.35	0.60	1.09	0.80	0.18
Jugglers	18,000	0.30	0.53	0.94	0.66	0.28	>0.14
Users	100,000	0.12	0.23	0.35	0.22	0.08	>0.02

[a]Calculated on the assumption that arrests for different charges are distributed among levels in the following way:

	Loitering	Misdemeanors (Possession)	Felony
Importers, kilo connections, connections, weight dealers	0	0	0
Street dealers	0	5%	25%
Jugglers	10%	15%	55%
Users	90%	80%	20%

New York State Permanent Committee on Investigations and the Knapp Commission.[3] Through extensive interviews with employees and the examination of the organization's records, the commissions documented the following charges:

1. Significant levels of corruption (e.g., accepting bribes extorting money, perjury, subverting planned investigations, and illegal possession and use of drugs).[4]
2. Inadequate procedures for selecting targets and coordinating the activities of different investigating units.[5]
3. Poor personnel systems that created inappropriate incentives (e.g., quotas) failed to train investigators and failed to maintain high morale within the division.[6]

In the view of the investigating commissions, these factors led to an enforcement program that was inefficient and targeted at the wrong levels of the distribution system.

In response to these criticisms, significant reforms were made within the Narcotics Division. The most important reforms included the following:

1. The personnel were almost entirely replaced over several years as a result of a large influx of new personnel and the gradual attrition of old personnel.[7]
2. Arrest quotas were eliminated to reduce incentives for illegal arrests and perjury and to provide adequate time to work on extended investigations leading to higher level violators.[8]
3. A large amount of "buy money" was made available to permit extended, high-level undercover operations.[9]
4. A system requiring the registration of informants was established to insure control over the buy money. It had the additional effect of allowing the division to monitor the effectiveness of its use of informants.[10]
5. A small amount of intelligence work was accomplished to identify major figures who appeared to be vulnerable to police efforts.[11]
6. The Narcotics Division relaxed its commitment to respond to complaints in order to provide more time for investigations based on better information, and directed at higher level violators.[12]

These changes had a dramatic effect on the level and pattern of cases produced by the Narcotics Division.

Figure 4-5 presents data on the level and distribution of Narcotics Division arrests for 1971-74. This table shows a dramatic decline in the level of arrests and an *increase* in the *proportion* of felony arrests. It is not clear how we should value this change in the pattern of arrests. Of course, the increase in the *proportion* of felony arrests is desirable. However, the *absolute level* of felony

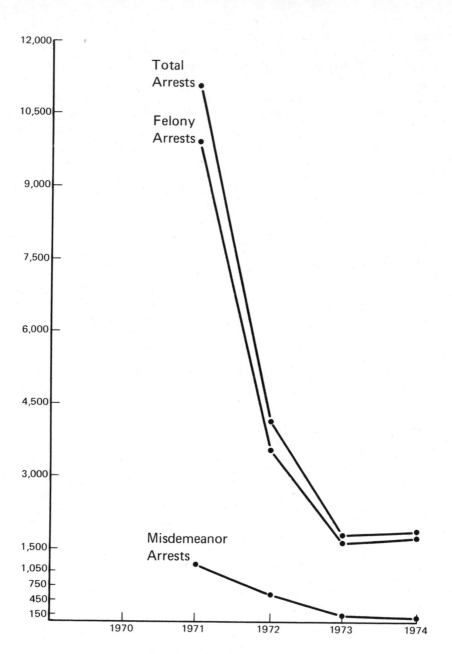

Source: *Statistical Reports*, New York City Police Department, 1967-74.

Figure 4-5. Trends in the Levels and Distribution of Arrests by the Narcotics Division: 1971-74

arrests also declined over this period in spite of the fact that the Narcotics Division had doubled in size. Unless there was a significant increase in quality *among the felony arrests*, it is possible to conclude that the effectiveness of the Narcotics Division diminished over this period.

Fortunately, some data exist that allow a glimpse into the quality of the felony arrests. Figure 4-6 presents data on the size distribution of undercover buys made by the Narcotics Division from 1971 to 1974. The table illustrates a significant change in the level of buys made by the Narcotics Division. Of course, changes in the quantity purchased do not necessarily imply changes in the level of the distribution system that is attacked.[g] Consequently, an increase in the proportion of "buys" in the 10 to 54 grain level compared with the 109 grain level is not all that important. What *is* important is the steady growth in the number of buys in the categories of 55 to 439 grains, 1 ounce to 1 pound, and over 1 pound. These buys probably do indicate cases at higher levels. At a minimum, the cases are made against careful street dealers. It is more likely that the cases are made against weight dealers or connections.

In addition to more effective undercover operations, there is some evidence of increased reliance on more sophisticated techniques for developing cases. For example, wiretaps increased from 30 in 1971 to 72 in 1972. Search warrants declined from 2,468 in 1971 to 672 in 1972.[13] Moreover, prosecutors in New York City testifying before the Senate's Government Operations Sub-Committee in 1972 described improvements in City Police capabilities in the following terms:

In the past, we have relied primarily on the federal agencies to perform these tasks. Recently, we have been fortunate to receive assistance from local enforcement agencies which have also conducted electronic and physical surveillance. In fact, the indictments naming a total of 86 defendants which were filed last month depend greatly on the efforts of the New York Police Department. These cases are presently pending and I will not get into a detailed description of the investigative tools used; however, it is a matter of public record that we have 106 reels of films of some of the defendants actually transacting narcotics business on Pleasant Avenue in upper Manhattan, all taken by the Police Department.[14]

Thus, it seems clear that the Narcotics Division has broadened its array of tactics for making cases, and succeeded in making cases against higher level violations.

The magnitude of the threat posed by the Narcotics Division can be gauged by calculations similar to those presented for the Patrol Bureau. Table 4-2 presents the calculations. Inspection of the table indicates the recent success of the Narcotics Division in reaching higher levels of the distribution system. However, the table also indicates that the Narcotics Division has only recently

---

[g]Larger buys could be the result of "building up" lower level dealers. For an example of this, see *Newsday, The Heroin Trail* (New York: Signet, 1973), p. 230.

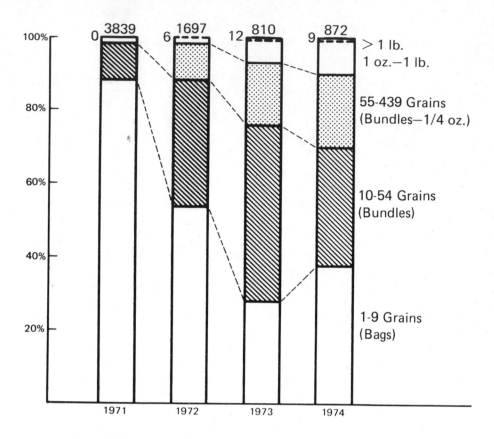

Source: *Statistical Reports*, New York City Police Department, 1967-74.

Figure 4-6. The Size Distribution of Heroin Buys Made by the Narcotics Division: 1971-74

achieved a plausibly effective scale of operations at mid-levels of the distribution system. Moreover, it is apparent that this gain was purchased at the price of significantly reduced pressure at lower levels. To the extent that the Patrol Bureau picked up the slack at the street level, the gain in pressure at lower levels would be a clear benefit. However, since we know that Patrol Bureau activity diminished throughout the period 1972-74, it is likely that gains in attacking mid-levels of the distribution system were partially offset by reduced pressure of street levels. In sum, it is possible that street-level dealers can now afford to behave very aggressively because neither the Narcotics Division nor the Patrol Bureau is paying much attention to them.[h]

---

[h]There are very important policy implications of slack efforts at street levels. See Chapters 5 and 6.

Table 4-2

The Estimated Expected Number of Arrests per Dealer at Each Level from Narcotics Division: 1971-74

Level of Distribution System	No. of Dealers	Expected No. of Arrests Per Year			
		1971	1972	1973	1974
		9,800 Felony 90% Jugglers 10% Street Dealers 1,200 Misdemeanors 60% Jugglers 40% Users	4,000 Felony 60% Jugglers 38% Street Dealers 2% Weight 6 Connections 600 Misdemeanors	1,600 Felony 40% Jugglers 55% Street Dealers 5% Weight 12 Connections 100 Misdemeanors	1,700 Felony 45% Jugglers 45% House 10% Weight 9 Connections 100 Misdemeanors
Importers	25	0	0	0	0
Kilo connections	25	0	0	0	0
Connections	125	0	0.05	0.10	0.07
Weight dealers	750	0	0.10	0.11	0.23
Street dealers	6,000	0.16	0.25	0.15	0.13
Jugglers	18,000	0.53	0.15	0.04	0.04
Users	100,000	0.005	0.002	0	0

1.3 Interactions in a Specific Copping Area

The data presented above indicate the magnitude of the threat facing the distribution system as a whole. In developing a good sense of the intensity and character of this attack, it is useful to focus on arrest activity in a specific, well-known "copping area" of New York City.[15]

Fortunately, the intelligence unit of the Narcotics Division maintains geographic files of arrests in specific areas. Due to the procedures for constructing the files, the files are likely to undercount the overall police activity and to overestimate the proportion of arrests made by the Narcotics Division.[i] Still, a review of the files can provide a rough picture of New York City Police Department activity of a specific location.

The Lennox Avenue File for 1972 indicated some 250 to 350 arrests. Thus, a narcotics arrest on Lennox Avenue was almost a daily event. Table 4-3 shows the distribution of types of arrest for a sample of 50 arrests chosen at random from the files. These data suggest that arrests for the possession or loitering by the Patrol Bureau occurred more often than every other day. Arrests by the Narcotics Division for sale or large possession cases occurred about every third day. Narcotics arrests by the Patrol Bureau incidental to other arrests also

Table 4-3
Distribution of Types of Arrests on Lennox Avenue near 116th Street: 1972

Type of Arrest	Quantity Seized or Purchased			
	<5 bags	5-15 bags	>15 bags	Total
Narcotics Division	2%	8%	20%	30%
Undercover buys	2	6	2	10
Observation sale	0	2	6	8
Possession	0	0	12	12
Patrol Bureau	36	16	18	70
Observation sale	0	0	0	0
Possession	8	14	16	38
Incidental to other arrests	8	2	2	12
Loitering	20	0	0	20
Total	38	24	38	

[i]The file probably underestimated the total number of narcotics arrests on Lennox Avenue because the Narcotics Division did not reliably receive arrest reports from other units.

occurred about once a week. The overall impression is one of an intense, broad-scale attack on a local copping area.

2.0 Federal Enforcement Agencies

Federal narcotics-enforcement efforts have been reorganized often.[j] A brief chronology of the reorganization since 1968 suggests the turmoil.

1. In 1968 the Federal Bureau of Narcotics (Treasury) and the Bureau of Drug Abuse Control (HEW) were combined in a new agency called the Bureau of Narcotics and Dangerous Drugs within the Department of Justice. Customs, which also had a narcotics-enforcement jurisdiction, remained within Treasury.[16]
2. In 1972 the new offices were created within the Department of Justice to assist Nixon's "war" against drug abuse. The Office of Drug Abuse Law Enforcement was established to field combined federal, state, and local task forces in major cities of the United States.[17] The Office of National Narcotics Intelligence was established to develop a national narcotics intelligence data base. Customs and BNDD continued their normal operations.
3. In 1972 Re-Organization Plan #2 combined BNDD, ODALE, ONNI, and 500 agents from Customs in a new organization within the Department of Justice called the Drug Enforcement Administration. A major purpose of the reorganization was to reduce destructive competition and bickering between Customs and BNDD over narcotics investigations. DEA was to have sole jurisdiction over narcotics *investigations*. Customs was to be responsible for *interdiction*.[18]

The frequent reorganizations make it difficult to present and support powerful generalizations about the shape of federal-enforcement efforts in New York City over a long period. There is a presumption that procedures have changed, but since reporting procedures have also changed, it becomes difficult to plot the magnitude and direction of the changes. To reduce the problem of generalizing about a changing system on the basis of a changing data base, we restrict our attention to the period since the last major reorganization, that is, from 1972 to 1974.[k] Although many things have changed even within this short period, the fluctuations are relatively small.

[j]In describing the activities of federal-enforcement agencies, I am relying primarily on my experience as the chief planning officer of DEA from January 1974 to September 1975.

[k]The exception to this statement is that we rely primarily on data *prior* to 1971 in describing Customs' activity.

2.1 The Drug Enforcement Administration

The Drug Enforcement Administration (DEA) is the federal agency primarily responsible for narcotics enforcement. The agency as a whole is significantly smaller than the New York City Police Department. It has approximately 4,000 people (2,000 special agents), and a budget of approximately $150 million.[19] These resources were allocated to many functions besides enforcement against heroin-distribution systems and are deployed throughout the world. In the New York Regional Office (which includes district offices in Buffalo and Newark as well as New York City), DEA has roughly 300 special agents.[20] Thus, the federal investigative presence in New York City is probably less than half the size of the Narcotics Division of his NYCPD, and a very tiny fraction of the size of the Patrol Bureau.

DEA relies primarily on the strategy of prospective investigations and the tactic of extended undercover operations. In addition, in New York City, retrospective-conspiracy investigations have begun to emerge as a significant component of DEA's investigative capabilities.[l] Possession cases, observation-sale cases, and buy and bust operations are usually not made by DEA. The only conditions under which these kinds of cases will be made is a situation where the existing stock of informants is not sufficient to maintain higher level investigations.

To support these operations, DEA leans heavily on a large supply of money to purchase evidence and information (PE/PI). Approximately $700,000 is spent on information or evidence within the New York Regional Office each year.[21] In addition, DEA depends on a large stock of defendant-informants produced partly by their own operations and partly by the operations of the City Police Department and Customs. Finally, they make a relatively large investment in intelligence to guide the development of the case.[m]

Figure 4-7 illustrates the level of narcotics arrests produced in recent years by this commitment of manpower, PE/PI money, capital equipment, and supporting personnel. Figure 4-8 illustrates the distribution of arrest across different classes of violators. The different classes of violators represent DEA's efforts to calibrate the relative importance of the violators they arrest. The distinctions are drawn partly on the basis of quantitative indicators (e.g., the amount and purity of the drug seized; the amount and purities of the drug purchased), and partly on the basis of intelligence information on the role of the arrested individual in trafficking operations.[22] Table 4-4 presents the criteria for assigning arrested individuals to the different classes. The impression created by these tables is a steady increase in the number of arrests, and a reduction in the

---

[l]Within DEA, it is well-known that the southern and eastern districts of New York are the leaders of conspiracy investigations and prosecutions.

[m]DEA's overall investments in intelligence include the following major components: the NADDIS system (basically an automated index system to cases), small regional intelligence units staffed by analysts; and a headquarters intelligence unit of approximately 100 professional analysts.

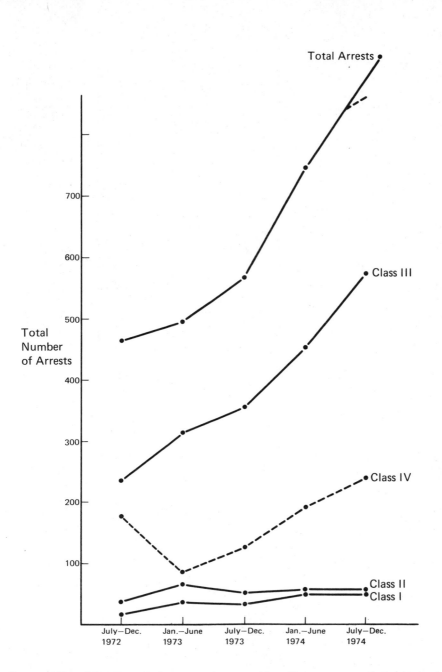

Total Number of Arrests

Total Arrests

Class III

Class IV

Class II
Class I

| July—Dec. 1972 | Jan.—June 1973 | July—Dec. 1973 | Jan.—June 1974 | July—Dec. 1974 |

Source: DEA, "Geo-Drug Enforcement Program: First Year Assessment" (Washington, D.C.: Department of Justice, 1974).

Figure 4-7. Levels of Narcotics Arrests Produced by DEA's New York Regional Office: 1972-74

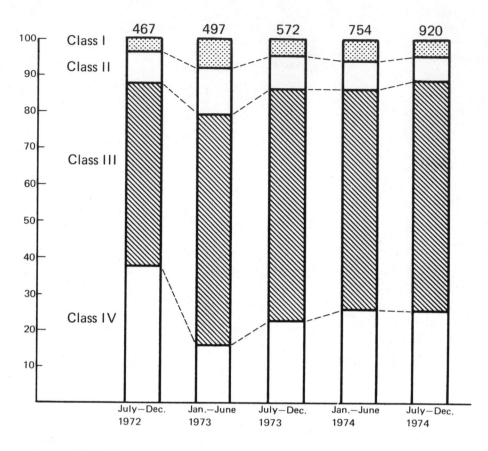

Source: DEA, "Geo-Drug Enforcement Program: First Year Assessment" (Washington, D.C.: Department of Justice, 1974).

Figure 4-8. Distribution of DEA Narcotics Arrests among Classes of Violators: 1972-74

proportion of class I and II arrests, though no reduction in the *absolute number* of class I and class II arrests.

Again, a key issue is how significant is the threat created by the observed level of enforcement effort. The calculation of the expected number of arrests as different levels of the distribution system proves even more difficult for DEA than the other enforcement organizations. The reason is simply that one must gauge the fraction of the narcotics arrests in the *regional* office that occurred within New York City, and the fraction of the arrests that were made for heroin offenses rather than cocaine or other drugs. There is some information to guide

Table 4-4
Criteria for Assigning Arrested Traffickers to Different G-DEP Classes

Class I: (Two or more criteria required)	a. Sale or seizure of 2.2 pounds or more of heroin or cocaine, 70% pure or higher b. Sale or seizure of 100,000 dosage units or more of clandestinely manufactured dangerous drug c. Laboratory operator d. Head of criminal organization e. Financier f. Drug-smuggling head
Class II: (Two or more criteria in class II or one each in class I and class II required)	g. Sale or seizure of at least 1.1 pounds of heroin or cocaine, 35% pure or higher h. Sale or seizure of 250 pounds of marijuana or more i. Sale or seizure of 100,000 dosage units of dangerous drugs or more j. Sale or seizure of 30,000 dosage units of hallucinogenic drugs or more k. Head of a class III drug organization or any identified organized crime subject not listed in class I
Class III: (Any one of the criteria in class I, II, or III required)	l. Sale or seizure of 2 ounces or more of heroin or cocaine m. Sale or seizure of 100 pounds of marijuana up to but not including 250 pounds n. Sale or seizure of 10,000 dosage units of dangerous drugs up to but not including 100,000 dosage units o. Sale or seizure of 1,000 dosage units of hallucinogenic drugs up to but not including 30,000 dosage units
Class IV:	All others

Source: Comptroller General of the U.S., "Efforts to Immobilize Major Traffickers," B175424 (Washington, D.C.: General Accounting Office, 1973).

these estimates. Figure 4-9 presents the number of heroin-cocaine arrests made by the New York Regional Office. However, one must still separate New York City from the rest of the region, and the heroin arrests from the cocaine arrests. Table 4-5 presents calculations of the expected number of heroin arrests taken by dealers at different levels by the Drug Enforcement Administration. The table is based on uncertain estimates of heroin arrests within New York City and uncertain assignment of arrested individuals to different levels of the distribution system. Still, to the extent there are reasonable estimates, the table indicates a significant risk to high level dealers in New York City from DEA.[n]

[n]Recall that our estimates of the number of dealers in New York City do *not* include people who transship drugs. Because these dealers are often the targets of DEA investigations, we have probably overestimated the expected number of arrests.

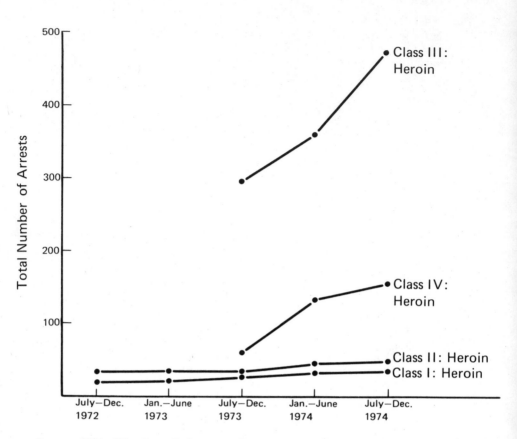

Source: DEA, "Geo-Drug Enforcement Program: First Year Assessment" (Washington, D.C.: Department of Justice, 1974).

Figure 4-9. Heroin-Cocaine Arrests Made by DEA's New York Regional Office: 1972-74

2.2 The U.S. Customs Service

The U.S. Customs Service has a budget of approximately $300 million and approximately 13,000 positions.[23] About 2,700 of these positions are allocated to Region II, which includes part of New York State and part of New Jersey.[24] Of the 2,700 positions in region II, approximately 1,000 are inspectors who examine passengers, cargo, and baggage; 185 are customs patrol officers, who conduct uniform and plainclothes patrols and surveillance; and 120 are special

Table 4-5

The Estimated Expected Number of Arrests per Dealer from DEA-Enforcement Efforts in New York City

		Expected Number of Arrests per Dealer per Year[a]		
		1972	1973	1974[b]
Level of Distribution System	No. of Dealers	30 Class I 45 Class II 225 Class III 90 Class IV	35 Class I 50 Class II 375 Class III 60 Class IV	40 Class I 60 Class II 420 Class III 150 Class IV
Importers	25	0.6	0.7	0.8
Kilo connections	25	0.6	0.7	0.8
Connections	125	0.36	0.40	0.48
Weight dealers	750	0.30	0.50	0.56
Street dealers	6,000	0.007	0.01	0.025
Jugglers	18,000	–	–	–
Users	100,000	–	–	–

[a]The following assumptions are made in calculating the expected number of arrests:
1. Class I arrests = 50% against importers; 50 % against kilo connections
2. Class II arrests = connections
3. Class III arrests = weight dealers
4. Class IV arrests = street dealers
5. Heroin arrests = 2/3 heroin-cocaine arrests
6. Arrests in NYC = 3/4 of arrests by regional office

[b]Figures here are converted to annual figures by doubling 6 months total.

agents, who conduct antismuggling investigations.[o] Thus, the organization in New York City is roughly comparable in size to DEA, and significantly smaller than the NYCPD.

Although the size of the organization is roughly comparable to DEA, its responsibilities and style of operation are much different. The U.S. Customs service in region II is responsible for inspecting the following volume of material:

1. 1 - 2 million cargo invoices
2. 6 - 8 million crew members and passengers
3. 500 million pieces of mail.[25]

Moreover, in examining this enormous volume of material, the customs inspectors must be looking for many different things: false declarations, fraudulently

[o]Comptroller General of the United States, "Heroin Being Smuggled into New York City Successfully," B-164031(2) (Washington, D.C.: General Accounting Office, 1972), pp. 18, 63. These numbers are not current. They are likely to overestimate the number of investigators and underestimate all others.

undervalued material, and contraband other than drugs.[26] Thus, the problems of discovering several kilos of heroin are simply staggering—particularly when one realizes that a single "cargo invoice" can cover a shipment of tens or hundreds of thousands of cans and bottles, any one of which could contain a kilo or more of heroin.[27]

The obligation to inspect this enormous volume of material with limited resources necessarily forces Customs into patrol strategies and tactics: a large fraction of their resources must be devoted to relatively superficial observations of the entire space of possible offenses. However, in seeking to maximize their effectiveness (within the constraint of covering all possible spaces with at least a thin screen), they make marginal, tactical adjustments to give greater attention to areas or activities that are relatively likely to contain offenses. Note that these tactical adjustments are guided by very general "leads." In effect, surveillance resources are shifted from haystacks that contain 1 needle to haystacks that contain 100 needles: they are not focused on a single tiny container filled entirely with needles. These general leads come from a variety of sources: internal analyses of arrests to discover general smuggling patterns, complaints or information from private citizens, debriefings of defendants to discover smuggling procedures, and maintenance of files on suspected smugglers. These "leads" can motivate shifts of manpower allocations from one area to another, the design of tactical programs to concentrate on some areas and activities rather than others, or merely heightened awareness to particular events among Customs' personnel.[28] All of these devices have the effect of marginally increasing the surveillance given to areas with marginally higher probabilities of containing offenses.

The available resources deployed according to these strategies result in the seizure of 100 to 1,000 pounds of heroin nationwide.[29] In New York City in 1971, Customs made 38 seizures of heroin totalling 540 pounds of heroin.[30] Although the amount of heroin seized in recent years has declined significantly, it has never dipped below 70 pounds of heroin.

It is interesting to note that five seizures accounted for 537 of the 540 pounds of heroin seized in 1971. Moreover, of these five seizures, three were made as a result of routine examinations without prior information, two were made as a result of a tactical program that intensified examinations of privately owned vehicles, and none were made on the basis of specific prior information.[31]

These data and observations are obviously too thin to support powerful generalizations about the impact of the U.S. Customs Service on the distribution of heroin in New York City. However, stretching this data beyond the breaking point and relying on the general analysis of enforcement efforts, I would offer the following judgments about the role of the U.S. Customs Service in pressuring illicit-distribution systems in New York City.[p]

---

[p]These judgments are primarily simple extensions of a more detailed analysis of Customs operations on the Southwest border. See DEA Survey Group, "An Analysis of DEA

First, it is apparent that Customs can make seizures sufficiently large to produce substantial direct effects on the distribution of heroin. Five hundred forty pounds of heroin represents a substantial share of the estimated annual consumption of heroin in New York City. Even if one assumes that much of the national supply of heroin passes through the port of New York, and that some of the heroin seized was destined for other markets, it is reasonable to suppose that some 10 to 20 percent of the locally destined heroin was seized. Although inventories and new orders may diminish the long-run impact of these seizures, in the short run, seizures of this magnitude can have a large, direct effect.

Second, the Customs Service produces significant indirect deterrent effects as well. The Customs' screen forces all smugglers to invest in more or less sophisticated hiding places. At a minimum, this threat makes transactions among illicit dealers slightly more complicated. Moreover, smugglers may be forced to search for specialists—thereby making themselves vulnerable to exposure or penetration by police.[32] At most, the requirement may deter some smugglers entirely.

Third, like the patrol efforts of the NYCPD, Customs' inspections of passengers and cargo produce defendants who are potentially valuable as informants. Although only a fraction of these defendants turn out to be valuable, several major cases have begun with a Customs seizure and arrest.[33] Moreover, at a minimum, these patrol efforts will check the comprehensiveness of the investigative intelligence systems.[34]

Fourth, these valuable effects of Customs' efforts are probably maximized when Customs relies on patrol strategies rather than investigative strategies. Both the deterrent effects and the intelligence-checking effects are maximized with strictly random patrols. One can do slightly better in terms of seizures by making tactical adjustments guided by *general* patterns of smuggling activity. However, Customs cannot narrowly focus its efforts without giving up the significant benefits associated with monitoring (however superficially) the entire space of possible offenses.[35]

Fifth, due to the somewhat random character of Customs patrol strategies, there will be significant variability in the amount of heroin seized, and the value of Customs' defendants in making other cases. Some years, Customs will make many seizures and turn up valuable defendant-informants. Other years, with similar investments in Customs efforts and similar volumes of heroin moving across the border, less will be seized, and fewer defendants will turn out to be cooperative and valuable.

Thus, Customs makes a substantial, but somewhat variable contribution to narcotics-enforcement efforts in New York City. Moreover, the average impact of the Customs efforts will be maximized when Customs relies on patrol strategies.

Coordination with Patrol Forces on the Southwest Border" (Washington, D.C.: Drug Enforcement Administration, 1974).

3.0 Coordinating Mechanics among Enforcement Agencies

The large number of enforcement organizations creates a presumption that coordination will be a major problem. In fact, the actual requirements for coordination may be exaggerated. The major costs associated with failures of coordination are redundant investigations, or investigations that are prematurely surfaced by unilateral actions of one group that is ignorant of the ongoing investigation of a different group. Even with no formal coordinating mechanisms, these events may be rare—particularly if there are a large number of dealers compared to the number of enforcement operations. Moreover, one may *like* some redundant investigations as a check on corruption problems. Finally, one may be able to minimize these kinds of failures by dividing the world up on simple dimensions. If the police agencies tend to specialize in one tactic or another, and this specialization limits their operations to specific geographic areas or specific levels of the distribution system, the frequency of redundant investigations may be very low. In short, even with the large number of enforcement organizations, it is not immediately evident that detailed coordinating mechanisms are required.

The specific features of the narcotics-enforcement situation that indicate a need for coordination are (1) the large scale of the police activity relative to the number of dealers and (2) the fact that several different organizations conduct investigations directed at similar levels of the distribution system where there are a small number of dealers. These facts suggest a need for coordination, particularly between the Narcotics Division and the Drug Enforcement Administration. They need a way to discover if they are working on similar cases and to bring all the information they have together to bear on tactical choices in developing cases. To fill these needs, they have established two different institutions: the Joint Task Force and the Unified Intelligence Division. Each is described briefly below.

3.1 The Joint Task Force

The Joint Task Force combines federal narcotics agents with city policemen in a separate enforcement unit. The basic idea is to achieve coordination between the city police and the federal-enforcement agencies by combining some portion of their personnel. The problem with this concept is that the Joint Task Force operates under its own command structure. Consequently, the unit ends up being an *additional* enforcement unit that must be coordinated with the city police and the federal-enforcement agencies. As a result, the unit may exacerbate rather than solve coordination problems.

Of course, this conclusion is overstated. However, it does serve to focus attention on what the *real* coordinating value of the Task Force will be. The real coordinating value has very little to do with the specific operations mounted by the Joint Task Force. It has everything to do with the personal relationships established among the personnel of the different units. Because federal agents and city policemen will have worked closely together in the formal task-force institution, in the future, coordination between agencies can occur *outside* of the structure of the Task Force. Policeman Jones will call Agent Smith even when both are back in their own units. If these observations are correct, there are significant implications for the management and operations of the Task Force. The Joint Task Force should have frequent turnover of personnel, and the managers of the Task Force should concentrate on establishing personal relationships as much as on making specific cases. In effect, the Task Force should become an occasion for establishing personal relationships among individuals in the different agencies rather than a significant mechanism for coordinating overall enforcement efforts.

It is not clear whether the Joint Task Force has achieved these purposes or not. My impression is that the personnel have been fairly consistent from the beginning, that the managers have concentrated on making impressive cases, and that city-federal antagonisms continue to flourish even within the structure of the Task Force. If these impressions are accurate, some of the potential coordinating value of this institution has been lost. Indeed, the Task Force may exacerbate the coordination problem by establishing yet another enforcement unit and by intensifying antagonisms among the personnel of the different agencies.

3.2 The Unified Intelligence Division

Most major cities have serious coordination problems between federal- and city-enforcement agencies. Many have tried to resolve them with the task-force concept. New York City has, in addition, created a unique institution—the Unified Intelligence Division.[36] The basic idea of the division is that all the enforcement agencies should indicate the set of cases they are currently working so that the various agencies can discover whether they are both working the same case.

There are enormous bureaucratic and technical problems in operating this unit. There are bureaucratic problems with motivating agencies to identify current cases. They have a strong incentive to keep their own cases secret, and are able to justify this action by expressing concern about the integrity of the other enforcement units.[q] In addition, there are technical problems with getting timely information on the full set of cases being worked by investigators, and with identifying cases on enough dimensions so that cases that are in fact related

---

qThis complaint and criticism was made frequently within DEA.

can be discovered to be related. These problems suggest that the case files of the Unified Intelligence Division will include only a small fraction of the current hot cases, and will be filled primarily with old cases that did not break quickly. Moreover, even within this limited file, it may be difficult to discover that cases are related.

Given these constraints on the potential effectiveness of a unified intelligence system, it would be surprising if it turned out to be an important coordinating mechanism. However, it turns out that the unit has prevented redundant investigation in a significant fraction of the cases known to the unit. Table 4-6 presents data on the number of duplicated cases in the period September 1972-January 1973. Note the number of different enforcement agencies that were active in this period. The fact that this much duplication was revealed by a limited system indicates the scope of the problem of redundant investigation. The Unified Intelligence Division has apparently played a major role in improving coordination among the enforcement agencies in spite of its limitations.

4.0 The Prosecutors and Courts

The data presented above on the scale of police activity suggest impressive levels of pressure on the distribution system. A significant fraction of the dealers are

Table 4-6
Duplication among Cases Known to Unified Intelligence Division: September 1972-January 1973

Agency	Number of Subjects Forwarded	Number of Verified "Duplications"	Fraction of Cases Duplicated
Narcotics Division	1,083	56	5.2%
Federal Bureau of Narcotics and Dangerous Drugs	1,278	97	7.6
U.S. Customs Service	1,717	141	8.2
U.S. Office of Drug Abuse Law Enforcement	190	37	19.5
New York Joint Federal-City Task Force	559	26	4.6
Total (5 agencies)	4,827	357	7.4

Source: Deputy Commissioner of Organized Crime Control, "Activity of the Narcotics Division for 1972," Internal Memorandum 90-73 (New York City: Police Department, 1973).

arrested each year, and those who remain on the street must fear arrest and behave cautiously. However, the impact of these arrests depends critically on effective prosecution and sentencing. Although arrests impose some sanctions in and of themselves, the magnitude of the deterrence and incapacitation effects from these arrests depends primarily on what prosecutors and courts do with the cases. Identifying what happens to narcotics arrests in the courts of New York City is the major purpose of this section.[r]

In 1970, the peak year of both concern about the heroin problem and police arrests, an analysis of the processing of narcotics cases in New York City courts was undertaken by the New York City Police Department.[37] They surveyed the disposition of 46,000 possession and sale cases arraigned in New York City courts from August 1, 1969 to August 1, 1970. Figure 4-10 illustrates the flow of cases for felonies (including some possession cases), and Figure 4-11 illustrates the flow for misdemeanors. In the terse words of the informal report, "the picture is one of breakdown."[38] The breakdown is apparent in the following areas.

First, there are large numbers of dismissals and reductions of charges throughout the process. Among felonies, about one-quarter of the cases are dismissed or reduced (18% discharged at arraignment, 1% discharged by Grand Jury, 1% reduced to misdemeanors by Grand Jury, 3% dismissed or acquitted at later charges). Among misdemeanors, about half of the cases are discharged (48% dismissed at arraignment, 2% acquitted after trial).

The dismissals and reductions in charges could be attributed either to poor arrests by the police or the congestions in the courts. The available evidence suggests that both play a role. Table 4-7 presents the results of a separate analysis of the reasons for dismissal for 774 narcotics cases (primarily possession cases) in a single court in New York City. To the extent that this court is representative of the courts in New York City, one can say that *dismissals* appear to be primarily a problem of police procedure, but that confused administrative procedures within the courts also play a role. Less direct evidence is available in seeking to explain the observed *reductions in charges*. However, it seems likely that many of the reduced charges are the result of plea bargaining rather than poor arrest procedures. We know that plea bargaining is a common practice in the New York City courts.[39] In addition, the fact that approximately 2,000 misdemeanor sentences were given in the Supreme Court, which handles only felony indictments, strongly suggests a major role for plea bargaining in causing reduced charges. Thus, although dismissals may be primarily a problem of police

---

[r]In writing this section, I have relied heavily on the following documents: Drug Law Evaluation Project, "Convictions and Sentences under the 1973 New York State Drug and Sentencing Laws: Drug Offenses" (New York: Association of the Bar and the Drug Abuse Council, 1975). New York State Commission of Investigations, "Interim Report Concerning the Operations of Special Narcotics Parts of the Supreme Court" (New York: 1973); Henry Ruth and Arthur Grubert, "Memorandum to Narcotics Control Council re Statistics on Dispositions of Narcotics Cases" (New York: Criminal Justice Coordinating Council, 1971).

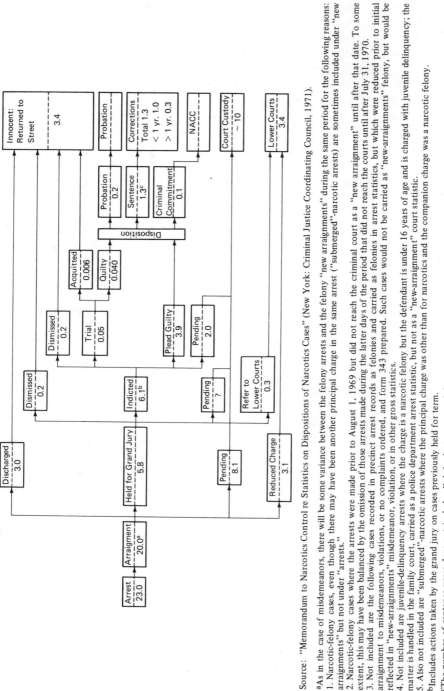

Source: "Memorandum to Narcotics Control re Statistics on Dispositions of Narcotics Cases" (New York: Criminal Justice Coordinating Council, 1971).

[a]As in the case of misdemeanors, there will be some variance between the felony arrests and the felony "new arraignments" during the same period for the following reasons:
1. Narcotic-felony cases, even though there may have been another principal charge in the same arrest ("submerged"-narcotic arrests) are sometimes included under "new arraignments" but not under "arrests."
2. Narcotic-felony cases where the arrests were made prior to August 1, 1969 but did not reach the criminal court as a "new arraignment" until after that date. To some extent, this may have been balanced by the omission of those arrests made during the latter days of the period that did not reach the courts until after July 31, 1970.
3. Not included are the following cases recorded in precinct arrest records as felonies and carried as felonies in arrest statistics, but which were reduced prior to initial arraignment to misdemeanors, violations, or no complaints ordered, and form 343 prepared. Such cases would not be carried as "new-arraignments" felony, but would be reflected in "new-arraignments" misdemeanor, violation, or in other gross statistics.
4. Not included are juvenile-delinquency arrests where the charge is a narcotic felony but the defendant is under 16 years of age and is charged with juvenile delinquency; the matter is handled in the family court, carried as a police department arrest statistic, but not a "new-arraignment" court statistic.
5. Also not included are "submerged"-narcotic arrests where the principal charge was other than for narcotics and the companion charge was a narcotic felony.

[b]Includes actions taken by the grand jury on cases previously held for term.

[c]The number of sentence users does not include all defendants sentenced for narcotic offenses since, if there was a multiple or combined sentence, the entry will be against the offense for which the sentence was most severe. Frequently, this offense is other than a narcotic offense, or there may be a sentence for lesser offense than a narcotic felony.

Figure 4-10. Disposition of *Felony* Arrest for Narcotics Offenses in New York City Courts: August 1969-August 1970 (in Thousands of Defendants)

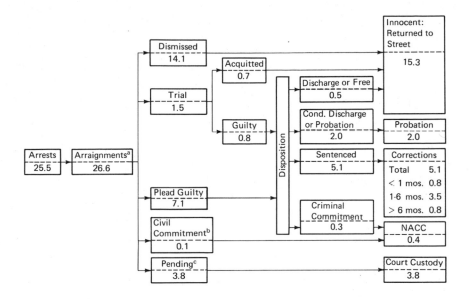

Source: "Memorandum to Narcotics Control Council re Statistics on Dispositions of Narcotics Cases" (New York: Criminal Justice Coordinating Council, 1971).

[a]The "New-arraignment" figure will differ from the misdemeanor-arrest figure in the corresponding period for the following reasons:
1. Narcotic-misdemeanor cases, even though there may have been another principal charge in the same arrest, ("submerged"-narcotic arrests) are sometimes included under new arraignments but not under "arrests."
2. Narcotic-misdemeanor cases where the arrests were made prior to August 1st, 1969, but did not reach the criminal court as a "new arraignment" until after that date. To some extent, this may have been balanced by the omission of those arrests made during the latter days of the period, which did not reach the courts until after July 31, 1970. This will be skewed to a greater loss of arrest cases from the last month's "new arraignments" since there were more narcotic-misdemeanor arrests in July 1970 than in July 1969.
3. Cases that were recorded in precinct arrest records as felonies, upon examination by assistant district attorneys in the court complaint room, or at prearraignment facility, resulted in misdemeanor complaints being drawn up. These cases were then recorded as "new arraignments" in the misdemeanor category even though arrest statistics carry them as felonies.
4. Arrests recorded at precincts as narcotic misdemeanors, but upon review by the assistant district attorney, prior to arraignment, result in complaints being drawn for a felony violation, or even no complaints being drawn because no crime or violation was shown. The felony and violation cases would be included under "new arraignments," felony, or violation, as the case may be. When no complaints were drawn, and form 343 was prepared, this would not show up in any narcotic "new-arraignment" date but eventually would be merged in with other gross statistics kept by the court.
5. Juvenile-delinquency arrests. Where the charge is a narcotic misdemeanor but the defendant is under 16 years of age, and is charged with juvenile delinquency, the matter is handled in the family court carried as an arrest statistic but not as a new arraignment.
[b]Under section 210 of the Mental Hygiene Law, "an addict-defendant may petition for his own civil commitment. He is eligible for this option only if he has no prior felony conviction, and if his present charge is a felony, the District Attorney's consent is required. This petition leads to a civil commitment for a maximum of three years and dismissal of the criminal charge. The proceeding remains in Criminal Court rather than transferring to Supreme Court where the civil commitments under S206 take place; in all other respects the addict is treated as though he were an unarrested self-petitionist under the civil provisions." This description occurs in New York City Criminal Justice Coordinating Council, *Criminal Commitment of Narcotic Users Under State Law* (New York City: Office of the Mayor, 1971, p. 9.
[c]This category includes youthful offenders (which go through a separate court process) as well as those whose cases have not yet been heard.

Figure 4-11. Disposition of *Misdemeanor* Arrests for Narcotics Offenses in New York City Courts: August 1969-August 1970 (in Thousands of Defendants)

Table 4-7

Causes of Dismissals: Bronx Criminal Court November-December, 1970

Reasons for Dismissal	Number	Percent
I. Police practices	450	58.1
1. Search not based on probable cause	94	12.1
2. Violation of search warrant	4	0.5
3. Failure to give Miranda warning	3	0.4
4. No probable cause for arrest found at arraignment	15	2.2
5. Prosecution unable to prove possession at arraignment	31	4.0
6. Several defendants arrested; only 1 connected to drugs at arraignment	244	31.5
7. Failure to mark evidence	3	0.4
8. Officer fails to appear	19	2.5
9. Conflicting police testimony	2	0.2
10. Court disbelieves drop-see testimony	33	4.3
11. Other	2	0.2
II. Court practices	271	35.0
1. Grand jury fails to indict as felony; no misdemeanor charge	6	0.8
2. Defendant charged with two offenses: pleads to nondrug charge	62	8.0
3. Several defendants arrested; one pleads guilty; other dismissed	29	3.7
4. Officers fail to appear due to court administration failures	28	3.6
5. Complaint drawn incorrectly	1	0.1
6. Diverted to youth programs	96	12.4
7. Diverted to mental health program	46	5.9
8. Other nonjail disposition (job corps; army)	2	0.2
9. Paroled defendant returned to jail	1	0.1
III. Other problems	53	6.8
1. Lab reports reveal no drugs	45	5.8
2. Officer fails to appear due to death, resignation, suspension	6	0.8
3. Defendant has prescription for drugs	2	0.2

Source: "Memorandum to Narcotics Control Council re Statistics on Dispositions of Narcotics Cases" (New York: Criminal Justice Coordinating Council, 1971).

procedures and only secondarily a problem of court congestion, *reduced charges* appear to be primarily the result of congestion-induced plea bargaining.

Second, a large number of cases are pending. About 60 percent of the felony cases and 20 percent of the misdemeanor cases have no dispositions. These figures suggest the significant congestion in the courts at that time, and also indicate that arrested traffickers are either in jail without a conviction (in the case that they failed to make bail), or on the street for long periods following arrest. Neither situation is desirable. The explanation for this problem is partly a very large number of arrests, partly a problem of inadequate court resources, partly a problem of inefficient scheduling of cases, and partly a result of strategic maneuvering by either defense or prosecutors to gain some advantage in the case.

Third, given *convictions* for drug offenses, the sentences are fairly lenient. Among convicted felons, about 25 percent escape jail altogether, about 50 percent receive jail terms of less than one year, and only 25 percent receive sentences of more than one year. Among people convicted for misdemeanors, about 35 percent escape jail altogether; about 40 percent serve for less than three months; about 15 percent serve for three to six months; and only 10 percent serve for more than six months.

Again, lenient sentences could be attributed to police, prosecutors, or judges. Some evidence exists that suggest these sentences are primarily the result of prosecutorial and judicial policies. Table 4-8 presents the dispositions of 175 undercover-buy cases made by the Narcotics Division. Given the procedures for making these cases, they are likely to be strong felony cases. Yet only 10 of the 89 defendants sentenced received jail sentences of more than one year. This evidence suggests that plea bargaining or judicial leniency are more likely to explain lenient sentencing than police procedures.

Thus, in 1970 there were serious problems in prosecuting narcotics cases. Since many cases were dismissed, had charges reduced, or were pending; and since even convictions rarely carried a jail term, a narcotics arrest was hardly a disaster for a narcotics dealer. Arrests neither deterred nor immobilized dealers.

Since 1970 two major policy initiatives have been launched to strengthen narcotics prosecution in New York City. In June 1971 the legislature established twelve Special Parts to handle only narcotics cases within New York City.[40] In September 1973 a new statute became effective that changed the classifications of drug offenses, created mandatory minimum sentences, and restricted plea bargaining.[41] The rationales and results of these two initiatives are described below.

The objectives of the Special Narcotics Parts were to reduce dismissals, plea bargaining, and "soft" sentences by generally increasing existing court resources; by earmarking a relatively large portion of the new court capacity for narcotics cases; and by developing a prosecutorial unit that would be accountable for narcotics prosecutions, would develop expertise in prosecuting sophisticated narcotics cases, and would develop close liaison with major enforcement units in the city.[42] The specific plan for the Special Parts was formulated by the five district attorneys of New York City. The plan established 12 special parts: 5 "centralized parts" in New York County; 2 "decentralized parts" in Bronx, Kings, and New York Counties; and 1 "decentralized part" in Queens County. In addition, a special assistant district attorney would monopolize prosecutions in the "centralized parts" and would "coordinate" narcotics prosecutions in the "decentralized parts." The special assistant district attorney was authorized to establish policies and collect information about all narcotics prosecutions in the city.[43]

In practice, the plan was only partly successful. The special assistant established tough policies with respect to plea bargaining[44] and managed the schedules of the centralized parts so cases were quickly resolved. However, since

Table 4-8
Dispositions of Undercover Cases Made by the Narcotics Division: 1970

	Number Arrested	Number Dismissed	Number Pending	Number Convicted
Group 1	25	0	7 (28%)	18 (72%)
Group 2	24	3 (12%)	2 (8%)	19
Group 3	25	0	2	23
Group 4	25	0	9	16
Group 5	25	1	3	21
Group 6	25	1	9	15
Group 7	25	4	13	8
Total number	174	9	45	120
Fraction of total arrests		(5%)	(26%)	(26%)
Fraction of those convicted & sentenced				

the prosecutors in the decentralized parts were not specialists hired by and loyal to the special assistant district attorney, but rather regular members of the district attorneys' staffs who rotated through the assignment, the special assistant failed to influence many of the narcotics cases and prosecuted them in roughly the same way as they did before the creation of the special parts.[45] Moreover, even within the centralized parts, nothing much changed with respect to sentencing. Roughly 60 percent of those convicted in the centralized Special Parts avoided jail.[46]

Thus, although the special assistant district attorney sought to upgrade narcotics prosecutors throughout New York City, his influence turned out to be sharply limited. With respect to prosecutorial policy, he influenced five to seven of the new parts. With respect to judicial policy, he seemed not even to influence policies within the centralized parts, much less the decentralized parts.

In 1973 a new effort was made to strengthen prosecution and sentencing of

	Number Awaiting Sentences	Number Sentenced	Sentences		
			No Jail	Jail ≤ 1 Year	Jail ≤ 1 Year
Group 1	0	18 (72%)	3 (12%)	13 (52%)	2 (8%)
Group 2	1	18 (72%)	6 (24%)	10 (40%)	2 (8%)
Group 3	1	22 (88%)	3 (12%)	16 (64%)	3 (12%)
Group 4	9	7	1 (4%)	6	0
Group 5	2	19 (78%)	14 (64%)	1 (4%)	4 (10%)
Group 6	0	15 (60%)	12 (48%)	3 (12%)	0
Group 7	0	8	6	1	1
Total number	13	107	45	50	12
Fraction of total arrests	(7%)	(61%)	(26%)	(29%)	(7%)
Fraction of those convicted & sentenced			(42%)	(47%)	(11%)

Source: "Memo re Statistics on Dispositions of Narcotics Cases."

narcotics offenses in New York. The laws defining narcotics offenses and establishing sanctions for offenses were modified.[47] First, many offenses were upgraded in their classification. Table 4-9 indicates some of the major changes in the classification of offenses. Second, minimum mandatory sentences were established for class A, B, and C drug felonies (except for offenses involving marijuana). Table 4-10 indicates the changes in sentencing requirements. Third, plea bargaining for defendants indicted for class A felonies was restricted to reductions to other class A felonies. The charges could not be dropped below an A felony. Fourth, plea-bargaining restrictions and minimum mandatory sentences were established for defendants indicted for narcotics felonies who had previously been convicted for a felony. In addition, to assist the courts in applying these new provisions, court resources were once again expanded. Figure 4-12 illustrates increases in the number of parts operating in New York City from 1971 to 1975.

Table 4-9
Major Changes in Classification of Heroin Offenses under Rockefeller Drug Laws

Crime Event	Classification Under "Old" Laws	Classification Under "New" Laws
I. Possession (heroin)		
1. More than 16 ounces	A felony	A = I felony
2. 8-16 ounces	B felony	A = I felony
3. 2-8 ounces	C felony	A = I felony
4. 1-2 ounces	C felony	A = II felony
5. 1/8-1 ounce (plus prior conviction)	D felony	B felony
6. 1/8-1 ounce (first offense)	D felony	C felony
7. Less than 1/8 ounce	A misdemeanor	A misdemeanor
II. Possession plus intent to sell (heroin)		
1. No quantity limitation	D felony	A = III felony
III. Sale (heroin)		
1. More than 16 ounces	A felony	A = I felony
2. 8-16 ounces	B felony	A = I felony
3. 1-8 ounces	C felony	A = I felony
4. 1/8-1 ounce	C felony	A = II felony
5. Less than 1/8 ounce	C felony	A = III felony
6. Sale to a minor	B felony	N.A.

Source: Drug Law Evaluation Project, "Convictions and Sentences Under the 1973 New York State Drug and Sentencing Laws: Drug Offenses" (New York City: Association of the Bar of the City of New York and the Drug Abuse Council, 1975). Reprinted by permission.

Unfortunately, it is early to evaluate the impacts of these laws on court processing. Table 4-11 indicates that the court "pipeline" is still filling with cases prosecuted under the new laws and emptying of cases prosecuted under old laws. Consequently, we are going through a period when the aggregate statistics of court processing reflect both new and old laws, and it may be difficult to see the full effects of the new statutes.

Fortunately, the Bar Association of the City of New York has sponsored an evaluation of these laws, and the project staff has undertaken a survey and a comparison of prosecutions under new and old laws in New York City.[48] indictments, fraction going to trial, etc.). But even this survey is limited in terms of what can be said about the effect of the law on later stages of processing (e.g., average time to disposition, patterns of sentencing, actual lengths of sentences served). There are simply not enough new drug cases through the process to have experience with the effects. Moreover, it is reasonable to assume that those cases that are already through the process (the quickly resolved cases) are likely to differ from the cases that will come later (the difficult-to-resolve cases). Consequently, all statements about the impact of these laws on later stages of processing must be received with caution.

Table 4-10

Major Changes in Restriction on Sentencing and Processing under Rockefeller Drug Laws

Area of Sentencing or Processing Restriction	"Old" Laws	"New" Laws
I. Allowable alternatives to prison:		
A. Defendant category and crime		
1. Narcotics addict-A felony	None	None
2. Narcotics addict-B, C, or D drug and violent felonies	DACC (NACC, DDAS)	None[a]
3. Nonaddict-B, C, or D drug and violent felonies	Probation[c]	None[b]
4. Second felony offense-B, C. D, or E felony	Probation[c]	None
II. Allowable plea bargains:		
A. Crime		
1. A felony, any class	Any	A-III
2. B, C, D, E felony, second offense	Any	E
III. Allowable minimum sentences for recidivists		
A. Current crime		
1. A felony	15-Life	1-Life
2. B felony	Probation	4 1/2-12 1/2
3. C felony	Probation, etc.	3-7 1/2
4. D felony	Probation, etc.	2-3 1/2
5. E felony	Probation, etc.	1 1/2-2

Source: Drug Law Evaluation Project, "Convictions and Sentences Under the 1973 New York State Drug and Sentencing Laws: Drug Offenses" (New York City: Association of the Bar of the City of New York and the Drug Abuse Council, 1975). Reprinted by permission.

[a]Class D convictions may result in a probation sentence with a treatment requirement.

[b]Class D drug convictions may receive probations, definite prison sentence, conditional or unconditional discharge.

[c]Prior to 1973, if a nonaddict was convicted of a non-drug felony, he could receive a sentence of conditional or unconditional discharge or intermittent imprisonment as well as probation.

Probably the most immediate and dramatic effect of the new laws resulted from the upgrading of various offenses. Figure 4-13 presents data on the distribution of adult, felony-drug arrests in New York City from 1973 to 1974. The differences are striking: 40 percent "A" felonies in 1974 compared with 3 percent in 1973. Nearly all of that change reflects upgrading of particular offenses rather than new police procedures producing higher level defendants.

Equally dramatic is the increase in the proportion of felony indictments that go to trial. Figure 4-14 presents data on the fraction of narcotics-felony cases going to trial. Although trials continue to be a small proportion of the total

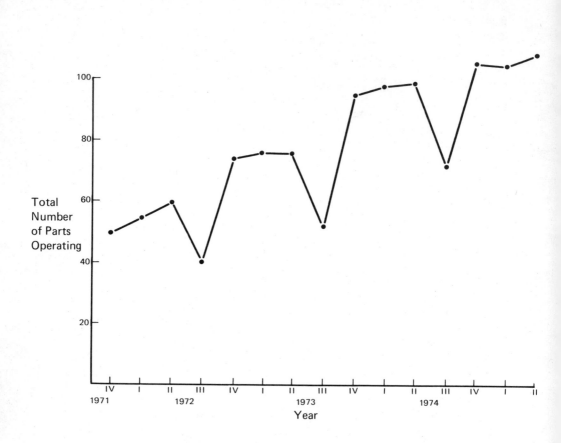

Source: Drug Law Evaluation Project, "Convictions and Sentences under the 1973 New York State Drug and Sentencing Laws: Drug Offenses" (New York City: Association of the Bar and the Drug Abuse Council, 1975). Reprinted by permission.

Figure 4-12. The Growth in Court Resources: 1971-75

disposition, the proportion of trials has increased by a factor of 4. Given stiff sentences for felony offenses and restricted plea bargaining, the increase in the number of trials was to be expected—the defendant has little to lose by going to trial.

The major anticipated result of the new laws was to stiffen the sentences for convicted narcotics violators: a large share would go to jail, and the terms in jail

Table 4-11
Share of Old-Law and New-Law Cases in Court Pipeline: 1972-75

Year	Arraignments		Disposition	
	Old Laws	New Laws	Old Laws	New Laws
1972	4,268	N.A.	3,654	N.A.
1973	3,081	197	2,869	5
1974	585	2,490	1,492	719
1975	185	2,649	465	2,044

Source: Drug Law Evaluation Project, "Convictions and Sentences under the 1973 New York State Drug and Sentencing Laws: Drug Offenses" (New York City: Association of the Bar and the Drug Abuse Council, 1975). Reprinted by permission.

would be longer. This result seemed to be guaranteed by the combination of upgrading offenses, restricting plea bargaining for class A felonies, and establishing minimum mandatory sentences for class A felonies. However, a superficial analysis of sentences under the new law suggests that nothing has changed with respect to sentencing. Table 4-12 indicates that the proportion of convicted felons going to jail has remained constant over time and through the change in statutes. This is an astonishing result. It suggests that the new sentencing provisions are ignored by judges.

In fact, a more detailed analysis of available information suggests that the sentencing provisions are having a substantial effect, and that the apparent constancy of sentencing patterns is both accidental and temporary. Table 4-13 indicates the fraction of convicted felons receiving jail sentences for class A felonies (where jail sentences are required), and class B and C felonies (where they are suggested). The table shows that the sentencing requirements for class A felons are being complied with by judges. Figure 4-15 compares the fraction receiving jail sentences under the new law with the fraction that would have been sentenced for similar *acts* under the old laws. The clear implication of these tables is that a large share of narcotics violations are being treated more harshly under the new laws.

Given the evidence of harsh treatment of convicted "A" felons, and given the large share of class A felony indictments, why has the aggregate sentencing pattern not changed? Two factors explain this result. First, the class A felony convictions and sentences have lagged behind indictments: as of December 1975, class A felonies constitute 74.5 percent of the indictments and only 64.9 percent of the convictions. This has occurred because these cases take longer to process than other cases. As class A felony convictions and sentences reach their share of indictments, the fraction of people receiving jail sentences will increase— probably dramatically.[49] Second, sentencing for class B and C felonies has apparently become less severe under the new laws. Figure 4-16 indicates the

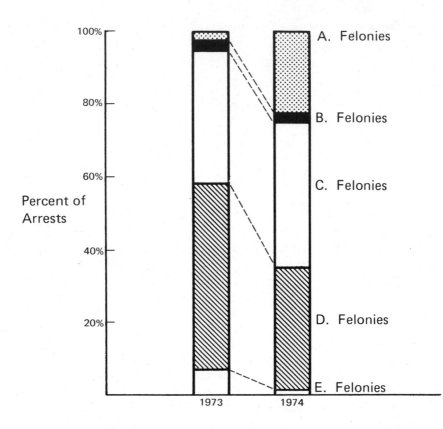

Source: Drug Law Evaluation Project, "Convictions and Sentences under the 1973 New York State Drug and Sentencing Laws: Drug Offenses" (New York City: Association of the Bar and the Drug Abuse Council, 1975). Reprinted by permission.

Figure 4-13. The Distribution of Adult Felony Arrests before and after Reclassification of Offenses

share of convicted offenders receiving jail sentences for acts classed as B and C felonies under the new law. The table indicates increased leniency for these acts. This increased leniency is difficult to explain. It could be the result of general congestion forcing more plea bargains in the small area where prosecutors retain discretion, or it could be a judicial reaction to the harshness of the sentences they are forced to hand out in class A felony cases. In any event, it is clear that many narcotics offenses are being dealt with more harshly, that some offenses are also being treated more leniently, and that, over time, the aggregate pattern

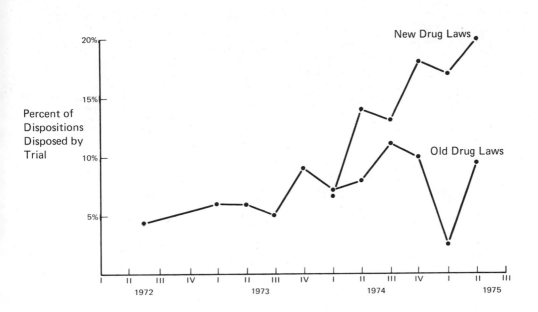

Source: Drug Law Evaluation Project, "Convictions and Sentences under the 1973 New York State Drug and Sentencing Laws: Drug Offenses" (New York City: Assocation of the Bar and the Drug Abuse Council, 1975). Reprinted by permission.

Figure 4-14. Percentage of Felony Drug Dispositions Disposed by Trial

will probably change in the direction of harshness as the class A felonies come out the end of the pipeline in greater numbers.

In sum, the court processing of narcotics cases has changed dramatically over the last few years. In 1970 the picture was one of general breakdown. By 1974 the system has been stiffened significantly. The stiffening resulted from reduced congestion (itself the result of reduced arrests, increased general court resources, and earmarking of court resources for narcotics cases); tougher and more consistent prosecutorial policy (itself the result of the establishment of the special narcotics prosecutor and the Special Parts); and the upgrading of narcotics offenses, the establishment of minimum mandatory sentences, and the restruction on plea bargaining (the result of new statutes). These changes have increased the deterrent and incapacitation value of an arrest, and applied more pressure on the distribution system.

Table 4-12

Proportion of Convicted Felons Receiving Prison Sentences under Old and New Laws: 1974-74

Year	Total Convictions	Total Prison Sentences	Percent Receiving Prison Sentences
1972: old law	5,162	2,279	38.9
1973: old law	4,725	1,719	36.4
1974: old law	1,613	561	34.8
1974: new law	1,473	536	36.4

Source: Drug Law Evaluation Project, "Convictions and Sentences Under the 1973 New York State Drug and Sentencing Laws: Drug Offenses" (New York City: Association of the Bar and the Drug Abuse Council, 1975). Reprinted by permission.

Table 4-13

Fraction of Convicted A Felons Receiving Jail Sentences Compared with Other Convicted Felons: 1974

Charge	Total Convictions	Total Prison Sentences	Percent Receiving Prison Sentences
Total	1,473	536	36.4
Class A felonies	330	306	92.7
Other felony convictions	1,143	230	20.1

Source: Drug Law Evaluation Project, "Convictions and Sentences Under the 1973 New York State Drug and Sentencing Laws: Drug Offenses" (New York City: Association of the Bar and the Drug Abuse Council, 1975). Reprinted by permission.

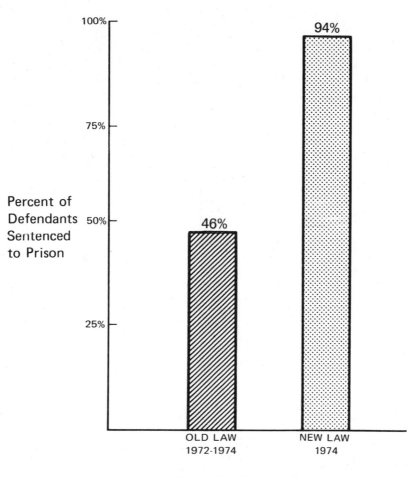

Cases Equivalent to New Law
CLASS A FELONY

Source: Drug Law Evaluation Project, "Convictions and Sentences under the 1973 New York State Drug and Sentencing Laws: Drug Offenses" (New York City: Association of the Bar and the Drug Abuse Council, 1975). Reprinted by permission.

Figure 4-15. Comparison of Sentences for Class A Offenses under New Laws with Sentences for Similar Offenses under Old Laws

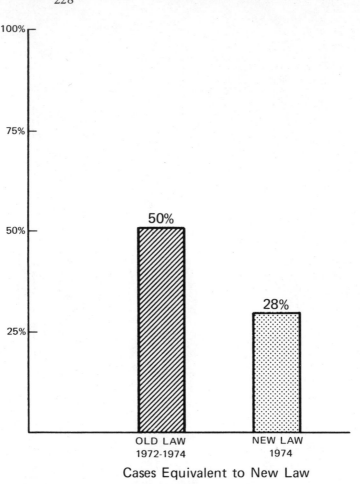

Cases Equivalent to New Law
CASES BELOW CLASS A FELONY

Source: Drug Law Evaluation Project, "Convictions and Sentences under the 1973 New York State Drug and Sentencing Laws: Drug Offenses" (New York City: Association of the Bar and the Drug Abuse Council, 1975). Reprinted by permission.

Figure 4-16. Comparison of Prison Sentences for Less than Class A Felonies under New Laws with Sentences for Similar Offenses under Old Law

Notes

1. Executive Committee, Criminal Justice Coordinating Council, *1973 Criminal Justice Plan*, New York City, 1973, p. 5.

2. New York State Commission of Investigation, *Narcotics Law Enforcement in New York City*, (New York: 1972), p. 50.

3. Commission to Investigate Allegations of Corruption, *Commission Report* (New York: 1972); New York State Commission of Investigation, *Narcotics Law Enforcement.*

4. *Narcotics Law Enforcement*, New York State Commission of Investigation, pp. 122-203.

5. Ibid., pp. 81-84, 106-107, 111-113.

6. Ibid., pp. 50-81.

7. William P. McCarthy, Deputy Commissioner of Organized Crime Control. Personal communication.

8. Ibid.

9. Deputy Commissioner of Organized Crime Control, "Activity of the Narcotics Division for 1972," New York City Police Department, Internal Memorandum No. 90-73, 1973.

10. Deputy Commissioner of Organized Crime Control, "Proposed Organized Crime Control Bureau Memo: Subject; Cooperating Individuals," New York City Police Department, Internal Memorandum, 1973.

11. Personal examination of intelligence files in "100 Major Violators" program, 1972.

12. William P. McCarthy, personal communication.

13. Deputy Commissioner of Organized Crime Control, "Activity of the Narcotics Division for 1972," p. 8.

14. Walter M. Phillips, Assistant United States Attorney for the Southern District of New York, "Statement Before the Government Operations Committee of the U.S. Senate," New York City, May 14, 1973.

15. Patrick H. Hughes et al., "The Social Structure of a Heroin Copping Community," *American Journal of Psychiatry* 128:5 (November 1975).

16. John Finlator, *The Drugged Nation* (New York City: Simon and Schuster, 1973), pp. 54-55.

17. Executive Office of the President, "Drug Abuse Prevention Program: Briefing Book," 1972, p. 25.

18. U.S. Congress, United States Senate, Subcommittee on Legislation and Military Expenditures, "Hearings on Reorganization Plan No. 2," 93rd Congress, 1st Session (April-May 1973).

19. U.S. Congress, House of Representatives, Committee on Appropriations, Subcommittee on Department of State, Justice, Commerce, the Judiciary, and Related Agencies, "Appropriations Hearings for 1976," 94th Congress, 1st Session, p. 780.

20. Drug Enforcement Administration (DEA), "Geo-Drug Enforcement Program: First Year Assessment" (Washington, D.C.: U.S. Department of Justice, 1974), p. 16.

21. DEA, "Geo-Drug Enforcement Program," p. 8.

22. DEA, "Geo-Drug Enforcement Program."

23. Executive Office of the President, "The Budget of the United States Government: Fiscal Year 1977," pp. 610-611.

24. Comptroller General of the United States, "Heroin Being Smuggled into New York City Successfully," B-164031 (2) (Washington, D.C.: General Accounting Office, 1972), p. 8.

25. Ibid., pp. 13-16, 33-34, 57.

26. Ibid., pp. 20-21.

27. Ibid., p. 16.

28. Ibid., pp. 23-28.

29. Ibid., p. 27. See also Office of Statistical and Data Services, Drug Enforcement Administration, "Drug Enforcement Statistical Report" (December, 1974).

30. Ibid., p. 29.

31. Ibid.

32. See above, pp. 26-27.

33. Evert C. Clark and Nicholas Horrock, *Contrabandista!* (New York: Praeger, 1973).

34. See above pp. 132-133.

35. DEA Survey Group, "An Analysis of DEA Coordination with Patrol Forces on the Southwest Border," (Washington, D.C.: Drug Enforcement Administration, 1974), p. 11.

36. New York City Police Department, "The Establishment of a Cooperative Narcotic Intelligence Committee" (Undated).

37. Criminal Justice Co-ordinating Council, "Memorandum to Narcotics Control Council re Statistics on Dispositions of Narcotics Cases" (New York: Criminal Justice Coordinating Council, 1971).

38. Ibid., p. 1

39. Ibid., p. 11.

40. New York State Commission of Investigations, "Interim Report Concerning the Operations of the Special Narcotics Parts of the Supreme Court" (New York: 1973), p. 1.

41. Drug Law Evaluation Project, "Convictions and Sentences under the 1973 New York State Drug and Sentencing Laws: Drug Offenses," (New York: Association of the Bar and the Drug Abuse Council, 1975), p. 1.

42. New York State Commission of Investigations, "Interim Report," pp. 2-8.

43. Ibid.

44. Ibid., p. 9.

45. Ibid., pp. 4-7.

46. Ibid., p. 16.

47. Drug Law Evaluation Project, "Convictions and Sentences under the 1973 New York State and Sentencing Laws: Drug Offenses."

48. Ibid.

49. Ibid., p. 7.

Part III
Policy Recommendations

Introduction to Part III

The analysis of parts I and II relied on a neutral style and language. However, it should be clear that we are dealing with an ugly and dangerous piece of the world. Violence, misery, and injustice are daily events of that world. One wishes there was an easy way to make it all go away.

Unfortunately, we live in a world where heroin exists, where its use is sufficiently widespread and contagious that many are threatened and its effects sufficiently intoxicating and demanding that individual lives are disrupted. Moreover, we live in a world where we have laws against the sale and use of heroin, and where police organizations are obligated to enforce the laws. Consequently, we cannot dispose of the problem. We must decide how to cope with it and how to enforce the narcotics laws in a way that improves rather than worsens the problem.

Part III tackles the policy problem of designing an effective narcotics-enforcement program within the context of an overall policy toward heroin use. The style and language continues to be neutral—precisely to control the enormous variety of considerations that should influence policy choice. However, given that we prescriptively analyze policy choices, we bear a special responsibility to insure that the categories and terms of the analysis capture the complexity of the situation and reflect the large, individual consequences at stake.

The analysis of Part III is in two sections. First, the role of narcotics enforcement within the overall strategy is generally defined. Second, a more detailed specification of an appropriate enforcement strategy is offered. Limitations of the recommended strategy and likely implementation problems are noted.

The Role of Narcotics-
Enforcement Strategies
in an Overall Policy

This chapter defines a limited but important role for narcotics enforcement (in an overall policy towards heroin use). The major conclusions are the following.[1] Enforcing narcotics laws is very important in *preventing* heroin use (i.e., in reducing the rate at which new people become users). However, enforcing narcotics laws will fail to prevent heroin use in areas where heroin use is endemic. Moreover, enforcing narcotics laws has very bad effects on the behavior and condition of people who are committed heroin users. Consequently, narcotics-enforcement efforts must be complemented by: (1) additional prevention programs in areas where heroin use is endemic, (2) a variety of programs for treating current users, and (3) legal devices that keep *users* arrested on narcotics charges out of jails and unblemished.

Note that the dilemma faced in enforcing narcotics laws are common to all negative incentive systems. To the extent that people notice and respond to the incentives, a desirable result occurs: people are deflected from using heroin. However, for the people who do *not* respond and begin using heroin in spite of the incentive system, there is a deadweight loss in punishing them: the reason for having the policy has already been negated, and there is little to be gained by further action. Still, to maintain the incentive system, one must go ahead and inflict the loss. The problem is fundamental: the desire to have the incentive conflicts with the desire to minimize the damage done to people who do not respond to the incentive.[a] One cannot lessen the adverse effects on current users without having some effect on the magnitude of the incentives facing nonusers. One cannot alter the incentives facing nonusers without having some effect on the consequences for current users. The policy problem is to decide how valuable the incentives discouraging heroin use are compared to the bad effects of these same incentives on current users. The answer implicit in this analysis is that one needs only a modest disincentive to discourage users, and, therefore, that one can do a great deal to dampen the adverse consequences of the incentive system on current users.

There are two key concepts that must be kept in mind throughout this analysis. First, a fundamental distinction is drawn between "current users" and "not-yet users." To some extent, the populations are socially and geographically distinct. However, the more important distinction is that they react much differently and take different consequences as a result of narcotics-enforcement

---

[a]I am indebted to Professor Thomas C. Schelling, Lucius N. Littauer Professor of Political Economy, Harvard University, for emphasizing this point.

efforts. When I use the word prevention, I am referring *only* to reducing the probability that not-yet users begin use. I am not referring to reducing levels of consumption among current, committed users. In effect, then, prevention programs are only those that reduce the flow of new users into the population of users. The analysis of the impact of narcotics-enforcement efforts is done separately for not-yet users and for committed users.

Second, I define the *effective price* of heroin as an index of all the things that make heroin difficult, inconvenient, risky, or otherwise "costly" for individuals to consume.[2] Thus, the index includes at least the following components: dollar price, amount of pure heroin, toxicity of adulterants, the expected time necessary to find heroin, the threat of arrest, and the risk of victimization by criminals. To some extent, market forces will cause these components of the effective price to be correlated. However, it should also be clear that some of the components will be fairly independent, and that they can be separately attacked by different policy instruments. Among these components of the effective price, dollar cost is likely to be relatively unimportant. Consequently, although I use the word "price" for analytic convenience, I mean to imply the concept of an "effective price."

1.0 Narcotics Enforcement as a Prevention Program

The single, most important objective of a narcotics-enforcement strategy is to discourage people who are not now using heroin from beginning to do so. If the police cannot achieve this objective at a reasonable cost in terms of public resources and maintenance of civil liberties, the prohibition policy ought to be abandoned. There are too many bad side effects of the policy and too few direct benefits other than preventing new use to warrant continuation of the policy if it cannot discourage new use.[b]

1.1 Models of the Relationship between Narcotics Enforcement and New Use

Several different models lead to a prediction that enforcing narcotics laws will reduce the rate at which new people become users. The first model could be called the *good-citizen model*. The basic idea is that criminalization of heroin use creates a presumption among most citizens that heroin use is dangerous and inappropriate. Consequently, many people decide not to use heroin. In effect,

---

[b]Many people are willing to argue that motivating users to seek treatment is also a substantial benefit of the policy. Although that this effect occurs, it is small relative to the costs of the prohibition policy. Consequently, the major justification for the prohibition policy must be to discourage new use.

the law operates as an educational program influencing individual values about the activity.

The second model is the more familiar *deterrence model*. The basic idea is that enforcing narcotics laws confronts all users with the risk of arrest, jail, and stigmatization. Confronted by these contingencies, many nonusers will decide not to experiment.[c]

The third model is the *inconvenience model*. The basic idea is that enforcing narcotics laws increases *many* of the components of the effective price of heroin. Indeed, the most important effect is likely to be increasing the time it takes to find heroin, and increasing the probability that a new user will fail to "score" after a long search. Facing this inconvenience, most new users, most of the time, decide that "copping" is not worth the effort.

Of these models, the strongest case can be made for the inconvenience model. The good-citizen model may describe a real effect, but it describes a mechanism that discourages heroin use among a population that is not likely to be tempted in any event. The value of this effect is roughly analogous to snapping one's fingers to keep elephants out of New Jersey: if it has an effect, it is largely redundant. The deterrence notion seems fairly implausible. The risk of arrest for experimenting users is not that high and could not be made high without very oppressive enforcement procedures. The risk of arrest enters as a component of the effective price, but it is not likely to be the most important component for new users. Consequently, if there is an argument for narcotics enforcement as a prevention program, it must rest on the truth or falsity of the inconvenience model: one must decide whether one believes that, on the margin, new users will be discouraged by increases in the effective price of heroin.

Of course, there is a trivial sense in which convenience matters in determining the probability of use. If a potential user cannot obtain heroin at any level of effort, he will obviously never become a heroin user. The real issue is more subtle: how the probability of use changes as the effective price varies over a reasonable range.[d]

We consider three hypotheses about the shape of this relationship. One hypothesis is that the effective price has no impact. People who use heroin are so strongly motivated to experiment that they will absorb enormous inconvenience and substantial risk to do so. A second hypothesis is that price and inconvenience have an effect, but only after the effective price reaches high levels. Potential users are not deterred by the prospect of a four-hour search and a

[c]In the terms of the analysis presented here, this model says that only one component of the "effective price" is important in influencing the probability of use. If true, this finding would dictate an enforcement strategy directed at users.

[d]Note that enforcement capabilities within existing constraints of legal procedures, resources, and bureaucratic procedures will define the limits of the "reasonable range." My own view is that narcotics enforcement can easily raise the time it takes a new user to find heroin from five minutes to two hours.

one-in-a-hundred chance of being arrested or mugged. However, they are deterred by the prospect of a ten-hour search and a one-in-five chance of being arrested or mugged. A third hypothesis is that inconvenience has an effect and that the strongest effects occur as the level of inconvenience rises from very low levels. Most potential users will be deterred by the expectation of a two-hour search and a very small chance of being arrested or mugged. A few users will not be screened out until the expected level of inconvenience rises to fairly high levels. Figure 5-1 illustrates the alternative hypotheses.

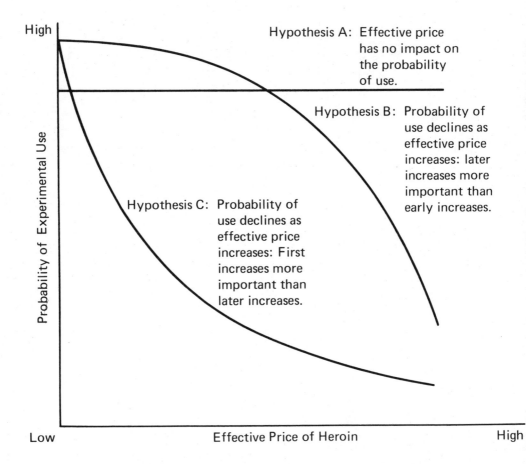

Figure 5-1. Alternative Hypotheses about the Relationship of the Effective Price of Heroin to the Probability of Experimental Use

1.2 Evidence Supporting the Hypothesis that Modest Levels
of Inconvenience are Sufficient to Discourage New Use

Two kinds of evidence are available to be considered in choosing among these alternative hypotheses. One kind of evidence comes from analyses of aggregate patterns of heroin use. If heroin is used more frequently in times, places, or populations where heroin is more available, then one can plausibly draw the inference that levels of accessibility do influence the probability of use. This kind of evidence presents problems of validity and interpretation: it is difficult to develop accurate measures of levels of heroin use, to separate the effects of accessibility from other predisposing factors, and to identify whether use is affecting accessibility or accessibility is affecting use.[e] Still, several findings are worth reporting. The findings should shift one's judgment in the direction of believing that levels of accessibility *do* influence the probability of use.

First, recent analyses indicate that the availability of heroin on the East Coast declined during the period 1972-73.[3] These decreases in availability coincided with decreases in both the incidence and prevalence of heroin use. Figure 5-2 reveals increases in price and decreases in purity for retail purchases of heroin from 1972 to 1973. Figure 5-3 shows decreases in levels of serum hepatitis (indicating new use) during the same period. Although the causation is not clear, the evidence is suggestive.

Second, a definitive analysis of drug-use patterns among Vietnam veterans indicated that levels of heroin users were very high in Vietnam (where heroin was conveniently available), but decreased dramatically among the same population when they returned to the United States (where heroin was less conveniently available).[4] Table 5-1 presents evidence on charges in levels in drug use. Of course, one can plausibly attribute this decline in use to dramatic improvements in the living conditions of the soldiers. However, when asked to give reasons for abandoning heroin use, many users indicated that risk of arrest and expense were important deterrents in the United States.[5]

Third, by interviewing addicts and enforcement personnel; and by reviewing court and police records, newspaper accounts and legislative hearings, analysts reconstructed by the sequence of events in a postwar epidemic of heroin use in Chicago.[6] The evidence indicated that an epidemic began shortly after World War II, reached its peak in 1949, and declined in the early 1950s. In looking for factors associated with the rise and fall of this epidemic they noted that: "The decline of this epidemic . . . [was] . . . most closely associated with decreased quality and increased cost of heroin."[7]

---

[e]It turns out that all documented cases of changes in levels of use for a given population, or comparisons among populations, cannot distinguish between changes in levels of "pressure and tension" and changes in "availability." They always seem to move together. This is true for Vietnam soldiers before and after Vietnam, for medical doctors compared with other professions, and for ghetto residents compared with other populations. Thus, we cannot conclusively exclude the hypotheses that levels of tension are more important than access in influencing levels of use.

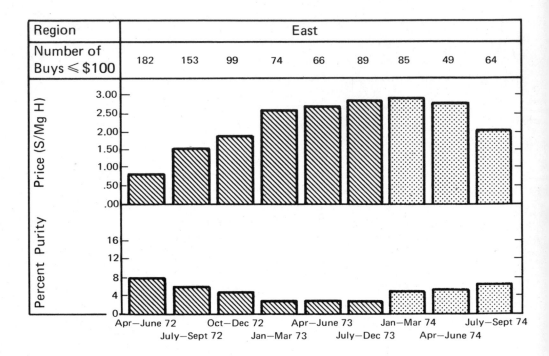

Source: Institute for Defense Analyses, "Trends in Heroin Indicators—January to September 1974: Availability Sources, Supply, and Use" (Washington, D.C.: Drug Enforcement Administration, 1975), p. 15.

Figure 5-2. Retail Heroin Availability April 1972-September 1974

Fourth, doctors and paramedical personnel have unusually high levels of opiate use. Doctors represent 1.5 percent of all admissions to federal hospitals treating narcotics addiction.[8] This is roughly ten times the proportion of physicians in the general population. Although one might hypothesize that doctors suffer from unusually severe pressures, it seems more than likely that some of their unusually high rates of use may be attributed to unusually low effective prices.

A second kind of evidence comes from an examination of the conditions under which individual users initiate and cease heroin use. This evidence suffers from uncertain biases in the sample of the interviewed users, and problems of interpretation. Still, the evidence is valuable in deciding whether modest or

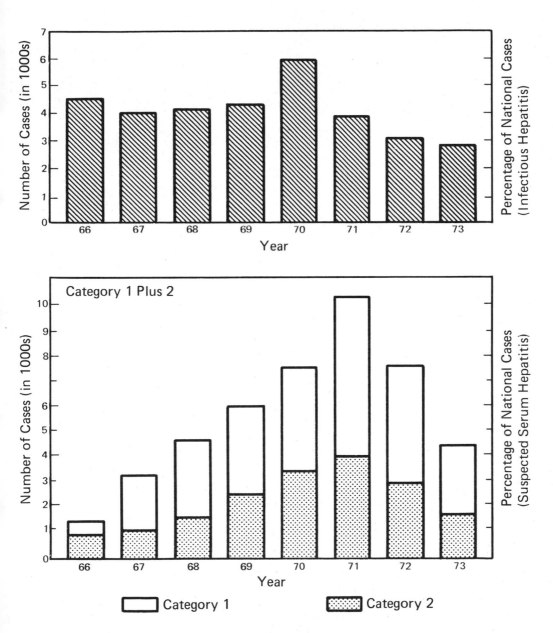

Source: Institute for Defense Analyses, "Indicators of Intravenous Drug Use in the United States: 1966-1973" (Washington, D.C.: Drug Enforcement Administration, 1975), p. 41.

Figure 5-3. Annual Trends in Hepatitis Reporting in the Middle Atlantic Census Division

Table 5-1
Dangerous Drugs Used In and Since Vietnam

	General Sample (N = 451)		Drug-Positive Sample (N = 469)	
	In Vietnam (Percent)	Since Vietnam (Percent)	In Vietnam (Percent)	Since Vietnam (Percent)
Any drug: narcotics, amphetamines, barbiturates	45	23	97	55
Narcotics	43	10	97	33
Amphetamines	25	19	59	38
Barbiturates	23	12	77	30
Combination of drug types				
All 3: narcotics, amphetamines, barbiturates	18	6	54	14
Amphetamines and barbiturates	0	3	0	6
Narcotics and amphetamines	6	2	4	7
Narcotics and barbiturates	5	1	23	6
Narcotics only	15	1	15	7
Amphetamines only	2	9	0	10
Barbiturates only	a	2	a	5

Source: Lee N. Robins, "The Vietnam Drug User Return," Special Action Office for Drug Abuse Prevention, Monograph: Series A, No. 2 (May 1972). Reprinted by permission.
aLess than 0.5%.

extreme levels of inconvenience are necessary to discourage experimentation with heroin. Two different findings can be reported.

First, studies of the onset of heroin use have discovered that virtually no users engage in a persistent search to find heroin during the early stages of use. Indeed, it seems that most users made no effort to find heroin. For example, in a definitive study of the causes of addiction in New York City, Isidor Chein found that:

The first opportunity [to use heroin] came about in a simple and casual way. . . . Very few actively sought the first opportunity. . . . In most cases, the heroin was obtained easily and without cost.[9]

Similarly, in a detailed study of the incidence of heroin use in Chicago, Patrick Hughes, and Gail Crawford discovered that:

Most frequently, the initiate is introduced to heroin when he meets a friend who is on his way to cop or is preparing to "fix"; he rarely seeks out the drug the first time. Thus, initiation depends more on fortuitous circumstances than on a willful act by the new user."[10]

One possible inference from these findings (although not the only possible inference) is that if heroin users had to look hard for heroin, they would not do so.

Second, there is one small study of people who experimented with heroin, found it pleasurable, but gave it up shortly after their first use.[11] These former experimenters were asked to state their reasons for abandoning heroin use. Table 5-2 presents the distribution of their responses. The fact that 55 percent of the experimenters stopped using heroin because their supply of heroin was interrupted casts doubt on the hypothesis that convenient access has no impact on the probability of use.

The experimenters also asked about the level of effort made to find a new source of heroin. Of the 9 former experimenters who had moved from their old neighborhood, 7 (78 percent) reported no efforts to find a new source, and 2 (22 percent) reported a small effort abandoned "because they could not find

Table 5-2
Significant Factors in Abandoning Heroin Use for Neophyte Users

Significant Factors in Abandoning Use	Number	Percent
I. Persuasion by others	2	5
a. Pressure from girl friend	2	5
II. Deterrence (anticipation of bad consequences of heroin use)	16	40
a. Experienced physical addiction	9	23
b. Friend convicted of narcotics charges	4	10
c. Subjects arrested for track marks	2	5
d. Friend died of overdose	1	2
III. Interruption of supply	22	55
a. Supplier arrested	9	22
b. Subject moved from neighborhood	6	15
c. Subject moved from town	3	8
d. Supplier lost his heroin source	3	8
e. Supplier moved from town	1	2
IV. Total	40	100

Source: Reprinted from Robert Schasre, "Cessation Patterns of Heroin Use Among Neophyte Users," *International Journal of the Addictions* 1:2 (1966): 27-28, by courtesy of Marcel Dekker, Inc.

anyone who could tell them how to go about getting stuff."[12] Of the 13 experimenters who reported that their connection was arrested, lost his source, or moved, 2 (15 percent) reported no effort to find a new source, and 11 (85 percent) reported efforts that "varied in intensity from two or three inquiries over as many days, to fairly extensive efforts lasting two to four weeks before 'losing interest,' or 'giving up.' "[13] If we pool these data, we observe that 9 of 22 experimenters who lost their connection (40 percent) made *no* effort to find a new source. Others made only a feeble effort, and some made a substantial effort. This evidence suggests there are many users who try heroin and like it, but are unwilling to look hard for it if it becomes difficult to find. It also shows that there are *some* who are willing to search intensively.

These former experimenters were identified by having *current* users have a friend who had started using heroin at the same time they did, but who had abandoned heroin use shortly after beginning. Consequently, the experimenters had a group of current users who had been associated with the *former* users at the time the former users stopped using heroin. This allowed the experimenters to address the question of why these current users continued to use heroin when their friends stopped. Of particular interest are the current users who were associated with the former users who lost their connection. The current users must also have suffered an interruption in their heroin supply. Why weren't they discouraged from use? Did they search longer than their friends?

Of the 13 people who became *chronic* users in spite of the loss of their connection at an early stage of use, 5 (38 percent) continued to search after their friends had stopped and eventually discovered a new source; 8 (62 percent) gave up heroin use at the same time as their friends and resumed heroin use later. However, for these 8 "introduction . . . reflected a common element of casualness and a lack of personal initiative in seeking out a new heroin source: 'I was at a party and one of the guys had stuff' was a typical explanation."[14] For the current users, then, disruption of the supply failed to discourage 5 of the 13 users. Disruption would have deterred the remaining 8 but for a chance encounter with heroin some time later. This evidence again indicates that convenience can affect the probability of use, that there are many experimental users who will not look hard for heroin, and that there are a minority who will.

The findings that practically no one searches intensively for heroin and that inconvenience is a major factor discouraging neophyte users from continuing heroin use suggest, but do not prove, that relatively modest levels of inconvenience may be sufficient to discourage use among new users.

Given both kinds of evidence, it seems reasonable to believe that the level of inconvenience in purchasing heroin can have an important effect on the probability of use. It is riskier, but not without some justification, to believe that the probability of use is more importantly influenced by the *first* increases in the level of inconvenience.

Since these arguments and evidence cannot be conclusive, it is prudent to ask how much is lost if we act on the basis of an incorrect hypothesis. The major policy choice that is influenced by a judgment about the importance of the effective price in discouraging experimentation is the decision about how strongly to enforce laws against the unauthorized use of narcotics. If convenient access does not matter, restricting access by aggressive attacks on the distribution system will not result in any prevention benefits. If access does matter, restricting it will have an important preventive effect. Moreover, if the first increases in the effective price are the most important, the enforcement effort does not have to be very successful in restricting access to have an important prevention effect.

Table 5-3 summarizes the consequences of working to restrict access at three levels for each hypothesis about the impact of the effective price on the probability of use. I find it difficult to evaluate this table simply because the stakes are so large and the differences in the probability that the hypotheses are true are so small. However, I am fairly confident that access has some effect. Consequently, I would be reluctant to relax our current efforts to restrict access to heroin.

This leaves us with the decision of how much we should attempt to restrict access. I recommend a moderate effort for three reasons. First, I think there is a reasonable chance that small levels of inconvenience are sufficient to deter many experimenters. Second, these moderate efforts to restrict access are not beyond our current bureaucratic capability and do not impose intolerable burdens on those who are already addicted. Third, we can increase our efforts to restrict access if it appears that moderate efforts are not enough. If we begin with very strenuous efforts, we may never discover that moderate efforts would have been just as successful.

Thus, it seems reasonable to act now "as if" access to heroin had an important effect in the probability of use and "as if" the first increases in inconvenience are more important than later increases, even if later, more definitive research indicates that these hypotheses are false.

1.3 Limitation of Narcotics Enforcement as a Prevention Program

The analysis above disguises a major problem in relying on narcotics enforcement as a prevention program. The problem has to do with the role of friends in spreading heroin use to nonusers. In stark terms, the problem is the following. Due to the difficulty of observing or infiltrating transactions among close friends, narcotics enforcement will be ineffective in discouraging transactions among close friends and relatives. Significant evidence indicates that nearly all users receive their early doses of heroin from friends and relatives. Consequently, it would appear that narcotics enforcement would be ineffective in preventing a

Table 5-3

Outcomes of Policies to Restrict Access under Alternative Assumptions about Role of Access in Affecting Probability of Use

	Policy I: Aggressive Efforts to Restrict Access: (Significant Expansion of Current Law-Enforcement Efforts)	Policy II: Moderate efforts to Restrict Access (Maintain Current Scale of Enforcement Activities)	Policy III: Relaxed Efforts to Restrict Access (Diminish Current Efforts to Restrict Access)
Hypothesis A: Effective price has no impact on probability of experimental use.	Outcome IA 1. *Few* are prevented from heroin use. 2. Current users harassed and stigmatized frequently. 3. Increased motivation to seek treatment.	Outcome IIA 1. *Few* are prevented from heroin use. 2. Current users harassed and stigmatized occasionally. 3. Small increase in motivation to seek treatment.	Outcome IIIA 1. *Few* are prevented from heroin use. 2. Current users' enjoyed increased comfort. 3. Slight decrease in motivation to seek treatment.
Hypothesis B: The probability of experimental use declines with increases in the effective price: later increases in effective price are important.	Outcome IB 1. *Many* are prevented from heroin use. 2. Current users harassed and stigmatized frequently. 3. Increased motivation to seek treatment.	Outcome IIB 1. Same as outcome IIA.	Outcome IIIA 1. Same as outcome IIIA.
Hypothesis C: probability of experimental use declines with increases in effective price: first increases in effective price are important.	Outcome IC 1. Same as outcome IB.	Outcome IIC 1. *Many* are prevented from heroin use. 2. Current users harassed and stigmatized occasionally. 3. Small increase in motivation for treatment.	Outcome IIIC 1. Same as outcome IIIA.

great deal of heroin use. It turns out that this general conclusion is wrong. However, the particular way in which heroin use spreads does establish some significant limitations on the effectiveness of narcotics enforcement as a prevention program. The issue is sufficiently important that it deserves close analysis.

There is overwhelming evidence that friends play an important role in spreading heroin use to new users. Specific findings are the following. First, surveys of users generally find that about 80 to 85 percent of the users report that their first dose of heroin was provided and administered by a close friend or relative.[15] Table 5-4 presents the findings of several studies of the circumstances surrounding the first use of heroin. The evidence is remarkable for its consistency, and provides overwhelming support for the proposition that friends have an important role in predisposing others to experiment and in facilitating their experimentation.

Second, two detailed analyses of the spread of heroin use in communities have documented the contagious character of heroin use and suggested that the contagion works primarily through friendship groups.

One study was conducted in a provincial town in England.[16] Figure 5-4 shows the observed pattern. The fact that 40 to 52 out of the 59 current users in the town could be traced back to only 2 initial users of heroin dramatically illustrates the contagiousness of heroin use. However, it does not necessarily show that the contagion works primarily through friends.

The hypothesis that friends play the role of infections agent is supported by the two pieces of evidence. The first piece is the author's observation that: "In every case between the initiators and the initiated there had been a long standing or current link of common school and neighborhood, or common haunts of amusement."[17] This evidence is not sufficient to allow to say that the initiator was a friend of the initiated, but it is suggestive.

A second piece of evidence is the particular pattern of introduction revealed in Figure 5-9. If one examines the map closely, one observes that an initiator typically initiates one to four people in a short period, and then introduces no new person. Drug use spreads only if one who was recently initiated initiates new additional people. There is no individual who initiates more than six people and most initiate one or less. This is the pattern one would expect if friends were important in the mechanism. An experimenter with drugs would quickly inform and tantalize his close friends, but *only* his close friends. Drug use would spread beyond that group of close friends only if the groups had some interlocking members. Thus, one would expect clusters of drug-use initiation, followed by lapses until a drug user moved into the periphery of a nondrug-using group, or a nondrug user who was in a group moved into the periphery of a drug-using group. This pattern is what one observes in the Crawley map. B4, B8, A3 and A8 are the most important "linkers" or interlocked friendship group members.

The above study was replicated in Chicago.[18] Figure 5-5 presents the

Table 5-4
Conditions of Initiation to Heroin Use

Locale	No. of Addicts Surveyed	Percentage of Addicts Started by a Drug User	Percentage of Addicts Started by a Drug-User-Initiator Who Was a Friend of the Same Age	Percentage of Addicts Started by a Drug Pusher	Percentage Who Started Out of Curiosity Due to a Friend's Influence
Los Angeles	321	87	63	2	81
D.C.	734	89	86	2	80
Chicago	348	77	75	4	60
New Jersey	995	90	87	1	64
New York City	3,566	89	86	2	63
San Antonio	352	91	80	–	53—curiosity 23—kicks

Source: McGlothin et al., *Alternative Approaches to Opiate Addiction Control*, Bureau of Narcotics and Dangerous Drugs (Washington, D.C.: U.S. Department of Justice 1972), Appendix B, p. 10. Reprinted by permission.

251

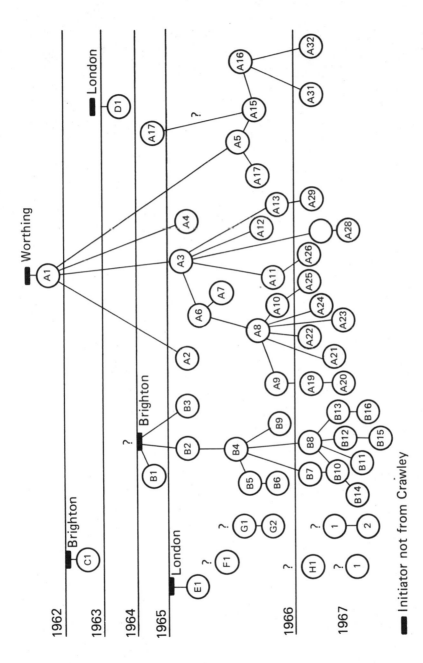

Source: R. de Alarcon, "The Spread of Heroin Abuse in a Community," *United Nations Bulletin on Narcotics* 21:3 (July-September 1969): 17-22. Reprinted by permission.

Figure 5-4. The Spread of Heroin Abuse in Crawley, New Town, England

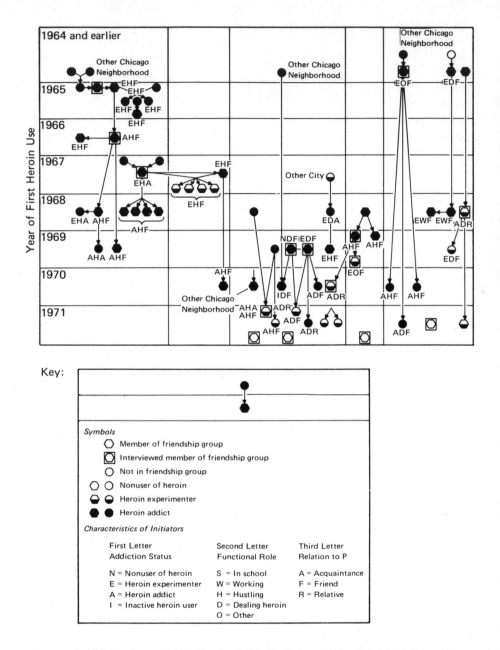

Source: Patrick Hughes and Gail Crawford, "A Contagious Disease Model for Researching and Intervening in Heroin Epidemics," *Archives of General Psychiatry* 27 (August 1972): 152. Copyright 1972, American Medical Association. Reprinted by permission.

Figure 5-5. The Spread of Heroin Use in a Neighborhood in Chicago, Illinois

pattern observed. Contagiousness is apparent, but to a lesser degree than in the English study. More importantly, the Chicago study presents direct evidence on the relationship between the initiator and the initiated. In the 50 cases for which this information is recorded, 40 (80 percent) were friends of their initiators, 4 (8 percent) were related to the initiator, and 6 (12 percent) were merely acquaintances.[19]

These detailed studies of the spread of heroin use give strong support to the proposition that friends spread heroin use to other friends. Indeed, it is hard to imagine more compelling evidence on this issue.

The importance of friends in spreading heroin use creates a dilemma for narcotics enforcement. It seems clear that transactions among friends are relatively impregnable to narcotics-enforcement efforts. The distribution system is vulnerable to legal arrests only if the police observe the transactions. Since it is easy to conceal the transactions, it is difficult to demonstrate that a transaction has occurred unless one has been a party to it. If participants in the transaction are always close friends, the police will not be able to insinuate themselves or informers into the distribution system. Consequently, enforcement activities tend to affect transactions only among relative strangers. If it is true that law-enforcement tactics are ineffective against transactions between close friends, and if it is true that nearly all users obtain their early doses of heroin from a close friend, the inevitable conclusion seems to be that narcotics enforcement will fail to prevent heroin use—in spite of the evidence that levels of convenience and accessibility seem to influence the probability of use.

However, the issue turns out to be slightly more complicated than the simple syllogism presented above. The issue that must be investigated is the relative importance of transactions among strangers in determining the rate at which heroin use spreads through a neighborhood, given that we know nearly all users get their first doses of heroin from a close friend or relative. A simple analytic model is helpful.

Imagine a neighborhood of 100 adolescents. We will assume that all are vulnerable to heroin use. To accommodate the proposition that convenient access affects the probability of use, we will make the probability of use a function of contact with other heroin users. To accommodate the proposition that experienced users play an important role in predisposing and facilitating use among nonusing friends, we will divide the society into ten groups, each with ten individuals. Each person in a group is considered a friend to all others in his group and a stranger to all outside the group. The probability of use is a function of contacts with heroin using friends and with heroin using strangers. One can think of these contacts as encounters that have the potential for being a first experience with heroin, for example, an encounter at a party in which a user has heroin to spare, or an encounter on the street when the user is going to score. In general, we assume that the probability of use given contact with a heroin-using friend is higher than the probability of use given contact with a heroin-using stranger. In the simple model, there are two parameters: the probability of use given contact with a heroin using *friend*, and the probability of use given contact with a heroin using *stranger*.

Using this model, we would like to investigate the value of restricting access through aggressive law enforcement when the enforcement cannot affect transactions among friends. The effect of law enforcement is captured by a decrease in the probability of use given contact with a heroin using stranger. The impregnability of transactions among friends is captured by keeping the probability of use given contact with a friend constant for all levels of enforcement. Thus, the analytic strategy will be to observe differences in the rate at which heroin use spreads through this community as we allow the probability of use, given contact with a heroin-using stranger to vary from low levels (which would occur if law enforcement was very effective) to levels close to the probability of use, given contact with a heroin-using friend (which would occur if enforcement efforts were so lax as to make a user not care whether he revealed his use to a friend or a stranger).

Figure 5-6 will aid in interpreting the results of this model. On the vertical axis of this figure is the proportion of people who have begun to use heroin. On the horizontal axis is time. We assume a constant probability of use, given contact with a heroin-using friend. We are interested in the rate at which heroin use spreads as we allow the probability of addiction, given contact with a heroin-using stranger to vary. Two possible outcomes are sketched. If curves L aggressive and L lax represent the differences between the spread of heroin use when law enforcement was aggressive and when it was lax, we will be inclined to believe that the value of the aggressive law enforcement in preventing heroin use is low. If curves L aggressive and L' lax represented the differences, we will be inclined to believe that the prevention benefits of aggressive law enforcement are large. In effect, we are interested in the sensitivity of the rate of spread to changes in the probability of use given contact with a heroin-using stranger.

Table 5-5 presents the results of repeated runs of the model. We have used two different indicators for the "sensitivity" of the rates of spread. One is changes in the average length of time for different proportions of the population to become addicted. The other is changes in the average length of time until each friendship group has at least one heroin-using member. In general, the results show that the rate at which heroin use spreads is quite sensitive to changes in the probability of use, given contact with a heroin-using stranger. When this parameter has a low value, the epidemic barely struggles along. When this parameter has a high value, there is an epidemic.

This result might be puzzling. However, two observations about the mechanism will clarify the findings. First, imagine what would happen if the probability of use given contact with a stranger were zero, that is, if it were impossible to score from anyone but a friend. In this case, everyone in the group with the initial user would be quickly become a user, and no one else. The

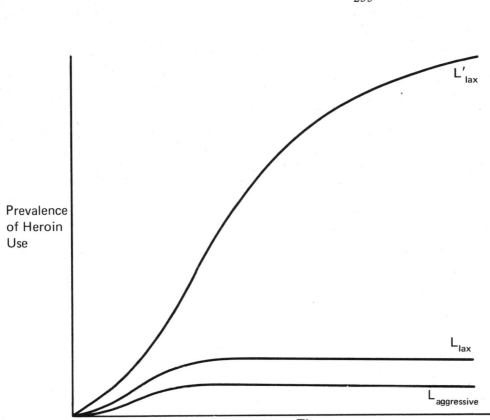

Figure 5-6. Possible Results of the Analytic Model

epidemic would have no way to get beyond the initial group of friends. This suggests that contacts with heroin-using strangers affects the spread of heroin use by allowing heroin use to leap out of one friendship group into another. Each time it does leap out, the rate at which heroin use spreads is increased via two different mechanisms; a new friendship group *tips* into heroin use, and the proportion of heroin using strangers in the population increases, thereby making the next leap more likely to occur.

Second, consider what proportion of the users have been initiated by strangers in a case where the epidemic never gets off the ground and in a case where it takes off quickly. In the case where the epidemic never takes off, we know that the probability of use given contact with a heroin-using stranger was low. Consequently, one might expect that a very small proportion were initiated

Table 5-5
Outputs of the Analytic Model of the Spread of Heroin Use

Assumed Parameters of the Model	No. of Periods Until X% of Population Has Experimented with Heroin			Length of Time Until Each Group Has 1 Using Member
	X = 25%	X = 50%	X = 75%	
I. $P(A\|F)$* = 0.05				
1. $P(A\|S)$** = 0.0005	8	>9	>9	>9
2. $P(A\|S)$ = 0.0010	7	9	>9	>9
3. $P(A\|S)$ = 0.0030	5	6	8	6
4. $P(A\|S)$ = 0.0050	4	5	6	4
II. $P(A\|F)$ = 0.10				
1. $P(A\|S)$ = 0.0005	5	9	>9	>9
2. $P(A\|S)$ = 0.0010	5	7	9	>8
3. $P(A\|S)$ = 0.0030	4	5	5	4
4. $P(A\|S$ = 0.0050	3	4	5	4
III. $P(A\|F)$ = 0.150				
1. $P(A\|S)$ = 0.0005	4	6	8	>9
2. $P(A\|S)$ = 0.0010	4	6	7	6
3. $P(A\|S)$ = 0.0030	3	4	5	4
4. $P(A\|S)$ = 0.0050	3	4	5	3

*$P(A\|F)$ = Probability of heroin experimentation given contact with a heroin using friend.
**$P(A\|S)$ = Probability of heroin experimentation given contact with a heroin using stranger.

by a stranger. Similarly, we know that in the case where the epidemic took off quickly, the probability of use given contact with a heroin-using stranger was high. Consequently, one might expect that a large proportion were initiated by strangers. What we find is that although there is some variation in the proportion initiated by a stranger, the variation is remarkably small. Both in the case where an epidemic takes off and in the case where it struggles along, the proportion of people initiated by a stranger ranges between 10 and 15 percent.

The reason for this result is that once there is one heroin user in a friendship group, it becomes much more likely that the others in the group will be initiated by a friend than by a stranger. It is only the *first* user in each group who needs to be initiated by a stranger. All the others can be more conveniently initiated by a friend. Since it is only the first user who is initiated by a stranger, the proportion of those who are initiated by strangers tends to be near $1/n$ where n is the average number of people in a friendship group for all probabilities of

[f]The proportion does not precisely equal $1/n$ because there is some possibility of becoming addicted from a stranger.

heroin use given contact with a heroin-using stranger.[f] Thus, there tends to be little difference in the proportion of users initiated by strangers between a virulent epidemic situation and a mild epidemic situation. The only difference between the two situations is the *absolute number* of successful stranger to stranger transactions that occurred. This observation emphasizes the importance of small increases in the absolute number of stranger to stranger transactions.

Thus, the simple model suggests that even if narcotics-enforcement strategies are limited to deterring stranger to stranger transactions, narcotics enforcement can have a significant impact on the rate at which heroin use spreads.

Note, however, that the model also suggests some conditions will decisively limit the potential effectiveness of narcotics enforcement in preventing heroin use. In some neighborhoods, heroin use is endemic. Virtually everyone in the neighborhood knows someone who uses heroin. Moreover, there are strong norms against cooperating with the police. In such neighborhoods, the distinction between friends and strangers blurs, and it becomes difficult for the police to reduce the probability of chance encounters with heroin. In other neighborhoods, no heroin use yet exists, people are more isolated, and existing norms encourage cooperating with the police. In such areas it is relatively easy for the police to control chance encounters. The implication of these observations is that narcotics enforcement will fail to prevent new heroin use in areas where heroin use is already endemic. In effect, narcotics enforcement can prevent heroin use in Richmond, New Jersey but not in Harlem.

The problems created by this limitation on the effectiveness of narcotics enforcement are exacerbated by the fact that the law-enforcement efforts will necessarily be targeted on endemic areas. It is in the endemic areas that the police will have to operate to make dealers and experienced users leery of strangers and to disrupt established markets and ways of doing business. Thus, the endemic area must take a lot of the pressure of the law-enforcement strategy but receive only a small amount of its benefits. The areas that really benefit are the areas that do not yet have the problem.

Efficiency may demand the law-enforcement strategy. It is a strategy that results in many people being protected from convenient access to heroin. However, equity demands that we do at least as much to prevent heroin use among people living in endemic areas. Indeed, since they will bear the brunt of the law-enforcement strategy, and since they tend to be among the most economically deprived in any case, it seems necessary that we do much *more* for them than for the others. Thus, in endemic areas, it will be necessary to complement narcotics-enforcement efforts with other programs to prevent heroin use among nonusers. One must provide jobs, schools, and recreation opportunities that can compete with heroin use as compelling alternative uses of adolescents' time. Law enforcement can contribute to prevention objectives in these areas by making the alternatives *relatively* more attractive, but it cannot be expected to do the whole job.

2.0 Impact of Narcotics Enforcement on Current Users

The analysis above indicates it is likely that moderate narcotics-enforcement efforts can reduce the rate at which new people living in nonendemic areas using heroin. A major price we pay for relying on narcotics-enforcement efforts to achieve this limited objective is that the enforcement efforts have very bad effects on the behavior and condition of current users. The purpose of this section is to gauge the effects of narcotics enforcement on current users and to identify policy instruments that can reduce the bad side effects of narcotics-enforcement policies.

2.1 Effects on Current Users

Enforcing narcotics laws has both direct and indirect effects on current users. The direct effect is that users are confronted by the threat of police harrassment and jail. In the short run, this means that users are intimidated, imprisoned, and made to feel powerless. In the long run, the arrests imply that users will be stigmatized, discriminated against in labor markets, exceedingly vulnerable to rearrest, and develop a conception of themselves as deviant.

The indirect effects are associated with having to consume heroin in the black market where the effective price is very high. Unpredictable quantities of heroin and toxic adulterants threaten the health of current users.[20] The high-dollar cost of heroin forces users both to spend less on housing, food, and other necessary items; and to work harder at illegal occupations that impose costs on others in the society.[g] Difficult and irregular access to heroin makes it difficult for users to hold regular jobs and leaves them little time or energy to devote to family and friends. In the long run, the life-style that was initially stimulated and sustained by the requirements of consuming heroin in a black market become deeply rooted in the skills, habits, and attitudes of the users. Thus, high, effective prices to current users produce broad, long-run, adverse effects on the behavior and condition of users.

The conventional analysis of these effects probably exaggerates the difference between the behavior of current users facing high, effective prices in black markets and the behavior of the same users facing low, effective prices in legitimate heroin-distribution systems. There is evidence that indicates users with access to low-cost heroin are *almost* as unhealthy, economically dependent, and dangerous as users forced to consume black-market heroin.[h] Apparently,

---

[g]For anecdotal accounts of this pressure, see Seymour Fiddle, *Portraits from a Shooting Gallery* (New York: Harper and Row, 1967); or Jeremy Larner and Ralph Tefferteller, *The Addict in the Street* (New York: Grove Press, 1964).

[h]See, in general, English studies of English users. The following sources are particularly good: Thomas H. Bewley et al., "Morbidity and Mortality from Heroin Dependence," *British Medical Journal*, March 23, 1968; M.M. Glatt et al., *Journey Into Loneliness: The Drug Scene in Great Britain* (London: Edward Arnold, 1967); and G.V. Stimson, *Heroin and Behavior* (New York: Wiley and Sons, 1973).

long-term, intravenous heroin use creates significant problems for individual users even when the society refrains from making heroin use even more disruptive by making it illegal, expensive, and unsterile. Still, in spite of this evidence, there is no doubt that high, effective prices for heroin to discourage experimental use impose significant costs on current users. Consequently, it is essential to find a way of reducing these costs.

Note that efforts to reduce the adverse consequences of narcotics enforcement on current users also reduce the incentive value of a high, effective price for heroin. If the bad consequences of using heroin are reduced, incentives to avoid experimentation and to abandon use are correspondingly reduced. As a result, flows into the population of users may increase, flows out of the population of users through treatment and voluntary abstinence may decline, and the equilibrium number of current users may increase. One cannot avoid this result. One must choose an appropriate level of incentive: one that is sufficient to discourage experimentation and encourage cures, but does not inflict too great a cost on current users. In my judgment, the policies proposed below reduce the adverse effects of the prohibition policy on current users, and retain sufficiently strong disincentives both to discourage experimentation and encourage decisions to seek treatment or voluntarily abandon heroin use.

2.2 Strategies to Reduce Adverse Effects on Current Users

Basically, there are three, broad strategies for reducing the adverse effects of narcotics-enforcement policies on the behavior and condition of current users. First, one can design the narcotics-enforcement policy to create two different effective prices—a very high, effective price for experimental users and a moderate, effective price for current users.[21] Second, one can make available a wide variety of treatment programs to soften the indirect, adverse effects of narcotics-enforcement efforts, and to respond to the "voluntary" demand of users who can no longer stand the hassle created by indirect effects. Third, one can soften the direct effects of narcotics-enforcement efforts by establishing diversion systems that keep arrested users out of jail. Each of these strategies is discussed briefly below.

The possibility of creating two effective prices resolves a cruel dilemma in the design of heroin policy. We would like a high, effective price to new users to reduce the probability that they become regular users. We would like a low, effective price to experienced users to reduce the pressure to commit crimes and to restore some dignity and comfort. Without the possibility of price discrimination, we would face a difficult trade-off between the prevention objective and the crime-reduction objective. With price discrimination, we can pursue both objectives simultaneously.

Ordinarily, it is difficult to create two prices for the same commodity. The reason is that if price differentials exist, there will always be incentives for arbitrage: people will buy in an inexpensive market and sell in the expensive market. The increased supply to the expensive market will gradually lower the price in that market until it equals the price in the cheaper market.

However, it is possible to design a narcotics-enforcement strategy that creates price discrimination between new and old users. As we have seen, illegal dealers wish to maximize a utility function that includes income and the probability of arrest as arguments.[22] This utility function gives them clear preference for certain kinds of customers: Those known not to be undercover police, those known to be stand-up guys (i.e., nonsquealers), and those who buy large quantities at each transaction. These customers yield higher incomes at lower risk. A less desirable customer is one who has no solid reputation, who buys irregularly, and who buys little. Since the characteristics dealers prefer in customers are positively correlated with duration of use, even though dealers may be indifferent on the issue of selling to new or old users, they have incentives to discriminate on the basis of characteristics correlated with a customer's previous experience as a user. A de facto discrimination against inexperienced users and in favor of old users results.

Similarly, one can separate new users from markets by making it difficult for them to observe and contact dealers. If copping areas are disrupted by combinations of police pressure and treatment intervention, users who do not currently have good connections will find it difficult to contact a broker or a dealer.

The observation that new users face relatively higher, effective prices gains added importance when one observes that at any given price the elasticity of demand for heroin is likely to be greater for new users than for experienced users. The reason is simply that new users are not yet addicted to heroin. Consequently, when supplies are restricted, new users are the first to disappear from the market.

Thus, in designing narcotics-enforcement strategies, it is both desirable and possible to create two effective prices—a high, effective price for new users to secure the prevention objective, and a moderate, effective price for old users to maintain some incentives for the old users to seek treatment while reducing some of the adverse effects on current users.

If the enforcement strategy is designed to create price discrimination between new and old users, some of the adverse effects of the enforcement strategy are reduced. However, there remains the problem of responding to increased demand for treatment from moderately harassed current users. This demand should be met by a wide variety of treatment programs. Current programs include therapeutic communities, methadone-maintenance programs, ambulatory-detoxification programs, and sheltered workshops. In addition, variants of current programs such as therapeutic communities that provide methadone maintenance, sheltered workshops for methadone patients, and therapeutic communities that require less rigorous psychological exercises should be tried as experiments. Given that by maintaining a high, effective price for heroin we inflict substantial losses on current users, and encourage them to seek treatment, we are obligated to make available to users a wide variety and adequate supply of treatment facilities.

Finally, the narcotics-enforcement strategy guarantees that users will be arrested. Some will be arrested for narcotics offenses as a direct effect of narcotics-enforcement efforts. Others will be arrested for property and violent crimes as an indirect effect of narcotics-enforcement efforts. Since jail terms do little to improve the behavior and condition of users, and since the stigma of arrest records constrains the future opportunities of the current users, these arrests inflict substantial losses on current users. These losses can be reduced by developing programs that divert arrested users from the criminal-justice system into treatment programs, which are more pleasant, more effective, and less expensive than jails. Because many of these arrests have only marginal value in efforts to increase the effective price, and since they inflict substantial losses on individual users, it is desirable to do as much as possible to reduce these losses.

3.0 Summary: What We Want Narcotics Enforcement to Do and What We Must Do in Addition

In sum, law enforcement has two very important contributions to make to our overall heroin policy. First, it prevents heroin use. Second, it motivates users to seek treatment. However, law enforcement is only *part* of a strategy. It prevents heroin use only among those not living in endemic areas. To protect those who do live in endemic areas we must provide attractive, competitive uses of their time. In addition, narcotics enforcement has disastrous effects on the behavior and condition of already committed heroin users. To cope with these disastrous effects, we must provide a rich array of treatment programs and invent procedures for diverting arrested narcotics users from jail. We should strengthen law enforcement to secure the benefits that law enforcement permits. However, it is important to keep constantly in mind that although law enforcement is an important instrument, it is only part of a strategy for controlling the heroin problem.

Notes

1. Mark H. Moore, "Testimony Before the Government Operations Committee of the U.S. Senate" (New York: May 1973).

2. Mark H. Moore, "Policies to Achieve Discrimination on the Effective Price of Heroin," *American Economic Review* 63: 2 (May 1973).

3. Robert L. DuPont, director of the Special Action Office for Drug

Abuse Prevention, "Statement Before the Senate Permanent Subcommittee on Investigation," Committee on Government Operations (June 1975), pp. 1-5.

4. Lee N. Robins, The Vietnam Drug User Returns, Special Action Office for Drug Abuse Prevention Monograph: Series A, No. 2 (May 1974).

5. Ibid., p. 58.

6. Patrick H. Hughes et al., "The Natural History of a Heroin Epidemic," *American Journal of Public Health*, July 1972.

7. Ibid., p. 999.

8. William H. McGlothlin et al., "Alternative Approaches to Addiction Control: Costs, Benefits, and Potential," Bureau of Narcotics and Dangerous Drugs (Washington, D.C.: U.S. Department of Justice, 1972), Appendix B, p. 8.

9. Isidor Chein et al., *The Road to H* (New York: Basic Books, 1964), pp. 150-151.

10. Patrick Hughes and Gail Crawford, "A Contagious Disease Model for Researching and Intervening in Heroin Epidemics," *Archives of General Psychiatry* 27 (August 1972): 152.

11. Robert Schasre, "Cessation Patterns Among Neophyte Users," *International Journal of the Addiction* 1:2 (1966).

12. Ibid., p. 29.

13. Ibid.

14. Ibid., p. 30.

15. McGlothin et al., "Alternative Approaches to Addiction Control," Appendix B, p. 10.

16. R. de Alarcon, "The Spread of Heroin Use in a Community," *United Nations Bulletin on Narcotics* 21:3 (July-September 1969).

17. Ibid., p. 21.

18. Hughes and Crawford, "A Contagious Disease Model for Researching and Intervening in Heroin Epidemics."

19. Ibid., p. 152.

20. Donald Luria, Terry Hensle, and John Rose, "The Major Medical Complications of Heroin Addiction," *Annals of Internal Medicine* 67:1 (July 1967).

21. Mark H. Moore, "Policies to Achieve Discrimination on the Effective Price of Heroin."

22. See Chapter 1.

6

A Specific Enforcement
Strategy for New York City

Given this role for narcotics enforcement in an overall policy towards heroin use, what specifically should state and local police do? What levels of the distribution system and what kinds of dealers should be their targets? Which strategies and tactics should be employed to create important indirect effects? What problems will the existing organizations face in implementing a specific strategy?

One can make some rough calculations about these issues through a process of "backward mapping." One begins with a description of specific objectives to be achieved in influencing the shape of the distribution system. Then, by reasoning backwards, one can identify the strategies and tactics we are likely to achieve those objectives. Finally, one can match specific organizational capabilities against the required strategies and tactics.[a]

1.0 Specific Objectives of an Enforcement Strategy

The overall objective of the narcotics-enforcement strategy should be to create discrimination on the effective price of heroin by maintaining a moderately high, effective price for old users, and by choosing enforcement tactics that have the effect of creating very high effective prices for new users. By discouraging a large amount of new use, and by maintaining some modest incentives for old users to abandon heroin use without subjecting the users to the full set of consequences of enforcing narcotics laws, this strategy maximizes the contribution of narcotics enforcement to an overall heroin policy.

The overall objective implies three more specific operational objectives. The first objective is to minimize the supply of heroin reaching illicit markets. Basically, the enforcement agencies must find efficient ways to constrain the throughput capacity of the production-distribution systems. Achievement of this objective insures a moderately high, effective price for both new and old users.

The second objective is to motivate retail dealers to discriminate against new users. The enforcement agencies can achieve this objective by choosing tactics that motivate dealers to screen out young strangers and by arresting dealers who fail to behave in this cautious way. Achievement of this objective guarantees that new users will face unusual difficulty in "copping."

[a]I am indebted to Richard E. Neustadt, professor of government, and Graham T. Allison, professor of politics, both of Harvard University, and the Faculty Seminar on Bureaucracy and Politics for encouraging me to make these calculations of bureaucratic feasibility in this particular style.

The third objective is to make it difficult for new users to locate "copping areas." There should be no area to which an inexperienced user could come and expect to find heroin. The markets should be small, concealed from public view and forced to move frequently. Because new users are usually less able to obtain accurate, current information about heroin markets than older, more experienced users, the disruption of stable copping areas inflicts greater losses on new users than old users.

Note that achievement of the first objective (i.e., limiting supplies of heroin) facilitates achievement of the second and third objectives. The reason is that since heroin dealers maximize a utility function that includes both money and security, their decisions on marketing strategies takes both factors into account. In a world of limited availability and high prices for heroin, dealers may find that they can satisfy absolute profit objectives easily, but may not be able to improve their profit position easily. As a result, money profits become less influential in guiding the selection of marketing strategies. The corollary of this observation is that the risk of arrest becomes a more influential guide to marketing strategies. In effect, in a world of tight supplies, dealers can *afford* to become cautious and deliberate. In this world, dealers will react much more dramatically to changes in levels or types of enforcement efforts. Since the second and third objectives (e.g., making dealers leery of strangers and disrupting stable copping areas) depend on dealers reacting to enforcement efforts, it will be easier to achieve these objectives in a world of limited heroin availability and high prices.

2.0 Optimal Strategies and Tactics for Achieving Operational Objectives

The strategic calculation about how best to achieve these objectives differs for each of the objectives. The calculation of efficient strategies for reducing the aggregate supply of heroin is very complex. The calculation of strategies to motivate retail dealers to discriminate against new users and to disrupt stable copping areas are more straightforward.

The most effective strategy for reducing the aggregate supply of heroin has long been the subject of heated controversy.[1] Viewed from the perspective of the federal government, the range of strategic possibilities is very broad. One can choose to strike at different factors of production or distribution (e.g., raw materials, processing facilities, inventories, or transactions that knit the entire system together). Within distribution systems one can strike at different levels or at different kinds of organizations (e.g., street levels v. higher levels, cautious organizations v. aggressive organizations). Finally, one can choose different geographic areas and different institutional mechanisms for mounting an attack. Given the lack of empirically verified models of international production-distribution systems, the calculation of the optimal strategy from such a broad array of possibilities is extremely complex.

Viewed from the perspective of state- and local-enforcement agencies, the design of a strategy to reduce aggregate supplies is more constrained, and therefore, more straightforward. Typically, state- and local-enforcement agencies face local-distribution systems. They must decide which level to attack and which tactics to employ in seeking to constrain the throughput capacity of the local-distribution systems. In making this decision, they should consider the magnitude of the direct effects (e.g., the arrest of dealers representing specific distributional capabilities and the seizure of inventories), the magnitude of the indirect effects (e.g., the incentives created for dealers who remain on the street to behave cautiously and, therefore, inefficiently), and the costs of the strategy (e.g., the resources consumed in making the case). In addition, to the extent that the federal strategy for reducing aggregate supplies is known, state and local agencies should design their strategy to assist the federal effort.

It is likely that the most effective strategy for reducing aggregate supplies of heroin within the constrained set of alternatives facing state- and local-enforcement units is to arrest dealers and confiscate supplies at medium levels of the distribution system (e.g., weight dealers). To make such arrests, they will typically have to rely on a combination of extended undercover operations, search-warrant and wiretap arrests based on information from high-level informants, and retrospective-conspiracy investigations. This level is the right level to attack for three reasons.

First, the arrests can be made fairly inexpensively. The level of the distribution system is low enough to be making frequent transactions, and to lack some of the most expensive defensive strategies (e.g., a capacity to kill or maim informants, a capacity to pay large bribes to police and court officials, and very extensive screening of customers). Consequently, with modest levels of effort, the police can make arrests at this level.

Second, the *direct* effects of arrests at these levels are not insignificant. This level is sufficiently high for dealers to be dealing in reasonably large quantities of heroin and to be reasonably difficult to replace. Consequently, the removal of these dealers involves a fairly large and durable reduction in the capabilities of the system.

Third, the *indirect* effects of arrests at these levels are also considerable. There are sufficiently few dealers at this level for them to notice when one of their peers is arrested and to react dramatically. The dramatic response will usually be in the areas of tighter screening and closer disciplining of their customers. This will reduce their efficiency in distributing heroin and force some of them out of business. Thus, the indirect effects will have a significant impact on the total throughput capacity of the system.

In sum, arrests at this level are likely to produce the largest reduction in throughput capacity (via both direct and indirect effects) per dollar expended. If one worked at higher levels, the costs would go up dramatically without necessarily producing greater local results. If one worked at lower levels, costs would decrease, but both direct and indirect effects on throughput capacity would decrease even faster.

Note that it is likely that this local strategy will fit in well with the national strategy to reduce aggregate supplies. A major piece of the federal strategy to reduce the supply of heroin will be to immobilize major trafficking networks.[2] Given that transactions will be as great a problem at the international level as they are at local levels; that criminal organizations will be established to routinize these transactions; and that, once established, these organizations may succeed in concentrating a substantial fraction of the distribution under their control, the federal strategy must be directed at immobilizing large organizations. To accomplish that objective, they will rely primarily on defendant-informants. The source of the defendant-informants will often be arrests by state and local police. Thus, the arrest of local "weight dealers" will not only produce an immediate reduction in local supplies of heroin, it will also create the possibility of enforcement actions that will reduce national supplies of heroin. Insuring this complementary relationship between local efforts to reduce aggregate supplies and national efforts to reduce aggregate supplies should be a major objective of state and local efforts.[b]

The most effective strategies for motivating retail dealers to discriminate against new users is to make large numbers of undercover purchases at retail levels. In making these arrests, one should rely on undercover police who have the characteristics of the vulnerable population. The police should look young, and should reflect the ethnic characteristics of the people in the neighborhoods where they conduct operations. An overrepresentation of white undercover police will result only in greater protection for white teenagers.

Note that achievement of the objective of making dealers leery of strangers will depend on the scale of police operations. There are a large number of retail dealers. Moreover, they are easily replaced. Consequently, one cannot count on the direct effects of arrests at this level to accomplish a great deal. The impact of the indirect effects is more important. If dealers are risk averse, marginal increases in the indirect effects of this strategy will increase as the proportion of retail dealers arrested by this tactic increase. Consequently, there are economies of scale in the overall effectiveness of this strategy: there are likely to be minimum economic levels in using this strategy, and once one has passed this minimum economic level, there are strong incentives to go even further.

The strategy to disrupt stable copping areas relies primarily on police patrol activities and casual surveillance by investigators. Patrol forces should maintain a strong presence in areas known to be copping areas and should respond to most narcotics complaints. Investigative forces should maintain surveillance of known copping areas and make occasional observation-sale arrests. These tactics will

---

[b]The major problem here is operational coordination among the organizations.

result in the arrest of brazen, aggressive dealers and will provide incentives for other dealers to be discrete. As a result, dealers will be moved off regular street corners and out of regular bars.

Note that the disruption of stable copping areas will depend on scale even more critically than the strategy to motivate dealers to be wary of new users. The reason is simply that the direct effects of these tactics will be very small. The charges against the dealers will not be serious, and the cases will be weak. As a result, the expected sanctions will be small, and the deterrent value of the strategy minimal. Thus, to disrupt stable copping areas, one must maintain a very high level of police activity.

Fortunately, these enforcement efforts can be complemented by other programs to disrupt stable copping areas. One tactic is to use the licensing powers of the state to threaten the owners of bars, restaurants, or cigar stores where heroin is routinely sold. A more effective and less oppressive tactic is simply to recruit large numbers of local users into treatment programs. In fact, a detailed study of a local epidemic of heroin use in a Chicago neighborhood showed that a combination of enforcement efforts and aggressive outreach by treatment programs could shut off the flow of new users in a local area.[3] Thus, these complementary efforts will be necessary to achieve the objective of disrupting stable copping areas.

Achievement of the objective of disrupting copping areas requires not only an impressive scale of enforcement efforts, but also effective *geographic* deployment. A major potential problem is that the police will be prohibited from operating within institutions such as schools and treatment programs. Of course, it is obvious that a police presence will adversely affect the operations of these institutions. However, it is also obvious that keeping the police out of such institutions may create "safe havens" within which drug selling to new users can easily occur. Indeed, once it becomes known that the police are not allowed to operate in these areas, the areas will attract aggressive dealers, or will permit dealers already operating there to become aggressive. An adequate solution to this problem depends on straightforward negotiations between managers of schools, treatment programs, and the police. The negotiations should concern the magnitude of the dealing problem, and possible ways to minimize the disruptive impact of police operations. Although cultural differences among the different professions make such negotiations exceedingly difficult, the public interest probably requires that neither group be able to determine policy unilaterally for all cases.

Thus, the optimal strategy for state and local police is a three-pronged attack:

1. Arrests made at medium levels of local distribution systems through extended undercover operations, search-warrant and wiretap arrests, and retrospective-conspiracy investigations

2. Arrests made at retail levels by undercover police who have the characteristics of new users of heroin
3. Arrests made at retail levels through patrol responses to complaints and investigative surveillance of suspect locations

Note that this strategy differs significantly from the strategies often implicitly or explicitly proposed for state- and local-enforcement agencies. It is worth sketching the difference and the rationale for the differences.

First, the objective of the strategy proposed here is to discourage experimental use and to maintain modest incentives for current users to abandon heroin use. The objective is not to eliminate all use. This objective seems more appropriate than complete elimination for two reasons. It is consistent with an overall policy toward heroin use. The police can achieve this objective without requiring enormous expenditures of public resources or eroding civil liberties.

Second, the strategy proposed here is designed to exploit both direct and indirect effects of enforcement efforts. It is designed not only to produce large numbers of arrests and seizures, but also to shape the behavior of dealers who remain on the street. In terms of the pipeline metaphor, not only are pieces of the pipeline dismantled, but the remaining pieces are both constricted and directed by the particular way in which the other pieces were dismantled. Since these indirect effects occur regardless of whether we take them into account, and since they are likely to be significant, it is probably worthwhile to take them explicitly into account in designing the strategy.

Third, the strategy proposed here tolerates a large amount of police activity at retail levels of the distribution systems. Activity at this level is justified partly by the objective of creating very high, effective prices for new users and partly by the potential value of these arrests in higher level cases. In addition, an effort is made to minimize the adverse effects of this policy by recommending that a large supply of treatment programs be available to users, and that there be a system for diverting arrested users from the criminal-justice system.

Fourth, the strategy proposed here makes no distinction between addict-dealers and profiteers. Although we might have very different ideas about how addict-dealers and profiteers should be treated once they are arrested, this law-enforcement program commits one to arresting *all* dealers. Indeed, in an important sense it is the smallest, sloppiest, least careful dealers that should bear the brunt of this law-enforcement effort simply because it is these casual dealers who are most likely to accommodate inexperienced users.

Thus, in its objectives and tactics, this program differs significantly from the law-enforcement program usually recommended.

3.0 Obstacles to Effective Implementation in New York City

Given the potential value of this strategy, what can be done to implement the various components? What organizations will be involved? How will the resources and capabilities of the different organizations match up against the performance requirements? Does effective implementation require a massive redirection of current agencies combined with large amounts of additional resources, or are current operations close to what is required?

Several different organizations will necessarily be involved in the implementation of the different components of the strategy. The first component (e.g., arrests at medium levels of the local-distribution system) should be primarily the responsibility of the Joint Task Force. The reasons for assigning this mission to the Joint Task Force are the following.

First, the prestige of this group has attracted some of the most experienced investigators from NYCPD, and enabled them to secure greater cooperation from judges in seeking wiretaps and from prosecutors in bringing conspiracy cases. As a result, this unit is equipped to undertake both wiretap and conspiracy investigations.

Second, association with federal-enforcement agencies insures an adequate supply of money to purchase evidence. As a result, the Joint Task Force will be able to use extended undercover operations.

Third, adequate mechanisms exist for insuring that cases being developed by the Joint Task Force will not become entangled with federal cases also being developed in New York City. Given that this component of the state and local strategy involves cases at medium levels of the distribution system, and that federal agencies will also be operating at this level, the risk of duplicated effort is a matter of concern. Consequently, it is desirable to confine these cases as much as possible to a unit that has close cooperation with federal-enforcement agencies.

Fourth, the possibility that these medium-level defendants could be effectively used in federal efforts to immobilize major trafficking networks is maximized by making these cases within the Joint Task Force. The prestige of the unit and New York State's drug laws allow them to threaten long prison sentences. Federal resources allow the group to offer money and protection to informants. The federal intelligence systems and jurisdiction insure that the potential of the defendant-informants can be fully exploited. Thus, the Joint Task Force can manage the kinds of investigations that are required and can maximize the chance that city operations will contribute to federal efforts to reduce aggregate supplies.

The second component of the strategy (large-scale undercover purchases of heroin at retail levels) should be primarily the responsibility of the Narcotics Division of the New York City Police Department. Both the personnel system and the standard operating procedures of this unit are well designed to conduct a large number of short undercover operations. They lack the intelligence systems, investigative procedures, and personnel to manage many extended undercover operations or retrospective conspiracy investigations. Currently, however, the Narcotics Division is occupied with tasks other than *undercover* narcotics arrests. To some extent these other tasks (e.g., jump collars, observations sales, investigation of complaints, etc.) contribute to the objective of additional undercover sales (e.g., they turn up additional informants to lead the undercover men to new dealers, they provide information useful to other cases, etc.). Also to some extent, these other tasks contribute to the third police objective (i.e., breaking up stable copping areas). However, the mission of the Narcotics Division ought to be primarily to make street-level dealers leery of strangers by making large numbers of arrests through undercover arrests.

The third component of the strategy (e.g., disruption of stable copping areas) should be primarily the responsibility of the Patrol Division of the New York City Police Department. This organization is large enough and has sufficient tactical mobility to achieve the necessary scale of arrests. Moreover, it is primarily the Patrol Division that receives and responds to narcotic complaints. Patrolmen receive specific reports from individual citizens via radio dispatches, and are alerted to chronic "narcotics situations" identified in reports from the intelligence section of the Narcotics Division on the basis of citizen complaints. The captains of precincts receive general reports and complaints from organized community groups. Size, mobility, and frequent direct relations with local communities make the patrol force the only organization that could conceivably keep narcotics markets "on the run" and more or less undercover.

Although organizations exist that can take responsibility for the different components of the strategy, there are several possible bureaucratic and political obstacles to implementing this program. We can identify obstacles at three levels: those that affect the individual policeman's incentives to take the action necessary to implement the recommended program, those that set constraints on the scale at which the program will be operated, and those that set constraints on the amount of coordination that can be achieved among police agencies and among police and the courts and other groups that can impose penalties for wrong-doing (e.g., alcoholic beverage control commissions, health boards, housing authorities, etc.). Table 6-1 flags obstacles at each of these levels for the three components of the law-enforcement program.

It is difficult to judge how serious these obstacles are to the success of the program for several reasons. First, it is difficult to know how sensitive the outcome of the program is to the existence of these obstacles. For example, it is not clear how much of the preventive value of the program is lost if the courts fail to impose high sentences, if the police officers occasionally work on the same case, or if uniformed patrolmen will simply not make more than one or two narcotics arrests per week.

Second, it is not clear what works in overcoming these obstacles. For example, it may be the creation of special narcotics courts will result in stiffer sentences on narcotics charges and that a law requiring mandatory sentences will not. Similarly, it may be that the insistence of the precinct captain that all narcotics complaints be investigated will result in a higher rate of narcotics arrests, or it may also be that their arrests will only increase when there is a large-scale, effective, anticorruption program.

Table 6-1
Bureaucratic Obstacles to Proposed Law-Enforcement Program

Police Objective and Tactic	Obstacles Affecting the Motivation and Capability of Individual Police Officers to Make Arrests	Obstacles Affecting the Motivation and Ability of the New York City Police Department to Maintain Aggregate Level of Effort	Obstacles to Coordination between Police Department and Other Agencies that Could Contribute to Police Efforts
I. Disrupt stable "copping areas" with narcotics misdemeanor arrests made by Patrol Division of NYCPD.	1. Inability to distinguish activities around stable "copping areas" from "normal community life."	1. Insufficient community pressure to mobilize precinct commanders to keep pressure on narcotics cases.	1. Courts unwilling to prosecute narcotics misdemeanors.
	2. Heroin users regarded as dangerous and unpleasant to handle compared with other arrestees.	2. Need to maintain statistics of arrests in areas other than narcotics.	2. Licensing agencies of both city and state refuse to take police guidance and information in inspecting and revoking licenses for bars, restaurants, night-clubs, etc.
	3. Arrests made in a crowd or in view of large numbers of people are considered dangerous.	3. Reluctance to pressure patrol since anticipated effects include: a. Harassment complaints b. Corruption c. Low morale d. Loss of time to court proceedings	3. Community groups fail to mobilize and support police.
	4. Misdemeanor narcotics arrests are not important for promotion and do not require "real police work."	4. Widespread corruption or inadequate internal instruments to control corruption.	
	5. Low morale associated with court's unwillingness to prosecute these cases.	5. Patrol Division is not currently responsible for responding to narcotics complaints.	
	6. Corruption.		

Table 6-1 (cont.)

Police Objective and Tactic	Obstacles Affecting the Motivation and Capability of Individual Police Officers to Make Arrests	Obstacles Affecting the Motivation and Ability of the New York City Police Department to Maintain Aggregate Level of Effort	Obstacles to Coordination between Police Department and Other Agencies that Could Contribute to Police Efforts

II. Make heroin dealers leery of "strangers" with arrests based on sales to undercover police in the Narcotics Division of the NYCPD.	1. Lack of performance standards (quotas).
	
	2. Much of the division's time is devoted to "nonproductive" activities (e.g. responding to complaints, time spent in courts).
	
	3. Informants who affect pace of operations are unreliable and nonpunctual.
	
	4. Widespread perception among undercover officers that low rates of arrests are less likely to "burn" them than high rates of arrests.
	
	5. Transfer of men out of narcotics division as anticorruption tactic has resulted in low morale and a significant loss of experience.
	
	6. Corruption.
		1. Insufficient supply of undercover police to maintain or expand pace of Narcotics Division operations.
		  a. Limited pool of officers who are suitable candidates for undercover work.
		  b. Recent reduction in incentives for doing undercover work. Undercover work used to be "fast track" for promotion to detective.
		  c. Inadequate representation of ethnic groups in Narcotics Division.
		
		2. Insufficient supply of "buy" money.
		
		3. Insufficient supply of "informants" to mobilize and guide operations.
		
		4. Lack of central control over targets and pace of Narcotics Division operations:
		  a. No operational role for intelligence section. No strategic plan.
			1. Courts unwilling to prosecute narcotics misdemeanors.
			
			2. Licensing agencies of both city and state refuse to take police guidance and information in inspecting and revoking licenses for bars, restaurants, night-clubs, etc.
			
			3. Community groups fail to mobilize and support police.

| III. Reduce aggregate supplies by arresting medium-level distributors in local-distribution system | b. No central participation in registration of informants.

5. Currently, the Narcotics Division has responsibility for responding to all narcotics complaints.

1. Inadequate supply of informants.

2. Inadequate intelligence systems to facilitate development.

3. Inadequate supply of personnel to conduct retrospective conspiracy and wiretap investigations. | 1. Inappropriate performance standards rewarding quantity of arrests.

2. Failure to use intelligence systems for coordination and development of case.

3. Unreliable informants.

4. Corruption. | 1. Courts unwilling to impose heavy sanctions.

2. Federal-enforcement agencies fail to provide resources or effectively use defendants developed by joint task force. |

Third, it is not clear how expensive it is to overcome these obstacles. It may be very difficult to set up special narcotics courts and much easier to pass a law requiring mandatory sentencing. It may be hard to motivate and train rookies to be effective undercover policemen and easier to increase the quota for undercover arrests. Notice that to some extent, expense can be calculated in budget terms. However, the more important currency is often the commitments and incentives of individuals who might shoulder the responsibility of implementing the program. Consequently, without viewing the problem of implementation from a particular position, it is difficult to know in whose currency one should be calculating the expense.

For all these reasons, we can do nothing more than simply *flag* these problems of implementation. However, the problems do not seem so crippling as to consign the proposed strategy to the realm of wholly impractical policies. Indeed, the strategy proposed here might be the rarest of all phenomena a policy that is both effective and feasible.

Notes

1. U.S. Congress, Senate Committee on Government Operations, Permanent Subcommittee of Investigations, "Hearings on Federal Drug Enforcement," 94th Congress, First Session (June-September 1975).

2. Domestic Council Task Force on Drug Abuse, *White Paper on Drug Abuse* (Washington, D.C.: U.S. Government Printing Office, 1975), pp. 39-41.

3. Patrick H. Hughes and Gail A. Crawford, "A Contagious Disease Model for Researching and Intervening in Heroin Epidemics," *Archives of General Psychiatry* 27 (August 1972).

Bibliography

Ackerloff, George. "The Market for Lemons: Qualitative Uncertainty and the Market Mechanism." *Quarterly Journal of Economics* 84 (August 1970).

Addiction Research and Treatment Corporation Team, Columbia University School of Social Work. *Progress Report.* U.S. Department of Justice, 1971.

Afflerback, Lee, et al. *Vehicle Tracking and Locating Systems*, The Mitre Corporation, 1974.

Amsel, Zili, et al. "The Development of a Case Register." Paper presented at the 31st Annual Meeting of the Committee on Problems of Drug Dependence, Division of Medical Science, National Academy of Sciences, February 1969.

Aronowitz, Dennis. "Civil Commitment of Narcotics Addicts." Columbia Law Review 67 (March 1967).

Babst, Dean V; Glaser, Daniel; and Inciardi, James. *Predicting Post-Release Adjustment of Institutionalized Addicts: An Analysis of New York and California Parole Experience and California Civil Commitment Experience.* Albany, New York: Narcotic Addiction Control Commission, 1969.

Ball, John C., and Richard Snarr. "A Test of the Maturation Hypothesis." *Committee on Problems of Drug Dependence.* National Academy of Science. Washington, D.C.: National Research Council, 1969.

Berg, Dorothy F., and Broecker, Linell, P. *Illicit Use of Dangerous Drugs in the United States, A Compilation of Studies, Surveys and Polls.* Bureau of Narcotics and Dangerous Drugs, June 1972.

Bewley, Thomas H., et al. "Morbidity and Mortality from Heroin Dependence." *British Medical Journal*, March 23, 1968.

Blum, Richard H. *The Dream Sellers: Perspectives on Drug Dealers.* San Francisco: Jossey-Bass, 1972.

_____. "Drug Pushers: A Collective Portrait." *Transaction* 8 (July-August 1971).

Blumenstein, Alfred; Sagi, Philip; and Wolfgang, Marvin E. "Problems of Estimating the Number of Heroin Addicts." Mimeographed. University of Pennsylvania, 1973.

Brecher, Edward H. *Licit and Illicit Drugs.* Boston: Little, Brown and Co., 1972.

Brotman, Richard, and Freedman, Alfred M. *Continuities and Discontinuities in the Process of Patient Care for Narcotic Addicts.* New York: New York Medical College, 1965.

Burroughs, William. *Junkie.* New York: Ace Books, 1953.

Chambers, Carl. *An Assessment of Drug Use in the General Population.* Albany: New York State Narcotics Addiction Control Commission, 1971.

Chein, Isidor, et al. *The Road to H.* New York: Basic Books, 1964.

Clark, Evert, and Horrack, Nicholas. *Contrabandista!* New York: Praeger Publishers, 1973.

Commission to Investigate Allegations of Police Corruption and the City's Anti-Corruption Procedures." *Commission Report.* New York: Fund for the City of New York, 1972.

de Alarcon, R. "The Spread of Heroin Use in a Community," *United Nations Bulletin on Narcotics* 21:3 (July-September 1969).

DeLong, James. "Drugs and their Effects." Drug Abuse Survey Project. *Dealing with Drug Abuse.* (New York: Praeger Publishers, 1972.

Dole, Vincent, et al. "Narcotics Blockade." *Archives of Internal Medicine* 118 (October 1966).

Drug Law Evaluation Project. "Convictions and Sentences under the 1973 New York State Drug and Sentencing Laws: Drug Offenses." New York: Association of the Bar and the Drug Abuse Council, 1975.

DuPont, Robert L., and Greene, Mark H. "The Dynamics of a Heroin Addiction Epidemic." *Science* 181 (1973): 716-722.

Duvall, Henrietta; Locke, Ben; and Brill, Leon. "Following-up Study of Narcotic Drug Addicts Five Years After Hospitalization *Public Health Reports* 78:3 (March 1963).

Edwards, Griffith. "The British Approach to the Treatment of Heroin Addiction." *Lancet*, April 12, 1969.

Eszterhas, Joe. *Nark!* San Francisco: Straight Arrow Books, 1974.

Fels Center of Government. University of Pennsylvania. "Heroin in Philadelphia: Reports of a Student Research Workshop of Heroin Abuse, Programs and Policies, March 1972.

Fiddle, Seymour. *Portraits from a Shooting Gallery.* New York: Harper and Row, 1967.

Finlator, John. *The Drugged Nation.* New York: Simon and Schuster, 1973.

Fishman, J.J., and Conwell, D.P. "The Narcotics Register: Problems in Data Interpretation." Paper presented at the 32nd Annual Conference of the Committee on Drug Dependence, National Research Council, 1969.

Gearing, Frances. "Evaluation of the Methadone Maintenance Treatment Program." Columbia University School of Public Health and Administrative Medicare. Albany: New York State Narcotic Addiction Control Commission, 1969-72.

_____ . "Successes and Failures in Methadone Maintenance Treatment of Heroin Addiction in New York City." In *Proceedings of the Third National Conference on Methadone Maintenance.* Washington, D.C.: National Institute for Mental Health, 1970.

Georgetown Law Journal 60 (1971). "Police Perjury in Narcotics Dropsy Cases: A New Credibility Gap."

Glatt, M.M., et al. *Journey into Loneliness: The Drug Scene in Great Britain.* London: Edward Arnold, 1967.

Goffman, Irving. *Strategic Interaction.* Philadelphia: University of Pennsylvania Press, 1969.

Harvey, Malachi L., and Cross, John C. *The Informer in Law Enforcement.* Springfield, Mass: Charles C. Thomas, 1960.

Hayim, Gila J. "Changes in the Criminal Behavior of Heroin Addicts: A One-Year Follow-up of Methadone Treatment." The Center for Criminal Justice, Harvard Law School, 1972.

Hughes, Patrick et al. "The Impact of Medical Intervention in Three Heroin Copping Areas." Paper presented at the Fourth National Methadone Conference, January 1972.

_____. "The Natural History of a Heroin Epidemic." *American Journal of Public Health*, July 1972.

_____. "The Social Structure of a Heroin Copping Community." *American Journal of Psychiatry* 128:5 (1971).

Hughes, Patrick, and Crawford, Gail. "A Contagious Disease Model for Researching and Intervening in Heroin Epidemics." *Archives of General Psychiatry* 27 (August 1972).

Inciardi, James A., and Chambers, Carl D., eds. *Drugs and the Criminal Justice System.* Beverly Hills, Calif.: Sage, 1974.

Institute for Defense Analysis. *Trends in Heroin Indicators: Availability, Sources, Supply, and Use.* Washington, D.C.: Drug Enforcement Administration, 1975.

Israel, Jerold H., and Wayne, R. La Fave. *Criminal Procedure in a Nutshell.* St. Paul, Minn.: West, 1975.

Kandel, D. "Stages in Adolescent Involvement in Drug Use." *Science*, 1975.

Klockars, Carl B. *The Professional Fence.* New York: The Free Press, 1974.

Kornblum, Alan. *The Moral Hazards.* Lexington, Mass.: D.C. Heath and Co., 1976.

Koval, Mary. "Differential Estimates of Opiate Use in New York City." Mimeographed. New York: Narcotic Addiction Control Commission, 1971.

_____. "Drug Users among Police Department Arrestees and Arrests for Narcotic Offenses in New York City." Mimeographed. New York: Narcotics Addiction Control Commission, 1969.

Langrod, John. "Secondary Drug Use Among Heroin Users." *International Journal of the Addictions* 5:4 (December 1970).

Larner, Jeremy, and Tefferteller, Ralph. *The Addict in the Street.* New York: Grove Press, 1964.

Leslie, Alan Craig. "A Benefit/Cost Analysis of New York City's Heroin Addiction Problems and Programs—1971." Teaching and Research Materials, Public Policy Program, Kennedy School of Government, Harvard University, 1972.

Lindesmith, A.R. *The Addict and the Law.* New York: Vintage Books, 1965.

Logan, Albert B. "May a Man be Punished Because He is Ill?" *American Bar Association Journal,* October 1966.

Lorrin, Donald; Hensle, Terry; and Rose, John. "The Major Medical Complications of Heroin Addiction." *Annals of Internal Medicine* 67:1 (July 1967).

McGlothin, William H., et al. *Alternative Approaches to Opiate Addiction Control: Costs, Benefits and Potential.* Washington, D.C.: Bureau of Narcotics and Dangerous Drugs, 1972.

McLean, Robert. "Drug Use Among the Sentenced Population of the New York City Department of Correction." Mimeographed. New York City: RAND Corporation, 1970. Internal document D20131.

Mellonics Systems Development Corporation. "Project Impact," Drug Enforcement Administration, 1975.

Minichello, Lee. "Indicators of Intravenous Drug Use in the United States: 1966-73." Washington, D.C.: Drug Enforcement Administration, 1975.

Moore, Mark H. "Anatomy of the Heroin Problem: An Exercise in Problem Definition," *Policy Analysis* 2:1 (1976).

_____. "The Economics of Heroin Distribution." Teaching and Research Materials No. 4, Public Policy Program, Kennedy School of Government. Cambridge, Mass.: Harvard University, 1971.

_____. "Policies to Achieve Discrimination on the Effective Price of Heroin." *American Economic Review* 63:2 (May 1973).

_____. *Policy Towards Heroin Use In New York City.* Ph.D. diss., Harvard University, 1973.

Moore, Robin. *The French Connection.* New York: Bantam Books, 1971.

Nash, George, and Cohen, Eli. "An Analysis of New York City Police Statistics for Narcotic Arrests During the Period 1957-1967." Mimeographed. New York: Columbia University Bureau of Applied Social Research, 1969.

New York City, Addiction Services Agency. *Report of City-Wide Census of Drug Treatment Programs.* New York, 1972.

New York City Criminal Justice Coordinating Council. *Criminal Commitment of Narcotic Users Under State Law.* New York: Office of the Mayor, 1971.

New York City Criminal Justice Coordinating Council, Executive Committee. *1973 Criminal Justice Plan.* 1973.

New York State Narcotic Addiction Control Commission. *First Annual Statistical Report.* Albany, 1968.

New York State Narcotics Addiction Control Commission and New York City Narcotics Register. *Opiate Use in New York City*. New York, 1969.

New York State Permanent Commission of Investigations. "Interim Report Concerning the Operations of Special Narcotics Parts of the Supreme Court." New York, 1973.

_____. *Narcotics Law Enforcement in New York City*. New York, 1972.

New York University Law Review 43 (December 1968): 1172-1193. "Due Process for the Narcotic Addict? The New York Compulsory Commitment Procedures."

Newsday, Staff and Editors of. *The Heroin Trail*. New York: Signet, 1973.

O'Donnell, John. "The Relapse Rate in Narcotics Addiction: A Critique of Follow-up Studies." Albany: Narcotic Addiction Control Commission, 1968.

_____. "A Follow-up of Narcotic Addicts: Mortality, Relapse and Abstinence." *American Journal of Orthopsychology* 34 (1964).

Perkins, Marvin, and Bloch, Harriet. "Survey of a Methadone Maintenance Treatment Program." *American Journal of Psychiatry* 126:10 (April 1970).

Phares, Donald. "The Simple Economics of Heroin and Organizing Policy." *Journal of Drug Issues*, Spring 1973.

Preble, Edward, and Casey, John. "Taking Care of Business—The Heroin User's Life on the Street." *International Journal of the Addictions* 4:1 (March 1969).

Proceedings of the Third National Conference on Methadone Maintenance. National Institute for Mental Health, 1970.

Public Research Institute of the Center for Naval Analysis. *Heroin Supply and Urban Crime*. Washington, D.C.: Drug Abuse Council, 1976.

Rachin, Richard L., and Czakjowski, Eugene H. *Drug Abuse Control*. Specifically Blumberge, Abraham S. "Drug Control: Agenda for Repression." Lexington, Mass.: D.C. Heath and Co., 1975.

Raiffa, Howard. *Decision Analysis*. Reading, Mass.: Addison-Wesley, 1968.

Reuter, Peter. "Gambling Prohibition: Unenforced or Unenforceable Laws." Paper prepared for the Meeting of the American Society for Criminology. Washington, D.C., 1975.

Richman, Alex. "Utilization and Review of Methadone Maintenance Patient Data." In Proceedings of the Third National Conference on Methadone Maintenance. National Institute for Mental Health, 1970.

Robins, Lee N. "The Vietnam Drug User Returns." Special Action Office for Drug Abuse Prevention Monograph." Series A, No. 2 (May 1974).

Robins, Lee N., and Murphy, George. "Drug Use in a Normal Population of Young Negro Men." *American Journal of Public Health* 57:9 (September 1967).

Rottenberg, Simon. "The Clandestine Distribution of Heroin, Its Discovery and Suppression." *The Journal of Political Economy* 76 (1968).

Rubinstein, Jonathan. *City Police*. New York: Farar, Straus and Giroux, 1973.

Ruth, Henry, and Grubert, Arthur. "Memorandum to Narcotics Control Council re Statistics on Dispositions of Narcotics Cases." New York: Criminal Justice Coordinating Council, 1971.

Schasre, Robert. "Cessation Patterns among Neophyte Users." *International Journal of the Addictions* 1:2 (1966).

Schecter, Leonard, with Phillips, William. *On the Pad*. New York: Berkeley, 1973.

Schelling, Thomas C. "Economics and Criminal Enterprise." *The Public Interest*, no. 7 (Spring 1967).

_____. "What is the Business of Organized Crime." *Journal of Public Law* 20 (1971): 1.

Singer, Max. "Addict Crime: The Vitality of Mythical Numbers." *Public Interest*, no. 23 (Spring 1971).

Skolnick, Jerome M. *Justice Without Trial*. New York: Wiley and Sons, 1966.

Spence, Michael. *Market Signalling*, Discussion Paper No. 4. Public Policy Program, Kennedy School of Government. Cambridge, Mass.: Harvard University, 1972.

Stanton, John M. *Lawbreaking and Drug Dependence*. State of New York: Bureau of Research and Statistics, Executive Department, Division of Parole, 1969.

Steinberg, Hannah. *Scientific Basis of Drug Dependence*. New York: Gruen and Stratton, 1969.

Stimson, G.V. *Heroin and Behavior*. New York: Wiley and Sons, 1973.

Stone, Robert. *Dog Soldiers*. New York: Ballantine, 1974.

Teresa, Vincent, with Renner, Thomas C. *Vinnie Teresa's Mafia*. Garden City: Doubleday and Co., 1975.

Thalinger, Alan. "A Study of Deaths of Narcotic Users in New York City— 1969." Mimeographed. New York City: Health Services Administration, Health Research Training Program, 1970.

Thomas, Piri. *Down These Mean Streets*. New York: Signet Books, 1967.

U.S. Bureau of the Census. *Statistical Abstract of the United States, 1973*. 94th Edition. Washington, D.C., 1973.

U.S. Comptroller General. "Difficulty in Immobilizing Major Traffickers." B-175424. Washington, D.C.: General Accounting Office, 1973.

_____. "Heroin Being Smuggled into New York City Successfully," 1972.

U.S. Congress, House of Representatives, Committee on Appropriations, Subcommittee on Departments of State, Justice and Commerce, the Judiciary and Related Agencies. "Hearings on Appropriations for 1976." 94th Congress, 1st Session, 1976.

U.S. Congress, House of Representatives, Committee on Government Operations. "Law Enforcement on the Southwest Border: Hearings Before a Subcommittee." 93rd Congress, 2nd Session, July-August 1974.

U.S. Congress, House of Representatives, Select Committee on Crime. *Drugs in Our Schools*. 92nd Congress, 2nd Session, 1972.

U.S. Congress, House of Representatives, Select Committee on Intelligence. "Hearings on U.S. Intelligence Agencies and Activities: Domestic Intelligence Programs." Testimony of Mark H. Moore. 94th Congress, 1st Session, November 1975.

U.S. Congress, Senate Committee on Government Operations. Permanent Subcommittee on Investigations. *Hearings*, Part I. 88th Congress, 1st Session, 1963.

_____. "Federal Drug Enforcement; Hearings Before the Permanent Subcommittee on Investigations." 94th Congress, 1st Session, 1975.

_____. Testimony of Robert L. DuPont, Director of the Special Action Office for Drug Abuse Prevention, June 1975.

_____. Subcommittee on Legislation and Military Expenditures. "Hearings on Reorganization Plan No. 2." 93rd Congress, 1st Session, April-May 1973.

Drug Enforcement Administration. "Geo-Drug Enforcement Program: First Year Assessment." Washington, D.C.: Department of Justice, 1974.

_____. Office of the Chief Counsel. "Disclosure of Informants." DEA Legal Comment No. 5, May 1974.

Office of Congressional Relations, Drug Enforcement Administration. "Report on Post Arrest Drug Trafficking," 1974.

Office of Statistical and Data Services, DEA. "Drug Enforcement Statistical Report," December 1974.

Survey Group, DEA. "An Analysis of DEA Coordination with Patrol Forces on the Southwest Border," 1974.

U.S. Department of Justice. "Handbook: Proving Federal Crimes." Washington, D.C., 1971.

U.S. Executive Office of the President, Domestic Council Drug Abuse Task Force. *White Paper on Drug Abuse*. Washington, D.C.: U.S. Government Printing Office, 1975.

U.S. Executive Office of the President, "Drug Abuse Prevention Program: Briefing Book." Washington, D.C., 1972.

Vaillant, George. "The Natural History of a Chronic Disease." *New England Journal of Medicine*, December 8, 1966.

_____. "A Twelve Year Follow-up of New York Narcotic Addicts: The

Relation of Treatment to Outcome." *American Journal of Psychiatry* 122 (1966).

Votey, Harold L., and Phillips, Llad. "Minimizing the Social Cost of Drug Abuse: An Economic Analysis of Alternatives for Policy." *Policy Sciences* 7:3 (September 1976).

Whitebread, Charles B., and Stevens, Ronald. "Constructive Possession in Narcotics Cases: To Have and Have Not." *Virginia Law Review* 58 (1972).

Wilson, James Q. *Varieties of Police Behavior.* Cambridge, Mass.: Harvard University Press, 1968.

Winick, Charles. "Maturing Out of Narcotic Addiction." *United Nations Bulletin on Narcotics* 14:1 (January-March 1962).

Winterbotham, F.W. *The Ultra Secret.* New York: Harper and Row, 1974.

Woodley, Richard. *Dealer.* New York: Holt, Rinehart and Winston, 1971.

Yale Law Journal 76 (1967). "Civil Commitment of Narcotics Addicts."

Index

Index

Abstinence, 8, 69, 70, 82, 245-247, 268

"Accommodating" sale, 39, 40, 41, 42, 123, 141, 143

Amphetamines, 53n, 244

"Anti-Crime Squads," 130n

Arbitrage, 260

Authority, abuse and subversion of, 139, 141

"Bad actors," 40

"Bag followers," 49n

"Bags." See "Habit size"

Bail, 178n, 216

Bar Association, 220

Barbiturates, 53n, 244

Bator, Francis M., 13n

Bedford-Stuyvesant, 78

Blackmail, 47, 142

Blum, Richard, 51n

"Brand names," 49n

Bribery, 30-38, 42, 111. See also Corruption

"Brokers," 31n, 49n, 50

Bronx Criminal Court, 216

Brotman, Richard, 8n

Buffalo, N.Y., 202

"Bugs," 171n

Bureaucracy, 145-146, 148, 168-169, 172, 270-274

Bureau of Drug Abuse Control (HEW), 201

Bureau of Employment Statistics (BES), 77

Bureau of Narcotics and Dangerous Drugs (BNDD), 70, 72n, 73n, 74, 75, 187n, 201, 212

"Burn," 140, 142, 143, 272

"Burned-out" users, 83, 84, 89, 90, 92, 93, 96, 97, 98

"Bust," 51n

"Buy and bust" cases, 140-143, 179, 181, 183, 184

"Buying up the ladder," 22n

"Buy money," 176-178, 179, 183, 195, 202, 269, 272

"Buys," level of, 197, 198

"Caches," 27-28, 41

Caffeine, 104

California, 68n

Chaiken, Jan, 157n

Chein, Isidor, 244

Chicago, 78, 241, 244, 249-253, 267

Civil commitment petition, 215n

Cocaine, 51n, 79n, 204-205, 206

Coercion of defendants, 163-164

College students, 79

Complaints, private citizen, 157-158, 182, 271, 273

"Connections," 17, 54, 57n, 59-60, 100, 108-114 passim, 134, 194, 199, 207

Conspiracy cases, 28, 124-125, 126, 133-135, 169, 180, 181, 182, 183, 184, 202, 265, 269, 273

"Constructive possession," 122, 125

Contract enforcement, 43-45

"Copping areas," 101, 200-201, 260, 263, 264, 266-267, 270, 271

Corruption, 30-38, 42, 139, 141-142, 177, 195; anticorruption procedures, 156, 272

Courts, 187n, 222, 271, 272, 273; authorizations, 122n, 127, 171; congestion, 213-216, 220, 223, 225; corruption, 32, 33; and defendant-informants, 122n, 127, 171; and police testimony, 29, 131, 175

"Cover," 142, 144

Crawford, Gail, 244

Crawley, England, 249, 251

Crime, 41-47, 82-91 passim, 109, 114

Criminal commitment procedures, 73n

Cutting operation, 100n

Dallas, 79

"Dangerous drugs," 53n, 68n, 205, 244

"Days on street," 90n, 114
Decision analysis, 10-12
Demand elasticity, 6-10, 13, 14, 260
Demographic characteristics: police,
    152-154; users, 86-87
Denver-Boulder metropolitan area, 79
Detoxication, 8, 260
Diagnostic tests and procedures, 71,
    74, 174-175, 216
Dilution process, 90n, 104-105, 106
"Dirty:" location, 139; urine, 8n
Discovery motions, 165
District attorneys, 217
Doctors, 241, 242
Documentary evidence, 169, 183
"Dropping a dime," 142n
"Drop" systems, 28-29, 41, 43
"Drop-use testimony," 122n, 216
Drug and Sentencing Laws of 1973,
    217, 219-225, 226, 227, 228
"Drug dabblers," 83, 84, 89-98 passim
"Drug dependents," 83, 84, 89-98
    passim
Drug Enforcement Administration
    (DEA), 129n, 137n, 173n, 174n,
    175n, 176n, 178n, 187, 201; G-
    DEP arrests, 202-206, 207; intelli-
    gence systems, 155n, 167n, 202
DuPont, Robert L., 73n

East Coast, 134n, 241, 242
East Village Other, 78
Economic theory, 5-6, 10-12
"Economies of scale:" enforcement
    policy, 144, 266; heroin industry,
    52, 55
"Effective price," 238, 239-240, 242,
    247, 248, 258-260, 263, 268
Electronic devices, 126, 127, 135n,
    171n, 173-174
Enforcement agencies, 120, 178-184;
    coordination, 148-149, 167, 195,
    266n, 269, 271, 272, 273; corrup-
    tion, 30-38; equipment, 170-176,
    183; federal, 187, 201-209, 273;
    intelligence, 156-169, 182, 183;
    legal constraints, 121-128; person-

nel, 150-156, 181; reforms, 195;
    strategies and tactics, 22n, 128-149,
    180, 181, 182, 183
Enforcement policy, xxn, xxi, 20n,
    36, 46, 237-261; changes in, 80,
    181; and distribution system, 37,
    60-61, 264-266, 273; impact on
    users, 19n, 248, 258-261; NYC,
    263-274; as prevention program,
    238-257; and price increases, 5-15
England, xxi, 249, 258n
"Entrapment," 125, 141, 143
Equality before the law, 153-154
Error, sources of, 71-75, 80, 85
Evidence, 125, 131, 132, 138, 139,
    165, 216; documentary, 169, 183;
    legal restrictions, 126-128; recollec-
    tions, 133-134, 135; recording de-
    vices, 174-175
Extortion, 36, 44, 141n, 142

Federal Bureau of Narcotics (Treasury
    Department), 201
Federal enforcement agencies, 187,
    201-209, 273. See also Drug En-
    forcement Administration; United
    States Customs Service
Felonies, 189-199 passim, 214,
    219-228 passim
Fencing operations, 20n, 24n, 27n,
    42n, 91, 114n
"Fingering," 34
Fixed-cost strategies, 12-13
"Flaking," 131n, 141, 142n
Florida, 79, 173n
Foreign language problem, 173n
Forensic tests, 71, 74, 174-175, 216
Fourth Amendment, 126
France, 135n
"Franchise" system, 31n, 36. See also
    "Licenses"
Frauds (nondealers), 142-143
Freedman, Alfred M., 8n
"Free lance" dealers, 39, 40, 41, 42,
    56, 101
French Connection, 26n
Friends, role of, 247-257

"Fringe" groups, 152-153
"Frisk," 122n

Gamblers, 36n
Gearing, Frances R., 8n
Geo-Drug Enforcement Program (G-DEP), 202-206
Ghettos, 19, 78, 241n
"Giving up," 144, 161
Goffman, Irving, 27n, 173n
"Good" sample, 88
Grand jury, 132n, 216
"Gumshoeing," 151-152, 181

"Habit size," 8, 69-70, 80-81, 83, 84, 86-87, 90, 114
Hallucinogenic drugs, 205
Hand, Learned, 163-164
"Hanging out," 50n
Hayim, Gila J., 7n
Health Center districts, 77
Health factors, 83, 241, 243, 258
Hearsay rule, 124
Hepatitis, 241, 243
Heroin, 49, 53, 90n, 241; adulterants, 49n, 104, 258; dilution process, 104-105; legalization, 91-92, 258-259; prices, 5-15, 48, 242; quality control, 98-105, 106, 107; substitutes, 69, 70, 82, 90n; tolerance and withdrawal, 6-7, 81
Heroin dealers, 122, 123, 139n, 177, 178n, 267; agents, 21-22, 30, 40, 44-45; bribes, 30-38; collective action, 37, 46; concealing and dispossessing of heroin, 23-30, 41; concealment of identity, 15-23, 41, 58; defense strategies, 15, 38-41, 51-52, 179; employees, 45-47; high-level, 54-56, 58, 84, 96, 99, 125, 134-135, 143, 179, 180, 195, 205; incautious, 19n, 37, 39, 40, 41, 42, 58, 268; low-level, 56-58, 84, 96, 130-131, 138, 142, 143, 179, 191, 197, 198-200, 268; marginal, 14n, 18, 101; nondealers (frauds), 142-143; in NYC, 68n, 92-114 pas-

sim; and NYC police, 191, 194, 195, 197, 198-200; and other criminals, 41-47; and price increases, 5-15; "protection" and "muscle," 43-45; relatives, 28, 47; screening of customers, 18-21; types and distribution levels, 38-41, 42, 268; wholesale/retail, 39, 40, 41, 42, 93
Heroin industry: competition, 14, 44, 57-58; distribution system, 37, 51-61, 63-65, 94, 134-135, 162, 209, 263, 265, 269, 273; employees, 45-47, 98, 111; equipment, 15-16, 111; and heroin supply, 52, 53n, 55-56, 264-266, 273; and legitimate businesses, 43, 93, 98, 109-110; "lot sizes," 106-108, 112, 113; market practices, 17-19, 40, 50-51, 91, 97-110; middle level of, 265, 269, 273; monopoly and monopsony, 14, 47, 50, 53, 54, 55, 57, 111; in NYC, 67-114; profits, 10-15, 39, 92-93, 96n, 105-108, 111; "tax" structure, 11-15
Heroin users: abstainers, 8, 69, 70, 82, 245-247, 268; aging, 80, 82; arrests, 72, 73n, 74, 81, 86, 90n, 194, 199, 207; characteristics, 80, 82-98 passim; consumption rates, 6-10, 69-92, 114; criminal activity, 42n, 48, 82, 83, 85, 86-87, 109; deaths, 70, 71, 72, 73n, 74, 78; effect of enforcement policies, 19n, 238-257; employment, 77, 78, 80, 83, 84-98 passim, 114; friends' role, 247-257; health, 83, 258; initiation, 241-245, 250; institutional confinement, 8, 69, 70, 91; male/female, 76, 77, 78, 88; non-addicts, 9, 10n, 18, 21, 75, 91-92, 101; prevalence in NYC, 70-75, 76-77, 78-79, 85-92, 99, 100; and price of heroin, 6-10, 14, 48, 259-260; problems of obtaining heroin, 47-51, 239-247
Heroin-using communities, 19, 46, 58-59, 78, 79, 152-153, 241n; epidemics, 241, 249-257, 261, 267

High-school students, 76, 79
"Hippies," 78
"Hot shot," 49
"House connections," 176
Hughes, Patrick, 7n, 18n, 244
"Hustlers," 83, 84, 89-98 passim

Immunity, legal, 125, 161
Importers, 95, 96, 100-114 passim,
    194, 199, 207
Income sources of users, 77, 84-97
    passim, 114, 258
"Inconvenience" model, 239-247
Informants, 18, 29, 44n, 126,
    127-128, 132, 135, 139-140, 144,
    154-156, 182, 183, 265, 272; and
    criminal justice system, 162-165; as
    defendants, 159-166, 179, 180,
    182, 202, 209, 269, 273; as nonde-
    fendants, 159, 166, 176-177, 182;
    registration of, 195, 273
Information sources: enforcement,
    156-169, 183; users, 49-50
Intelligence systems, 54n, 155-156,
    166-169, 182-183, 195, 200, 202,
    273
Investigating commissions, 193-195

Joint Task Force, 187, 210-211, 212,
    269, 273
"Joy poppers," 83, 84, 89, 90, 91, 92,
    93, 94
"Jugglers," 95, 100, 108-114 passim,
    194, 199, 207
"Junkies," 28, 153
Juvenile-delinquency arrests, 214, 215

Kilo, 106, 108
"Kilo connections," 95, 96, 100,
    108-114 passim, 194, 199, 207
Knapp Commission, 195
Koval, Mary, 73n

Lansky, Meyer, 134n
"Leads," 136-137, 208
Legal constraints, 121-128, 162-164,
    171, 173

Lennox Avenue File, 200-201
"Licenses," 30-32, 33, 34, 35, 42
Licensing authority, 267, 271, 272
Loitering, 190, 192, 194, 200
Los Angeles, 250
"Lot sizes," 106-108, 112, 113
Lump-sum tax, 12-13, 14

Marginal: dealers, 14n, 18, 101; users,
    18, 21, 91, 101
Marijuana, 205
Marseilles, 135n
"Maturing out" phenomenon, 8n, 82n,
    83, 84, 89-98 passim
McGlothin, William H., 8n
Mental health programs, 216
Mental Hygiene Law, 215n
Methadone, 8, 260
Mexico, 68n, 134n
Michigan, 79
Military personnel, 78, 241
Miranda warning, 216
Misdemeanors, 189-196 passim, 199,
    215, 220, 271, 272
Money to purchase evidence and infor-
    mation (PE/PI money), 142, 166,
    176-178, 179, 181, 183, 195, 202,
    269, 272
Monopoly, 14, 50, 53, 54, 57-58, 111
Monopsony, 47, 55
Montgomery Co., Md., 79
Moore, Mark H., 8n
Mortality rate, 70, 71, 72, 73n, 74, 78
"Mules," 161
Multiple-drug abuse, 82, 83, 86-87
"Muscle," 43-45

NADDIS intelligence system, 167n,
    202n
Narcotics Addiction Control Commis-
    sion, 80
Narcotics cases, 121-125, 128; classes
    of violators, 202-204, 205, 206,
    207; disposition, 189, 213-225
    passim; felonies/misdemeanors,
    189-200 passim; types, 138-147
Narcotics distribution by heroin users,
    88, 89, 94, 98

Narcotics investigations, 133-147, 180, 181, 182, 183, 184; prospective, 129-130, 136-147, 193; retrospective, 129, 133-136, 169, 179, 202, 265, 273

Negroes, 78

New Jersey, 206, 250

New York City, 67n, 68n, 134n, 244, 250; courts, 187, 212-228; enforcement agencies, 187, 210-228; enforcement policy, 263-274; heroin consumption, 75-92; heroin users, 70-75, 76-79, 99, 100; Narcotics Register, 72, 73n, 74, 75; Rockefeller Drug Laws, 217-228 passim

New York City Police Department, 177n, 187, 188-201; budget and procurement, 172, 188; Narcotics Division, 187, 193-201, 212, 269-270, 272, 273; Patrol Bureau, 187, 188-193, 197-201, 270, 271

New York State, 78, 123n, 206; Drug and Sentencing Laws of 1973, 217-228 passim; Narcotics Addiction Control Commission, 73n; Permanent Committee on Investigations, 195; Special Narcotics Parts of the Supreme Court, 217-218

Newark, N.J., 202

Newspapers, 20

Night operations, 176n

Nixon administration, 201

"Noise," 25, 58, 150

Oakland, Calif., 78

"Observation-sale" cases, 138-139, 141, 184, 200

Office of Drug Abuse Law Enforcement (ODALE) (Justice Department), 201, 212

Office of National Narcotics Intelligence (ONNI) (Justice Department), 201

"Opportunity costs," 14n, 111

"Organized crime," 44n, 54, 205

"Overt act," 124n

"Pads," 33, 36n

Parole, 216

Patrol strategies, 129, 130-133, 136-137, 161-162, 179-184 passim, 266

"Patting down," 122n

"Penetration" tactics, 132n, 161-162, 184

Pennsylvania, 79

PE/PI (purchase evidence-purchase information) money, 176-178, 179, 183, 195, 202, 269, 272

Perjury, 29, 131, 139

Philadelphia, 79n

Phillips, William, 31n

Pickpockets, 31n

"Plain-view" search, 126-127

Plea bargaining, 213-216, 217, 219, 221

Police, 44, 45, 101n, 130n, 138, 267; "buy and bust" cases, 140-143, 152-153; and community, 19, 58-59, 157-158, 189, 271, 272; corruption, 32-33, 34-36, 141-142, 156, 177, 271, 272, 273; danger, 158n, 176n, 271; discretion, 29n, 32, 153; and distribution system, 53-54; homogeneity, 152-154, 172n, 181, 266, 272; and informants, 154-155; intelligence, 155-156, 181, 272; and money transactions, 142, 166, 177-178; practices, 213-216; protective devices for, 175-176; quotas (arrests), 160, 195, 272, 273; search authority, 24, 26, 29; testimony, 29, 131, 139, 174-175, 216

Possession cases, 28, 29, 61n, 122, 139, 190, 192, 193, 194, 200, 216, 220

Prevention program, 238-257; "inconvenience" hypothesis, 239-247; limitations, 247-257; models, 238-240

Price of heroin, 5-15, 48, 241, 258; discrimination between old and new users, 259-260, 263; "effective price," 238, 239-240, 242, 247,

Price of heroin (cont.)
    248, 258-259; undercover "buys,"
    101, 102
Prison, alternatives to, 216, 221, 259,
    261, 268
"Probable cause," 138, 216
Procaine, 104
Procurement policies, 172n
"Produce differentiation," 148n
Profits, 10-15, 39, 93, 96n, 105-108,
    111, 114. *See also* "Utility" func-
    tion
Proof, burden of, 125-126
Proprietary interest, 125
"Protection," 43-45
Protective custody, 165
Protective devices for policemen,
    175-176
Punishment, threat of, 162-164
"Pushing," 18

Quinine, 104

Recidivists, 221
Recording devices, 174-175, 183, 197
Reforms, 195
Relatives: of dealers, 28, 47; of users,
    88, 89, 92, 96
Richman, Alex, 8n
Ricord, Auguste, 125n, 134n
"Rip-offs," 28, 42n, 43, 101
Risk: dealer, 10-13, 18-19, 39, 111;
    informant, 144, 165
Rockefeller Drug Laws, 217-218 *passim*
Ruth, Heather, 8n, 85

St. Louis, 78
Sale offense, 122-124, 125, 220. *See
    also* "Buy and bust" cases; "Obser-
    vation-sale" cases
San Antonio, 250
San Mateo Public High School, 79
Schools, 79, 267
"Score," 33, 50n, 59, 144
Screening customers, 18-21, 40, 44-45,
    47, 146, 152, 153, 260
Search authority, 122, 126-127, 131

Search-warrant cases, 122n, 139-140,
    141, 184, 197, 216, 265
Self-incrimination, 125
Sentencing policy, 81, 86, 217, 219,
    221, 222-224
Sex of user, 76, 77, 78, 88
Sheldon, Donald, 174n
"Signals," 20n, 25, 150
Skolnick, Jerome M., 29n
Smuggling, 25-26, 205, 208, 209
Southwest border of United States,
    68n, 208n
"Space," 129, 137, 161
Special Narcotics Parts (NYS),
    217-218
Spence, Michael, 20n
"Stake-out," 170-171
"Stand-up guys," 46
"Sting," 48
"Stoned," 82
"Stop and frisk" rules, 127
"Straight" users, 85
"Street" transactions, 36-37, 49n, 85,
    95, 100, 108-114 *passim*, 158n,
    194, 197, 199
"Strip searches," 27n
"Submerged" narcotics arrests, 214n,
    215n
Surveillance, 126, 127, 170-174, 183,
    208, 266
"Syndicate," 44

"Tagged sample," 71, 74
"Take a fall," 44
"Take-off artists," 146
"Tax" structure, 11-15
TECS intelligence system, 167n
Tedesco, Willie, 85n
Teenagers, 79n
Testimony, 122n, 123, 132; perjured,
    29, 131, 139; recorded, 174-175
Thalinger, Alan, 73n
Thefts, 43, 45, 48, 85, 114n, 142,
    146; types, 88, 89, 91, 93, 97
"Tipping," 45
"Touts," 49n
Traffic offenses, 127n

Transmitters, personal, 174
Transshipment of drugs, 67n, 68n, 205n
"Traps," 27n, 139
Treatment: motivation, 80n, 83, 90n, 238n, 248; programs, 7-8, 73n, 81, 82, 86, 242, 259, 260-261, 267, 268

"Ultra Secret," 47n, 164n
Undercover operations, 18, 61n, 101, 126, 193, 195; "bust and buy" cases, 140-143; long-term, 146-147, 202, 265, 269; money for, 176-177, 181, 184; NYC "buys," 102, 103, 104, 105; short-term, 144-146, 181, 200, 266, 269-270, 272; skills, 151-152
Unified Intelligence Division (NYC), 187, 211-212
United States: Customs Service, 26, 131, 137n, 161, 167n, 187, 201, 206-209, 212; HEW, 201; Justice Department, 201; Marshal's Service, 165n; Senate Sub-Committee on Government Operations, 197; Supreme Court, 127n; Treasury Department, 201
University of Maine, 79

University of Michigan, 79
Urinalysis, 8n
"Utility" function, 10-11, 13, 14, 96n, 260

Valliant, George, 73n
"Value added," 96-105, 108, 109, 110, 114
Variable-cost tax, 12-13, 14
Vehicle-surveillance systems, 172-173, 183
Vehicle-tracking technology, 170n
"Victimless crimes," 128
Vietnam veterans, 78, 241
Vigilante groups, 44
Violence, 39, 42n, 43-45, 144n, 146, 165n

"Wads," 35n
Washington, D.C., 73n, 78, 250
"Weight dealers," 95, 100, 108-114 passim, 194, 199, 207, 265, 266
Welfare payments, 88, 89, 92, 96
Wilson, James Q., 187n
"Wiretaps," 135n, 171n, 173-174, 197, 265, 269, 273
Woodley, Richard, 51n

Youth programs, 216

About the Author

Mark H. Moore is currently an Associate Professor of Public Policy at the Kennedy School of Government, Harvard University. His major substantive interests are drug abuse and crime. His major methodological interests include analyses of implementation problems, and the development of forms of policy analysis that integrate the disciplines of economics, political science, operations research and statistics. He has been a consultant to the New York City Addiction Service Agency, the New York City Police Department, and the National Advisory Council on Drug Abuse Prevention. In addition, he served as Chief Planning Officer and Special Assistant to the Administrator of the United States Drug Enforcement Administration.